Latin American Party

D0783415

Political parties provide a crucial link betweei takes a variety of forms in democratic regimes, cal machines built around clientelistic networks to the establishment of sophisticated programmatic parties. *Latin American Party Systems* provides a novel theoretical argument to account for differences in the degree to which political party systems in the region were programmatically structured at the end of the twentieth century. On the basis of a diverse array of indicators and surveys of party legislators and public opinion, the book argues that learning and adaptation through fundamental policy innovations are the main mechanisms by which politicians build programmatic parties. Marshaling extensive evidence, the book's analysis shows the limits of alternative explanations and substantiates a sanguine view of programmatic competition, while nevertheless recognizing that this form of party system organization is far from ubiquitous and enduring in Latin America.

Herbert Kitschelt is the George V. Allen Professor of International Relations in Duke University's Political Science Department. He has published widely on comparative political parties and party systems in Western Europe and post-communist Eastern Europe and is a member of the American Academy of Arts and Sciences.

Kirk A. Hawkins is Assistant Professor of Political Science at Brigham Young University. He is the author of *The Discourse of Populism: Venezuela's Chavismo in Comparative Perspective* (Cambridge University Press). He has published work on political parties and populist movements, and his current research focuses on the analysis of political culture.

Juan Pablo Luna is Associate Professor of Political Science at the Pontificia Universidad Católica de Chile. His dissertation on party voter linkages in Chile and Uruguay won the 2008 Juan Linz Best Dissertation Award of APSA's Comparative Democratization Section.

Guillermo Rosas is Assistant Professor of Political Science at Washington University in St. Louis. He is the author of *Curbing Bailouts: Bank Crises and Electoral Accountability in Comparative Perspective*. His research interests center on political economy and legislative politics.

Elizabeth J. Zechmeister is Assistant Professor of Political Science and Assistant Director of the Latin American Public Opinion Project at Vanderbilt University. She is the author, with Jennifer Merolla, of *Democracy at Risk: How Terrorist Threats Affect the Public*. Her research interests are in comparative political behavior, with a regional focus on Latin America.

Cambridge Studies in Comparative Politics

General Editor
Margaret Levi *University of Washington, Seattle*

Assistant General Editors
Kathleen Thelen *Massachusetts Institute of Technology*
Erik Wibbels *Duke University*

Associate Editors
Robert H. Bates *Harvard University*
Stephen Hanson *University of Washington, Seattle*
Torben Iversen *Harvard University*
Stathis Kalyvas *Yale University*
Peter Lange *Duke University*
Helen Milner *Princeton University*
Frances Rosenbluth *Yale University*
Susan Stokes *Yale University*

Other Books in the Series

David Austen-Smith, Jeffry A. Frieden, Miriam A. Golden, Karl Ove Moene, and Adam Przeworski, eds., *Selected Works of Michael Wallerstein: The Political Economy of Inequality, Unions, and Social Democracy*

Andy Baker, *The Market and the Masses in Latin America: Policy Reform and Consumption in Liberalizing Economies*

Lisa Baldez, *Why Women Protest: Women's Movements in Chile*

Stefano Bartolini, *The Political Mobilization of the European Left, 1860–1980: The Class Cleavage*

Robert Bates, *When Things Fell Apart: State Failure in Late-Century Africa*

Mark Beissinger, *Nationalist Mobilization and the Collapse of the Soviet State*

Nancy Bermeo, ed., *Unemployment in the New Europe*

Carles Boix, *Democracy and Redistribution*

Carles Boix, *Political Parties, Growth, and Equality: Conservative and Social Democratic Economic Strategies in the World Economy*

Continued after the Index

"In this study of 12 Latin American countries, Kitschelt, Hawkins, Luna, Rosas, and Zechmeister show that programmatic party competition constitutes a rather unusual principal-agent mechanism linking politicians and voters. Programmatic linkages require that parties distinguish themselves along major issue dimensions, that they employ clear informational shortcuts to describe their positions to citizens, that they reflect the preferences of their voters, and that they remain ideologically cohesive. The first part of the book compares programmatic linkages cross-nationally: the authors employ extensive surveys of Latin American legislators conducted by the University of Salamanca in Spain to compare the level of programmatic politics achieved by Latin American party systems in the late-1990s. The second part of the book explores the historical origins and consequences of programmatic politics in the region. The authors conclude that programmatic party structuration is quite fragile: it emerged in few countries that experienced early economic development and partisan competition after long political struggles that involved a redefinition of social welfare, and it eroded under the pressure of negative economic trends in the 1980s and the 1990s. The book combines multiple perspectives, quantitative as well as qualitative, and incorporates Iván Llamazares and Scott Morgenstern as co-authors in two important chapters. This may be the most ambitious book on Latin American party systems since the publication of Mainwaring and Scully's *Building Democratic Institutions*."

– Aníbal Pérez-Liñán, University of Pittsburgh

"This book will be essential reading for students of Latin American politics. It introduces an important new dimension, programmatic party structuration (PPS), and it uses a wealth of data to demonstrate the considerable variation in PPS that exists in Latin America. The book offers a compelling historical explanation for why a few Latin American party systems, such as those in Chile and Uruguay, are organized along relatively coherent programmatic lines while many others are not. It argues persuasively that programmatic party structuration is rooted in historical and structural conditions that date back to the initial decades of the twentieth century, and that these historical causes are far more important in shaping contemporary Latin American party systems than are commonly cited factors such as short-term economic conditions and electoral rules. The book's argument has important implications for our understanding of new patterns of party competition that emerged with Latin America's turn to the Left in the 2000s."

– Steven Levitsky, Harvard University

Latin American Party Systems

HERBERT KITSCHELT
Duke University

KIRK A. HAWKINS
Brigham Young University

JUAN PABLO LUNA
Pontificia Universidad Católica de Chile

GUILLERMO ROSAS
Washington University in St. Louis

ELIZABETH J. ZECHMEISTER
Vanderbilt University

CAMBRIDGE
UNIVERSITY PRESS

CAMBRIDGE UNIVERSITY PRESS
Cambridge, New York, Melbourne, Madrid, Cape Town, Singapore,
São Paulo, Delhi, Dubai, Tokyo

Cambridge University Press
32 Avenue of the Americas, New York, NY 10013-2473, USA

www.cambridge.org
Information on this title: www.cambridge.org/9780521132664

First published 2010

Printed in the United States of America

A catalog record for this publication is available from the British Library.

Library of Congress Cataloging in Publication data

Latin American party systems / Herbert Kitschelt . . . [et al.].
p. cm.
Includes bibliographical references and index.
ISBN 978-0-521-11495-0 (hardback) – ISBN 978-0-521-13266-4 (pbk.)
1. Political parties – Latin America. 2. Latin America – Politics and
government – 1980– I. Kitschelt, Herbert. II. Title.
JL969.A45L37 2010
324.2098 – dc22 2009016392

ISBN 978-0-521-11495-0 Hardback
ISBN 978-0-521-13266-4 Paperback

Additional resources for this publication at www.cambridge.org/9780521114950

Contents

Tables

Figures

Preface

This book is the result of a long, didactic, and collegial process. In the time between the start and finish of this project, we experienced significant changes in our academic careers and our personal lives. Four of us made the transition from graduate student to assistant professor during the course of writing this book. As a group tally, we began the project with one little girl in our midst and ended with eight young children. At the project's start, we all lived a distance of roughly ten miles from each other around Duke University; at one point toward the project's end, we were spread across three continents.

Our research cluster gathered for the first time in the spring of 1998 in the office of the only author of this study who then already held a faculty position, Herbert Kitschelt. We had recently been given an early peek at a significant new dataset, the first round of the Parliamentary Elites of Latin America survey, created by scholars at the University of Salamanca under the leadership of Manuel Alcántara Sáez. Most of us present at this meeting were second- and third-year graduate students whose research interests focused on Latin America. The project would be to undertake a thorough investigation into the nature of programmatic party competition in Latin America, an analytical question on which Kitschelt had just completed a book with data from postcommunist Eastern Europe. It is hard to overemphasize the importance of the fact that most of us were in the early stages of our Ph.D. studies when this project started. It was partly through our work on this project that those of us who were graduate students at the time improved our capacity for various aspects of data analysis and, more generally, social science. The camaraderie that the group exhibited and experienced has been a very enjoyable aspect of this project and, we hope, has resulted in a better final product than we might otherwise have produced.

Our thanks for having made this project possible extend first and foremost to Manuel Alcántara Sáez, who created the dataset with his students and colleagues at the University of Salamanca. Manuel is a tireless academic entrepreneur with a keen sense that one of the most important tasks – and also most difficult and least rewarding in terms of academic accolades – is the provision of novel measures of political phenomena and their assembly in datasets that are open to inspection by the academic community. He has done the profession a great service not only in getting the Latin American legislators' surveys under way but also in publishing his own pertinent research based on this dataset. We submit our investigation as further testimony to the tremendous value of his undertaking. We are confident that many scholars will follow in our footsteps and build on these data, and we can only hope that Manuel and the Salamanca team will continue to deliver these vital surveys.

Over the years, we have collectively presented various parts of this project to individuals and groups at university workshops. Among those who gave us important feedback, we would like to express our gratitude to the following in particular. We thank Scott Mainwaring (who, incidentally, directed us to the Salamanca surveys) and Susan Stokes for their careful attention to the project in its very early stages, which included sponsoring a very useful meeting during the 2000 American Political Science Association (APSA) conference in Washington, D.C. We also thank several scholars for engaging us in productive conversations at various times at Duke, including Michael Coppedge, Jorge Domínguez, and Steven Levitsky. We thank our colleagues Jonathan Hartlyn, Evelyn Huber, and John Stephens at the University of North Carolina at Chapel Hill for their suggestions in a seminar on our project in 2001 and in subsequent years when they took the time to comment on papers coming out of the project.

We are thankful to Margaret Levi and all the participants in the Center for Comparative and Historical Analysis of Organizations and States workshop in December 2004 at the University of Washington, where we first presented a more or less complete set of chapters of our investigation. In addition to Margaret's leadership at this workshop, we would like to acknowledge the critical contributions of John Ahlquist, Christian Breunig, Tony Gill, Stephen Hanson, Steve Pfaff, and Eric Wibbels. Over a two-day period, participants took turns to discuss and dissect the various draft chapters of our book and to give us numerous recommendations. This often-challenging process unquestionably made the ultimate product much stronger, at least in our eyes. Needless to say, all remaining weaknesses are our own responsibility. After the Seattle event, we had one more opportunity to present our project collectively, this time at the University of New Mexico in Albuquerque, thanks to an invitation extended by Ken Roberts. We owe thanks to Ken and his departmental colleagues for their feedback at our May 2005 meeting on their beautiful campus.

In addition to feedback, some individuals have generously provided us data that have helped our project in specific ways. We thank Michael

Coppedge and Ken Roberts, both of whom gave us access to their datasets for particular analyses in this book. We also thank Hans-Dieter Klingemann for support in obtaining data from the Latinobarometer and Marta Lagos and her assistants for providing us with these data.

We have, individually or in subgroups, presented portions of the project to various audiences. We thank our discussants and the active participants in these sessions for their honest and helpful comments. We presented early drafts of our work at APSA meetings in 2000 and 2001. A very early draft of the empirical analyses that became Chapters 2 and 3 was presented at the 2000 Latin American Studies Association (LASA) Congress. An updated version of Chapter 3 was then presented at the following LASA Congress, in 2001. Early work on the project that became Chapter 4 was presented at the 2001 meeting of the Southern Political Science Association and again at the 2003 LASA Congress. A later version of Chapter 4 was presented to the Stanford Comparative Politics Working group in 2004. We also want to acknowledge that some of the work in this book has been published in journals. Specifically, an article based in part on Chapter 2 was published in *Comparative Political Studies* in 2005, and an article that draws on Chapter 4 was published in that same journal later that year. We thank the editor and the anonymous reviewers for their support of the project and the helpful comments they provided during the review process.

While the final product of our research was produced by five coauthors, we want to recognize the contributions made by several additional scholars. First, in the very initial stages of the project, our team included Sarah Brooks (then a graduate student at Duke, now a faculty member at Ohio State University), who thus gave input into the initial ideas and analyses that we circulated and discussed. Second, Scott Morgenstern (University of Pittsburgh), Iván Llamazares (University of Salamanca), and Marisa Ramos (University of Salamanca) participated in modules of our project. In Scott's and Iván's cases, this participation was sufficiently strong to recognize them as coauthors of Chapters 4 and 8.

In pulling together the final drafts of the manuscript, we had tremendous assistance from several individuals. We would like to acknowledge the help of Sergio Toro, who formatted the manuscript for submission to Cambridge, and the staff of administrative assistants in Brigham Young University's Department of Political Science, who helped review and edit the bibliography. Juan Pablo Luna acknowledges financial support from the Fondo Nacional de Desarrollo Científico y Tecnológico (FONDECYT Regular Projects 1060760 and 1060749), which helped with various aspects of the project. Finally, we thank Lew Bateman and the two anonymous reviewers at Cambridge for their careful reading of the entire manuscript and their insightful, critical, and also supportive comments.

The fact that this project had a gestation of more than a decade means that in some places our recall may be less than perfect. We apologize for any errors or omissions in this preface and are sincerely grateful for all the support and critical feedback we have received along the way. Finally, we would not have completed this work without our families' support and patience; we owe them an enormous debt of gratitude.

Introduction

Party Competition in Latin America

Herbert Kitschelt, Kirk A. Hawkins, Guillermo Rosas, and Elizabeth J. Zechmeister

By the end of the twentieth century, most Latin American countries could look back on their longest uninterrupted and, as of this writing, still open-ended period of political democracy. No country except Chile and Uruguay had enjoyed a longer run of full or even constrained democratic competition in any previous era. Before 1980, only five Latin American countries had achieved episodes of more than twelve continuous years of democratic or semidemocratic rule,[1] but by 1999 that threshold had been crossed by no fewer than six additional countries.[2] By the turn of the millennium, four of the five countries with comparatively durable democratic experiences before 1970 had once again accumulated a record of more than twelve years of continuous democracy since their most recent democratic transitions.[3] Consequently, Latin America stands out as the most uniformly democratic region on earth behind the established Western democracies and Japan. This is evidenced in Table I.1, which is based on Larry Diamond's recoding of Freedom House regime scores (Diamond 2002: 29–30, table 2).[4]

Because of the regional prevalence and durability of democracy in Latin America since the 1980s, research on the region has begun to move away since the mid-1990s from the theme of political regime change and has started to focus more on the empirical "quality" of democratic institutions

---

[1] They were Argentina (1912–30), Brazil (1946–63), Chile (1932–72), Costa Rica (1949–), and Uruguay (1942–73). On this scoring of countries, see Mainwaring, Brinks, and Pérez-Liñán (2001: 49).

[2] These countries were Bolivia (1982–), Colombia (1974–), Dominican Republic (1978–), Ecuador (1979–), Venezuela (1958–), and arguably Peru (1980–). Our scoring follows Mainwaring et al. (2001: 49).

[3] Argentina (1983–), Brazil (1985–), Costa Rica (1949–) and Uruguay (1985–).

[4] Contrary to reputation, Latin America was never exceptionally authoritarian relative to the economic affluence of its various countries. As Mainwaring and Pérez-Liñán (2003) show, if anything, Latin America has been more democratic than a simple GDP per capita variable would lead one to predict.

TABLE I.1. *Latin American Political Regimes in Global Comparison (2001)*

Region	Average Regime Score[a]	Standard Deviation	Number of Countries (Full Democracies)[b]
Western democracies	6.0	0.0	24 (24)[c]
Latin America[d]	4.92	1.22	25 (9)
Postcommunist region	4.33	1.71	27 (11)
Sub-Saharan Africa	3.31	1.60	48 (5)
Asia (East, Southeast, South)	3.16	1.95	25 (3)
Middle East–North Africa	2.05	1.31	19 (1)[e]

[a] Liberal democracy = 6; electoral democracy = 5; ambiguous regime = 4; competitive authoritarian regime = 3; hegemonic electoral authoritarian = 2; politically closed authoritarian = 1.
[b] Total countries followed by number of full democracies in parentheses.
[c] Twenty European countries plus four Anglo-Saxon settler democracies.
[d] Includes Caribbean and Central American countries, excluding eight Caribbean micropolities.
[e] Israel is the only full democracy.
Source: Coded from Diamond (2002: 29–30).

and processes of authoritative decision making. Our study contributes to this field of investigations. Although most Latin American polities may be democratic in a broad sense, there are still great differences in the ways citizens and politicians enact relations of democratic accountability in each polity. Our study explores this topic by analyzing patterns of party competition in twelve Latin American democracies in the late 1990s. We do so by creating indicators of programmatic party structuration primarily on the basis of elite and also mass surveys collected in the years 1997 and 1998. To understand these patterns, we introduce and test general theoretical arguments about the capacity of actors to develop democratic accountability relations. From the perspective of general theorizing, the geographic region and the point in time we employ as empirical material for our analysis are therefore almost purely coincidental and unimportant. At the same time, however, our investigation yields strong substantive implications for anyone who cares about the past and future of Latin American politics.

A traditional image of Latin American democratic politics suggests that parties in the region cannot produce relations of democratic accountability between citizens and politicians. They have shallow roots in society and cannot organize constituencies in support of alternative policy programs offering contrasting visions of societal development, distributive justice, and associated democratic institutions. According to this image, Latin American parties generate at most relations of accountability around clientelistic-selective material inducements. This proposition is true to a considerable extent for some Latin American countries. In line with much of the recent scholarship on Latin American democracy and political economy, our study is more impressed by the profound variance in the practice of democratic politics that can be encountered across Latin America. But we also have a somber message that results from our theoretical analysis. Because it takes a long time and requires crystallizing, protracted political struggles to build strong programmatic relations of democratic accountability, those we are empirically able to detect in Latin America in the late 1990s are built on political-economic conflicts belonging to a bygone era. Programmatic alternatives built on these conflicts are destined to erode in the political-economic environment of domestic and global market liberalization that has begun to take shape at least since the 1980s. At the same time, our study cannot (yet?) detect the emergence of new programmatic divides that may align coalitions of voters around political parties responding to the more recently emerging political-economic conflicts and challenges. As we discuss in the conclusion to our study, our data from the late 1990s may have some prognostic value at least for subsequent developments in the first decade of the new millennium. At the same time, our baseline data for the late 1990s put into sharper relief the new programmatic departures that may be emerging in the region.

The focus of our investigation is *programmatic party structuration* (PPS) in Latin America. As a first, rough approximation, consider *programmatic coordination* to indicate the extent to which politicians employ party labels to develop coherent policy alternatives in their public appeals. These alternatives define the competitive space of democratic electoral contests. Moreover, on the basis of their capacity to coordinate around programmatic appeals, parties may build *programmatic linkages* to voters by assembling distinctive electoral coalitions such that each party's voters are on average closer to that party's programmatic appeals than to the rival appeals of any other party. Programmatic coordination and programmatic linkages taken together constitute programmatic party structuration, measured at the level of entire party systems or individual parties. PPS, in the sense of both programmatic coordination and programmatic linkages, is a precondition of, albeit not identical with, "responsible partisan government," an attribute of democracy highlighted by political science for generations (APSA 1950). At a minimum, it says that a democracy's policy outputs vary with the partisan composition of its governments, which, in turn, is a function of voters' choices among programmatic parties that announce different policy packages they intend to implement in the event of their being elected to government. The anticipation of party responsibility motivates citizens to cast their vote for the party that most closely relates to their own personal policy preferences. Where PPS is weak or absent, politicians may seek to mobilize electoral constituencies on the basis of direct selective incentives and exchange relations that target individuals and small groups (clientelism, with office patronage and other currencies) or by purely emotional appeals to symbols, group identification, or the charisma of a candidate.

A substantial part of this book develops novel and informative measures of components of PPS and a combined index of PPS. We hope they may serve to inspire researchers of party systems dealing with other regions of the world so that they will eventually facilitate interregional comparison. In the subsequent part of the book, we account for cross-national variance in patterns of PPS. Programmatic party structuration in the late 1990s tends to be comparatively strong only in those Latin American polities where momentous mass mobilization, led by parties that date back at least to the era immediately following World War II but may even go back to the nineteenth century, managed to assert the interests of urban citizens working in manufacturing and services, sometimes against agrarian oligarchies, by instituting welfare states benefiting urban wage earners. Where this shift in political mobilization occurred *in combination with* social policy innovation, it realigned politics around resilient political parties that directly or through successor parties have continued to shape their polities' profiles of democratic contestation until the late 1990s.

Where the initial political-economic and regime shift failed to occur, party systems have remained either fluid and "inchoate" (Mainwaring and Scully 1995) over the decades or institutionalized around thoroughly clientelistic parties. More recently, the profound dislocations of the "lost decade" of the 1980s and the aftermath of painfully slow and halting recovery in most Latin American countries are also beginning to leave a footprint on Latin American party systems. However, the processes by which politicians and voters update their strategies and techniques of democratic competition in light of new political-economic challenges are glacially slow. Particularly fierce economic crises in the 1980s have precipitated the erosion of programmatic party systems where they once were anchored in comparatively favorable conditions, but better economic performance in the 1980s and 1990s has not led to improved programmatic party structuration in other countries where capacities for PPS were traditionally weak or flared up only in brief historical episodes, such as in Bolivia or Peru. New programmatic alignments may require the emergence of new political-economic distributive institutions, and the neoliberal reforms by themselves have neither delivered consistent economic results nor produced such institutions and political alignments. Our study offers a first glimpse at different pathways of party system development that might become more consequential in Latin America in the future. We are thus arguing not that Latin American party systems are "frozen" but that the disappearance of existing programmatic alignments and the emergence of new programmatic alignments require political-economic innovations that have yet to germinate. We leave it to other studies to explore which countries will have an easier or harder time to find new political-economic formulas and institutions to set themselves on a course of sustained economic growth: countries that had a party regime with a modicum of programmatic competition in the past or those polities that start "from scratch" against the background of inchoate or clientelistic institutionalized party systems.

Our study covers a set of twelve Latin American countries in which more than 90 percent of the region's population resides. Primarily because of data constraints, we could not include further cases, particularly in Central America. Table I.2 lists the countries covered here and shows their Freedom House democracy status measured right before the data on which our study is based were gathered and at the most recent time of observation (2006–7). In a second column, for each period the table also includes the Central and South American countries on which we did not obtain suitable data. It shows that our sample generally covers the range of regime variance encountered in the region. In the time period on which our study focuses (the years 1997–98, when the survey data we examine were collected), electoral competition was on shaky ground in Peru and, because of a quasi–civil war, also in Colombia. In all the countries we cover, the quality of democracy in terms of civil liberties and political rights has subsequently improved or stayed constant (Ecuador alone), with the exceptions of Bolivia and Venezuela (Table I.2).

Our study differs from previous work in its choice of data, inclusiveness of comparative design, analytical techniques, and specification of causal hypotheses.[5] Nevertheless, its key findings contribute to the collective knowledge about the diversity of Latin American party democracy resulting from research undertaken over the past few decades. In terms of past descriptive regional analysis of party systems, the cross-national documentation of such diversity using quantitative measures by Mainwaring and Scully (1995), Coppedge (1998b), and Roberts (2002) stands out. Qualitative characterizations of diversity in the Latin American region result from a host of studies that typically examine the career of individual parties or of several parties in individual countries. Our study picks up the systematic efforts by Mainwaring and Scully and Coppedge but also attempts to describe and compare the profiles of programmatic party competition with the finer quantitative measures on which our study is based. We make the diversity of politicians' efforts to structure programmatic party competition across Latin American party systems more visible with the aid of analytical concepts never before applied to democratic polities in this region.[6] For a subset of nine countries, we also explore the extent to which programmatic coordination by political

---

[5] It is worth mentioning that data from the same congressional elite survey we use here were extensively analyzed in a recently published book (Alcántara 2008). The work edited by Alcántara, who funded and directs the Universidad de Salamanca congressional elite survey, provides a more comprehensive examination of all the questions and cases included in the study from its origin in the 1990s to the most recent wave of interviews. Here we privilege focus over scope and concentrate our efforts at measuring and explaining PPS.

[6] For a previous application of these concepts to various postcommunist countries, see Kitschelt et al. (1999) and Kitschelt and Smyth (2002).

TABLE I.2. *Political Regimes in Latin America: Political and Civil Rights, 1997–1998 and 2006–2007*

Freedom House Democracy Status: Civil and Political Rights Scores[a]	1997–98		2006–7	
	Countries in Study	Countries Not in Study	Countries in Study	Countries Not in Study
Liberal democracies	Costa Rica (1,2) Uruguay (1,2) Bolivia (1,3) Chile (2,2)	Belize (1,1) Trinidad & Tobago (1,2) Guyana (2,2)	Chile (1,1) Costa Rica (1,1) Uruguay (1,1) Argentina (2,2) Brazil (2,2) Dominican Republic (2,2)	Belize (1,2) Panama (1,2) Antigua Barbuda (2,2) Suriname (2,2) Trinidad & Tobago (2,2)
Electoral democracies	Argentina (2,3) Venezuela (2,3) Dominican Republic (3,3) Ecuador (3,3) Brazil (3,4) Mexico (3,4)	El Salvador (2,3) Honduras (2,3) Jamaica (2,3) Panama (2,3) Nicaragua (3,3) Suriname (3,3) Guatemala (3,4)	Mexico (2,3) Peru (2,3) Bolivia (3,3) Colombia (3,3) Ecuador (3,3) Venezuela (4,4)	El Salvador (2,3) Guyana (2,3) Jamaica (2,3) Honduras (3,3) Nicaragua (3,3) Paraguay (3,3) Guatemala (3,4)
Ambiguous regimes	Colombia (4,4)	Antigua & Barbuda (4,3) Paraguay (4,3)		
Competitive authoritarianism	Peru (5,4)	Haiti (4,5)		Haiti (4,5)
Hegemonic electoral authoritarianism				
Politically closed authoritarianism		Cuba (7,7)		Cuba (7,7)

[a] Low scores indicate extensive civil rights (first score in each bracket) or political rights (second score). Scales range from 1 to 7.

elites actually yields principal-agent relations of democratic representation (or programmatic linkage), at least in the weak sense of a correspondence between electoral constituencies and legislators on preferences over salient policy issues.

In an effort to explain these cross-national PPS country profiles, we develop a theory of partisan divisions and voter-politician linkages that highlights how long-term investments by political entrepreneurs and citizens in political alignments come about, fade away, and are displaced by new investments. By focusing on long-term processes of political adaptation and reform in the construction of Latin American party systems, we take inspiration from the works of authors such as Remmer (1989: chap. 3), Collier and Collier (1991), Hagopian (1996), Coppedge (1998a), and Roberts (2002). "Critical junctures," to employ Collier and Collier's (1991) key concept, are embedded in a lengthy prior process of collective action and mobilization that eventually results in party system innovation. That innovation "locks in" because it is associated with a reconfiguration of political-economic institutions that constitute the actors' "stakes" in the struggle over political control. Where such configurations of investments in vehicles of collective action and political-economic institutions occur, they create a "stickiness" of party systems that makes them hard to dislocate. While not frozen, party alignments fade away gradually and only under the impact of dramatic political-economic or cultural changes.[7] Such adaptation results from the interplay of citizens' and politicians' capabilities, their opportunities to engage in the iteration of the competitive electoral game, and the emergence of new "stakes" of conflict that result from the existing distribution of scarce materials and symbolic resources in a polity.

With the benefit of hindsight, processes of party system change that stretch over several decades may be highlighted by sudden "critical junctures," but they are intricately tied to long periods of mounting mobilization for change before the juncture and a lock-in of new patterns of political competition and social organization thereafter. Consider Juan Perón's Justicialist Party in Argentina. Perón came onto the scene with a sudden splash, but these events were preceded by decades of constrained democratic competition (1912–30), the growth of industrial unionism, and the grappling for an alternative to export-led growth starting with the Great Depression. In this sense, institutional and political-economic change is not adequately characterized by sudden processes of radical change, as suggested by the "punctuated equilibrium" perspective of political and institutional change.[8] Our account of the temporality of political adaptation in Latin

---

[7] For a critique of the literature on the sudden realignment of party systems, see Mayhew (2000).

[8] For a critique, see Thelen (1999; 2003), Kitschelt (2003), Pierson (2000; 2004), and Roland (2004).

American party systems suggests the adequacy of a more incremental model. This is not to say that all party system change requires long-term incremental buildup. But it is useful to distinguish between processes that result from proximate causal mechanisms and processes that work over a long duration.

Both short-term and long-term mechanisms of constructing, maintaining, dismantling, or preventing programmatic principal-agent linkages in partisan politics presuppose some purposive, deliberate political action on the part of citizens and politicians. The difference between the two basic families of theoretical models concerns what exactly the cues, conditions, and capabilities are that enable actors to devise strategies and the time horizons involved in their choices. At the core of the long-term perspective are iterative processes of learning democratic politics through repeated efforts of mobilization and electoral competition. These processes are made possible against the backdrop of economic resource development and catalytic but protracted periods of societal struggle about political economic reform that crystallize political camps. The result is the electoral enfranchisement of hitherto excluded groups, often followed by a political redistribution of property rights, earnings opportunities, and state-administered income flows. Because of the high costs of collective action sunk into the construction of political organizations as well as the cognitive formation of reputations and expectations about the likely behavior of political actors, the past strongly affects the current generation of citizens and politicians.

By contrast, the short-term perspective on political adaptation and strategic choice discounts the importance of sunk political investments and focuses on the currently available capabilities of the actors; the institutions governing the political game (e.g., electoral laws) and the unfolding political-economic developments. Even in the world of long-term, path-dependent political investment in patterns of democratic competition, the cumulative impact of economic shocks and societal dislocations eventually leaves its mark on party systems and political voter alignments. But the short-term perspective expects much faster adjustment by politicians and voters to new conditions and opportunities. Whereas long-term perspectives count in terms of several decades and whole generations, short-term perspectives focus on annualized changes, legislative terms, and conditions and strategic alignments unfolding over the course of less than a single decade.

Our empirical analysis suggests that, even in the late 1990s, contrasting profiles of programmatic party competition across Latin American polities still exhibit the marks of long-term, path-dependent, but incrementally innovative collective action and political "learning" that began to emerge as far back as the 1930s and that were embedded in a distinct political-economic context. Specifically, we find that only those Latin American polities which experienced a relatively high level of economic development already before World War II, longer periods of democratic competition after 1945, and the implementation of comparatively broad policies of social protection for at least the urban population in that time period were able to lock in patterns of programmatic party competition that still persist into the late 1990s. By contrast, polities that lacked one or more of these experiences and consequently developed less institutionalized parties in the course of the twentieth century still exhibit much lower PPS in the late 1990s, even if societal and institutional conditions for the development of programmatic linkages have recently become more favorable.

By emphasizing cumulative adaptation, our investigation affirms the presence of a dynamic of change that erodes old citizen-politician alignments in light of changed political-economic realities. In a sometimes glacial but at other times accelerating process, party systems reshape themselves. Our empirical snapshot of Latin American party systems in the late 1990s permits us to gauge the relative weight of cumulative historical adaptation and the power of current updating of party systems only at a single point in time. Dynamic studies with panel data will have to improve on this cross-sectional research design by showing how new societal developments and political strategies modify or trump existing patterns of citizen-politician linkage, yet then become components of a cumulative stock of political experiences and organizational investments that continuously (re)shape the cross-national diversity of party competition in Latin America.

Long-term processes are certainly not prisons of path dependence. Citizens and politicians have frequent opportunities to update such patterns, particularly in light of new economic and political challenges that make existing arrangements appear obsolete. Although Coppedge (1998a) emphasizes long-term developments of Latin American party systems, he also correctly warns against an exclusive preoccupation with long-term learning models of political competition and partisan organization. At the end of a descriptive account of Latin American party system diversity, he draws our attention to short-term political and economic events and politicians' strategic moves as forces that mold Latin American politics:

Party systems as diverse and dynamic as these will not be easily explained. The explanatory factors in the standard toolkit – levels of development, class structure, ethnic cleavages, demographic change and electoral laws – change too slowly or gradually to capture much of the variance described here. Explanations that work in Latin America are more likely to concern factors that are more easily, rapidly and completely manipulated by governments, party leaders, and other elites. These factors include party splits, mergers and alliances; campaign tactics; programmatic shifts; perhaps short-term economic performance; and in isolated cases, election boycotts and the proscription of certain parties or candidates. (Coppedge 1998b: 563)

While we would consider some of the items on Coppedge's list of short-term causes of party system change (party splits, mergers and alliances, campaign tactics, and programmatic shifts) as aspects or close correlates of our dependent variable – the programmatic structuring of partisan alternatives – others clearly are serious candidates to serve as causes for such patterns. Among the forces exogenous to party systems, yet potentially consequential for them, may be the new institutions that emerged from the democratic transitions of most Latin American countries in the 1980s, as well as the different countries' trajectories of economic policy reform and performance (inflation, growth, employment) throughout the "lost decade" of the 1980s and after.

In the final analysis, short-term political and economic experiences may complement long-term forces shaping the structuration of Latin American party systems, even if such experiences are sometimes hard to identify. Given the small number of cases (twelve) and the purely cross-sectional design of our study, it is fiendishly difficult and somewhat hazardous to assign relative explanatory power to long-term and short-term causal variables because of the familiar problems of collinearity, endogeneity, and overdetermination. Nevertheless, without doing too much violence to our close scrutiny of the evidence, let us offer a simple heuristic formula as summary and prospect. Where long-term regime and political-economic developments have favored strong PPS in some Latin American polities, sharply negative short-term economic and political conditions may nevertheless erode PPS substantially over the course of a few electoral terms. Programmatic party structuration proves to be quite fragile. Conversely, where long-term political developments have been inauspicious for strong PPS in Latin America, comparatively favorable short-term economic and political conditions in the 1980s or 1990s did fairly little to boost PPS by the end of that decade. Programmatic party competition is a fragile achievement that is more easily destroyed than constructed. What new programmatic alignments, if any, might result from the dismantling of import-substituting industrialization was a matter of speculation at the end of the 1990s and still is, in many regards, a decade later. We revisit this topic in the Conclusion.

Let us close our Introduction with three clarifications and caveats. First, when we say that our study focuses on the "quality" of democracy in Latin America, we employ that notion in a purely positive – that is, descriptive and analytical – sense. It concerns the identification of attributes and features of democratic processes of interest articulation, aggregation, decision making, and policy implementation in Latin American polities. We do not subscribe to a unified normative scale of "high" or "low" quality against which existing democracies can be judged, nor do we attempt to create a parsimonious set of multidimensional "types" of democracy under which empirical cases can be subsumed. Instead, we identify specific dimensions and attributes of democratic "quality" with regard to one key feature of contemporary democracies, that of party systems. We analyze empirically how different features of party systems hang together. In the course of this endeavor, we characterize each quality at a level of measurement beyond a simple nominal scale (high-low). In other words, in order to achieve precision in our comparative analysis, we attempt to move from "quality" to "quantity" through ordinal or interval scaling of our concepts.

Second, our study focuses exclusively on the quality of the democratic process without probing into the consequences of different patterns of democratic competition for public policy and political regime stability or volatility. It is *descriptive* in characterizing different patterns of competitive alignments in Latin American democracies at a time when many of these countries could look back on a longer uninterrupted run of democratic elections than in any previous period. It attempts to be *explanatory* in terms of accounting for such patterns in light of rival theories of democratic politics. Our study thus brackets the theoretically and politically salient question of whether the features of the democratic process shape the outputs and outcomes of authoritative political decision making, such as economic performance, levels and distributions of life chances, and ultimately the public approval ("legitimacy") and survival of a democratic regime. Only in Chapter 9 do we turn to public opinion and political-economic correlates of different patterns of programmatic party structuration, and even then our analysis cannot make strong causal claims.

Within the field of political processes, the focus of our investigation is the causal analysis of features exhibited by party systems, and in some instances of individual parties, in Latin American democracies. Thus, we set aside other potential chains of interest articulation, aggregation, and decision that may affect the authoritative allocation of scarce resources, such as those which run through the mobilization of social movements and interest groups. In our study of Latin American party systems, we do draw on scholars who have examined the role of political institutions in shaping democratic processes across Latin America, such as electoral institutions (e.g., Jones 1995; Carey 1996), executive-legislative relations in presidential systems (Shugart and Carey 1992; Mainwaring and Shugart 1997; Carey and Shugart 1998; Haggard and McCubbins 2001; Morgenstern and Nacif 2002), and federalism (Wibbels 2005). Latin American party systems themselves and their circuits of accountability and responsiveness have not yet attracted a sizable community of scholars probing into patterns of democratic competition in an encompassing comparative fashion. To be sure, there are thorough and insightful monographs that are centered on the politics of individual countries. Often, they provide theoretical frameworks that, in principle, should permit interesting cross-national comparative tests (e.g., Ames 2001; Bruhn 1997; Coppedge 1994; Gibson 1996; Levitsky 2003; Mainwaring 1999; McGuire 1997; Samuels 2003). But there are few genuinely comparative quantitative studies of Latin American party systems. Dix (1989; 1992) was one of the first to theorize about the institutionalization and cleavage structure of Latin American party systems, but he offered only a smattering of empirical evidence. Coppedge (1998b) and Mainwaring and Scully

(1995) provided a descriptive framework and comparative data to characterize party system institutionalization across Latin American democracies. They did not push, however, toward a causal analysis of what produces party system institutionalization, its correlates, or its consequences. Roberts and Wibbels (1999) published a sophisticated analysis of electoral volatility in Latin America, and Roberts (2002) examined patterns of working-class mobilization and party systems in order to explain trajectories of economic reform in the 1980s. Moreno (1999: 106–49) produced the first survey of evidence-based comparative investigations of issue divisions and partisan alignments in Latin America countries. Furthermore, some important monographs and edited volumes compare the fortunes of individual party families across several Latin American countries (e.g., Mainwaring and Scully 2003; Middlebrook 2000; Roberts 1998).

Third, while our study of Latin American party systems is encompassing, it is confined to a single point in time. Our investigation cannot capture the intertemporal change of party systems that is often obvious to observers of Latin American democracies. Consider countries such as Bolivia, Ecuador, Peru, or, most dramatically, Venezuela over the short span of the ten-year period starting in 1995. In all of them, party systems have been severely shaken or altered and have approached the brink of democratic rupture. A purely cross-sectional analysis can assess only the extent to which political economic developments in individual countries in the 1980s and 1990s cumulatively affected the broad cross-national pattern of programmatic party competition that we observe with data from 1995 to 1998. It may even postulate factors that contribute to the likelihood of brittleness and volatility in a specific polity. Factors that may explain cross-national patterns of partisan politics, however, do not necessarily explain the details of intranational dynamics over time, and vice versa. This does not rule out, of course, that mechanisms operating within each polity to modify programmatic partisan politics over time may eventually also produce a different cross-national pattern of democratic party competition.

Nevertheless, studying attributes of democratic party competition at a single time is a useful exercise for at least two general reasons. First, comparative studies of party systems in Latin America have to start somewhere. Why not with one point in time? Future research can then compare the state of party systems at earlier or later points with our findings and directly try to account for systemic dynamics. Second, our study is not exclusively descriptive but is also explanatory. We want to probe into the causes of different quality features in Latin American party democracies. Some of these potential causes are historically deep and enduring, whereas others are temporally shallower, short-term, and contingent. To the extent that our causal analysis uncovers the continuing relevance of deeper, intertemporally more robust, if not "structural" determinants of party system features, such causes should also affect Latin American party systems at other points in time. Our analysis thus provides input for further studies probing the resilience of causal patterns.

In Chapter 1, we first motivate a comparative analysis of parties and party systems, then present a range of rival or complementary theories that may account for alternative patterns of party structuration, and finally characterize the causal argument of the book in greater detail. Part I of the book describes the patterns of programmatic party structuration observed in Latin America in the late 1990s by measuring the issues that divide politicians and parties (Chapter 2), the use of left-right labels by politicians (Chapter 3), the congruence between legislators' and voters' positions on key issues (Chapter 4), and the degree of ideological cohesion within parties (Chapter 5). As these chapters demonstrate, party systems in Latin America revolve almost exclusively around economic-distributive conflicts, whereas religion and regime constitute only minor divides. Part II then moves on to examine long-term determinants of economic PPS in the region (Chapter 6), short-term forces exogenous to these long-term developments but with the potential to disrupt them (Chapter 7), the conditions of the minor programmatic divides of religion and regime (Chapter 8), and correlates of different levels of PPS in the current operation of democracies in Latin America (Chapter 9). In the Conclusion, we discuss the future comparative research agenda concerning programmatic party structuration across time within Latin America and in a cross-regional, global perspective.

Patterns of Programmatic Party Competition in Latin America

Herbert Kitschelt, Kirk A. Hawkins, Guillermo Rosas, and Elizabeth J. Zechmeister

Most democracies have a representative format such that citizens as "principals" entrust politicians as "agents" with the business of making binding, authoritative decisions for all members of the polity. Democracy is a political regime that specifies formal procedures of political participation and electoral contestation, together with guarantees of civil and political rights and basic resource endowments, that allow citizens to engage in this process effectively and without constraint. Through periodic elections, agents are held accountable to the mass public. In anticipation of such accountability, agents may be responsive to the principals' demands and preferences. There is plenty of debate about this normative and positive characterization of such "first principles" of democratic contestation (cf. Collier and Levitsky 1997; Held 1987; Dahl 1989; Shapiro 2003), but in this study we are concerned with the more specific question of how democratic polities express circuits of accountability and responsiveness in light of their existing institutions and the nature of the political actors who inhabit them. Even more specifically, our study examines how political parties – as collective actors involved in the process of interest articulation and aggregation – affect the positive quality of democracy by shaping circuits of accountability and responsiveness in Latin American polities.

In populous democratic polities, political parties – as coalitions of ambitious, office-seeking politicians – may be indispensable elements of any political process that organizes circuits of accountability and responsiveness. This, of course, does not rule out the presence and significance of other types of collective actors, such as interest groups and social movements, in the political decision-making process. Moreover, how parties serve as agents for democratic principals may take many different forms and may be limited by numerous constraints.

At a basic level, voters enact accountability by deciding whether to reelect their agents. But "throwing the rascals out" is a blunt, uninformative tool for citizens to express their displeasure with agents. If citizens could vote on policies rather than representatives, however, chances are their preference schedules would be so complex that simple democratic decision procedures would yield not stable binding collective decisions but cycles of collective choices (Arrow 1963 [1951]). Further, democratic accountability relations can cause informational asymmetry between citizens and politicians on the basis of the complexity of political decision making (Kiewiet and McCubbins 1991; Moe 1984). This makes opportunistic politicians inclined to claim responsibility for popular outcomes they did not affect but to conceal responsibility for unpopular outcomes they promoted.

Characterizing citizen-politician relations as principal-agent games suggests that misalignments between the preferences and interests of citizen-principals and those of politician-agents are ubiquitous. Where such preferences are aligned and yield a relationship of preference representation, the mode and substance of this representation may vary profoundly across polities. Typically, treatments of democratic accountability home in on a single mode that we call programmatic accountability, which is closely wedded to what is commonly known as the "responsible partisan model of democratic governance." Politicians fight for or deliver club and collective goods ("policies") more or less congruent with citizens' preferences. On the basis of their perceptions of the policy-making record and more or less credible electoral promises of politicians, voters decide on the (re)election of incumbents or their challengers. Programmatic accountability, however, may occur only under very specific conditions. And there may be alternative modes of accountability that we need to introduce in order to appreciate the uniqueness of the responsible partisan model.

Because of informational constraints and the complexity of political decision making, programmatic accountability cannot work practically at the level of individual representatives and on individual policies. It compels politicians to organize themselves in teams (parties) whose members pool resources in pursuit of votes and assemble joint aggregate policy schedules to simplify the alternatives for the voters, who tend to be information misers with limited attention to political matters. In other words, to solve the *principal-agent problem* between citizens and politicians in the programmatic mode of linkage, politicians first have to *solve coordination and collective action problems among themselves*. In modern mass democracies, programmatic accountability is conceivable only in terms of competition among a very restricted number of political teams that have mastered the challenges of collective action and coordination around joint preference functions that can be mapped on a very low dimensional programmatic preference space. To a lesser or greater extent, individual politicians subordinate their personal preference rankings to the collective preference schedule endorsed by the party.

When the conditions prevail that facilitate this programmatic mode of party formation, we may conceive of political agency as a capacity not just of individual politicians but of "parties as teams" capable of enforcing collective agency against individual dissenters. In this instance, the use of a collectivist language that attributes agency and the ability to learn to a corporate entity is not a misleading reification of collective actors but is a shorthand way to characterize the coordinated movement of actors in a situation of programmatic competition.

In the first section of this chapter, we discuss programmatic principal-agent relations of accountability and responsiveness and their alternatives in democratic politics. In the second section, we advance hypotheses about the conditions under which politicians are likely to make programmatic appeals and to build *sustained* relations of voter representation based on programmatic linkages. In the third section, we present our favored theoretical perspective in greater detail and preview how it applies to the experience of Latin American party politics toward the end of the twentieth century.

NATURE AND SIGNIFICANCE OF PROGRAMMATIC LINKAGES AND PARTY SYSTEM STRUCTURATION

Parties and party systems are *programmatically structured* if teams of politicians compete for votes by offering citizens alternative packages of policies that they commit to enact if elected to political office with sufficient support. Policies are proposals to issue binding authoritative decisions that incur costs and award benefits to citizens regardless of whom they voted for in the election. Vote- and office-seeking politicians may tailor their proposals such that they benefit electoral constituencies that support them already or whose support they consider decisive for their party's success in future elections and government formation. In programmatic competition, politicians cannot verify which individuals and groups actually supported them and hence cannot target benefits to their current or prospective supporters. Voters, conversely, are "free riders": They enjoy benefits regardless of how they voted but also suffer costs independent of whether they supported or opposed the politicians whose parties form the executive.

A *programmatic linkage* between voters and politicians presupposes that citizens make electoral choices contingent upon the competing parties' programmatic record and proposals. By relating the parties' perceived collective policy ideal points, discounted by the credibility of the parties that offer them, to their personally preferred policy ideal points, "rational" citizens choose the partisan alternative that somehow maximizes their personal utilities.[1] Principals are represented by their agents through programmatic

---

[1] It is irrelevant for us in our study whether this proximity model relies on a spatial operationalization in terms of Euclidean geometric distance or a directional model computing the

linkage if there is *congruence* between the policies preferred by each party's voters and its corresponding politicians and if there is between-party *divergence* such that each party appeals to a different subset of voters. Thus, *programmatic coordination* of politicians within each party and differentiation across parties is a necessary, but not sufficient, condition for the emergence of a programmatic principal-agent linkage. The latter is consummated as *programmatic representation* only if voters act on politicians' programmatic cues and align themselves with parties by comparing personal and partisan programmatic packages.[2] If all or most relevant parties seek to maximize their votes or control of political office by building programmatic linkages, we are dealing with high *programmatic party structuration* (PPS) within the party system. PPS becomes a systemic property and *is sustained over time*.

PPS occurs at the level of individual party, measured by the coherence of the programmatic messages created by politicians running under a single party label, or at the systemic level, based on the discernible differences among parties' programmatic appeals that matter for citizens' party choices. When we use the abbreviation PPS, the semantic context makes clear whether we refer to it as systemic property or as property of individual parties.

Of course, demand and supply of programs are not entirely exogenous to each other. It is safe to presume that there is an ongoing process of mutual adjustment in which politicians cater to voters' preferences, and voters in turn modify their preferences in view of politicians' appeals. What matters to us is the identification of empirical tracers of sustained PPS as elite coordination and citizen-politician linkage and to explain the extent to which PPS varies across polities, parties, and time.

Let us relate our notion of programmatic party system structuration to two other features that play a role in the comparative party system literature: "polarization" between parties and "cleavages" that structure party alignments. Party polarization is a special case of PPS, namely a programmatic structuration of partisan alternatives in which the announced positions of relevant competitors are very far apart. Imagine a unidimensional 10-point left-right scale with four parties of equal size; a system in which the central appeal of the two outlying parties is at 2 and 8 is more polarized than a system in which the outlying parties are at 4 and 6, with the remaining

---

scalar product of distance and direction where voters support the party that articulates a clear position on the same side of issue divides they are supporting as well. For a comprehensive analysis, see Merrill and Grofman (1999).

[2] How exactly citizens and politicians relate to each other in representative relations is a complicated matter (see Chapter 4). Suffice it to say here that there are many variants of program-based representation and accountability, the weakest of which is a simple correspondence between citizens' and politicians' programmatic preferences (cf. Przeworski, Stokes, and Manin 1999; Powell 2000, 2004b; Mansbridge 2003).

two parties always located between these extremes. Not every programmatically structured system is polarized. Programmatic structuration requires that party positions are identifiable, that is, that politicians provide similar assessments about the location of their own parties and that voters perceive clear and distinct party positions. Polarization concerns the distribution of parties' mean positions, whereas PPS is about the spread of voters' beliefs and politicians' assessments about the location of those positions.

Political cleavages are durable alignments that link political parties to electoral constituencies characterized by specific traits (attributes, policy preferences, associational practices). Stable alignments can be based on non-programmatic linkages between politicians and voters. But the presence of clear programmatic partisan profiles makes the formation of durable cleavage alignments in party systems more likely. Parties gather particular types of voters around their programmatic appeals. They build electoral coalitions of supporters that are pitted against those of other parties, and they compete by issuing programmatic appeals for segments of the electorate that are situated between the partisan camps. Both partisan cleavage and party system polarization are related to programmatic party system structuration, yet are not identical to that concept. High PPS is a necessary, but not sufficient, condition for polarization and durable cleavage formation, but it may occur also under conditions of moderate, centripetal political competition. Political cleavage alignments definitely lend stability to PPS, as will be evident in the cases we discuss in this study. Yet not all polities with high PPS may feature sharp cleavage alignments.

We make four points in this section. First, programmatic party competition constitutes only one of several principal-agent linkage mechanisms that establish accountability in democratic politics. Second, programmatic party competition is, however, a particularly consequential linkage mechanism from the perspective of normative and positive democratic theory. Third, for a variety of reasons, the presence of institutionalized parties is a facilitating, if not indispensable condition for the programmatic structuring of party competition and for the development of citizen-politician linkages. And, fourth, programmatic party competition is both feasible and real, although some scholars may challenge that claim on the basis of well-known results from formal theories of party competition going back to Downs (1957) or Riker (1982).

Alternative Modes of Linkage in Democracies

Democratic linkages between citizens and politicians come in nonrational, affective and in rational, deliberative variants. Among the former, citizens support candidates and parties on the basis of collective identification (party identification); the personal charisma of a politician, including her perceived moral rectitude;[3] or descriptive collective attributes (ethnic group, gender, class traits) shared by principals and agents. Rationalists have argued that even such affective bonds may betray self-interested calculus. Descriptive representation, for example, is rational, if it is based on the expectation that a group member is likely and able to pursue political group interests. And party identification may to a considerable extent be just a "running tally" of the cumulative services a party has delivered to a given constituency in the past (Fiorina 1997: 397). A politician's "charisma," finally, may reflect a specific expectation of competence and efficiency in delivering benefits to supporters, particularly in a time of crisis. In each instance, rationally calculating voters employ descriptive attributes, party labels, or politicians' personal moral stances as clues to their policy preferences, when politicians' intentions and empirical actions cannot be directly observed (Zechmeister 2003). While these rationalist accounts may be partially true, they are still likely to leave an irreducible affective element in many citizens' electoral choices.

Three variants may be distinguished among rational-deliberative linkages between citizens and politicians. Two of them are based on policy and one on contingent, targeted material advantages voters receive or expect in exchange for supporting a party. A first policy-based linkage mechanism concerns collective goods (nearly) everyone in a polity would like to see produced. Delivering economic growth, clean air, law and order, and external defense may come close to being collective or "valence" goods. Rather than taking opposite positions on what is to be delivered, politicians compete on valence goods by advertising their own or their party's unique competence to deliver the universally endorsed good. Voters then evaluate a politician on the basis of her proven record to deliver collective goods (retrospective voting) as well as the credibility of her promises to do so in the future (prospective voting).[4]

Most policies, however, only seemingly produce purely collective goods. On closer inspection, the operational pursuit of objectives such as economic growth, public safety, or environmental protection involves distributional choices that benefit some and hurt others. What politicians thus deliver tend to be "club" goods that advance the fortunes of only some. Beyond the veil of rhetoric, candidates and parties overwhelmingly rely on positional, directional stances rather than valence appeals. People and politicians struggle over the right kinds of policy instruments and their distributional implications to bring about seemingly collective goods.[5]

---

[3] This is what Fearon (1999) refers to as voters selecting a "good type."

[4] On the theory of valence competition and its relationship to spatial competition, see Schofield (2003; 2004), Schofield and Sened (2006), and Miller and Schofield (2003).

[5] The most recent literature has therefore ventured to combine spatial theory of competition with valence competition or an element of "partisan identification," broadly conceived, that

What unites both valence-based and position-based programmatic competition among parties and programmatic citizen-politician linkages, however, is that voters are *only indirectly compensated* for their support of winning candidates and parties. Winning politicians enact policies that (re)distribute costs and benefits among all members of broad citizen categories, regardless of whether specific individuals voted in favor of or against the winning party. Given the anticipated distribution of costs and benefits a policy imposes on citizens, politicians have a general idea of which categories of voters are more likely to support them. But they cannot reward only those individuals who actually do vote for them. The "contract" between voters and politicians through policy or promised policies ("programs") is at best incomplete. Yet it may also be an efficient, low-cost mechanism to establish accountability and responsiveness between principals and agents: few transaction costs are incurred in tailoring and targeting benefits to citizen categories, and there are also few monitoring and sanctioning costs for exchanges gone bad. Often enough, entrepreneurs might find programmatic politics less costly to produce than voter compensation through targeted personal or small-group favors.

Such costs are higher in the third mode of rationalist, deliberative citizen-politician linkage commonly referred to as "clientelistic."[6] This mode involves direct, targeted exchanges between principals and agents. The former provide above all votes but also labor and monetary inputs to advance a candidate's or party's chances to be elected. In case of victory, a candidate may compensate her clients directly by channeling jobs, contracts, or subsidies to them personally or to localized bands of identifiable supporters (e.g., extended families, streets, and neighborhoods). Constituents thus reap the windfall of having supported the winning candidate (party) as "private" or as decentralized small-scale "club" goods. Benefits do not accrue to broader socioeconomic, cultural, or geographic categories of citizens as large-club goods or collective goods. Clientelistic exchange requires some kind of monitoring and enforcement, if not in the form of doing away with the secrecy of the individual vote, then at least by monitoring turnout or relying on densely woven social and organizational networks that minimize defection from political exchange by detecting and excluding free riders (cf. Stokes 2005, 2007; Kitschelt and Wilkinson 2007; Nichter 2008).

Politicians and parties may combine different modes of accountability in complex "portfolios" in which different affective and rational mechanisms

---

also incorporates an "attribution of competence" to certain candidates based on their past record more than their current positions. See Adams, Merrill, and Grofman (2005).

[6] We do not have the space here to refine our distinction between programmatic and clientelistic linkages, representation, and competition. For access to the vast literature on this topic, see Kitschelt (2000b), Piattoni (2001), and Kitschelt and Wilkinson (2007). As is clear from our formulation, we do not deem clientelism to be wedded to older anthropological conceptions that characterized it through affective relations of identification between patron and client.

are deployed simultaneously or in a differentiated fashion targeted at different constituencies, for example, party programs and clientelistic exchange (cf. Magaloni et al. 2007). Nevertheless, parties, and often entire party systems, may exhibit different dominant profiles of accountability mechanisms. In some instances, clientelistic bonds may clearly outweigh programmatic bonds or vice versa. And beyond a certain production possibility frontier, constituted by a party's budget constraint on the use of human and financial assets or by the tolerance of its electoral constituency to different linkage mechanisms, parties do encounter trade-offs among the techniques deployed in linkage strategies (Kitschelt 2000). As we elaborate in the next section, it may require the presence of specific political and economic resources, strategic opportunities, and stakes of the political conflict over binding allocations of costs and benefits to further clientelistic, programmatic, or both kinds of linkage mechanisms. In a dynamic intertemporal perspective, these forces should also explain why different linkage mechanisms rise and decline within the same polity.[7]

Programmatic Linkages Are Consequential for the Operation of Democracy

If programmatic linkages are only one of many forms of democratic linkage, why focus an entire book about Latin American democratic principal-agent relations on just this one form? Normative democratic theorists as well as intellectuals in just about all democracies have invariably singled out programmatic accountability and linkage building as the most, if not the *only*, legitimate mode of organizing democratic principal-agent relations. In the spirit of enlightenment, they see its most basic superiority in the gain of rationality evidenced by actors who operate in a programmatic political world: first of all, both voters and politicians explicitly consider preference orders. Voters see politicians' ends (office control) as the means to advance their own ends, while politicians see serving the preferences of electoral constituencies as the means to promote their own ends of holding political office for policy purposes or for personal material or immaterial benefits. Rationality triumphs over affective impulses. Second, for many democratic theorists the *deliberative character* of the process of relating voters' and politicians' ends to each other is a desirable quality of democracy, as it considers values and ideologies. Third, programmatic linkages respect the *universalistic baseline of normative democratic theorists to treat all citizens equally under the rule of law*. Laws are general principles of allocating rights, resources, and obligations that apply to all citizens equally. No one is treated differently simply because of their partisan preferences. Fourth, as a special

---

[7] For a study of the decline of clientelism in contemporary affluent democracies, see Kitschelt (2007).

corollary of equal treatment, programmatic linkages preserve the secrecy of the vote and thus the personal rational autonomy of the citizen. And, fifth, because of the universalistic, nondiscriminatory nature of the process, ambitious politicians have incentives to offer and realize broad club goods or pure collective goods that advance the welfare of many, if not all, citizens.

But why should normative theorizing matter for an empirical world of democratic politics where clientelistic practices, just as voting based on affective, unreflective identification, are ubiquitous? Indeed, clientelism does constitute a principal-agent relationship with a circuit of accountability and responsiveness that has proved to be quite durable. Voters keep supporting a political agent as long as they obtain material compensation for their effort. There are empirical conditions, however, when normative theorizing that condemns clientelistic practices becomes a political rhetoric that actually resonates with large audiences and becomes part of a dynamic to undo clientelistic politics. Identifying the circumstances under which party politicians adopt or abandon clientelistic practices is a good point of departure to investigate the presence of programmatic party competition.[8]

Programmatic Competition through Political Parties

Building on extensive literature, we argue here that programmatic principal-agent relations in democratic party competition require party organization and institutionalization, but also acknowledge that not all institutionalized parties are programmatic. Following Aldrich (1995), we conceive of parties as organizations that pool the resources of a multitude of political activists, at least some of whom pursue electoral office. Resource pooling creates scale economies in the pursuit of voters, as organizations can present and advertise multiple candidates under the same label or brand name or organize the turnout of supporters more efficiently. Party organization also permits the distribution of resources to target constituencies with less effort than most candidate-centered, stand-alone organizations. Often politicians implement clientelistic exchange through large political machines that may execute the costly tasks of directly or indirectly monitoring and enforcing targeted exchange relations, particularly under conditions of ballot secrecy (cf. Kitschelt and Wilkinson 2007).

Organizing collective action alone, however, does not make parties programmatic. This occurs only when parties coordinate their politicians' pursuit of policies around a collective preference function that overrides all the diverse idiosyncratic personal preference functions held by each individual politician. These reasons have to do with problems of *information*, *coordination*, and *credible commitments* (avoidance of opportunism on the part of

---

[8] For summaries of the literature, see Kitschelt (2000b) and Piattoni (2001). For a further development of theories, see Kitschelt and Wilkinson (2007) and the essays in that volume.

agents) in programmatic electoral competition. Because the organizational costs of programmatic competition are so formidable, politicians will organize such linkages only when other more expedient and direct linkages that do not require the creation of a collective choice function around partisan labels, such as clientelism, are unattractive to most voters.

The capacity of voters to process *information* is a constraint that makes collective policy choice functions identifiable by partisan labels a requirement for programmatic party competition. As Downs (1957) argues, even rational voters who intend to compare their own salient preferences to the parties' announced programs have only limited attention spans and resources for the acquisition of information that prevent them from scrutinizing the detailed appeals of large fields of candidates. Partisan labels assemble politicians under collective choice functions that reduce voters' search costs. Furthermore, the imperatives of limited information processing even by rational voters ("information misers")[9] encourage parties to summarize their policy preferences under the umbrella of simple encompassing formulas invoking principles of economic, political, and cultural organization that sometimes are called ideologies (cf. Hinich and Munger 1994). Political competition then becomes a matter of ideological signaling among a handful of "teams" (parties) in an extremely low-dimensional space.[10]

Politicians make strenuous efforts to map salient issues onto such simple ideological dimensions and to build a *reputation* (brand name) for espousing distinct positions on these dimensions, so that they will appear on the radar screen of information misers in the electorate. Even if voters do not know most of a party's positions on individual issues, they can infer such positions from the parties' general ideological dispositions. If voters cannot treat the parties' simple ideological messages as reliable tracers of their actual policy commitments, programmatic citizen-politician linkage will eventually fail. Voters may accept a certain level of discrepancy between a party's rhetoric and the realities of its policy making in legislatures and executive politics. But when there is a consistent and wide discrepancy between appeal and practice on the few salient policy issues on which at least some rational voters collect a modicum of information, then the programmatic linkage of

---

[9] There is a vast theoretical and empirical literature on the limits and capabilities of voters to process political information. For key statements on which we build, see Zaller (1992) and Lupia and McCubbins (1998).

[10] We leave it open here how many divides (or cleavages) a party system can support. In Stimson's (2005) theory of issue evolution, two-party systems gravitate toward unidimensional competition. As new crosscutting issues appear, politicians in established parties have strong incentives to assimilate them to the existing programmatic packages and modify the latter so as to incorporate the new issue into a unidimensional arrangement. Because of voters' information constraints, it may be the case that even in multiparty systems with relatively easy entry the parties coordinate around one or at most two basic dimensions of competition on which they seek linkages with electoral constituencies.

policy accountability will break down. Party organization plays an important role in preventing such breakdown by *coordinating* politicians and
demonstrating to voters a *credible commitment* to a minimal set of salient
policies. Party organizations address both challenges simultaneously: by
enforcement of coordination among politicians, they create credible commitments of parties to policy positions on which voters may count.

Politicians elected to legislative or executive office run in territorial districts and are charged with representing their constituents for a fixed period
of time on a thematically uncertain and unrestrained range of issues. How
can voters be assured that individual representatives will not defect from
the general appeals they endorsed at the ballot box? Noncompliance with
general partisan appeals by individual politicians would void the informational value of programmatic partisan labels. Intraparty disagreements hurt
a party's support in elections, because rational information misers in the
electorate stay clear of internally divided parties; given that the latter cannot
make credible commitments to a specific future course of policy making,
a vote for such a party would be wasted (Caillaud and Tirole 2002). Programmatic linkages thus presuppose a certain ideological cohesiveness of
parties and the enforcement of discipline in their legislative delegations and
executive cabinet members.[11]

Horizontally, party unity is threatened by competing factions of actual
and aspiring party leaders for control of the party. Vertically, party unity is
endangered by the disparity between the ideological radicalism of middle-
level activists who participate in a party's mobilizational effort for purposive, programmatic reasons, but do not aspire to electoral political office,
and the more moderate opinion profile both within a party's electoral and
membership rank and file at the bottom and its leadership in electoral office
at the top (Aldrich 1983).[12] Several formal mechanisms are available to
enforce compliance and lend credibility to a party's collective programmatic
stance. First of all, this role may be played to a certain extent by the specific
democratic institutions that govern the recruitment of legislators and executives. Electoral systems with multimember district closed-list proportional

---

[11] At the same time, as Caillaud and Tirole (2002) argue formally, hierarchical-authoritarian
parties that suppress conflict are not conducive to electoral success either, because the
internal process of party politics sends voters no reliable signal about the probability of
the party's opportunistic or nonopportunistic behavior after elections. From the vantage
point of rational information misers in the electorate, parties that institute a modicum of
internal party democracy, but nevertheless remain cohesive, are most attractive. When the
option to dissent is not exercised, voters have some reassurance that there is sufficient
internal support for a party's program to prevent it from acting opportunistically. Party
organization enhances the credibility of a party's programmatic appeal.

[12] For the contingent validity of the "law" of curvilinear disparity, see Kitschelt (1989b). As
the work of May (1973) and Robertson (1976) suggests, curvilinearity typically assumes a
two-party system with high barriers to entry.

representation, for example, strengthen the hand of party leaders vis-à-vis individual legislators, as does a parliamentary form of government in which the governing parties' cabinet members have to rely on the disciplined support of their parliamentary caucuses to stay in office.

Second, organizational mechanisms within parties may be called for to ensure the credibility of a party's collective choice function. Party membership may be made costly for aspiring politicians, and such costs may discourage individuals who find they are not close enough to the party's current platform from getting involved. Furthermore, even after politicians become members, the party may screen out potential electoral candidates who diverge from its platform in order to make its external programmatic voter appeals informationally valuable (cf. Snyder and Ting 2002). Organizational screening devices – such as a powerful central party leadership that controls material resources employed throughout the organization – influence the nomination of candidates running on the party's label for electoral office and set the agenda for national party conferences in ways that counteract horizontal and vertical sources of internal heterogeneity. Special caucus organizations in legislatures may further enhance the homogeneity of a party's programmatic appeals by imposing discipline on its representatives that is revealed in their roll-call voting behavior. Ideological cohesiveness and legislative discipline of a party are not identical. Obligations associated with the membership role, screening techniques in the recruitment of party leaders, and organizational discipline imposed on members of a party's legislative caucus are procedures that may complement each other in cultivating a party's programmatic profile.[13]

Of course, power concentration in a party can be a mixed blessing. Without making available opportunities to change its strategy through entry and internal competition, a party may lose transparency and adaptability to new political demands, all developments that hurt its credibility and external accountability.[14] Programmatic party competition thus entails that parties be internally cohesive in terms of the issue positions supported by their officers and elected representatives, yet sensitive to changing external demands and sufficiently differentiated from other parties in their ideological positions so that voters are able to distinguish which parties are closer to their own stances.

---

[13] Under specific conditions of competition, however, politicians may choose to render their party's programmatic message on salient issues vague and diffuse. Party system format matters. Where only two parties compete for the median voter, it is more likely that parties announce vague programmatic positions to catch the greatest possible share of the electorate; in fragmented party systems, individual parties may have to invest in greater policy specificity and "product differentiation" to carve out their electoral market niche.

[14] See Kitschelt (1994: chap. 5) on organizational conditions of strategic flexibility and Caillaud and Tirole (2002) on opportunities for internal contestation of a party's strategic stance.

Even where parties can create the appearance of cohesiveness and discipline, the value of the information they send out is insecure because parties, as collective actors, may behave opportunistically and abandon their programmatic appeal after elections ("policy switching"). Because the electoral "contract" between politicians and voters is temporally disjointed and incompletely specified, a party may always be tempted to change its mind ex post and pursue a programmatic strategy different to the one endorsed by voters. What prevents parties, as unitary actors, from opportunistically defecting from the programmatic positions they stake out before elections and instead pursue, for example, the enrichment of their leadership or the demands of an electoral constituency different from the one that elected them? Put differently, how do parties make it credible to voters that their relative programmatic cohesiveness before elections will be consequential for their legislative and executive conduct after elections?

One barrier to opportunism in party strategy is the iterative nature of the electoral game. As long as agents compete repeatedly for political office, they build up and may care about a reputation for nonopportunistic conduct in order to attract rational information misers in the electorate. Parties as teams of politicians with an internal organizational structure of interest aggregation have an advantage over individual politicians in this regard. Party organizations consisting of overlapping generations of members compete for an indefinite number of rounds of elections and therefore have longer time horizons than individuals with finite biological lives and career expectancies. The latter might always be tempted to defect in what they choose to become the "final round" of competition in their biographies. If a party has a reputation for expressing and acting time and again on programmatic appeals, rationally deliberating information misers in the electorate may attribute more credibility to established rather than to newly founded parties or to programmatically volatile or internally divided parties.[15]

The intertemporal programmatic credibility of a party may also be strengthened by the way investments in party organization are intertwined with ideological commitments. The medium of organization becomes part of the message. Both the process and the content of a party's "ideology work" affect the credibility of its programmatic appeals to voters. Committing organizational resources to the collective deliberation of political programs and ideological training of party members, activists, and leaders delivers the corporate equivalent of what Fearon (1999: 62) described as the individual candidate quality of moral honesty and consistency that

---

[15] Note that the emphasis here is on voter rationality and information processing in the construction of credible programmatic parties over longer periods of time. Converse (1969) employs time and repeated electoral contests precisely to make the opposite argument for the creation of nonprogrammatic linkages, namely a claim that the passage of time yields strong affective, nonrational linkages between citizens and parties ("party identification").

might make politicians attractive to voters, net of their substantive policy positions.

Some political ideologies may enhance corporate organizational credibility and cohesiveness more so than others. An ideology of solidarity and equality, such as provided by Marxism or social democracy, may give rise to more cohesive and disciplined parties than liberal individualist or populist ideologies.[16] Parties with collectivist ideologies thus may enjoy greater programmatic credibility.

In summary, if voters are rational information misers who demand three things from a party before surrendering their vote to it – low-cost information about the party's policy objectives, capacity for coordination of the party's agents around the pursuit of those objectives, and the durable and credible commitment of the party to those objectives throughout an electoral term – the party may invest in a combination of the following three techniques to satisfy such demands. First, the development of programmatic platforms ("ideology") addresses all three problems of information, coordination, and credibility. Second, the construction of a collective formal organization that disciplines the conduct of politicians copes with the problem of coordination among politicians around such programs. Third, the durable institutionalization of such party structure over many iterations of electoral competition tackles the issue of credible commitments and minimizes the voters' preoccupation with absorbing a continuous stream of new information about the current political conduct of a party.

For politicians, developing organizational and ideational solutions to establish a workable principal-agent relation is an arduous process that takes plenty of time and material resources. This may in part account for the "stickiness" of programmatic divides that theorists of cleavage formation in European politics have claimed (e.g., Lipset and Rokkan 1967; Bartolini and Mair 1990; Lijphart 1999). External programmatic brand names clearly discernible to rational information misers in the electorate result from iteration of electoral competition over many rounds, coupled with intensive, exhausting programmatic "ideology work" and "organization work" over long periods of time ("institutionalization"). Of course, fundamental changes in the "stakes" of politics – for example, through new political economic challenges – may compel politicians and voters to rebuild programmatic linkages.

Is Programmatic Party Competition Feasible?

Even if politicians were to contemplate programmatic appeals, would programmatic party competition be at all feasible in a world where politicians are primarily vote or office seekers and rationally calculating voters

---

[16] As an empirical test, see Janda and King (1985).

are motivated by policy? Downs (1957) and Riker (1982) suggest not, at least in two-party systems and possibly beyond. In the two-party case, the median voter theorem tells us that partisan alternatives should converge on the median voter and/or offer a "mist of generalities" to win elections. In the case of multiparty competition, the exigencies of postelectoral coalition formation may undermine the credibility of all interparty differentiation of programmatic appeals (Riker 1982). The policy dictator will be the party controlling the median voter and catering to her policy preferences. Rather than proposing diverging programs, politicians might not offer policy alternatives but immediately resort to direct targeted side payments in order to attract support.

An extensive empirical and theoretical literature, however, ably summarized in Grofman (2004), argues against Downs's median voter theorem and in favor of the feasibility of programmatic party competition with consequences for policy formation.[17] As indifferent or radical voters may selectively abstain from voting and as activists of different persuasions accede to parties and try to shape their platforms, politicians may have incentives to differentiate parties' programmatic appeals and see to it that such differences are reflected in "responsible partisan governments." Moreover, once programmatic profiles are in place, parties cannot effortlessly relocate their appeal in the political issue space; they are constrained by the need to preserve their reputation and credibility in the eyes of electoral constituencies. Empirically, programmatic parties are well advised to change their policy positions only incrementally in order to maintain the electoral linkage to citizen constituencies. As a consequence, they may never find themselves in an equilibrium position in the strict formal sense of spatial models of party competition (cf. Laver 2005).

On the political demand side, programmatic competition becomes feasible if other options to organize principal-agent relations of accountability in democracies become unacceptable to the principals themselves. Politicians would rather avoid the arduous investment in "ideology work" and organizational coordination involved in programmatic competition and rely on affective bonds to electoral constituencies or on clientelistic targeted exchange. But they may not enjoy those options when parties and party systems based on such accountability mechanisms manifestly perform unsatisfactorily from the perspective of voters. Under some, albeit not all, political-economic conditions, clientelistic party systems may deliver distinctly worse economic outcomes, as they lead to an underinvestment in collective and large-club goods and tremendous costs of rampant political rent seeking, as

---

[17] For detailed arguments in recent theorizing, see Adams et al. (2005), Laver (2005), and Miller and Schofield (2003). Empirically, Powell (2000) finds that, contrary to Downsian logic, the policy positions of governments in the case of two-party competition diverge substantially.

the example of clientelism in affluent industrial economies such as Austria, Italy, and Japan illustrates (Kitschelt 2007). Under many, but far from all, circumstances, programmatic relations of citizen-politician linkage and democratic competition deliver results more acceptable to electoral constituencies than clientelistic or charismatic alternatives. As political scientists from Huntington (1968) to Linz and Stepan (1996) never tired of arguing, it is often the existence of at least moderately stable party systems with coherent programmatic alternatives that create the foundations of durable democracy with broad mass support. Conversely, the failure to produce such linkage mechanisms may often, but not always, breed cynicism about democratic politics, withdrawal, and ultimately a readiness to passively tolerate or actively support the installation of a nondemocratic regime. As we show in Chapter 9, Latin America at the turn of the millennium suggests a striking macrolevel correlation between cynicism about democracy and the absence of programmatic party competition.

Consider Levitsky's (2001: 93) recent assertion in the following quotation, which is typical for a broad literature on the topic of party competition and democracy. Substitute "programmatic" where the quotation associates adjectives such as "effective" or "strong" with the party noun:

Rarely in Latin America has effective democratic governance been achieved in the absence of effective [programmatic] parties. In the contemporary period, cases of party failure and party system decomposition have frequently been accompanied by regime crisis (Venezuela) or breakdown (Peru). By contrast, the region's most successful democracies (Argentina, Chile, Costa Rica, Uruguay) have strong [programmatic] parties.

Even though programmatic partisan competition may have, on average, better chances to maintain durable democracies than other linkage mechanisms, it does not always materialize. What are the conditions under which political actors bring about or fail to achieve programmatic relations of democratic accountability? Because this question is at the heart of the theoretical problem we examine in this book, let us turn to the conditions that promote or restrain the emergence of programmatic competition as a supplement to or substitute for other linkage mechanisms.

THE CONDITIONALITY OF PROGRAMMATIC PARTISAN COMPETITION

If we assume that voting is a costly activity, it is always rational for self-interested voters to abstain in elections with programmatic party competition. As long as no selective incentives are offered, the benefit of voting is always zero because individual voters have a vanishingly small chance of affecting the electoral outcome. Programmatic linkages are therefore much less plausible than linkages based on affective or communal solidary concerns or targeted material clientelistic side payments. Building programmatic parties is an arduous task for politicians, who have to overcome difficult challenges of collective action and social choice. And voters may enjoy the material inducements of clientelistic direct exchange or the entertainment value of politics as a personalistic spectacle among charismatic leaders.

Programmatic parties become feasible only if voting is a low-cost affair and voters attribute negligible or negative value to the selective incentives incurred by clientelistic or affective voting. The theoretical task then is to identify the contingent and unlikely circumstances under which voters demand and politicians supply programmatic parties. This is obviously not an "all-or-nothing" situation. To approach the task in a more realistic fashion, we might ask, When do politicians and voters shift their emphasis on charismatic or clientelistic linkage modes to a greater programmatic structuration of party systems?

Given the organizational and intellectual difficulty of establishing programmatic principal-agent linkages, such arrangements may require years if not decades of building, learning, teaching, and struggling on the part of both politicians and electoral constituencies. The trajectory of learning programmatic politics is a collective, adaptive process of trial and error. We do not see it as a purposive, anticipatory learning, teleologically directed toward the clearly conceived objective of deeper and better mastery of party competition, but more akin to an evolutionary process of variation, selection, and retention like the selection of organizational business models by the market success of firms (Alchian 1950). Multiple entrepreneurs and teams participate in the process and try out different ideas and arrangements. Given the costliness of experimentation, there is always a "fundamental asymmetry" (Greif 2006: 187–90) that favors learning by building on inherited practices and institutionalized rules over innovations that embark on radically new activities. Within these constraints, the electoral environment selects what works best for the success of political parties. The notion of organizational "learning" we employ in the context of partisan politics is thus a weak one akin to evolutionary adaptation under conditions of bounded innovation, even though individuals act intentionally and try to derive lessons from past experiences in order to generate better outcomes in the future.

Demands for the provision of collective goods or conflicts over the production and (re)distribution of large-club goods may constitute the "stakes" for adaptive organizational learning of programmatic politics. Parties that lock in policy solutions to such challenges may pattern programmatic alignments for some time to come ("cleavages"). Programmatic alignments thus may put political-economic and cultural arrangements in place that become sticky and durable. These institutions can degrade and dissipate over time, particularly as new challenges arise that have not been incorporated in the established political alignments. Yet the transaction costs of political innovation make rational politicians opt for perpetuating these linkage mechanisms, unless endogenous or exogenous challenges devalue their electoral payoffs and compel politicians to embark on a new trajectory of adaptive learning.

Because change is costly and slow, a theory of adaptive learning of programmatic party formation may rely on temporally distant causes of the observed patterns of interparty competition and principal-agent linkage. Even in the face of new challenges, such "deep" causes continue to produce lasting, cumulative effects by shaping the orientations and dispositions of political actors and their organizational practices.[18]

Three elements need to come together in order to create an adaptive learning process that produces lasting programmatic linkages. First, political actors must have the *capabilities* – in terms of material and cognitive resources – to process the information and build the organizations that make possible programmatic linkages. Second, they must have *opportunities* to engage in collective action and electoral competition to build programmatic linkages through an iteration of elections in which politicians and electoral constituencies can learn democratic accountability. Finally, neither capabilities nor opportunities will yield programmatic linkages unless citizens and politicians perceive *political stakes* – widely shared prospective material or cultural gains or losses imposed by authoritative policies and institutions locking in such policies – that motivate them to organize the political process around partisan alignments.

As a simple organizing scheme to identify mechanisms that interact in triggering and promoting adaptive learning of programmatic party structuration, we therefore arrange different causal forces and processes under the headings of capabilities, opportunities, and stakes for political action.[19] Of course, it is not always easy to disentangle capabilities from opportunities or perceived stakes empirically.[20] As Elster's (1979) rendering of the "sour grapes" parable illustrates, perceived capabilities and opportunities may shape the perceived stakes of an action, thus rendering the latter endogenous to the former.[21] But even if the causal relations among capabilities,

---

[18] For a discussion of temporal structures of causality, see Greif (2006: especially chaps. 7 and 12), Kitschelt (2003), Pierson (2003), and Roland (2004).

[19] Note that the literature on the cognitive political sophistication of citizens often employs the same triad of mechanisms (see, e.g., Luskin 1990; Gordon and Segura 1997; Zechmeister 2003). Whereas these studies operate at the individual level, our analysis tries to develop theoretical propositions about macrolevel forces and contexts that involve programmatic political sophistication on the part of citizens and politicians in the construction of linkages. In order to signal the level change, we replace the psychological concept of "motivation" with the notion of perceived "stakes" of political action.

[20] In the literature on social movements, for example, scholars have voiced a great deal of dissatisfaction about the indiscriminant use of the concept of opportunities. See Kriesi (2004) and Tarrow (1996).

[21] Of course, in this case the preference change is concealed (or at least mediated) by a change in the perception of the situation (cognition). The fox does not change her preference for

opportunities, and stakes is complex, we treat the distinction among these three categories of mechanisms as a heuristic organizing principle to identify conditions that favor the emergence of programmatic party competition and to avoid an omitted variable problem in causal analysis.

Capabilities, Opportunities, and Stakes: Short-Term and Long-Term Learning

An adaptive, trial-and-error learning and selection model of programmatic party structuration discounts the feasibility of building programmatic partisan linkages quickly. The emergence of available resources to initiate a search for programmatic party competition and the political-economic or cultural stakes that shape actors' preferences over programmatic alternatives may be gradual. It may require several iterations of party competition to organize programmatic alternatives, even if retrospectively the final crystallization of such competition is identifiable as a specific, sudden point in time at which different causal chains interacted (such as the emergence of Perón's Justicialists in the mid-1940s). For this reason, recently founded democracies that lack a prehistory of bottom-up collective interest mobilization in parties and associations, if not intermittent episodes of electoral competition, are unlikely to adopt programmatic party competition right away. Conversely, once citizens and politicians can draw on a stock of political practices and experiences that facilitates programmatic competition, exogenous shocks, whether economic or political, may produce only a gradual reversal and realignment of citizens' programmatic demands that are then incorporated into partisan alternatives.

As Pierson (2004) and others have argued, contemporary social science has privileged short-term causal mechanisms at the expense of longer-term processes of learning and adaptation. Thelen (2004: 30) correctly observes that this has led scholars to explain social change in terms of "stasis" and "radical innovation" ("punctuated equilibria") rather than "incremental change through periodic political realignment and renegotiation." Societies certainly experience periods of radical and rapid change, but these may be less important to account for variation among political institutions and processes, such as democratic accountability in party systems, than are adaptive, evolutionary learning and transaction-cost models in which both the learning of new and the "unlearning" of existing patterns are slow, gradual processes. Our study, in fact, argues that this last type of model is better at capturing the process of programmatic party structuration in the real world than models turning on the stasis–radical change dichotomy of punctuated equilibrium. What the literature refers to as "critical junctures" (Collier

(sweet) grapes but declares the available but distant grapes to be too sour, because her capabilities and the opportunities in her external situation fall short.

and Collier 1991) are often long, drawn-out processes of political struggle extending over several decades. Only with the benefit of hindsight can scholars identify such epochs as times of fundamental change for institutions and power alignments in a polity.

In order to show that long-term political adaptation and learning are key for programmatic party structuration, the empirical analysis has to consider alternative scenarios and assumptions carefully. Maybe citizens' and politicians' adaptive capabilities do permit the rapid construction and/or destruction of programmatic party systems. Maybe all actors (or at least a critical subset) can seize on sudden shocks almost instantly and update their democratic linkage practices and political alignments smoothly, as capacities, opportunities, and perceived stakes and conflicts of interests change. Furthermore, there may not necessarily be a full symmetry between actors' abilities to craft programmatic party structuration and their propensity to abandon such linkage mechanisms. New PPS linkages may be harder to establish if the actors' lack of experience can be overcome only through a lengthy process of trial and error. Conversely, external shocks and internal conflicts among actors and their constituencies may provide instant information and preference changes that precipitate the rapid destruction of artfully constructed linkage patterns.

In an ideal-typical fashion, Table 1.1 dichotomizes the options of revolutionary or incremental learning or unlearning (destruction or reconstruction) of PPS. First, the chance that external observers detect strong PPS polities is empirically greatest if political actors can quickly react to favorable conditions that enable them to build PPS, but mechanisms such as increasing returns to scale (sunk organizational costs) and positive feedback (oligopolistic party competition with high effective entry barriers) make the situation "sticky" against shocks that would otherwise erode achieved PPS and encourage actors to refashion party alignments (constellation B). In this instance, the life expectancy of parties is rather long. Second, individual party durability and PPS within party systems are also moderately high where it takes more time for politicians and voters to institute strong PPS, yet, once completed, such linkage patterns are resilient to external shocks and internal pressures for change (constellation D). Third, where external shocks can quickly destroy existing patterns of strong PPS, but actors have also great capacities to build up new PPS arrangements quickly (constellation A), levels of PPS and party life expectancy also tend to be moderately high. Finally, both PPS levels and party life expectancy tend to be lowest if it takes a long time and major effort to build up programmatic linkage mechanisms, but external shocks can quickly sweep them away (constellation C).

Where conditions for PPS become favorable but adaptive processes of building parties and interest associations are slow, observers should also see high levels of party system institutionalization in the sense developed by

TABLE 1.1. *Alternative Models of Political Learning and Programmatic Party System Structuration*

| | Destruction and Reconstruction of Existing Programmatic Linkages[a] | |
	Rapid and in Leaps	Gradual in Cumulative and/or Intermittent and Nonlinear Trajectory
Construction of new programmatic linkages[a]		
Rapid and in leaps	A Rapid adaptive learning, rapid destruction (new linkages appear quickly and existing programmatic linkages collapse rapidly): (1) Average PPS: moderately strong; (2) Average party age: intermediate	B Rapid adaptive learning, inertia of restructuring (new linkages appear quickly, but existing programmatic linkages fade away slowly: great stickiness): (1) Average PPS: strong; (2) Average party age: high
Gradual in cumulative and/or intermittent and nonlinear trajectory	C Slow adaptive learning, rapid destruction (new linkages appear slowly, after long trial and error, while existing programmatic linkages collapse rapidly): (1) Average PPS: weak; (2) Average party age: low	D Slow adaptive learning, inertia of restructuring (new linkages appear slowly, after long trial and error, and existing programmatic linkages fade away slowly: great stickiness): (1) Average PPS: moderately strong; (2) Average party age: moderately high

[a] Response to changing capacities, opportunities, and stakes of political controversy.

Huntington (1968: 409–12) and Mainwaring and Scully (1995). Institutionalized parties adopt organizational rules that make the survival of parties resilient to the turnover of leaders, particularly the passing away of a charismatic party founder. But high observed institutionalization of parties does not always imply strong PPS. Where conditions for high PPS are inauspicious and (un)learning of linkage patterns is incremental, durable parties may construct other linkage patterns, such as those relying on clientelistic exchange.

Mechanisms Supporting Programmatic Party Structuration through Long-Term Adaptive Learning

We now detail a variety of long- and short-term conditions that may affect programmatic party structuration. These conditions work through actors' capabilities, opportunities, and perceived stakes in political mobilization. In this section and the next, we provide an abstract analytical treatment of relevant long- and short-term mechanisms. We then preview the actual results of our empirical analysis.

Economic development may provide resources, and a democratic regime may create opportunities for politicians and citizens to invest in PPS. But it may ultimately take the perception of "stakes" in the political struggle by conflicting collective actors to trigger the tenacious construction of programmatic partisan appeals and citizen linkages. Because economic-distributive arrangements turn out to be most pertinent to account for differential profiles of PPS across Latin America, later in this chapter we lay out in some detail the logic that explicates what type of economic development strategy may be associated with greater or lesser emphasis on programmatic party competition in the electoral and legislative arenas.

While our account gives causal preeminence to economic-distributive issues, we hasten to acknowledge that much theoretical reasoning and some empirical evidence suggest that a sociocultural pluralization of a polity along alternative divides – religion, language, race, or ethnicity – often promotes clientelistic linkage patterns.[22] Mobilized sociocultural groups typically develop infrastructures of communication, if not patterns of residence, that facilitate monitoring and enforcement of clientelistic relations. Such practices should be even more pronounced where sociocultural divisions and patterns of economic distribution interact, for example, in a society with a ranked or segmented ethnic division of labor whose sociocultural groups are concentrated in specific economic sectors or occupations. Because distributive-economic appeals turn out to be the predominant ones in Latin America, in this general theoretical outline we do not discuss specific substantive mechanisms that would make political actors coordinate around sociocultural stakes. We revisit this question, however, in Chapter 8, where we explore the conditions under which religious and regime divisions emerge and align with economic-distributive dimensions of party competition.[23]

---

[22] For arguments, see the introduction to Kitschelt and Wilkinson (2007) as well as contributions by Chandra (2007), Krishna (2007), and Wilkinson (2007). The point has also been made more generally by Horowitz (1985).

[23] We will not, however, deal with racial, regional, and linguistic divides that may play a role in Bolivia, Ecuador, Mexico, and Peru, countries with large indigenous populations. Brazil is a unique case given its large African Brazilian population whose lack of political mobilization has been treated in detail (Marx 1997). Our late-1990s data do not suggest that such sociocultural divides pattern national party politics in any distinctive fashion. In the

Capabilities

As a way to discriminate between politicians' and voters' dispositions to build clientelistic or programmatic linkages, the level and distribution of socioeconomic development in a polity provide one important, albeit not fully determinative causal mechanism.[24] On the side of citizens' demand for politicians' services, preferences for clientelistic selective incentives decrease with economic affluence. On the supply side, politicians' abilities to provide selective incentives also fade beyond a certain point of economic development.

Demand-side mechanisms are multiple. Greater affluence coincides with higher levels of education and cognitive sophistication. With increasing education and understanding of the causal relations between general economic growth and personal material fortunes, citizens begin to value the material benefits of large-scale club goods and collective goods, as opposed to private goods and small-scale club goods. Furthermore, for educated citizens the opportunity costs of abandoning clientelism tend to approach zero, as many of the goods politicians can supply as material selective incentives become unattractive (e.g., low-skill public-sector jobs or jobs in public works projects contracted with private companies; mediocre public housing; consumer appliances).[25]

On the supply side, politicians are confronted with at least two problems. First, they discover that citizens' increasing physical and occupational mobility makes it difficult to maintain the associational networks that are vital for monitoring and enforcing their political support. As extended local kinship and associational networks break down and immigrant enclaves disperse, politicians find it much more costly to construct machines that can gather information about voting intentions and political participation. Second, as politicians struggle to mobilize the geometrically escalating resource quantities needed to sustain voters' interest in clientelistic benefits, they face a new constraint. Raising and diverting resources to clientelistic rent seekers at high levels of development may depress overall economic performance sufficiently to deprive politicians of the requisite means to sustain targeted clientelistic accountability.[26] Therefore, particularly in affluent democracies,

---

singular case where we do find some significance of ethnocultural divides in the late 1990s, Ecuador, the divide strongly overlaps with distributive-economic issues. As Yashar (2005: chap. 3) argues, the stakes and opportunities for ethnic minority mobilization increased only as a consequence of economic liberalization that endangered the local control of Indian minorities in the 1980s. Any impact of ethnic identity on the formation of partisan divides would thus have to be short-term.

[24] For more extensive discussion, see Kitschelt (2000b), Kitschelt and Wilkinson (2007), and especially Lyne (2007).

[25] Thus, Norris (2004: chap. 5) finds that political ideology as a predictor of people's partisan choice is more important in postindustrial than in less developed democratic polities.

[26] This constraint can be overcome only in polities whose main public revenue source is rents from the sale of natural resources. As OPEC countries demonstrate, the copious flow of

citizens tend to perceive clientelistic targeted benefits as "corruption" that deprives the economy of collective goods potentially enhancing economic performance. Citizens' interpretive dispositions to reject clientelism, in turn, enable the mass media to unleash a frenzy of sensational investigations about "scandalous" misappropriation of public funds and vote buying in clientelistic relations and contribute to a general alienation of many citizens from what is now labeled the "political class" of partisan officeholders in the legislature and the executive.

Opportunities

If the buildup of programmatic principal-agent linkages is a time- and resource-consuming process that enables politicians to go through long-term adaptive learning, two enabling conditions are essential to make this process possible. First, a modicum of *civil liberties* allows the formation of interest associations, such as unions and professional organizations, as well as that of diverse political parties. Second, repeated rounds of electoral contestation, even in a lopsided playing field with a hegemonic regime party, are helpful practice grounds for citizens and politicians to coordinate around programmatic demands and overcome collective action problems.[27] As the number of rounds of party competition played by politicians and voters rises, the opportunities for actors to learn programmatic principal-agent relations rise asymptotically to some threshold or ceiling value.[28] Iteration of the democratic contest enables both principals and agents to learn adaptively from each round of elections. Politicians can sharpen their appeal and craft a reputation over time. Rational information misers in the electorate should be able to update their understanding of each party's appeals while expending minimal resources on gathering information.

Frequent and prolonged interruptions of competition by authoritarian rule may arrest or even reverse capabilities for programmatic party competition. Yet even under conditions of authoritarian rule, submersed PPS capabilities may persevere through associational infrastructures and social networks and may even be transmitted intergenerationally. It takes extremely severe and durable repression – essentially the liquidation of an entire generation of political entrepreneurs who devised and practiced programmatic politics and their immediate offspring – to root out accumulated organizational and

petro-dollars fuels clientelistic politics, whether within a democratic or an authoritarian setting (cf. Ross 2001).

[27] In the same spirit, Geddes (2003: 153) emphasizes the presence of some degrees of competition, but not full democratization, as a conducive condition to political cleavage formation in her analysis of some implications of Lipset and Rokkan's (1967) account of European party system formation in Latin America.

[28] Gerring et al. (2005) have called the cumulative effect of democratic learning "political capital." Crafting reliable relations of electoral accountability in this sense may be a component of political capital that accrues only over time.

cognitive capacities for programmatic conceptualization of party competition in a polity. Capabilities for PPS can thus survive even lengthy periods of dire opportunities, provided the "stakes" of programmatic divides that inspired politicians originally to build programmatic alternatives are still relevant at the time democracy reemerges.

Stakes of the Political Battle

Political action requires sufficiently large stakes to make political entrepreneurs and citizens shoulder the costs of mobilization, whether or not selective incentives are provided. Such stakes may involve not only political-economic distributive outcomes but also the political and cultural governance of a polity and the fundamental assignment of rights and liberties. They may concern the scope of activities of cultural organizations, such as the Catholic Church in a country's education system and the congruence between the moral teachings of a cultural group and public law.

Our treatment here focuses primarily on questions of political-economic regime form because they turn out to be empirically the most critical ingredient of strong PPS linkages where they exist in Latin America. In this regard, politics ultimately involves authoritative rules that (re)assign property rights and regulate people's market behavior. Such institutions boost or reduce people's access to resources compared to some alternative set of rules. In the short run, the state of technology, levels and distribution of skills and knowledge, the availability of natural resources, and existing economic institutions are exogenous conditions that influence people's calculations of how policies affect their material well-being. In light of these background conditions, do conflicting collective economic distributive interests crystallize around factors of production, sectors, or geographic regions?

In the long run, constraints on political mobilization – such as economic institutions in particular, but also skill distributions, and to some extent even technological endowments and trajectories – are at least partially endogenous to political struggles and, even if exogenous, are subject to change by external shocks (e.g., a change in relative factor prices, whether because of technology, demographics, or new patterns of economic openness). Political "stakes" involve a protracted struggle over the very choice of economic regimes, particularly when existing regimes deliver bad performance for most actors. Such struggles tend to be intensely programmatic. Whether programmatic politics can be *sustained* over extended time periods may to a considerable extent be a consequence of the persistence of societal conflicts over scarce resources and of institutional mechanisms to cope with them in public policy. Conversely, where existing societal conflicts and challenges that generate conflicts subside or fundamentally change, political entrepreneurs' past investments in established political organizations enacting programmatic politics depreciate. In due course, politicians will be compelled to embark on the arduous trajectory of devising new programmatic appeals and corresponding institutional policy solutions, or quit the game of programmatic party competition altogether in favor of sole reliance on clientelistic and/or charismatic personal politics. Programmatic party alignments hence may not be forever.

In other words, dynamic periods of regime and institutional choice over fundamental distributive arrangements ("stakes") may give rise to programmatic politics, particularly if resources and opportunities are available and lock in policy solutions together with programmatic partisan alignment for some time to come. In that process, profound crises and dynamic situations may raise or lower the ability of political actors to articulate programmatic alternatives. From the perspective of long-term learning, it is difficult to predict the ability of political actors to make durable investments into crafting programmatic alternatives under such circumstances. We return to short-term learning predictions later.

Just as Przeworski et al. (2000) postulate that the fact of regime transitions to democracy is harder to predict than the lock-in of democracy, it is more difficult to predict programmatic party crystallization under conditions of political-economic turmoil than under conditions of relative stability. Nevertheless, even in crisis periods featuring new stakes and challenges, polities with more capabilities, opportunities, and a past record of developing organizational infrastructures of programmatically inspired partisan alternatives leave political entrepreneurs better equipped to devise new programmatic policy appeals than polities with unfavorable conditions and practices of programmatic partisan competition. Thus, where political entrepreneurs learned to solve problems of collective action and social choice once before, they are more likely to revamp their programmatic practices faster than to learn them against the backdrop of an experience with pure non-policy-based party competition, whether of a primarily clientelistic or an amorphous personalistic kind.

During periods of comparatively stable political-economic regimes, whatever political linkage mechanism dominates the exchange of political agents and their constituencies is also likely to remain in place. This may sometimes be an equilibrium of primarily programmatic party competition or an equilibrium with a preponderance of durable clientelistic politics.

Exceptional success of an institutional and political-economic framework put in place by competing programmatic parties, however, may undermine to a certain extent the very programmatic bases of competitive politics. Widely perceived policy success may shift public opinion so overwhelmingly in favor of the organizational principles on which it is based that parties can no longer compete for votes by developing alternative policy visions. Vote-seeking politicians are then compelled to differentiate their competitive appeals from those of other parties by embracing partisan stances on *secondary* programmatic policy dimensions that divide the population; by engaging in *valence* rather than *positional* competition by featuring the "competence" of a party's own candidates, as opposed to that of its competitors, to deliver the policies most voters would like to see continued or enacted; or by resorting to nonprogrammatic accountability mechanisms, such as affective party identification, clientelistic exchange, or the cult of the charismatic political personality. This perspective on the long-term learning of PPS implies that cross-national variance in PPS levels should mostly result from developments and regime attributes that precede observed competitive partisan interactions by a substantial amount of time. In other words, there should be *some "long-distance" causality*: political economic features established decades ago at time t_1 should still matter to account for variation in accountability mechanisms across polities decades later at time t_2. That said, at any particular point in time this expected robust relationship between antecedent causes and PPS consequences may be somewhat obscured by short-term bursts of programmatic competition in nonprogrammatic party systems and by party systems that were programmatic for long periods but generated a sufficiently broad, encompassing societal consensus forcing vote-seeking parties to engage in valence competition or nonprogrammatic modes of accountability. In a purely cross-sectional comparison, only thorough case knowledge can help to sort out patterns based on long-term relations from conjunctural measurement error.

Historically, the probability that party systems configure around programmatic divides for extended periods of time is associated with a number of baseline features, all of which have in common that they enable and involve the provision of large-scale club or collective goods through general rules of allocation rather than case-by-case decisions of politicians. Five in particular deserve to be highlighted. None of them may be a sufficient condition to maintain the "stakes" of programmatic politics, but each may contribute to its persistence:

1. Political authority is *centralized in larger territorial polities*, rather than delegated to localized entities where decision making is tailored to idiosyncratic relations between individual politicians and small groups of citizens. Localized politics tends to be more personalistic and clientelistic.

2. The *civil service is professionalized* through recruitment and promotion based on educational and occupational achievements rather than ascriptive criteria, compensation by salaries rather than client payments, and obligation to apply generalized legal prescripts, the compliance of which can be ascertained by transparency requirements of the administrative process (written communication) and checks through judicial review by impartial courts insulated from the influence of elected politicians.

3. The *economy is based on a capitalist foundation of property and competition* so that elected politicians or professional civil servants cannot directly decide or influence the terms of producing, allocating, or exchanging scarce economic resources in particular work organizations but are confined to issuing *general rules constraining the*

conduct of private market participants (entrepreneurs, wage earners, firms as a compact of entrepreneurs and wage earners). In contrast to universalistic-regulatory arrangements, large-scale public enterprise and "planned" political economies may promote personalistic and clientelistic politics. By involving politics in the case-by-case allocation of scarce resources and undercutting hard budget constraints, they are ultimately inimical to programmatic politics, even though they may originate from intensely ideological programmatic struggles about socialism, populism, or social democracy in periods of political-economic regime formation.

4. If programmatic party systems support wage earners against labor market risks, they adopt a more inclusive *social insurance–welfare state regime that covers and protects large categories of wage earners under generalized rules* within the framework of contributory insurance schemes codifying general benefit schedules. Conversely, narrow welfare regimes targeted to specific localized electoral constituencies, and particularly means-tested noncontributory arrangements that give bureaucrats and politicians a great deal of discretion over the selection of beneficiaries competing for rewards, are inimical to programmatic politics.

5. *Institutional rules of democratic competition*, such as electoral laws for legislative or executive national elections; the division of powers between legislature, executive, and judiciary; and the distribution of jurisdictions across national and subnational government levels may have an independent, exogenous effect in facilitating or impeding programmatic party competition, when kept in place for long time periods. One may also postulate a short-term, instant effect of political institutions, expecting actors to adjust to institutional rules quickly.

We specify the impact of "stakes" and political-economic regimes on PPS later for Latin America. In Latin American countries with more PPS at the end of the twentieth century, a particular kind of import-substituting industrialization – mated with social policies that protect a large share of the urban labor force but not informal and agrarian workers since the post–World War II era – constituted the stakes of political conflict that evolved in close interaction with resources and opportunities for partisan competition. All three components – stakes, capabilities, and opportunities – jointly nurtured a modicum of persistent programmatic contestation, even under conditions of political-economic adversity. In Latin American countries lacking these conditions and experiences, PPS remained weak, setting aside brief bursts of programmatic mobilization in crisis periods.

The Interaction of Capabilities, Opportunities, and Stakes
Economic capabilities, political opportunities for party competition, and the stakes of political conflict, as they result from actors' interests to promote or

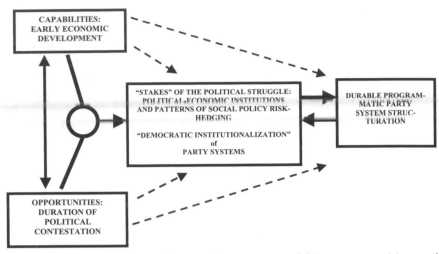

FIGURE 1.1. The interaction between long-term capabilities, opportunities, and stakes shaping principal-agent linkage patterns.

dismantle specific political-economic regimes, are interrelated without reaching complete mutual endogeneity. Economic development may historically go first and set the stage for political opportunities of electoral competition and collective mobilization around high-level political-economic stakes that crystallize partisan camps, but greater affluence and cognitive sophistication of urban citizens do not necessarily translate into the emergence of democracy and distinct political-economic modes of governance. Capabilities and opportunities may jointly promote the definition of political-economic "stakes" and their realization in institutions and policies, such as welfare state agencies. Figure 1.1 depicts these possible relations, without showing all the plausible feedbacks running from PPS back to capabilities and opportunities. Broken lines indicate that the main effect of capabilities and opportunities on durable programmatic party system structuration is not expected to be direct but is mediated through their interactive influence on the constitution of "stakes" of political conflict which then shape PPS directly. Needless to say, in an empirical world of high collinearity, it will be very difficult to sort out the precise causal mechanisms, as we illustrate in later chapters.

How does our treatment of long-term factors that influence contemporary PPS in democracies relate to Lipset and Rokkan's (1967) comparative analysis of party systems? Following their classic account, we focus on party system alignments, not the success of individual parties, and stress long-term processes of political mobilization. Both their analysis and ours reject economic development as the sole causal determinant and favor politics-centered arguments about opportunities for political mobilization and definition of collective stakes (state formation and centralization, church-state conflicts, or electoral enfranchisement). Social divides do not directly translate into political alignments, as political conditions and political mobilization intermediate.

Yet there are also differences between our approach and that of Lipset and Rokkan. While their argument appears to assume that all partisan alignments are programmatic, we question that premise and are concerned with the extent to which programmatic accountability matters and is nested within broader portfolios of democratic linkage mechanisms. When we deal with programmatic competition, however, the Latin American cases force us to be narrower than their theoretical scope allows. Our analysis revolves around distributive economic conflict, and we find relatively little evidence of religious or ethnocultural conflict, although the mobilization of indigenous Indian constitutencies has recently received considerable attention (cf. Yashar 2005; Van Cott 2005).

Our approach may also be somewhat more flexible than Lipset and Rokkan's in accommodating change. Our notion and measure of programmatic partisan divides lack the air of permanence and resilience of partisan alternatives that they associate with the notion of political cleavage. Partisan divides, in our sense, may or may not be durable. Certainly when the "stakes" of political conflict change, partisan alignments are likely to change as well, albeit with some lag as citizens and politicians learn how new appeals and new policies can translate into lasting electoral coalitions.

Mechanisms Affecting Programmatic Party Structuration through Short-Term Learning

Contrary to a cumulative-historical logic of trial-and-error learning, maybe politicians can craft programmatic alignments as a result of sudden changes in capabilities, opportunities, and political stakes. According to this alternative view, proximate causes reign supreme; citizens and politicians quickly perceive their interests in light of political-economic challenges. What counts to explain political alignments, then, are short-term causal mechanisms linking recent economic performance and development, opportunities to compete in the electoral arena, and the mobilization of stakes to the observed PPS outcomes. Short-term causal mechanisms require that actors quickly construct and destruct programmatic appeals and strategic alignments in response to changing capabilities, opportunities, and stakes in the polity. Where adaptation by existing parties to new environmental conditions is slow, new parties rush in to fill the void.

Capabilities
Levels and rates of change in the distribution of scarce material and symbolic resources may shake up existing principal-agent linkages. Countries that

were poor in the past but have recently and suddenly become affluent may
see a rebellion against clientelistic politics and a transformation of existing
party systems. Bursts of economic growth, sustained for only a few years,
may reduce the proportion of a country's electoral constituencies that are
amenable to selective material inducements. Conversely, democracies with
recently but precipitously declining standards of living may experience a
scramble of electoral constituencies for clientelistic special protections, as
citizens find politicians' traditional programmatic appeals hollow and less
than credible. Overall, this perspective postulates a short lag between large-
sale economic and cultural shifts and the response of party systems.

Opportunities

In the short run, authoritarian interruptions of democratic politics may da-
mage opportunities to develop PPS, while continuous multiparty competition governed by rules that promote team coordination among politicians without highlighting individual candidate quality or discretion will
improve it. The relationship between repression and PPS may be curvilinear, however. Mild authoritarians may buy off opposition forces, and such
quasi-clientelistic practices may preempt PPS under a subsequent democratic
regime. Conversely, very severe authoritarianism may physically liquidate
those who have the experience and social networks to build programmatic
parties after a return to democracy. Moderately intense repression, nurtur-
ing deep resentment that crystallizes around political ideologies, may therefore be most conducive to programmatic politics under subsequent democratic conditions. Of course, the impact of repression may be mediated –
or canceled out – by features of the pre-authoritarian party system, that
is, long-term mechanisms that come into play through submerged associational continuities and social networks even under moderately authoritarian
regimes (cf. Remmer 1989: 70).

In terms of democratic institutions, scholars have singled out *electoral
laws* as causal determinants of accountability mechanisms.[29] Targeted, clientelistic exchange is hypothesized to thrive under conditions of individual-
istic party competition rather than closed-list proportional representation.
Second, an *independently elected presidency* may promote clientelistic politics, particularly if it enjoys broad legislative and executive powers and
faces what Cox and Morgenstern (2002) call a "reactive" legislature with
weak capacities to set the political agenda. Presidents then have wide discretion to dole out patronage and build legislative coalitions on a case-by-case
basis among individual legislators or small bands. This practice disorga-
nizes the organizational discipline and programmatic cohesion of legislative
party caucuses and encourages party switching of legislators. Nonconcurrent

---

[29] As powerful statements of this perspective, see Ames (2001) and Mainwaring (1999) on
Brazilian politics.

elections of presidency and legislature further deepen the separation of executive and legislative parties. Presidents may calculate that their capacity to "buy off" legislative support and assemble changing coalitions of party factions is greater than their ability to dominate a majority party, or coalition of parties, in the legislature (cf. Mainwaring and Shugart 1997).

Third, the delegation of public authority to subnational territorial units with elected governments makes programmatic party cohesion more difficult. In all but the most developed polities with a full array of safeguards to ensure "market preserving" federalism, decentralization of political decision making promotes sectional subnational interests, targeted clientelistic principal-agent relations, and corruption (cf. Cai and Treisman 2001; Rodden and Wibbels 2002; Wibbels 2005: chap. 2). Unitary government, by contrast, may cut off elected politicians from particularistic constituencies and encourage them to engage in more programmatic competition.

Stakes of the Political Conflict

Citizens will challenge existing linkages to politicians primarily when politicians do not come through with expected benefits, be they private and small-club goods in clientelistic exchange relations, or large-club and collective goods in policy-based principal-agent linkages. For example, citizens abandon incumbent parties when macroeconomic performance – such as growth, employment, price stability, and external balance of accounts – weakens. Because economic market liberalization and privatization can undercut politicians' discretion over resource allocation in the economy and thus reduce opportunities for clientelistic politics, parties that undertake these reforms must often rely on good economic performance to maintain political allegiance. Where clientelism was formerly the dominant mode, economic troubles and the failure to deliver promised rewards can trigger a call of disgruntled citizens for more programmatic politics and the abolition of "cronyism." If programmatic linkages instead dominate, bad economic performance may make citizens initially support an opposition party with a different program, but repeated alternation in office with invariably unsatisfactory policy outcomes might lead citizens to resort to politicians and parties that rely on charismatic leadership or clientelistic lures.

Theoretically, linking economic performance to programmatic politics is complex and involves at least three elements. Politicians can maintain the full credibility of programmatic party competition only if parties first communicate distinctive preelection programmatic appeals; if the winning party or parties then implement these appeals consistently when in executive office, while nongovernmental parties continue to oppose such policies; and if governing parties achieve good economic performance (provision of collective or large-scale club goods) during their tenure. It goes without saying that government policies are only one of several forces that impinge upon economic outcomes.

TABLE 1.2. *The Effect of Policy Promises, Enacted Policies, and Policy Outcomes on the Programmatic Structuration of Partisan Alternatives*

	Consistency between Preelectoral Programmatic Appeals and Postelectoral Policies of Governing Parties	
	High[a]	Low[b]
Performance of government policy in eyes of electoral constituencies		
Strong	A Responsible partisan government I: sincere and effective policies	B Successful policy switching: policy is effective, but programmatic appeals are insincere
Weak	C Responsible partisan government II: sincere but ineffective policies	D Unsuccessful policy switching: disarray of programmatic politics . . . lack of effectiveness and sincerity in policy making

[a] No "policy switching."
[b] Common and profound "policy switching."

Table 1.2 lays out a simple scheme of alternative configurations of the three short-term variables – with values simplified to dummy alternatives – that may contribute to greater or lesser programmatic structuring of partisan competition. We ignore the possibility of coalition governments and the complexities that this may entail in citizens' perception of responsible partisan government.

As long as parties promise programmatic differentiation of policies and then do what they say if elected to office, responsible partisan governance and programmatic competition prevail (configuration A, Table 1.2). Where parties promise one type of policy ex ante during an electoral contest but then, as governing parties, deliver quite another policy, we are dealing with "policy switching" (Stokes 2001). Such switching may dilute PPS, as it discredits parties' programmatic sincerity and makes voters discount their proclamations (configuration B). If policy switching is practiced by successive governments under different partisan labels, citizens may become disaffected with democracy more generally, abstain from voting, or support maverick parties and charismatic politicians, often with an antidemocratic appeal.

Bad policy performance under a party government also erodes PPS, as it throws doubt on the capabilities of programmatic politicians, even where they are not insincere (configuration C, Table 1.2). Of course, failure after policy switching makes things worse (configuration D). And an iteration of such experiences over electoral terms makes things even worse.

Interaction of Capacity, Opportunity, and Motivation
Just as in the case of long-term facilitators of PPS, short-term mechanisms may bring about high structuration only where we encounter a confluence of capacities (resources), opportunities (democratic institutions, authoritarian regime experiences), and stakes (economic conditions and response by governing parties). More interestingly, there may be an interaction between long-term conditions conducive to high PPS and short-term stakes and opportunities. In countries where long-term conditions have promoted the programmatic structuration of current party systems, a recent spell of particularly bad economic performance, especially when it is associated with inconsistent policy promises ("policy switching," "betrayal"), may undermine the workability of programmatic competition and citizen-politician linkage. Yet without long-term favorable conditions and actual investments in high PPS by both politicians and voters, even favorable short-term economic circumstances may not yield a competitive polity following a model of responsible partisan government. Patterns of party competition with high PPS are easier to destroy than to build up anew.

THE GENERAL ARGUMENT APPLIED TO LATIN AMERICA

We do not claim there is anything unique to Latin American party systems per se. In principle, the general argument about the emergence of PPS should be applicable to a wide range of cases. Nevertheless, let us specify how the general forces discussed so far are likely to divide Latin American countries into polities with greater or lesser PPS by the end of the twentieth century. Identifying origins of differential PPS also enables us to consider forces of change that impinge on "sticky" party systems. In fact, it appears that the conditions that created variation across Latin American countries in levels of PPS observable in the late 1990s have by and large faded by the beginning of the new millennium, but that party systems had not (yet) reconfigured around new stakes and electoral coalitions, although the resources and opportunities to do so are clearly emerging.

The Emergence of Programmatic Parties in a Period of Urban-Centered Import-Substituting Industrialization with Social Policy

If long-term learning of democratic politics matters for its emergence, PPS can be expected to be strong in the end of the twentieth century primarily in those Latin American countries that expanded their economic resources fairly early in the first half of the century and that offered repeated, albeit sometimes intermittent or constrained opportunities for incipient political elites to coordinate around competing parties, even if the competition did not take place on a level playing field. In the absence of such resources and opportunities, only short-term surges of programmatic politics, followed by a quick collapse of the aspiring programmatic parties or the democratic regimes altogether, should be occurring.

In Latin America, early economic developers in the late nineteenth and first half of the twentieth century experienced a shift in the relevance and power of business from agriculture to urban-based manufacturing and services. The collapse of international trade during the Great Depression accelerated the relative loss of economic and political prowess by rural oligarchies of large-estate owners and promoted the adoption of new "import-substituting industrialization" (ISI) economic development strategies in many Latin American countries. ISI involves tariff protection for a wide array of domestic industries; the provision of loans and subsidies to specific industrial champion companies, if not their outright nationalization; and overvalued currencies that cheapened the import of select factor inputs, such as sophisticated capital equipment that could not be made at home, but also hobbled the exports of the agricultural economies. ISI strategies, however, were not by themselves necessary or sufficient causes for the development and lock-in of political mobilization with high PPS for the following reasons. While initially the shift from an agrarian export economy to an industrializing import-substituting strategy may have involved fierce programmatic politics, particularly promoted by the ascending camp of urban forces challenging the agrarian oligarchies, once instituted, ISI policies with their discretionary interventions in the economy offered plenty of opportunities for clientelistic politics and rent seeking. Often enough, politicians were likely to find it less arduous and costly to assemble electoral coalitions through the clientelistic distribution of material advantages than through the programmatic commitment to provision of large-scale club or collective goods.

ISI facilitated, but did not automatically produce, the critical ingredient we claim to have framed and then sustained programmatic party competition in those Latin American countries where it can be observed in the late twentieth century. The missing ingredient is the establishment of fairly inclusive urban welfare states that primarily benefited wage earners in formal labor markets in manufacturing and services through pension systems, health care, or unemployment insurance, but typically excluded the rural masses and the informal service economy.

Nowhere in Latin America were these systems of social security universalistic and encompassing in the sense of some West European welfare states (cf. Esping-Andersen 1990), but they varied in the scope of their benefits to large urban categories of wage earners (cf. Segura-Ubiergo 2007; Haggard and Kaufman 2008; Rudra 2008). Promoted by urban labor movements and, in a very few instances, agrarian smallholder movements, the resulting welfare states revolved around *defensive* insurance systems to maintain income when wage-earner jobs disappeared but not a *proactive* strategy of building human capital to enable people to compete in labor markets through broad-based education and preventive health care. Latin American social policies thus contributed to the construction of "consumptive" welfare states that subsidized labor when it could no longer be deployed in capitalist national or world markets, rather than "investive" welfare states that prepared workers through the acquisition of education and vocational skill formation or provided preventive health care – all programs that would enable workers to earn wages and to anticipate and to counteract the volatility of labor markets rather than to be compensated for the effects of such volatility.[30] Moreover, Latin American welfare states remained particularistic and exclusionary to the extent that neither most of the poor landless peasantry nor workers in the informal economy were covered.

The degree to which group claims were included in social policy varied remarkably even across the more developed and urbanized Latin American polities. More generous and more inclusive urban-targeted social policies were typically pursued under democratic regime conditions, a critical variable in both Segura-Ubiergo's (2007) and Haggard and Kaufman's (2008) extensive case treatments. Here "opportunities" and "stakes" for programmatic party politics interact. More encompassing social policies emerged primarily in the face of comparatively strong unions and working-class partisan mobilization. Costa Rica is a unique case in this regard, as it was poorer and economically more open but exhibited a greater share of small family farmers rather than a concentration of landholdings under the control of agrarian oligarchs commanding large armies of landless laborers or sharecroppers.

The more encompassing, but still exclusionary urban-based welfare states within Latin America created an electoral constituency for social reform that reflected the relatively small size and organizational capacity of the industrial working class, when compared to its counterparts in Western Europe. Among Latin American countries, financially weaker social policies with still narrower constituencies of beneficiaries emerged in traditionally more trade-open economies, under conditions of predominantly authoritarian politics and relatively weak labor unions and leftist parties (cf. Segura-Ubiergo

---

[30] For the development and profile of Latin American welfare state programs in comparative perspective, we rely especially on Segura-Ubiergo (2007) and on Haggard and Kaufman (2008). For a good exposition of these political-economic regimes, see especially Haggard (1990), as well as Collier (1979), Collier and Collier (1991), Haggard and Kaufman (1992; 1995), Teichman (2001), and Weyland (2002).

2007: chap. 2). In other words, political mass organizations locked in the "stakes" of a political struggle that involved large proportions of the electorate through the construction of urban-centered welfare states. The maintenance or expansionary orientation of social policy became a frequent bone of programmatic contention among parties, even though such policies tended to exclude large proportions of the poorest groups in society, especially the largely destitute rural peasantry and the informal service sector.[31] Nevertheless, the mobilizational capacity and organizational profile of popular leftist forces shaped the varying degrees to which the mostly more developed Latin American democracies established welfare states. These distributive institutions, in turn, reinforced and reinvigorated political mobilization and kept programmatic partisan alternatives in place.

Once politicians and voters had coordinated around social policy institutions, programmatic partisan alternatives also became sticky and hard to change. Where intense struggles about ISI development strategies crystallized around new political-economic institutions of governance and social policies in the transition from natural resource–based to industrializing economies, it is also more likely that political actors locked in programmatic alternatives that then survived until the end of the twentieth century. By contrast, poorer, non-ISI economies with weak urban sectors, particularly those relying primarily on raw materials exports and enclave sectors, never exhibited levels of political mobilization and social policy implementation that could have locked in programmatic partisan alternatives, especially where voters had few opportunities to participate in multiple rounds of democratic contestation. Here programmatic politics flared up occasionally and then subsided again, as political regimes failed to lock in and enshrine programmatic interests in their political-economic institutions. It is mostly the first cohort of ISI adopters after the Great Depression, rather than the "late" ISI adopters of the 1950s and 1960s, that developed greater PPS because it is only in these polities that the rise of ISI was actually associated with the rise of social blocs that pushed for and benefited from social policies at the heart of PPS.[32]

Period II: Erosion and Collapse of ISI Strategies and the Search for New Political-Economic Programs

With the political-economic exhaustion of the protectionist and state-centered ISI development trajectory in the 1980s – manifested through severe

---

[31] It is therefore not by accident that the size of the welfare state, measured by state expenditure, is often related to greater, rather than lesser inequality in less-developed countries, when compared to the opposite relations in Western OECD countries (cf. Rudra 2008: 61–70).

[32] We thank one of the anonymous reviewers of the book manuscript for suggesting this formulation.

financial crises, spiraling inflation, declining GDP, rising unemployment, and low productivity improvements – the foundations of the exclusionary urban welfare states were shaken through pressures to open economies to world trade and capital markets. ISI-based economies experienced a precipitous economic fall, particularly where they confronted international competition, because their wage levels were incommensurate with their productivity.[33] Given this situation, what would long-term and short-term theories of programmatic party system structuration predict?

Long-term theories would predict that a cumulative series of damaging events may be required to destroy existing patterns of PPS. Conversely, it will not be easy to construct new PPS alignments, particularly in polities that have no previous programmatic politics to build on, where parties primarily relied on the charisma of political leaders or clientelistic payoffs. As long as the old stakes – differential entrenchment of welfare states – persist, legacy alignments may stay in place. Even where they erode, such processes do not immediately translate into changing party alignments. In previously nonprogrammatic partisan polities, new parties may produce programmatic blips – say, with either neoliberal parties that radicalize economic reform or neopopulist parties that call for a resurrection of defunct ISI strategies when economic reforms appear not to deliver better economic results – but it is a different matter whether these surges actually "lock-in" new alignments configured around a lasting formula to produce economic growth and societal advancement.

Unless politicians find a new formula to deliver sustained socioeconomic improvement or cultural integration, it is unclear whether any new programmatic initiatives will be transitory or durable. In fact, as we argue in the conclusion, it is unlikely that Latin American polities have found such new political-economic formulas, a reason why it is difficult to institutionalize PPS where it was weak before and why old PPS divisions linger on that are rooted in welfare state construction during the ISI era. Thus, while programmatic partisan alignments are changeable, in practice such change is an arduous, protracted undertaking. Similar observations could be made about programmatic realignments in the party systems of advanced

---

[33] It is therefore not so surprising that Rudra (2008: 39–46) finds a negative association between the magnitude of social policy expenditure and the interaction between the countries' trade openness and their potential power of labor, measured by the ratios of skilled to unskilled labor in the country's entire labor pool. What this does not show, however, is if and how greater potential labor power actually works its effect on social policy through a political micrologic, for example, the weakening of labor unions and the waning of labor parties, or the "policy switching" behavior of parties and unions representing labor. Rudra does not associate the effect of trade openness with political regime status (democracy?), let alone the configuration of political parties, and particularly the strength of more leftist, socialist parties representing industrial working-class constituencies.

postindustrial democracies that have been stretching over decades.[34] Eventually, Latin America will also likely experience the rise of new alignments, particularly in countries where politicians and citizens have already gained some experience with programmatic politics in a previous era, but we may currently only speculate about the emerging shape of such alignments, as we do in the conclusion to our study. The old coalition of urban protectionist business and labor has exploded, but it may still take considerable time to see new political-economic arrangements germinate around which programmatic parties can build durable political alignments.

The long-term learning argument thus is far from suggesting that the level and content of programmatic alignments in party systems is immutable, determined once and for all in the distant past. The argument suggests only that it takes tenacity and strong effort to build or reconfigure programmatic party appeals. A short-term perspective on political learning of PPS takes a different position. Sharp economic reversals, sudden regime breaks, and especially policy switching by previously programmatic parties should be decisive events that undermine existing programmatic alignments or serve as catalysts to create new ones. Rapid domestic and international economic liberalization of markets for goods, services, labor, and capital, for example, may be expected to leave deep imprints on the programmatic appeals and electoral alignments of political parties in this perspective. Moreover, a short-term learning theory may be much more optimistic that political elites can quickly construct programmatic parties, particularly if institutional engineering comes to the aid of such efforts by supplying rules to organize electoral contests or legislative-executive relations that are said to promote programmatic partisan competition.

Relation of the Argument to Existing Literature on Latin American Party Systems

The most cited single piece on Latin American party systems is probably Mainwaring and Scully's (1995) treatment of party system institutionalization, conceived as the persistence and stability of partisan labels over time. Institutionalization may be a necessary condition for programmatic party system structuration, but it is not a sufficient one. Predominantly clientelistic party systems may also be highly institutionalized. Mainwaring and Scully provide no causal treatment that would explain why some party systems are more institutionalized than others, nor do they probe into the more programmatic or nonprogrammatic attributes of party systems

---

[34] In this regard, Kitschelt (1994; 1995a) report only snapshots or phases of ongoing transformations that took a long time to get under way and have continued on into the new millennium.

with higher institutionalization. If our long-term learning theory of programmatic partisan politics is correct, we should detect some correlation of institutionalization with our measures of PPS, but the correlation does not imply a causal account. In a more recent piece, Mainwaring and Zoco (2007) explore patterns of electoral volatility worldwide as indicators of the degree of institutionalization of party systems. They argue that the duration of democracy is not as important a determinant of volatility as the timing and sequence of democracy. In earlier times, political elites had an incentive to invest in party building, as this was the most expedient method to mobilize voters. Early party building endured across generations through processes of political socialization. In later times, especially after the advent of television, political elites have less incentive to invest in party building, as they can reach the electorate through direct, unmediated appeals. This argument suggests that time alone may not be sufficient to permit the creation of programmatic parties; instead, the cost of organizing programmatic parties may have increased in relation to other linkage mechanisms more recently, so no amount of time would allow elites and voters the opportunity to learn programmatic competition. Thus, their explanation is based on the interaction between openings of democratic contestation at times when parties were better able to develop organizational and mobilization strategies that might have helped to entrench them in society.

Coppedge (1998a) makes an explicit causal argument about the rise of party cleavages in Latin America. While not identical with programmatic structuring, Coppedge's dependent variable is sufficiently close to ours to merit a direct comparison of causal arguments. For Coppedge, programmatic divides emerged wherever democracy was preceded by stable oligarchical party systems that were trailblazers in sinking initial costs of collective political organization. Speed and timing of enfranchisement then did the rest to account for differences in cleavage formation, once democracy arrived. Coppedge rightly emphasizes the need for opportunities to exercise partisan competition (Coppedge 1998a: 172), but his opportunity-based analysis pays little attention to societal capacities of democracies and the national stakes of the political struggle. Poor, localized agrarian economies with large landholders facing a weak urban sector did not lend themselves to high PPS, even in the presence of a fairly long run of democracy. Until recent economic improvements, Colombia exemplified this configuration.

Whereas Coppedge (1998a) emphasizes opportunities of political partisan contestation as decisive for programmatic political divisions, Hagopian (1996) and Roberts (2002) put more emphasis on political-economic stakes and power relations. For Hagopian, the main issue is whether landed oligarchies were decisively sidelined by political rebellions in the twentieth century. Where such elites have remained strongest, "political parties are weakest, executive-legislative relations are at their worst and economic reforms have lagged" (Hagopian 1996: 78). Among cases with tenacious entrenchment with landed oligarchies, we find Brazil, Colombia, the Dominican Republic, and Ecuador. Class and cross-class parties sweep such oligarchies away in Argentina, Bolivia, Mexico, and Uruguay. Peru constitutes an intermediate case. Costa Rica and Venezuela do not explicitly figure into Hagopian's comparison.

In our own account, the countries Hagopian classifies as preserving oligarchical authority also turn out to be least conducive to high PPS. But the underlying mechanisms can be specified more precisely than in Hagopian's work by examining early capabilities, political opportunities arising with enfranchisement, and the development of social policies to limit the costs of urban and rural constituencies caught up in the process of ISI. Moreover, when taking these complex mechanisms into account, it becomes clear why at least two cases that Hagopian qualifies as having partially or entirely displaced incumbent oligarchical elites – Bolivia and Peru – should actually have developed only feeble programmatic partisan alignments and patterns of PPS that flare up only intermittently in moments of political-economic crisis.

A similar problem of not specifying different types of cases where oligarchical elites have been displaced in favor of new political-economic growth regimes characterizes Roberts's (2002) stimulating work on the intensity of ISI development trajectories, labor movements, and the costs of economic liberalization in the transition to market-liberalized political-economic regimes since the 1980s. For Roberts, intensive ISI strategies follow from the political mobilization of labor. At the same time, where labor mobilized most, we see the most wrenching economic crises in the 1980s and 1990s and consequently the greatest volatility and destruction of established political parties. But Roberts does not distinguish between countries in which labor mobilization is based on raw materials enclaves, surrounded by great poverty and labor repressive agriculture, and those where broader urban development took place and/or agrarian labor was organized less repressively. His categorization and the implied micrologic of political mobilization are therefore not theoretically and empirically adequate to account for cross-national variance in programmatic politics.

Obviously our critiques of Coppedge's, Hagopian's, and Roberts's comparative studies of Latin American party systems should not be taken as proof of their lack of validity. They try to explain somewhat differently conceived outcomes than our study. While they are adequate for these other explanatory objectives, they are not appropriate for our study.

THE SUBSTANTIVE ARGUMENT IN BRIEF

The next part of the book presents the descriptive profiles of programmatic party system structuration across our four cases. Chapter 2 analyzes the dimensionality of opinion and partisan divides among the parties represented in the legislatures of the twelve Latin American countries we could include in this study. We find that a single divide, which relates to issues of economic governance–property rights and/or income (re)distribution, has the capacity to articulate PPS in at least some Latin American countries. Economic partisan divides thus provide our main avenue for comparing party systems and probing into systematic explanations for greater or lesser degrees of programmatic party structuration in Chapters 6 and 7.

Additional programmatic partisan divides surface in some Latin American countries, but they are of two kinds. One kind maps directly onto divides concerning economic (re)distribution and governance, as is the case most of the time with religion; parties that promote reliance on markets also tend to be more religious and morally conservative. The other kind seems to be of a fleeting, transitory nature and largely cuts across economic policy divides. This other kind mostly concerns regime divides, which follow either from retrospective appraisals after repressive dictatorship or from prospective debates about alternatives to democracy in a crisis.

Chapter 3 investigates the extent to which politicians are able to give programmatic divides a sharp and simple focus by mapping alternative positions onto the formal semantics of "left" and "right," the ultimate unidimensional rendering of interpartisan divides. Whether and the extent to which issue positions und underlying dimensions of programmatic competition among parties explain how politicians place themselves and their parties on a left-right axis, however, also vary across countries. In general, the stronger the substantive programmatic economic divide, the larger the chance that parties' positions on this divide explain (i.e., covary) the variation in the left-right placements politicians attribute to political parties. Thus, left-right semantics and the dimensionality of the partisan issue space both seem to get at a common underlying attribute of the party system.

Our third measure of PPS, in Chapter 4, provides an empirical confirmation of the signaling process between voters and politicians that is presumed in the notion of programmatic party competition. The extent to which parties' elites and their voters express congruent issue preferences that set them apart from competitors varies across issues and across countries. Most of the time, parties with stronger programmatic divides and issue-based left-right labels also tend to develop more congruous relations between partisan elites and electorates. Programmatic party appeals can be communicated to voters, and they respond to it.

Chapter 5 probes into the most demanding measure of PPS: do parties distinguish themselves from competitors not only by differences in the mean values of their respective leaders' issue appeals and left-right placements but also by internal cohesiveness, that is, a small internal variance of the issue appeals expressed by each party operative? While Latin American parties tend to be internally much more diffuse than parties in the postcommunist region, we again find intraregional variation. Stronger partisan divides over

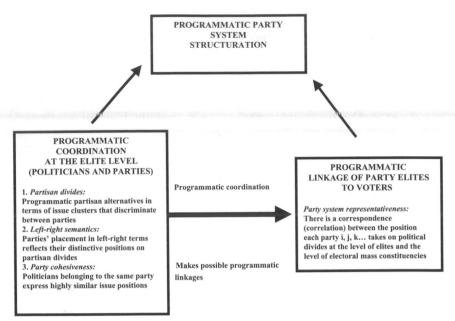

FIGURE 1.2. Concept formation: Labeling elements of programmatic party system structuration.

issues that can be mapped onto the formal left-right semantics coincide not only with more voter-politician congruence but also with less heterogeneity or more cohesiveness within political parties.

Figure 1.2 assembles our theoretical conceptual apparatus consisting of three terms, namely programmatic *coordination* at the level of partisan elites, programmatic linkage of party elites to voters, and programmatic party structuration as the overarching concept covering the former two. For each of the two conceptual components, the figure displays the operational-empirical elements in our twelve countries.

The next part of our study then explains cross-national variation in programmatic party structuration, with an exclusive focus on economic-distributive divides (Chapters 6 and 7). We show how differentials of long-term capacity, opportunity for democratic competition, and formation of political stakes, particularly those embodied in the development of more or less encompassing social policy arrangements for the urban electorates, go far toward explaining cross-national differences in PPS within the Latin American region. Without considering social policy, however, different pathways of ISI development or urban working-class mobilization leave little imprint on PPS. Chapter 7 then tests the robustness of our claims about long-term mechanisms of PPS formation around economic divides and introduces potential short-term mechanisms that can derail PPS or build new capacities, such as the number of continuous rounds of democratic elections in the most recent spell of democracy, or the nature of electoral laws currently used in national elections, or the power of policy switching in destroying programmatic partisan competition. In spite of strenuous efforts, we cannot systematically identify short-term mechanisms based on capabilities, opportunities, and stakes, either separately or jointly (cumulative or interactive effects) that could trump an explanation of current (i.e., 1997–98) cross-national patterns of PPS based on the configuration of long-term conditions laid out in Chapter 6. Where short-term mechanisms have even a semblance of explanatory power, they tend to be endogenous to prior long-term mechanisms. As an exception, consider the interaction between long-term prior conditions for PPS and short-term economic crisis. In some countries where these prior conditions are promising, very bad economic performance in the 1980s and 1990s may actually undermine PPS, but very good economic performance does not make a difference for PPS in countries where prior conditions for PPS are weak. We get here a glimpse of the beginnings of dynamic change in profiles of PPS over time and across countries, but our analysis also makes us appreciate how slow, sticky, and arduous such political change is. Politicians and voters may yet need to become excited about a new formula of economic development around which political-economic institutions and programmatic parties will be able to align.

Chapter 8 probes into the mechanisms that produce religious divides and, once again, finds long-term processes characterizing the interaction between the Catholic Church and the state responsible for shaping religious PPS. Countries with late, severe conflicts over Catholic prerogatives such as education and civil registries (the analogy to "stakes" in the case of economic partisan divides) are more likely to have strong religious partisan divides today, but only where long-term levels of economic development (capacities) and democratic experience (opportunities) permit the enduring crystallization of such conflicts. When it comes to the political regime dimension, by contrast, Chapter 8 shows that it is *recent* experiences with dictatorship and *prospective* problems of democratic performance rather than long-term conditions that affect the relative strength of a regime divide. This may explain why regime divides tend to be comparatively rare and unstable in party systems, Latin America included.

Chapter 9 probes the one ultimate intellectual justification for a comparative analysis of PPS profiles – namely, the extent to which different principal-agent linkages in democratic politics also shape policy outputs and outcomes. Our aspiration to demonstrate the policy relevance of differential patterns of PPS in this study yields only provisional results and must be pursued elsewhere. There are, however, striking associations between national patterns of PPS and features of democratic quality, such as political participation, governance, and regime support. While we are unable to make strong, unidirectional claims of causality, these associations suggest that programmatic structuration is an extremely important component of the circuit of accountability and responsiveness in a democracy.

Our concluding chapter takes stock of the progress that our project makes in regard to measuring, describing, and explaining programmatic party competition, but it also raises questions about the dynamic change of partisan alignments in Latin America. We do so through three lenses. First, we discuss the degree to which our causal story adequately explains programmatic party structuration in the late 1990s in Latin America. Second, we consider the findings of our within-region study in light of a cross-regional comparison, specifically with postcommunist Europe. Third, given that our data were collected in the last third of the 1990s, we examine the extent to which our findings would enable us to "predict" subsequent developments in the first postmillennial decade and what this might imply for the (re)building of programmatic party competition across Latin America in the new century.

DESCRIBING PROGRAMMATIC STRUCTURATION

In Part I we present data that describe the degree of programmatic structuration of Latin American party systems. Each chapter focuses on one of four indicators: the dimensionality of the issue space (Chapter 2), left-right semantics (Chapter 3), elite-mass programmatic linkage on key issues or representation (Chapter 4), and the ideological cohesion of individual parties (Chapter 5). The data that we use to measure each of these indicators come from the 1997 Parliamentary Elites of Latin America (PELA) project and, in the case of representation, are complemented by data from the 1998 Latinobarometer survey. Full descriptions of the PELA survey, the variables we use, and a discussion of several data issues are presented in Appendixes A–C and in Web Appendixes D and E (at www.cambridge.org/9780521114950).

Although many of our key findings are summarized in the introduction to the next section of the book, Part II, analysts of party systems more generally and of Latin American politics more particularly will want to inspect these data carefully. Many of our indicators are new and are better understood when analyzed in their appropriate context within each chapter. Moreover, the scope of each analysis is broad and, in several cases, unprecedented; the data permit the comparison of Latin American party systems not only to each other but to party systems in the advanced industrial democracies and the former communist regimes of Eastern Europe. This introduction to Part I begins by justifying our operationalization of each indicator. It then addresses two potential sources of measurement error peculiar to this set of survey data: the lack of true party-level indicators and the absence of measures of political salience.

EMPIRICAL INDICATORS OF PROGRAMMATIC PARTY COMPETITION

If politicians coordinate around party labels and engage in programmatic competition to attract voters, we should observe at least four features in their party systems: low dimensionality of the ideological space, informative left-right semantics, appropriate representation on issue dimensions, and ideological cohesion of political parties. As already detailed by Downs's (1957) lucid discussion of information processing and democratic party competition, these features facilitate the electoral conduct of minimally informed but rational-purposive voters who wish to base their electoral choice on the congruence between their own policy preferences and the parties' programmatic positions. Because these traits provide the framework for, and support, programmatic party competition, we also refer to the four traits as indicators of programmatic party structuration (PPS).

Ideological, Partisan, and Competitive Dimensions

According to the first of these four traits, parties should diversify their programmatic packages from one another on a single or a very small number of issue dimensions. Politicians simplify the world of interparty competition for themselves, their activists, and their electoral constituencies by "bundling" individual policy positions into a minimal number of underlying dimensions that relate issue stances to abstract normative political principles (Hinich and Munger 1994). We should expect differentiation of programmatic positions across one or several dimensions under moderately realistic behavioral assumptions about voters and politicians, and under both two-party and multiparty competition.

The exact nature of the political dimensions into which issue positions are bundled requires further specification; in particular, it is useful to discriminate among three levels or spaces of political articulation: ideological, partisan, and competitive. At the lowest level of political articulation, that of ideological divides, issue divisions run deep across individuals, very likely across social groups, but not necessarily across political parties. We infer the existence of an ideological dimension whenever a citizen's or politician's position on issue i may enable us to predict her positions on issues j, k, and so on. In our study, we measure ideological dimensions by performing country-specific factor analyses of all twenty-seven issue-oriented questions in our dataset; each of the strongest factors that emerge is treated as a possible ideological divide.

Ideological dimensions do not always translate directly into the arena of partisan politics. It might occur, for example, that knowledge of the issue positions i, j, and k of an individual does not help us predict her party preference or affiliation. Yet some ideological dimensions do translate into party preferences and give rise to political partisan divides at an intermediate level of political articulation. In this instance, a citizen's or a politician's ideological position (i.e., her stances on related issues i, j, k) enables us to predict her party preference or affiliation and vice versa. We measure the existence and strength of partisan dimensions by performing country-specific discriminant analyses of the same twenty-seven issues in our dataset.

At the highest level of political articulation, that of competitive dimensions, groups of citizens and politicians do not simply support parties because of their issue positions but are also willing to change their partisan choice contingent upon parties' evolving positions. Thus, changes in the programmatic positions of parties along the competition space translate into changes in electoral choices among voters. Unfortunately, most survey evidence about voters and politicians does not permit us to measure the competitive nature of these dimensions directly. We would require a panel design in which the political preferences and partisan messages of voters and politicians were measured over several rounds of electoral competition in order to calculate the elasticity of voters' preferences contingent upon politicians' programmatic positions. In a less demanding research design, one could presume partisan dimensions to be competitive if citizens and politicians attributed high salience to the issues that made up such bundles. But even this information is rarely available in surveys taken at the population or the political elite level, and our own comparative study of Latin American politics is no exception. What remains is the indirect inference about competitive dimensions from the strength of, and number of issues that make up, political partisan dimensions. This, then, is the focus of Chapter 2.

The Informational Value of Left-Right Semantics

According to the second trait, politicians should employ the semantics of "left" and "right" (or liberal-conservative) as information shortcuts that connect their programmatic packages to this single formal dimension. If minimally informed but intentionally rational voters need a low-dimensionality space of party competition, they also need easy reference points with which to identify and locate themselves and other political actors in this space. Left-right (or liberal-conservative) labels typically serve as such reference points, orienting individuals within the political space and facilitating efficient and meaningful communication of a party's program.

Theoretically, ideological labels may reference at least two components: symbolic and substantive.[1] The symbolic component references political groups without necessarily also being associated with the policy stances of those entities. Because the groups associated with this component typically are political parties, this component is generally conceptualized as partisan.[2]

---

[1] While not addressed here, it is worth acknowledging the left-right semantics might also contain a third component: affect. In short, political actors may attach affective or evaluative meaning to ideological labels and use this emotive content, such as hostility or warmth, as a decision-making heuristic (see Jacoby 2002; also see Cobb and Elder 1973; Conover and Feldman 1981).

[2] The significance of the partisan component is made clear by a quote that originates in Butler and Stokes (1969; cited in Inglehart and Klingemann 1976): "Voters come to think of themselves as Right or Left very much as a Conservative in Birmingham or Scotland used

The substantive component reflects policy divides within a society. A left-right label with significant substantive meaning allows one to predict a person's stance on a policy or bundle of policies, such as those belonging to the traditional economic state-market basket, simply by knowing her left-right self-placement. Overall, the value of left-right semantics for programmatic structuration depends critically on the interconnectedness between politicians' policy stances on key issues and their ability (and willingness) to place their party on the left-right dimension. The greater this constraint is, then the stronger the programmatic content of left-right labels is, the more efficient and useful left-right semantics are as communication devices, and the more the mass public can treat parties' left-right placements as reliable indicators of future conduct in legislative and executive office. Programmatic party structuration is fostered to an even greater degree when there is simultaneously a strong substantive and a strong symbolic partisan component to the left-right semantics: elites use the labels to simultaneously communicate their party affiliation and their party's programmatic stances on this abstract, simplified dimension of competition.

In Chapter 3, for each country, we measure the substantive component of left-right semantics by regressing legislators' left-right self-placements on, first, the ideological and, second, the partisan dimensions of issue conflict reported in Chapter 2. The explained variance from these two sets of regressions indicates the strength of these substantive components – that is, the extent to which legislators agree on the shared policy content of the left-right semantics. We further examine these substantive partisan connections as they also relate to the symbolic partisan component by including a second set of regressions of left-right self-placement on the relevant partisan dimensions of conflict and on the parties' true (mean) positions on the left-right scale. This analysis yields insight into which component of the left-right semantics – symbolic partisan or substantive partisan – dominates in which countries and, moreover, in which countries the two overlap in programmatically useful ways.

Representation on Issue Dimensions

If party elites successfully issue programmatic messages that can be easily decoded by rational information misers, then, according to the third trait, we should observe some correspondence between the programmatic

---

to think of himself as a 'Unionist,' because that is what his party is called locally" (p. 260). Thus, where the symbolic partisan component is strong, ideological labels act as alternatives to party labels. Theoretically, the symbolic component might reference other politically relevant groups or even individuals in a society such as "the rich," "the government," "the unions," or "President X" (see Zechmeister 2006).

preferences of political agents (voters) and those of their principals (legislative representatives) at least on some relevant issue dimensions. Such linking may be called mandate, or issue, representation. While we recognize that correspondence between preferences articulated by a party's voters and politicians constitutes a narrow measure of political representation, one that, for example, does not take into account cycles of accountability and responsiveness, issue representation is typically considered a sign of, or at least a factor enabling, democratic quality and more-robust forms of representation. Such a perspective is consistent with that of "responsible party government," in which voters (principals) select among parties (agents) according to the alternative policy packages they offer (APSA 1950; Adams 2001; Converse and Pierce 1986; Dalton 1985; Schmitt and Thomassen 1999; Thomassen 1994).

In examining issue representation among party elites and party electorates, two basic measures are of primary importance to us: the relative ordering of the mean party positions across party elites and party voters and the presence of significant divides among these positions. In other words, in order for relations of mandate representation to exist, both party elites and supporters must take issue stances that are coherent and distinct from those of their peers, and the positions of party elites and party electorates must be aligned in such a way that if voters of party B are to the right of voters of party A, then party elites also on average line up in this same ordering, for all parties A and B.

In Chapter 4 we measure programmatic linkages (representation) across five sets of issue bundles: general economic, foreign investment, religion, regime, and law and order–good governance. Complementing the elite survey data with Latinobarometer data from 1998, we create average policy positions for each party's legislators and electorate. For each country, our measure of representation is based on the degree to which these mean positions line up (i.e., the degree to which the mass positions are correlated with the elite positions for that party system) and the extent to which there exist significant divides among these positions at both the mass and the elite levels.

Ideological Cohesion of Political Parties

Finally, to the degree that parties organize around salient issue positions, party elites should be ideologically cohesive or exhibit only limited disagreement around those issues. Parties are cohesive when information about the position of legislator A on issue i allows a precise prediction of the positions of fellow partisan legislators B, C, and so on, on that same issue. In Chapter 5 we measure cohesion using the standard deviation of party members' issue positions. We do not measure cohesion in terms of party discipline. Although cohesion can contribute to party discipline, or the degree to which party members vote together in the legislature, we regard the two concepts as distinct (Ozbudun 1970: 305). Specifically, parties that are not particularly cohesive may still attain high levels of party discipline thanks to the incentives created by electoral rules or other aspects of party organization.

As with our other indicators, cohesion can be considered both an indicator and a facilitator of programmatic structuration. It is an indicator in that politicians are more likely to select themselves into ideologically compatible parties when their main legislative activities are concerned with the creation of policy rather than the distribution of selective incentives, that is, when they operate in a programmatically structured system. However, it is also a facilitator to the degree that voters are concerned about the potentially opportunistic behavior of their agents once in office. In the absence of other disciplinary tools, a robust consensus among party members and leaders on the policy content of their joint political undertaking can improve voters' confidence that the party will enact its policy platform once it occupies office (cf. Caillaud and Tirole 2002); cohesion will also act as a kind of insurance for those situations in which politicians act outside the watchful eye of the voters or their party leaders, or when new issues arise that were not originally foreseen in the party platform.

We should add that our measure of intraparty ideological cohesiveness probably puts the bar higher for what it means to have programmatic structuring in a party system than for any of our other measures. Because we include this criterion, parties must not only distinguish themselves from each other in their mean central tendencies of support with respect to a variety of policy positions (i.e., show divisiveness) but also display a more or less strong internal compactness of the policy range supported by its leaders and core activists. Whereas the discriminant analyses employed to test for partisan alignments tend to yield respectable discriminant functions provided there is some mixture of divisiveness and moderate cohesion of respondents belonging to the same party, our measure of cohesion moves beyond the divergence of means and concentrates entirely on the internal dispersion of a party's legislators, regardless of how the central tendency of their responses relates to those of other parties' agents.

TWO POTENTIAL SOURCES OF MEASUREMENT ERROR

Our desire to include all relevant information for measuring each of these four indicators of programmatic structuration (issue divides, left-right semantics, representation, and cohesion) was at times challenged by short-comings of the survey data. In this section, we discuss our solutions to two shortcomings related most closely to our efforts at description: our reliance on "personal" opinions as opposed to "party" opinions, and the lack of instruments to measure the perceived salience of policy issues.[3]

Personal Opinions versus the Party Line

Except in the case of left-right placements, the Salamanca survey generally asks respondents for their self-placement on issues rather than their estimations of where their party stands. By relying on these measures, we are assuming that personal preferences drawn from survey data are effective indicators of the degree of programmatic structuration of parties and party systems. Yet we can raise objections to both parts of this assumption. First, attitudes do not necessarily equal behavior. Even if individual party members are shown to have policy preferences that differ from those of the majority in the party, party leaders may be able to discipline members and force them to act as one in the pursuit of policies associated with the party line. This possibility is not just hypothetical. Recent studies of Latin American legislatures find extremely high levels of party discipline in countries such as Argentina, Mexico, and Venezuela that equal or rival those in advanced industrial democracies with parliamentary regimes (Jones 2002; Ames 2001: 188; Nacif 2002; Coppedge 1994), yet the attitudinal indicators explored in this volume show that these countries have only moderate levels of programmatic structure. Second, the whole matters more than the sum of its parts. While it seems unlikely, the personal opinions of party members may be different from the party platform, and it is ultimately the party platform, rather than personal preferences, that determines if a party is programmatic. A consistent party manifesto abounding in clear references to official party positions on policy issues may enhance the programmatic status of a party to a greater extent than having a collection of similarly minded legislators whose views are not generally known by the electorate.

We acknowledge these objections but suggest that survey-based measures of personal attitudes are still useful indicators of programmatic linkages and in some cases make for a superior choice. In response to the first objection, we make the very strong claim that attitudinal measures (similarity of opinions among party legislators) are actually better than behavioral ones (party discipline). This claim rests on several considerations. In the first place, unity of action is necessary but insufficient for programmatic structure. Various Latin American party systems are noted for having powerful political machines that enforce discipline through clientelistic rather than programmatic means; likewise, Latin American politicians working at the

---

[3] Two additional problems – sampling problems and missing values – lend themselves to a more technical discussion and are referenced in Appendix A.

behest of a feared or revered charismatic leader often show considerable una-nimity. As studies by Levitsky (2003) and Coppedge (1994) demonstrate, parties such as the Peronists, the PRI, AD, and COPEI were (or still are) patronage machines – highly disciplined, but maintaining political support primarily through the careful, conditional distribution of pork and partic-ularistic benefits. And the politicians who currently support Hugo Chávez in Venezuela are as disciplined as any of the traditional parties ever were, but their discipline might be based heavily on Chávez's role as a charismatic leader.

Another reason why attitudinal measures are superior indicators of PPS is that if a party system in fact embodies programmatic linkages – that is, if the legislative activity of parties is all about issues and policies rather than selective incentives or the faithful support of a particular charismatic leader – then individual politicians will tend to join a party whose pref-erences are close to their own; their opinions about one issue should be related to their opinions about other issues; and they should employ shared, issue-based meanings of party labels. Technically, it is true that politicians do not have to share the same views about particular issues in order to have a successful programmatic party – they only need to act as if they agree on the issues. This is another way of saying that politicians who form a pro-grammatic party are office-maximizing. However, it seems unrealistic to argue that politicians care only about winning public office. While we do consider politicians to be self-interested, office-seeking individuals, they have second-order preferences about the policy content of party platforms that affect them personally. Given a choice between two equally powerful par-ties, an office-maximizing politician will join the one closest to his views. Thus, unity of individual-level preferences and meanings seem to be likely outcomes of programmatic structuration.

Finally, the politicians' attitudes about issues should matter to voters because they reduce uncertainty. If a party has a homogeneous preference profile among its representatives, voters can predict what the party's leg-islative stance will be, even on new policy issues. If, however, a party is highly heterogeneous in the preferences of its individual legislators, voters cannot predict the collective position of the party on issues that were not originally included in the platform. Discipline then means only that the party can impose on its legislative agents whatever position it chooses in a very broad policy space, and voters still cannot anticipate that the party's collec-tive position will in any way resemble their own policy preferences. In this regard, voters probably prefer a relatively undisciplined, yet ideologically homogeneous party to an ideologically fractured party with great capacity to impose discipline on the rank and file (see Caillaud and Tirole 2002 for a similar argument).

While these considerations make attitudes rather than behavior the best indicators of programmatic structure, they do not respond to the second objection, that a measure of party attitudes – for example, "What is your party's position on the privatization of public utilities?" as opposed to "What is your opinion about the privatization of public utilities?" – would be a better measure of programmatic structure than a personal one. Our response to this objection is pragmatic. We agree that party placement measures would probably be superior indicators of programmatic structuration. However, the preceding arguments about the value of attitudinal measures also suggest that self- and party placement indicators are likely to be highly correlated with each other, insofar as programmatic structuration both encourages and is facilitated by individual-level cohesion around issues. In fact, the analysis in Chapter 3 shows that there is a fairly high degree of correspondence between self-placement and placement of the party on a left-right scale, with an average correlation of about $r = .70$ in each country in our sample.

Even if self-placement items provide somewhat biased measures of the real degree of programmatic structure in Latin American party systems, we know something about the direction of this bias: if there is more leeway for discrepancies between personal and party positions, then our indicators of self-placement are likely to underestimate the amount of party-level convergence among issue positions and ideological labels, that is, we will underestimate the degree of programmatic structuration. This conjecture seems to be borne out by the cohesion data on left-right placement found in Chapter 5. The results show that legislators are indeed more cohesive when asked about their parties' positions than when they are asked about their own.[4]

Lack of Salience Questions

An additional shortcoming of the Salamanca survey is the lack of questions on salience, that is, the degree to which respondents consider certain issues relevant for current national politics. While the survey includes a large number of questions about a wide range of issues, only a single series asks which of these issues are important in the respondent's country. The series includes just fourteen items, some of which (e.g., inflation and economic stagnation) have no match among the issue positions measured elsewhere in the survey. Thus, we cannot consistently and directly gauge the salience of most of our issues, and we ultimately include just two of these questions in our analysis (*violence is a problem* [v87] and *corruption is a problem* [v168] – see Appendixes A and B for a discussion of variables and an English translation of survey questions); even then, we include these as rough measures of issue

---

[4] A one-tailed test indicates that the difference between these two indicators of left-right cohesion (self-placement and party placement) is statistically significant at the $p < .02$ level for our twelve country cases.

position rather than measures of salience. The series does provide us with one highly useful piece of information that informs much of the design of our analysis, namely, the importance of economic issues across the region. Of the fourteen issues covered in the series, the seven most salient (all of which have a regional average of 3.9 or higher on a scale of 1–5, where 5 is "most important") include five relating to the macroeconomy and social programs (salaries, employment, economic stagnation, education, and heath care–housing). In contrast, of the seven least salient issues (with regional averages between 2.7 and 3.6), only two are economic issues (inflation and foreign debt). Issues of democracy and human rights in particular are among the least salient across the region, and questions about religion and "family values" are simply not included. We take this as support for our decision in much of the rest of this book to focus on programmatic structuration around economic policy.

The lack of data on salience can distort our descriptive findings in several ways. For example, our measures of programmatic structuration may be based on issues (e.g., environmental issues) that have not yet had any real political relevance in that particular legislature and which do not resonate strongly with existing partisan divides in Latin America. Because politicians' views will probably not coincide on these nonsalient issues, their inclusion is likely to lead to a "false negative" (i.e., to conclude that they are not particularly divisive when they are not even a matter of public debate), adding noise to our data and causing us to underestimate the actual level of programmatic structuration. Likewise, we may accidentally include valence issues or issues that once divided politicians and parties but have since faded in importance (e.g., traditional church-state issues or questions about the legitimacy of democracy). This error will lead to a "false positive," in that we are more likely to find a mistakenly high level of programmatic structuration. Finally, we may include latent competitive divides, that is, issues that do happen to map onto existing parties (partisan divides) but which have not yet become and may never become part of the political debate or policy agenda (e.g., the legalization of abortion). This error would again lead to a false positive finding.

Fortunately, we have means of eliminating some of these sources of bias. In our discussion of ideological and partisan divides, we make an attempt to correct for the lack of questions on salience by using discriminant analysis to determine the degree to which the party affiliation of respondents helps us predict their positions on different issues. The presumption is that issues that map onto parties have a much better chance of being politically salient. In Chapter 3, we use OLS regressions of these discriminant functions to measure the substantive component of the left-right semantics. Finally, in Chapter 5 we first measure the divisiveness of each issue by performing an analysis of variance (ANOVA) on each question from the Salamanca survey. Arguing that highly divisive issues have a greater chance of being politically salient, we refine our data on cohesion by considering only the most divisive issues for each country.

These correctives are very useful because they help to decrease two of the sources of bias mentioned previously: the tendency to underestimate salience by including irrelevant variables, and the tendency to overestimate salience by including valence issues. Unfortunately, they do not prevent us from including formerly salient issues or latent divides. As we argue in Chapter 5, divisiveness is an imperfect indicator of salience because some divisive issues may not have any actual bearing on current political debates; the discriminant analysis in Chapter 2 eliminates irrelevant and valence issues (by essentially taking into account both the parties' standard deviations and mean positions), but it lacks any way of distinguishing between actually salient issues, formerly salient issues, and latent divides that may or may not become competitive; and the techniques used in Chapter 3 can really show only whether the associations between certain issues and left-right semantics are statistically significant, not whether they are politically significant. Thus, the good news and the bad news are that we can probably eliminate the possibility of underestimating the degree of programmatic structuration, but we cannot eliminate the possibility that we have overestimated it. Because in all of these chapters we find only moderate levels of programmatic structuration in most Latin American countries, actual programmatic structuration may be even lower, and our estimates can best be seen as an upper bound.

Knowing this bias complicates our analysis somewhat because it seems to run in the opposite direction of what we expect from the discrepancy between personal and party assessments mentioned in the preceding section: the framing of the survey questions may cause us to underestimate programmatic structuration, but the lack of salience indicators may lead us to overestimate it. This is problematic for our efforts to describe the exact level of programmatic structuration in Latin America. Because we do not have an easy solution to this problem, we must simply encourage readers to keep these potential sources of bias in mind as they explore the following chapters.

The situation is not as problematic for our efforts to explain the patterns of programmatic structuration, which come in Part II. To the extent that the sum of these errors systematically affects all of our observations, our analytical findings – our explanations for the causes of programmatic structuration – remain unaffected (King, Keohane, and Verba 1994: 156). Specifically, in OLS regressions our estimates of the intercept may be wrong but our estimates of effect parameters will be unbiased, and correlation coefficients will be unchanged.

2

Issues, Ideologies, and Partisan Divides

Imprints of Programmatic Structure on
Latin American Legislatures

Guillermo Rosas

What political, economic, and social issues shape the political arena of Latin American legislatures? During the past two decades, dramatic changes have altered the economic and political makeup of Latin American societies, perhaps shifting the ideological bases of party competition. Though comparative researchers have delved into the deep cleavages that might shape politics in the region (cf. Dix 1989; Collier and Collier 1991), we know little about how these divides are mapped into political preferences at the elite level. Party systems are shaped by both societal cleavages and political institutions such as electoral rules (Lipset and Rokkan 1967; Cox 1997). In the stage set by cleavages and institutions, strategic politicians devise political programs to capture votes, sometimes energizing dormant societal divides to garner electoral support, sometimes reactively aligning their political platforms to shifting preferences in the electorate. In any case, politicians "map" multiple issues on essentially "either-or" propositions, in order to convey their own political preferences to cognitive misers in the electorate. The spatial analysis of politics refers to these issue bundles as "ideologies." This chapter explores Latin American legislatures by analyzing the structure and contents of issue bundles.

We begin our empirical analysis of programmatic structuration by focusing on the attitudes, values, and opinions of legislative elites. In doing so, we confirm that the contents and structures of what we call ideological and partisan spaces vary immensely throughout the region. At the most basic level, our analysis allows us to rank our twelve legislatures in terms of levels of programmatic structuration of beliefs and attitudes, from highest to lowest, in the following order: Chile, Uruguay, Mexico, Argentina, Venezuela, Ecuador, Colombia, Costa Rica, Peru, Bolivia, Brazil, and the Dominican Republic. We also find that two divides – economic-distributive and cultural-religious – strongly pattern attitudes and opinions in many Latin American legislatures but that these two divides translate into partisan divisions in only a handful of cases. Notably, these two divides tend to reinforce, rather than cut across, each other wherever they structure legislative party competition, so we can conclude that the space of party competition in Latin American legislatures is generally one-dimensional.

The next section presents an overview of the spatial approach to the study of legislative ideologies along with a factor analysis of twenty-seven issues in the Salamanca surveys. We then present a discriminant analysis of the partisan structures that underlie the policy preferences of Latin American legislators. In a Web appendix (Web Appendix 2.1 at www.cambridge.org/9780521114950), we compare the ideological and partisan spaces of Latin American legislatures. Web Appendix 2.1 speaks to an important debate regarding the possibility of party realignment and increased programmatic structuration in Latin America, but because our theoretical arguments do not depend on any of the measurements derived therein, this material can be skipped in a first reading without loss of continuity.

IDEOLOGICAL DIMENSIONS IN LATIN AMERICAN LEGISLATURES

In the rationalist approach to the study of politics, ideology is understood as a tool that allows voters to economize on information costs related to the policy positions of different political actors, particularly candidates for public office (Downs 1957; Converse 1964; Hinich and Munger 1994). Rather than investing limited time and resources in obtaining accurate information about the myriad policy stances that candidates hold, rational information misers will look only at the "ideological label" (e.g., liberal-conservative, left-right) attached to candidacies and use it to infer the policy preferences of politicians running for office. Rational voters will then form more precise expectations about a candidate's policy stances conditional on the candidate's ideological persuasion.

In strictly descriptive terms, rational-choice theories provide an excellent approximation of how voters cast their votes in settings rich in ideological content.[1] However, it is less obvious that the substantive contents of ideology are similar across countries, and even less obvious that ideologies exist as useful cost-saving devices in other nations. Thus, voters in Peru might be unable to agree on the meaning of "rightist," "progressive," or "libertarian," and therefore find little value in using these ideological labels as cues into the issue stances of candidates who run under these banners. We focus in this chapter on the existence of "ideologies" or "ideological organization" as a hallmark of the programmatic structure of party systems. Indeed, ideological organization at the elite level is a necessary condition for programmatic party competition. Where politicians are unwilling or unable

---

[1] For example, the liberal-conservative ideological divide in the United States is so entrenched and its connotations so widely shared that voters have a relatively good idea of the kind of issue stances that a "liberal" candidate might hold.

to coordinate around distinct party programs, voters will find it extremely difficult to understand what their vote buys and to hold incumbent politicians accountable for betraying policy promises; the quality of democratic representation and political accountability will diminish consequently.[2]

We consider four relevant levels or spaces of political organization, each of which conveys a different aspect of the programmatic structure of a party system (Kitschelt et al. 1999: chap. 7; Hinich and Munger 1994).[3] In our

---

[2] Indeed, the theory of conditional party government in the United States posits that ideological homogeneity within parties and ideological heterogeneity across parties is a sine qua non for party government (Aldrich and Rohde 2001). Note, however, that we do not consider ideological structure at the elite level to be a sufficient condition for programmatic party competition at the mass level: even if political elites are organized along relatively clear ideological lines, it does not necessarily follow that voters understand the meaning of basic programmatic differences in the party system or that their vote choice is determined by these programmatic differences. In other words, ideological organization does not entail policy voting (Adams 2001).

[3] This decomposition of the issue space adds one dimension to those described by Kitschelt et al. (1999). The difference is subtle, but it squares better with the choice of methods (especially discriminant analysis) employed here. Kitschelt et al. (1999: 224) disregard discriminant analysis because their purpose is "to determine dimensions on which party policies and voter preferences vary, independent of finding the technically most efficient tool to discriminate among party positions." We note, however, that discriminant and factor analyses differ not in their relative efficiency but on the information they provide about the structure of ideological and partisan spaces.

Note also that the literature on party competition employs notions such as "divide," "division," "dimension," and especially "cleavage," in widely varying ways. To advance some conceptual clarity in our study, we employ "dimensions" and "divisions" interchangeably as generic concepts and then make a semantic distinction between two categories, "divides" and "cleavages." Thus, "dimensions" or "divisions" refer to all sorts of disagreements over politically relevant issues or issue clusters we can observe among the citizens of a polity. Issues are politically relevant if at least one group calls upon the government for an authoritative, binding resolution of a disagreement. The distinction between divides and cleavages depends then on the persistence of these disagreements. If political issues are temporally fluid or transitional, we refer to them as "divides." In contrast, "cleavages" refer to those divisions that last over long periods of time. Usually, but not always, the persistence of divisions and their crystallization around cleavages goes together with one or all of the following attributes: (1) Cleavages involve conflict between societal groups that can be identified in sociodemographic categorical terms (e.g., class, occupation, ethnicity, region). (2) Cleavages express divisions not just on a singular issue that is of intermittent temporal relevance and separate from other issues in substantive respects; rather, cleavages are lasting divisions usually involving a cluster of issues that are organized in some systematic fashion around principles, interests, and values. (3) Cleavages coincide with the mobilization of civic associations on different sides of the issue, even outside and preceding electoral competition (Lipset and Rokkan 1967). In this volume, we do not attempt to determine whether our results describe cleavages or merely divides, and in any case our data rarely provide the evidence we would need to make the distinction. Hence, when we talk about "dimensions" or "divisions," we generally refer to "divides"; we use the term "cleavages" sparingly, and reserve it for those few situations where it truly applies.

database, each legislator's vector of twenty-seven issue stances is an element in the issue space, the most superficial level. The issue space is observable directly, in the sense that we know each legislator's actual responses to an interviewer's questions.[4] The rationalist account of ideology suggests that the extremely high dimensionality of the issue space imposes excessive informational costs on voters. However, a much simpler ideological space spans the issue space, providing summaries, as it were, of politicians' stances on different issues. These summaries consist of "issue bundles," sets of issue positions that "belong together" in the minds of politicians and voters. In practice, this means that, whether by accident or by design, issue stances are not distributed independently along each dimension in the issue space. On the contrary, legislators' positions tend to correlate even across issue dimensions that an outsider would not consider similar a priori. For example, it is understandable that a politician who believes that government should provide housing for the poor also believes that government should provide unemployment insurance. It is less obvious that a politician who holds both of these beliefs should also oppose the death penalty. Yet, that is what ideologies achieve: they provide an authoritative and reasonable account of how otherwise disparate issue stances "belong together" (Hinich and Munger 1994). In any case, the ideological space is of much lower dimensionality – two or three dimensions often suffice to summarize adequately the issue space – and it provides all the information that a citizen requires in making prospective voting decisions.

We refer to dimensions in the ideological space as "ideological dimensions," and we compare in this section both the substantive contents of ideologies and the simplicity of underlying ideological spaces across our twelve legislatures. In particular, we derive measures of the degree to which three substantive bundles – the economic-distributive, political-regime, and cultural-religious divides – structure legislators' opinions, even when they might not help discriminate among parties.

We are not entirely agnostic about how diverse issues might combine into different ideological dimensions. We believe that as many as seven issue bundles could make up the ideological spaces of some Latin American legislatures (see Web Appendix 2.1 at www.cambridge.org/9780521114950).

---

[4] To understand how a voter's decision problem is simplified by ideology, consider that our analysis is restricted to a relatively simple issue space with only twenty-seven dimensions. In order to carry out a maximally informed voting decision in this "simple" political world, each voter would need to inform herself about each candidate's vector of issue stances, and compare this information with her own policy positions in a twenty-seven-dimensional space to decide, whether by spatial proximity or general proclivity, which candidate to support. This problem is compounded by the fact that the number of relevant issues has no upper bound in the real world – and is likely much larger than twenty-seven.

However, this naive expectation is based solely on glimpses into the history of party formation and party competition in Latin America (Dix 1989; Collier and Collier 1991; Coppedge 1998b). The field of comparative Latin American politics lacks a coherent account of cleavage formation that would help us build theoretically sound expectations about the contents and form of ideological spaces in different countries in the region. Consequently, we have decided against use of statistical tools, like confirmatory factor analysis, that would allow us to test the fit of the data to the expectations embodied in our seven issue bundles. As Hinich and Munger (1994) suggest, deciding which dimensions, if any, shape up patterns of programmatic organization across countries is ultimately an empirical matter. In the face of theoretical paucity, we resort to the more inductivist tool of exploratory factor analysis.

Exploratory factor analysis, like other scaling techniques, aims to summarize variation in a large number of variables by constructing a smaller number of latent dimensions or "factors." Given the assumptions of factor analysis, the researcher faces a number of choices that introduce discretion into otherwise mechanical procedures. Two decisions are of utmost importance: the number of factors that are kept as a "summary" of the larger dataset, and the proportion of variation in each input variable (the twenty-seven issues in this case) that is considered "common."[5] In particular, decisions about commonality of variance are likely to have important interpretive consequences. Factor analysis assumes that only a fraction of the variation in any particular issue can be attributed to latent factors, whereas the rest of the variation should be considered idiosyncratic to each issue. Unfortunately, one does not know the size of the common variance of each variable beforehand. Thus, prior estimates about commonality become critical, especially in small samples.

We prefer a method of extraction – principal factor analysis – that uses the average squared correlations of variables as estimates of commonality. Given that the purpose is to explore the latent "ideological" space underlying the visible "issue" space, we feel justified in using principal factor analysis. The obvious alternative, principal component analysis, assumes that commonalities are 1, an assumption we do not find defensible.[6] Factor analysis makes the underlying dimensions more interpretable, because loadings for variables that contribute highly to a principal factor (common variance) are perforce larger than loadings for variables that contribute highly to a principal component (total variance). In a sense, then, we are presenting a

[5] Answers to both decisions are related. Justifying each and every one of our assumptions would lead us into a larger statistical debate that we prefer to circumvent. The interested reader is referred to Jolliffe (1986).

[6] In practice, other factor extraction techniques, like iterated principal factors or principal component factors, yield very similar results. Principal factors differ most from principal component results, as explained in the text, but even then the substantive conclusions are largely similar.

"best case" scenario, offering the best possible argument for the existence of programmatic structuration in Latin American ideological spaces.[7]

Table 2.1 displays summary results from factor analysis of each of the twelve country samples (full results are available in Web Appendix 2.2). Each column in Table 2.1 contains information that will aid in interpreting the substance of relevant ideological dimensions. In order to maintain cross-country comparability and keep the analysis within manageable proportions, we built Table 2.1 following simple guidelines. First, within each country, we report only information concerning "significant" ideological dimensions. This characteristic is captured indirectly by a factor's eigenvalue. Indeed, the "proportion explained" statistic next to each factor at the bottom of each column in Table 2.1 can be interpreted as the relative predictive power of each constructed factor. In Argentina – for example, factor 1 alone predicts 24 percent of common variance in the issue space, whereas factors 2 and 3 account for a further 14 and 12 percent respectively.[8] Thus, factor 1 is the most divisive ideological dimension in the Argentine legislature. Notice that some countries show similar predictive power across underlying factors. In Ecuador, for example, factors 1 through 3 each predict between 14 and 18 percent of common variance in the issue space (factors 4 and 5 are less important in this regard). In this case, it is difficult to infer the existence of a preeminent ideological dimension. Indeed, the structure of ideological spaces is sensitive to alternative scaling methods (principal factors or principal components), but only where factors show similar predictive capacity, such as in Ecuador. Even then, results vary mostly in the order in which factors appear, not necessarily in the content of variables that load highly on each factor.[9]

Second, we use factor loadings, which can be interpreted as correlations between inferred underlying factors and observed issue variables, to infer the meaning of each underlying factor. For the sake of simplicity, only factor loadings larger than 0.5 are shown in Table 2.1; the parenthetical number next to each loading corresponds to the factor on which the variable loads. We conclude that a discernible issue bundle makes up an ideological divide whenever we observe high factor loadings for a cluster of

---

[7] The discussion is based on the analysis of forty-one parties, excluding parties with less than seven respondents.

[8] This of course begs the question of what proportion of total variance in the original issue space is "common." In Table 2.1, the number that appears at the bottom of each column conveys this information. Thus, the estimated average common variance per variable is 0.49 in Argentina. Average common variance goes from a low of 0.29 in Venezuela to a maximum of 0.49 in Argentina.

[9] Where one ideological dimension appears as preeminent, alternative model specifications always return the same variables in the same factor and all factors in the same order, regardless of method of factor extraction. In other words, ideological dimensions in these countries are insensitive to alternative factorization methods.

TABLE 2.1. *Ideological Dimensions in Latin America (factor analysis)*

Issues	Argentina (54)	Bolivia (62)	Brazil (47)	Chile (89)	Colombia (55)	CR (48)	DR (61)	Mexico (122)	Ecuador (56)	Peru (71)	Uruguay (69)	Venezuela (66)
Privatize industry	0.63 (1)	−0.58 (2)		0.65 (1)	0.64 (1)			0.69 (1)		0.65 (1)	0.60 (4)	
Privatize services	0.58 (1)			0.64 (1)				0.67 (1)		0.69 (1)	0.59 (4)	
Don't control prices	0.53 (1)	0.60 (1)		0.57 (1)	0.60 (1)	0.83 (2)		0.76 (1)				0.60 (4)
Don't sponsor job creation	0.76 (1)	−0.57 (2)		0.61 (1)	0.66 (1)		0.51 (1)			0.58 (1)		0.59 (4)
Don't provide housing	0.77 (1)	0.55 (3)			0.74 (1)	0.60 (2)	0.65 (1)			0.65 (1)	0.72 (4)	0.72 (4)
Don't provide social security	0.62 (1)				0.65 (1)		0.66 (1)		0.63 (5)	0.58 (1)		0.53 (4)
No unemployment insurance	0.75 (1)	−0.64 (1)	0.78 (1)				0.60 (1)	0.63 (1)		0.57 (1)		−0.62 (2)
Don't subsidize basics	0.66 (1)			0.60 (1)	0.51 (1)	0.75 (2)	0.50 (1)	0.50 (1)				0.52 (1)
Let IMF in		−0.54 (2)					0.55 (3)					
US investment best	0.70 (5)		0.66 (2)	0.65 (3)		0.78 (3)	0.66 (4)		−0.71 (3)	0.59 (2)	0.80 (1)	0.60 (3)
EU investment best			0.58 (2)	0.62 (3)		0.93 (3)	0.56 (4)		−0.81 (3)	0.74 (2)	0.86 (1)	0.58 (3)
LA investment best		0.57 (1)	0.61 (2)			0.67 (3)	0.52 (4)	0.57 (3)	−0.51 (3)	0.55 (2)	0.73 (1)	
Justice doesn't work	0.61 (3)	0.78 (1)			0.54 (3)					0.58 (2)	0.53 (3)	
Crime is threat	0.63 (3)				0.62 (3)	0.51 (4)			−0.68 (1)			
Labor unrest is threat	0.52 (3)	0.71 (2)			0.59 (3)		0.56 (3)		−0.64 (1)		0.72 (2)	
Violence is a problem	0.57 (4)		−0.53 (1)		−0.63 (4)		0.75 (2)					
I go to church often	0.86 (2)	0.68 (3)	0.63 (3)	0.78 (2)	0.85 (2)	0.52 (1)		0.70 (2)	0.75 (2)	0.65 (3)	0.60 (3)	0.80 (1)
Abortion not allowed	0.66 (2)			0.74 (2)	0.80 (2)			0.72 (2)				
Divorce not allowed	0.58 (2)	0.50 (3)	0.50 (3)	0.64 (2)	−0.53 (3)	0.52 (1)	0.51 (3)	0.62 (2)	0.76 (2)			
I'm very religious	0.87 (2)	0.72 (3)	0.76 (3)	0.69 (2)	0.58 (4)			0.69 (2)		0.58 (3)	0.70 (3)	0.87 (1)
Minority rights not important	−0.65 (3)	−0.60 (2)	0.53 (1)	0.72 (1)	0.69 (4)	−0.78 (1)	−0.72 (2)	−0.68 (3)		0.58 (3)	−0.56 (2)	−0.59 (2)
Environment not important	−0.68 (4)	−0.54 (2)	0.70 (1)				−0.60 (2)		0.72 (5)			−0.50 (2)
Democracy always best				−0.50 (1)		0.50 (4)			0.50 (4)			
Elections always best				−0.48 (1)		0.55 (4)		0.50 (4)				
Parties not superfluous		−0.54 (1)		−0.58 (1)								
Corruption always existed		0.77 (4)				0.57 (4)	−0.51 (1)					
Army/welfare trade-off				0.69 (1)								
Factor 1	0.24	0.26	0.24	0.40	0.23	0.18	0.21	0.35	0.18	0.29	0.32	0.27
Factor 2	0.14	0.16	0.15	0.14	0.18	0.15	0.15	0.19	0.15	0.18	0.14	0.16
Factor 3	0.12	0.13	0.11	0.11	0.13	0.12	0.12	117	0.14	0.13	0.11	0.12
Factor 4	0.09	0.10			0.10	0.10	0.11		0.11		0.09	
Factor 5	0.09								0.11			
Common variance	0.49	0.40	0.32	0.36	0.37	0.38	0.34	0.31	0.40	0.31	0.41	0.29

Note: The sample size appears in parenthesis with the country name. Cells contain factor loadings greater than |0.5| (the relevant factor appears in parenthesis next to the factor loading). Full results appear in Web Appendix 2.2 at www.cambridge.org/9780521114950.

substantively similar issues. For example, factor 1 in Argentina can be easily interpreted as an economic-distributive ideological dimension: eight related issues (*privatize industry, privatize services, don't control prices, don't sponsor job creation, don't provide housing, don't provide social security, no unemployment insurance, don't subsidize basics*) show high factor loadings. Argentine legislators place themselves along the inferred economic-distributive ideological dimension, some of them espousing views that agree with statements regarding extensive state intervention in the economy, some disagreeing with those statements. Indeed, we can consider Argentine legislators with high scores on factor 1 to espouse economic views traditionally attributed to the right.[10] In this case, it is noteworthy that legislators who agree with statements regarding privatization of industry and services also tend to have similar opinions on government responsibility regarding price control, job creation, supply of cheap housing and social security, unemployment insurance, and subsidies to the poor. The "observed" stances of legislators on all of these issues correlate highly with their inferred stances along factor 1. In some cases, the 0.5 benchmark for factor loadings could be relaxed, as in the case of *let IMF in*, which shows a relatively large factor loading on Argentina's factor 1 (0.42). In this case, it is sensible to consider *let IMF in* as belonging to the economic-distributive ideological dimension just described, particularly because no other issues come close to the 0.5 yardstick (see Web Appendix 2.2 for details on all factor loadings).

Note as well that factor loading signs have no intrinsic meaning. Because there are an infinite number of solutions to a factor analytic problem, and because factor rotation is geared toward maximizing correlations for a group of variables without concern for the signs of these correlations, all loadings in Argentina's factor 1 could have conceivably been negative. In this case, we would have interpreted legislators with negative scores on factor 1 as belonging to the economic right. It would be strange, however, if variables that should intuitively relate to the same underlying ideological dimension appear with contrary signs. The correct interpretation in this case would be that legislators somehow manage to reconcile differing views about similar issues. As will become clear in the following paragraphs, however, this event is extremely rare and occurs only in issue bundles that do not turn out to have significant ideological dimensions.

Finally, we mentioned earlier that the factor analytic solution we chose includes rotating factors so as to maximize the correlation between inferred factor scores and actual legislator stances on relevant issues. This procedure

---

[10] To avoid prejudging the analysis that we present in Chapter 3, we mostly eschew use of the labels "left" and "right" in this chapter. Note as well that the inferred positions of legislators along different factors are constructed so as to yield approximately standard normal distributions. Thus, the mean of the distribution of legislators' inferred positions along Argentina's factor 1 is −0.06, its standard deviation 0.93.

merely increases the substantive interpretability of elicited factors. We also stipulated that constructed factors should not correlate with one another. This is again a consequence of theoretical paucity, as we have no way of telling, for example, that ideological stances concerning economic distribution should mildly correlate with views on religion and morality issues. Nor could we reasonably build expectations about how issue bundles would relate to each other in different countries. The solution then was to rotate factors using the "varimax" procedure, which yields latent dimensions that are orthogonal by mathematical construction; factor loadings would have been higher had we constructed oblique (i.e., correlated) factors.

The Substance of Ideological Dimensions

In this subsection, we explore in detail cross-country variation in the three most common ideological dimensions: the economic-distributive state-market dimension, the divide along religion-secularism, and the democracy-authoritarianism regime divide. Our main purpose is to build reliable measures of the importance of these divides cross-nationally; in later chapters, we use these measures as dependent variables in a study of the determinants of programmatic structure in Latin American party systems.

Before looking in detail at these three ideological dimensions, we look briefly at other issue bundles whose importance we had anticipated. As a matter of fact, two of these bundles fail to consistently structure the beliefs of legislators in the region. First, opinions on the desirability of allowing monitoring and financial assistance from the World Bank and the IMF (*let IMF in*) *do not* appear to be related to variables concerning foreign ownership of domestic industry (*US investment best*, *EU investment best*, *LA investment best*), as was just shown in the case of Argentina. Except in Ecuador's factor 3 and the Dominican Republic's factor 4, *let IMF in* seldom loads highly together with the other three indicators of what we expected to make up a financial isolation-integration ideological divide. Even in these two countries, however, the factor loading for *let IMF in* is small in comparison with those of *US investment best*, *EU investment best*, and *LA investment best*.

In most other cases, either *let IMF in* or the foreign investment variables load highly on some factor but never together. We have already discussed Argentina's factor 1 as an instance in which legislators hold different opinions on whether to allow IMF conditionality. In contrast, legislators in Brazil (factor 2), Chile (factor 3), Costa Rica (factor 3), Peru (factor 2), Uruguay (factor 1), and Venezuela (factor 3) differ markedly on their opinions regarding the desirability of allowing foreign investment, regardless of nationality, in the privatization of strategic industries. As a matter of fact (with the exception of Argentina), Latin American legislators seem to share a declarative consensus *against* the desirability of World Bank or IMF monitoring, which is substantiated by extremely lopsided and unimodal distributions of responses on *let IMF in* across countries (the exception to this is Brazil, where opinion is lopsided in favor of the IMF). Thus, the lack of association between *let IMF in*, on the one hand, and *US investment best*, *EU investment best*, and *LA investment best*, on the other, lends credence to the view that economic nationalism, not financial isolation-integration, still defines an ideological divide among political elites in Latin American countries. In other words, legislators seem to be divided not on whether foreign investment from some countries should be disallowed but on whether it should be permitted in strategic industries.

Second, the five law-and-order issues seldom load together in the same ideological dimension. In some cases, a single law-and-order indicator intermingles with other variables, adding noise to otherwise interpretable dimensions (e.g., *violence is an important problem* in Chile's factor 2, which we interpret as a religious-secular ideological divide; see Web Appendix 2.2 at www.cambridge.org/9780521114950). In other cases, at least two of these variables load highly on a single factor, suggesting an inchoate law-and-order ideological dimension. Among these, factor 3 in Colombia is probably the only one that could be interpreted unequivocally as a law-and-order dimension in which opinions on *justice doesn't work*, *crime is threat*, and *labor unrest is threat* are bundled together. Interestingly, indicators of law and order in Argentina, Brazil, and Mexico are bundled together with opinions on *minority rights not important* (factors 3, 1, and 3, respectively). In Colombia, a fourth factor also picks up *violence is an important problem* and *minority rights not important*. The simultaneous appearance in these countries of at least one law-and-order issue and *minority rights not important* suggests that legislators in these countries interpret minority rights as referring to human rights (the corresponding survey question lends itself to equivocal interpretations), and that they are willing to sacrifice protection of human rights to the extent that they see law-and-order issues as problematic. In these cases, we might interpret the issue bundle as a legislator's stance on how to combat the mounting challenge of organized crime (an interpretation substantiated by the relatively high loadings of *crime is threat* in Argentina and Mexico). However, the relatively high loading (0.48; see Web Appendix 2.2) of *environment not important* in Mexico's factor 3 casts doubt on this interpretation and suggests instead that legislators might be divided on their opinions about the rights of indigenous minorities, whose livelihoods are often tied to exploitation of natural resources. A similar pattern is observable in Colombia, where questions on human rights, violence, and environment load highly on factor 4.

We are mainly interested in the existence and shape of three ideological dimensions: an economic divide, which can be shaped by economic governance concerns, social protection issues, or both; a regime divide, which should include items relating to democracy as a desirable form of political

TABLE 2.2. *Importance of Economic Divides in Latin American Legislatures*

State/Market Dimension	Strong Social Protection Dimension	No Conspicuous Economic Divide
Argentina	Costa Rica (?)	Brazil
Bolivia (?)	Dominican Republic	Ecuador
Chile	Mexico	Venezuela
Colombia	Uruguay	
Costa Rica (?)		
Peru		

organization, and possibly items relating to law-and-order concerns; and a religious-secular divide, which should tap into legislators' behaviors and attitudes toward "morality" issues. As suggested by our discussion of economic nationalism and law and order, we consider individual factor loadings for all issues along with the context in which they appear in order to arrive at tentative interpretations of the substance of ideological dimensions across Latin America. Our main criterion to confirm the existence of these dimensions is that several issues load highly (preferably with a factor loading higher than 0.5) on the same underlying factor. The larger the number of similar issues that load on a single factor, the more confident we are about our ability to interpret that factor substantively as a genuine ideological dimension.

Among these three ideological dimensions, by far the most conspicuous across countries is the economic-distributive divide. As noted before, the economic factor does not share the same contents across nations. There are indeed marked differences in the issue bundles that make up the economic-distributive dimension in various countries, depending on the divisiveness of economic governance and social protection concerns. Economic governance issues relate to opinions about the ownership role of the state in a national economy. In contrast, social protection issues concern state intervention in the economy to sponsor social safety nets. In principle, any of four mutually exclusive outcomes can obtain: both economic governance and social protection reinforce each other (i.e., a state-market dimension); economic governance and social protection are equally divisive but cut across one another; only one of these ideologies appears as divisive; or neither economic governance nor social protection is divisive. In practice, we do not find instances of crosscutting economic dimensions in this sample. Table 2.2 classifies the twelve legislatures according to the contents of their economic-distributive divides.

On the basis of Table 2.2, Argentina, Chile, Colombia, and Peru, and possibly Bolivia and Costa Rica, display a deep ideological economic-distributive divide. In these countries, the "economic right" agrees to the following propositions: industry and services should be privatized, price controls are harmful, and social protection and basic subsidies should not be provided by the state. These results are in line with Huber and Inglehart's (1995) findings; their survey of experts documented that the "economic or class conflict" was the main political cleavage in Argentina and Chile in the 1990s.[11] In these two countries, and in Colombia, at least five out of eight tracers of economic disagreement obtain factor loadings higher than 0.5. The result is even more evident in Argentina, where all eight economic issues load highly on factor 1. Costa Rica (factor 2) can be tentatively categorized among legislatures structured by a state-market divide, except that factor loadings on questions of economic governance (*privatize industry*, *privatize services*) and on some of the social protection items fall slightly below the 0.5 cutoff in factor 2. In this group, Bolivia's ideological structure is confusing, because economic governance and social protection issues have high loadings in up to three different factors but are always combined with noneconomic issues that make the substantive interpretation of these dimensions difficult. More important, Bolivia's factor 1 shows opposite signs on *don't control prices*, on the one hand, and *don't provide social security* and *no unemployment insurance*, on the other. These opposite signs reveal a counterintuitive ideological organization of Bolivian legislators. "Leftist" legislators (particularly members of MIR, after closer inspection) tend to favor price controls but oppose the provision of social security and unemployment insurance, whereas "rightist" representatives tend to oppose price controls and favor unemployment insurance and social security. In Bolivia, economic governance and social protection stances might be at odds.

The Dominican Republic, Mexico, and Uruguay have legislatures clearly marred by ideological divisions regarding social protection. Any disagreements legislators might have about economic governance in these three countries are eclipsed by their less consensual stances on the provision of state-sponsored safety nets.[12] This is most clear in the Dominican Republic, where social protection items load highly on factor 1 to the exclusion of economic governance issues. A social protection divide similarly structures the opinions of Mexican legislators, though in this case economic governance items show loadings that are relatively higher than in the Dominican Republic. Uruguay displays a couple of economic indicators with loadings slightly below the cutoff mark in factor 1 (which, incidentally, also picks a strong

---

[11] Huber and Inglehart added Brazil and Mexico to this set, a conclusion partially supported in the case of Mexico but not in the case of Brazil. Norden (1998: 437–38) would agree with this conclusion: "Probably the most important of these divisions in Latin America is that between social classes, with many political parties defined primarily by their purported representation of working-class, middle-class or upper-class interests."

[12] In Mexico and Uruguay, the perceived lack of disagreement regarding economic governance is clearly a consequence of very narrow distributions of responses for variables 49 (*privatize industry*) and 50 (*privatize services*). Indeed, frequency distributions for these variables in Colombia, Mexico, and Uruguay are strongly unimodal, with most legislators choosing the middle point. Venezuela's distributions are slightly lopsided toward high scores.

economic nationalism dimension). However, three social protection traits appear even more starkly in factor 4 as manifestations of a social protection ideological dimension.

Finally, Brazil, Ecuador, and Venezuela lack economic structure at the ideological level. In these countries, isolated economic items achieve high factor loadings in one or two factors, but there is no systematic bundling of economic issues along any one factor, in contrast with the other nine legislatures in the sample. We conclude that whatever economic disagreements exist among legislators in these countries, they come to naught compared with ideological conflicts along noneconomic dimensions. We now explore the strength of these other divisions, starting with the religious-secular divide.

We mentioned in Chapter 1 that religion has left a strong identity imprint on twentieth-century politics in Latin America. Consistent with this presupposition, we find throughout that a behavioral divide separates Latin American politicians who regularly attend religious services from their less-devoted brethren. In most cases, this behavioral divide is reinforced by an attitudinal split, with the religiously inclined showing conservative stances on abortion and divorce. One interpretation is that this is a reminiscence of the reinforcing church-state, center-periphery cleavage that structured nineteenth-century politics (Dix 1989), manifested today in a lack of consensus on the role that the Catholic Church should play in public affairs; this finds some support in Chapter 8. An alternative interpretation is that this divide reflects a cultural division between secular, cosmopolitan legislators and traditional, parochial politicians. This interpretation downplays the political role of the Catholic Church and points to a conflict about the importance of religion (any religion) in public life.[13]

In one way or another, variables associated with a religious latent dimension are strong in all countries. In Costa Rica, Colombia, Ecuador, Peru, Uruguay, and Venezuela, attitudes toward abortion and divorce *do not* factor highly on any dimension, even when *I go to church often* and *I'm very religious* do. In other words, legislators in these countries share more consensual opinions about both abortion and divorce. This consensus is for a "liberal" position on divorce (i.e., admitting legislation that allows it); on abortion, most legislators declare that they favor it only in specific, legally sanctioned cases (the questionnaire is mute about what these cases might be). In Argentina, Bolivia, Brazil, Chile, and Mexico, there is much more variance on positions on abortion and divorce.

More interestingly, legislatures vary on whether the religious dimension cuts across or overlaps a different ideological dimension. The distribution of

---

[13] In this regard, it would be extremely informative to compare the countries in our sample with those countries, like Guatemala, where evangelical Protestants have successfully challenged Catholic dominance.

preferences in a body politic holds important implications for the character of political strife – possibilities for consensus building, fragmentation, and polarization of political party systems. The location of the religious dimension vis-à-vis other ideological bundles points to varying degrees of fragmentation across Latin American legislatures. To see this, consider the cases of Argentina, Brazil, Chile, Ecuador, Mexico, and Peru, where all religious variables appear in one factor, which is separate from all other dimensions. In these countries, the religious dimension cuts across the economic dimension, making for a more ideologically fragmented legislature. This means that there is little correlation between a legislator's position on economic governance and his religious stance. We underscore that the existence of two crosscutting *ideological* dimensions does not necessarily imply existence of two crosscutting *partisan* dimensions, as we explain in the next section.

Finally, we expected the authoritarian divide to be paramount in explaining variance in issue positions across Latin American legislatures. Although most Latin American societies have achieved progress in the consolidation of democracy, the relatively recent experience of harsh military dictatorships might have left indelible imprints on the minds of citizens and politicians. Be that as it may, we find that a systematic authoritarian divide is appreciable only in Chile, where it overlaps with the state-market dimension (consider the very high loadings on factor 1 for *democracy always best*, *parties not superfluous*, and *army/welfare trade-off*). One obvious explanation is that Chilean rightist parties have been successful in rallying supporters of Pinochet's regime after a very controlled transition to democracy. In contrast, supporters of the military regime in Argentina have not managed to gather around a focal political party, let alone have electoral success. As for other legislatures, only Bolivia and Costa Rica show traces of the authoritarian-democratic divide in any of their factors, and then only in conjunction with issues from other ideological bundles. Thus, we conclude that opinions on the desirability of democratic regimes, party competition, and electoral representativeness are not extremely divisive at the ideological level.

Comparative Strength of Ideological Dimensions

Levels of ideological divisiveness provide only one among several indicators of programmatic coherence that we explore in this book. In Part II, we carry out extensive analyses of the determinants of programmatic structure in Latin American legislative party systems. To further this purpose, we submit in the final paragraphs of this section a simple measure of the strength of the economic-distributive, political regime, and religious ideological dimensions across our twelve legislatures.

In principle, we want to construct measures that preserve comparability across legislatures. In doing so, we are forced to take a leap of faith, because any measures that we derive at the national level are obviously based on samples of twelve different populations. As explained before, factor analyses of the different national samples return results that vary in the estimated amount of common variance, the relative importance awarded to different factors, and the different factor loadings assigned to various issues. Under these circumstances, pretending that cross-national measures are perfectly comparable is folly. However, the task of arriving at general explanations to understand why some party systems coalesce around programmatic structures and why others fail to do so is extremely important and warrants more leisurely comparisons.

Thus, we have decided to base our cross-national measures of the strength of ideological dimensions on the factor loadings presented in Table 3.1. To make the most favorable case for the existence of programmatic structure, and to preserve the utmost degree of comparability, we calculated the average (absolute) factor loading of all issues that should load on a particular ideological dimension, across all factors with eigenvalues larger than 1.5 (i.e., the ones included in Table 2.1). We then kept the highest average factor loading as our "strength score," regardless of the relative importance (i.e., the eigenvalue) of the factor in which they load.

We carried out this procedure for the three ideological dimensions of interest on the basis of the following issues: for the economic-distributive divide: *privatize industry, privatize services, don't control prices, don't sponsor job creation, don't provide housing, don't provide social security, no unemployment insurance*, and *don't subsidize basics*; for the religious divide: *I go to church often, abortion not allowed, divorce not allowed*, and *I'm very religious*; and for the regime divide: *minority rights not important, democracy always best, elections always best*, and *parties not superfluous*. Consider thus the score for the strength of the religious divide in the case of Mexico: the average factor loadings (based on absolute values) of the four religious issues along Mexico's factors 1, 2, and 3 are, respectively, 0.173, 0.683, and 0.038. Thus, we keep 0.683 as Mexico's "religious strength" score. Note that these "strength scores" vary between 0 and 1, because they are averages of statistics (factor loadings) in the unit range. Table 2.3 gathers the ideological strength scores for all twelve countries along the economic, regime, and religious divides. Although the religious dimension has more weight than either the economic-distributive or political regime dimensions across all of our cases, this need not mean that religion is the most salient divide for purposes of party competition, as we emphasize in the next section.

PARTISAN DIVIDES IN LATIN AMERICA

In exploring the "ideological space" underlying legislators' opinions, attitudes, beliefs, and values, we have thus far concluded that economic-distributive, religious, regime, and economic-nationalism divides vary in

TABLE 2.3. *Ideological Strength Scores for Economic, Regime, and Religious Divides*

Country	Economic-Distributive Dimension[a]	Political Regime Dimension[b]	Religious Dimension[c]
Argentina	0.662	0.250	0.743
Bolivia	0.378	0.276	0.549
Brazil	0.331	0.390	0.599
Chile	0.487	0.571	0.713
Colombia	0.558	0.231	0.620
Costa Rica	0.532	0.328	0.467
Dominican Republic	0.439	0.317	0.423
Ecuador	0.285	0.261	0.556
Mexico	0.562	0.206	0.683
Peru	0.575	0.318	0.527
Uruguay	0.456	0.263	0.511
Venezuela	0.309	0.347	0.598

[a] Highest average of absolute factor loadings on *privatize industry, privatize services, don't control prices, don't sponsor job creation, don't provide housing, don't provide social security, no unemployment insurance,* and *don't subsidize basics.*

[b] Highest average of absolute factor loadings on *I go to church often, abortion not allowed, divorce not allowed,* and *I'm very religious.*

[c] Highest average of absolute factor loadings on *minority rights not important, democracy always best, elections always best,* and *parties not superfluous.*

their capacity to predict the stances of legislators on twenty-seven issues in twelve national legislatures.[14] If each of these four ideological dimensions or divides were to separate legislators perfectly into different political parties, and if every dimension were to cut across each other, we would encounter a configuration in which twenty-four ideological "blocs" could enjoy representation in the legislature. This number is greater than the largest number of parties in any Latin American legislature, Brazil included. In practice, the actual number of legislative parties is smaller because some ideological divides might be overlapping rather than crosscutting or because politicians might be constrained by the structure of citizens' preferences and thus be unable to choose positions freely.

More important, our ideological dimensions are designed by mathematical construction to comprise issues over which individual legislators disagree the most, regardless of their party membership. Although it might seem natural to ascribe similar ideological positions to politicians in the same party, whether political parties rally similarly minded politicians is ultimately an empirical question. In other words, ideological dimensions might

[14] An earlier version of this section appears in Rosas (2005).

be extremely divisive among legislators, but they need not divide parties[15] – hence, the need to explore a third level, the partisan space, which should be of dimensionality lower than or equal to that of the ideological space. We refer to the components of the partisan space as "partisan dimensions."

To find out the content of partisan dimensions, we essentially analyze the power of party membership to predict legislators' positions in the issue space; we do so through discriminant analysis of the original twenty-seven issues.[16] This technique is suited to classify observations into different categories from sheer knowledge of an observation's characteristics. In our case, individual legislators make up the set of observations, parties are the groups into which legislators are categorized, and each legislator is characterized by her issue stances. With knowledge about the issue positions and the party membership of each legislator, discriminant analysis constructs a new variable (a discriminant function) that is a linear function of the twenty-seven issue variables. More important, discriminant analysis also estimates weights (discriminant coefficients) on issue variables such that between-group separation along the constructed discriminant function is maximal. Intuitively, discriminant analysis places more weight on issues over which parties disagree and thus provides a glimpse into the issue bundles that separate parties from each other.[17]

---

[15] Consider religion, for example. Religious convictions and beliefs might very well separate individuals in a legislature. This need not mean that believers will self-select into party A, while atheists will join the ranks of party B. For all we know, both parties might have their share of believers and atheists.

[16] We checked discriminant analysis results against regression results by fitting one OLS model per factor per country. In each model, the continuous dependent variable comprised legislators' induced factor scores. We regressed these scores on a set of dummy variables, one for each party (an intercept was not estimated). Needless to say, these models are not full specifications of the variables that determine legislators' placements on underlying scores. Rather, they are measures of the strength of association between parties and factors. In practice, these models amount to using parties as predictors of a legislator's placement on different ideological dimensions; they are equivalent to ANOVA or to a difference of means test where the null hypothesis is that the party's mean position is equal to the overall mean – the mean placement of all legislators regardless of party. The results of this analysis are available from the authors. Kitschelt et al. (1999) follow the OLS strategy summarized here to infer the ideological dimensions that translate into political dimensions, but they are aided in this task by the availability of salience scores for each ideological dimension. The lack of salience scores is one reason to prefer discriminant analysis. The other reason is that the OLS strategy constrains the political space to have crosscutting dimensions. To see this, consider a case like Mexico. With the OLS strategy, one would conclude that religion-secularism and social protection are crosscutting political dimensions because party positions are significantly different on both axes. With discriminant analysis, we conclude that religion-secularism and social protection overlap in a single political dimension that divides the market-oriented, socially conservative PAN from the redistributive, socially progressive PRD and leaves PRI legislators occupying a middle position.

[17] The researcher can then use the model, with its emphasis on discordant issues, to classify out-of-sample legislators. See Klecka (1980) for an introduction to discriminant analysis.

Table 2.4 summarizes the discriminant analysis results (full results appear in Web Appendix 2.2 at www.cambridge.org/9780521114950). To facilitate the interpretation of results, Table 2.4 reports only discriminant functions with a statistically significant Wilks's Λ. (Only Chile and Mexico have more than one significant discriminant function by this account.) Table 2.4 also reports eigenvalues, which we construe as the proportion of between-party variance that is "covered" by each discriminant function, and canonical correlations, which convey the closeness of association between each discriminant function and the distribution of parties along that dimension. In general, significant discriminant functions with canonical correlations approaching "1" and large eigenvalues are indicative of divisive underlying partisan dimensions. Cell entries in Table 2.4 report the structural coefficient of each issue along the corresponding discriminant function.[18] In order to interpret the substantive meaning of each discriminant function, issues with large structural coefficients appear in the table (those with absolute values larger than 0.4). We use this arbitrary cutoff point to begin interpreting the substance of partisan dimensions within legislatures.[19]

The results show that some ideological dimensions, divisive as they are, do not translate into recognizable partisan dimensions. Argentina provides a useful illustration of this argument. Recall that factor analysis uncovered a well-defined religious dimension dividing Argentine legislators (factor 2), and that this dimension complemented a stronger state-market dimension (factor 1). Table 2.4 conveys a different story about Argentine parties. In particular, note that the first discriminant function (DF1) does not include any indicator of religiosity with a coefficient higher than 0.4 (though *abortion not allowed* has a structural coefficient of −0.34). We interpret this as evidence that religion in Argentina does not make up a partisan divide, despite its importance in shaping the ideological structure of the legislature. In other words, religion lacks capacity to predict partisanship. Table 2.4 reveals that Argentine parties can instead be placed along a continuum that includes the state-market dimension found in the first part of this analysis and an equally important concern with law-and-order issues.

The Structure and Substance of Partisan Dimensions

In this subsection, we describe both the structure of legislative partisan dimensions (number of overlapping or crosscutting divides) and the

---

[18] Structural coefficients are correlations between each of the twenty-seven variables, on the one hand, and induced discriminant scores, on the other. Large structural coefficients (close to 1 or −1) reflect a high degree of association between variable and discriminant function (Klecka 1980).

[19] Four indicators – *EU investment best, LA investment best, corruption always existed*, and *environment not important* – always had structural coefficients smaller than 0.4 and are thus excluded from Table 2.4 for the sake of brevity.

TABLE 2.4. Partisan Dimensions in Latin America (discriminant analysis: structural coefficients larger than |0.4| in cells)

Issues	Argentina	Bolivia	Brazil	Chile 1	Chile 2	Colombia	CR	Ecuador	DR	Mexico 1	Mexico 2	Peru	Uruguay	Venezuela
Privatize industry				0.75						0.53		0.40	0.44	
Privatize services	−0.45			0.64			0.42			0.56				
Don't control prices	−0.40			0.48			0.62							
Don't sponsor job creation	−0.43			0.54						0.47				
Don't provide housing							0.54			0.45				
Don't provide social security				0.60						0.51				
No unemployment insurance				0.45						0.40			0.54	
Don't subsidize basics				0.51			0.55			0.52			0.48	
Let IMF in							0.43						0.53	
US investment best													0.57	
Justice doesn't work	0.52										0.50			
Crime is threat	0.44		−0.44											
Labor unrest is threat	0.41								−0.43					
Violence is a problem				0.49					0.68					

I go to church often				0.43	0.66					0.75				
Abortion not allowed		−0.40		0.48	0.64					0.77				
Divorce not allowed				0.60						0.46			0.59	0.56
I'm very religious				0.40	0.65					0.65				
Minority rights not important	0.44							0.60					−0.50	
Democracy always best				0.63							0.67			
Elections always best				−0.53									−0.48	−0.63
Parties not superfluous								0.51				0.41		−0.55
Army/welfare trade-off				0.70					0.44		0.65		−0.45	
Number of respondents	54	62	47	89	89	55	48	56	61	122	122	71	69	66
Canonical correlation	0.97	0.84	0.91	0.92	0.81	0.82	0.87	0.89	0.85	0.87	0.67	0.70	0.90	0.87
Eigenvalue	7.011	2.394	4.701	5.262	1.868	2.051	3.107	3.733	2.699	2.975	0.805	0.985	4.164	3.006
Wilks's Λ	0.058	0.046	0.029	0.034	0.176	0.328	0.244	0.052	0.169	0.139	0.554	0.402	0.099	0.039
	$p < .01$	$p < .05$	$p < .05$	$p < .01$	$p < .01$	$p < .10$	$p < .05$	$p < .05$	$p < .05$	$p < .01$	$p < .01$	$p < .01$	$p < .01$	$p < .01$

Note: Full results in Web Appendix 2.2 at www.cambridge.org/9780521114950.

substantive importance of three of the issue bundles we identified earlier –
religion, economics, and political regime. The number of inferred discriminant functions in each legislature equals, by mathematical construction,
the number of parties in the analysis minus one. Thus, one should trivially
expect a strong association between the number of legislative parties in the
sample and the number of inferred partisan dimensions. However, we consider discriminant functions to be relevant partisan dimensions only when
they carry a statistically significant Wilks's Λ (at the 95 percent level or
better). Thus, the number of partisan dimensions need not depend on the
number of legislative parties. For example, three parties are represented in
the Argentine and Mexican legislative samples and consequently two discriminant functions are estimated in both countries. In Argentina, however,
only one discriminant function is statistically significant, whereas both are
in the Mexican legislature. We cannot reject the null possibility that a function does not add discriminant power to the model if Λ is insignificant;
therefore, we think that insignificant discriminant functions do not reveal
relevant partisan dimensions.

Table 2.4 confirms that partisan spaces reduce to a single partisan dimension in most Latin American legislatures.[20] The blatant exceptions to the
"one dimension" mode are Chile and Mexico, which are structured by two
partisan dimensions, and Colombia, where evidence about the existence
of partisan dimensions is inconclusive. Chile and Mexico provide useful
backdrops against which we can discuss the structure of partisan spaces in
Latin American legislatures. These two legislative party systems are each
structured by two partisan dimensions that blend religious, economic, and
political issues. On the first partisan dimension, Chilean legislators select
themselves into market-oriented, pro-authoritarian parties on the right, and
state-oriented, pro-democratic parties on the left, as confirmed by the mean
positions of the five Chilean parties along DF1 (see Table 2.5, which shows
the alignment of parties along inferred partisan dimensions in the twelve
legislatures). The second political dimension (DF2) discriminates between
pro-church and secular parties on issues of personal morality.[21]

Mexican legislative parties are separated along an economic governance
dimension that clearly overlaps with a religious partisan divide (DF1). In

---

[20] This is not out of line with findings in other legislative settings. In particular, Poole and
Rosenthal argue from their analysis of roll-call votes in U.S. Congresses that one political
dimension suffices to describe party stances among a variety of issues not only in present days
but throughout history (Poole and Rosenthal 1997). In a recent update, Poole and Rosenthal
confirm that ideology in the U.S. Congress can still be captured by a single dimension and
that low dimensional spaces (two dimensions at most) also characterize settings as varied
as France's Fourth Republic, the Czech Parliament, the 1841 British Parliament, and the
United Nations General Assembly (Poole and Rosenthal 2001).

[21] Londregan's analysis of the Chilean Senate uncovers a similar two-dimensional basic space,
with a first dimension comprising welfare state issues (labor relations, education) and human
rights, and the second concerning social and morality issues (Londregan 2000: 8).

TABLE 2.5. *Distribution of Parties along Inferred Partisan Dimensions*

Legislature	Party (Party Centroids)
Argentina	PJ (−2.27), UCR (2.32), FREPASO (2.92)
Bolivia	CONDEPA (−2.76), MIR (−2.59), ADN (−0.49), UCS (0.64), MNR (1.23)
Brazil	PT (−3.94), PSDB (−1.67), PFL (0.78), PMDB (2.17)
Chile (Dimension 1)	PS (−2.33), PFD (−1.99), PDC (−1.38), RN (2.55), UDI (3.30)
Chile (Dimension 2)	PS (−1.60), PPD (−1.21), RN (−1.06), UDI (1.32), PDC (1.42)
Colombia	PL (−0.92), PSC(2.77)
Costa Rica	PLN (−1.63), PUSC (1.82)
Dominican Republic	PRSC (−1.89), PLD (1.31), PRD (1.36)
Ecuador	PRE (−2.56), PSC (0.19), DP (1.76), Pachakutik (2.76)
Mexico (Dimension 1)	PRD (−1.79), PRI (−0.62), PAN (2.67)
Mexico (Dimension 2)	PRI (−1.01), PAN (0.39), PRD (1.14)
Peru	APRA (−2.13), UPP (−1.33), C95 (0.60)
Uruguay	FA (−2.84), PC (1.06), PN (1.66)
Venezuela	Causa R (−2.54), MAS (−1.55), Convergencia (−0.36), COPEI (0.87), AD (1.73)

Note: A party centroid is the average position of all legislators within the party.

contrast, the second partisan dimension includes several other issues – *justice doesn't work* (0.50), *minority rights not important* (0.67) and *army/welfare trade-off* (0.65) – that are reminiscent of the regime dimension that divided the governing PRI from the opposition PAN and PRD for most of the 1990s (Domínguez and McCann 1996; Magaloni 1997; Moreno 1998). The inferred spatial order of PRI, PAN, and PRD along DF2 is consistent with this interpretation (see Table 2.5).

As mentioned previously, the other exception to the "one dimension" rule is Colombia, where DF1 is only marginally significant (at the 90 percent level). More important, DF1 is difficult to interpret in substantive terms, as no single issue carries a structural coefficient larger than 0.4, though some of the religious traits and the indicator of opinions on violence are close to this benchmark. Note that by considering the substantive composition of discriminant functions, as in the discussion of Colombia's legislature, we are in fact introducing a second criterion, on top of Wilks's Λ, to describe partisan spaces. By this second criterion alone, Bolivia, Brazil, Ecuador, and Peru have legislative party systems that are only minimally organized along substantive dimensions, despite showing one statistically significant discriminant function (at the 95 percent level). In Brazil, *justice doesn't work* is the only indicator with a structural coefficient larger than the cutoff point, but *army/welfare trade-off* and *crime is threat* also have relatively large coefficients (−0.33 and −0.31, respectively), perhaps large enough to claim that Brazilian parties are organized along an inchoate law-and-order partisan dimension. However, this interpretation is not substantiated by the inferred distribution of parties along DF1, which has the PT and PMDB as opposite poles on law-and-order issues, and the PSDB and PFL somewhere in the middle (Table 2.5).[22]

In Ecuador and Peru, *minority rights not important* and *elections always best*, and *privatize industry* and *parties not superfluous*, respectively, have coefficients larger than 0.4; in Bolivia, only *abortion not allowed* has this characteristic. In Ecuador, other indicators lack structural coefficients as large as those on *minority rights not important* and *elections always best*, so we conclude tentatively that the legislative party system is organized along a partisan regime divide. In contrast, the Peruvian legislature shows several items with structural coefficients slightly below the benchmark value (*privatize services, let IMF in, labor unrest is threat,* and *I go to church often*), which makes this legislature difficult to categorize as organized along a clear partisan dimension. Indeed, to the extent that DF1 taps into a genuine partisan dimension at all, this is best interpreted as an economic cum regime divide that separates APRA and UPP from Fujimori's personalist vehicle, Cambio '95 (Table 2.5).

Regarding the substantive organization of partisan spaces, religion provides important bases of differentiation in some Latin American legislatures. To wit, consider those legislatures that display at least two "religious" indicators with coefficients greater than 0.4. A partisan dimension comprising varied stances along a secular-religious continuum then appears in Chile, as mentioned before, and overlaps with several political and/or economic issues in the legislatures of Bolivia, Mexico, and Uruguay. At least one indicator of religious stances carries a structural coefficient barely below the cutoff point in Argentina and even in Colombia. On the opposite end, religion does not seem to structure legislative party systems in Costa Rica, the Dominican Republic, Ecuador, and Venezuela.

In contrast with the religious issue bundle, an economic-distributive divide is clearly recognizable in the partisan spaces of a majority of legislatures. Indeed, Latin American legislatures can be grouped according to the content of their economic partisan divides. A first group comprises Argentina, Chile, Costa Rica, Mexico, and Uruguay, where various indicators of both economic governance and social protection show high structural coefficients, therefore revealing a deep state-market divide that provides a locus for party coordination. Legislative parties in these countries are aligned along a traditional left-right economic-distributive dimension (which

---

[22] The PFL should be to the right of the PMDB on law-and-order issues (Figueiredo and Limongi 2000; Mainwaring and Pérez-Liñán 1997). The mean position of PFL legislators is slightly to the right of PMDB legislators on *justice doesn't work* and *army/welfare trade-off*, but the PMDB's mean position is much more to the right than the PFL's mean position on *crime is threat*. This disparity is probably driving the results.

sometimes overlaps with religious or regime divides, as in Chile or Mexico). The inferred alignment of parties from left to right along the economic partisan dimension is as follows: PJ, UCR, and FREPASO in Argentina; PPD, PS, PDC, RN, and UDI in Chile; PLN and PUSC in Costa Rica; PRD, PRI, and PAN in Mexico; and Frente Amplio, Colorados, and Blancos in Uruguay (Table 2.5). Except in Argentina, where the left-right placement of Peronists along an economic dimension is debatable, these rankings correspond to commonsense views and expert interpretations of these party systems.

A second group would include legislatures divided by an economic partisan dimension that contains social protection issues or economic governance concerns, but not both. This is the case of Peru and Venezuela. Venezuela throws into sharp relief the problems posed by sticking to a fixed yardstick in order to interpret discriminant analysis results. In Venezuela, four indicators of social protection show high structural coefficients that still fall short of the baseline (*don't subsidize basics, no unemployment insurance, don't provide housing*, and *don't control prices*). However, the Venezuelan discriminant function is unarguably dominated by political regime issues, particularly topics that were hotly debated in 1997 as the country moved away from the AD-COPEI *partidocracia*. Peru offers a nice counterpoint to this discussion, because its legislative parties were divided on economic governance issues (*privatize industry* and *privatize services* display relatively large structural coefficients) but agreed on questions of social protection, which are not important in shaping the substance of its single partisan dimension.

Finally, a third group would comprise the legislatures of Bolivia, Brazil, Colombia, Dominican Republic, and Ecuador, where the partisan space is not structured by a clear-cut economic dimension. The inclusion of the Brazilian and Colombian legislatures in this group follows from the lack of organization that we noted at the beginning of this section. The weak partisan structure of the Brazilian legislature is hardly surprising. Scholars have looked into the electoral connection of legislators with their constituents for explanations of the absence of programmatic coherence among Brazilian parties during this period (Ames 1995). Analyses of roll-call votes and of turnover rates in the Brazilian Congress from this time also point to scant organization of legislative activity (Mainwaring and Pérez-Liñán 1997; Samuels 2000). The findings here confirm that legislative disorganization extends to the ideological realm. The Dominican Republic – and, to a lesser extent, Ecuador – contrasts with Brazil and Colombia in that parties there do not differ on their economic stances but are divided by law-and-order concerns; the Bolivian legislature, instead, appears to be divided on the contested issue of abortion, but no other religious issue appears as divisive as this one.

As we did earlier, we search for summary measures to convey variation in the degree to which religious, economic, and regime issue bundles structure the partisan space of Latin American legislatures, at the risk of losing some

TABLE 2.6. *Partisan Strength Scores for Economic, Regime, and Religious Divides*

Country	Economic-Distributive[a]	Political Regime[b]	Religious[c]
Argentina	0.325	0.250	0.245
Bolivia	0.166	0.163	0.188
Brazil	0.159	0.093	0.198
Chile	0.516	0.490	0.581[d]
Colombia	0.200	0.123	0.283
Costa Rica	0.361	0.085	0.208
Dominican Republic	0.130	0.195	0.028
Ecuador	0.134	0.320	0.210
Mexico	0.461	0.195	0.658
Peru	0.208	0.285	0.153
Uruguay	0.371	0.348	0.443
Venezuela	0.276	0.388	0.200

[a] Average of absolute canonical correlations (DF1) on *privatize industry, privatize services, don't control prices, don't sponsor job creation, don't provide housing, don't provide social security, no unemployment insurance,* and *don't subsidize basics.*

[b] Average of absolute canonical correlations (DF1) on *I go to church often, abortion not allowed, divorce not allowed,* and *I'm very religious.*

[c] Average of absolute canonical correlations (DF1) on *minority rights not important, democracy always best, elections always best,* and *parties not superfluous.*

[d] Average on DF2.

nuance in interpreting the substance of inferred partisan dimensions. We use the canonical correlations reported in Table 2.5 to construct "partisan strength scores" for the religious, economic, and regime issue bundles. These scores are reported in Table 2.6; they are similar to the "ideological strength scores" reported in Table 2.3 in that they obtain from averaging (absolute) correlation coefficients for each issue bundle along DF1 (and DF2 in Chile and Mexico). For example, Argentina's partisan strength score for the religious bundle is 0.245, which is the average of the absolute values of the correlation coefficients of *I go to church often, abortion not allowed, divorce not allowed,* and *I'm very religious.* In Part II, we also resort to these "partisan strength scores" as indicators of programmatic structuration in Latin American party systems.

CONCLUSION

Throughout this chapter, we have explored the ideological and partisan spaces that underlie legislators' beliefs, attitudes, values, and dispositions and found that levels of ideological and partisan organization vary widely across the region. We found that in most countries a single dimension generally suffices to account for variegated policy positions among partisan legislators. There are important exceptions to this pattern, particularly Chile and Mexico, where the positions of legislative parties cannot be reduced to a single dimension. In other countries – Bolivia, Brazil, Ecuador, and Peru – we could not assign unequivocal substantive meanings to partisan dimensions. Finally, we could not make a compelling case that a unidimensional partisan space structures Colombia's legislature.

To conclude this chapter, we present a rank order of Latin American legislatures based on the information provided in Table 2.6, in recognition of the fact that our indices are more trustworthy as ordinal than as interval scales. We computed the rank order of each legislature for each of the three measures presented in Table 2.6, from more to less programmatic structuration. The overall ranking of legislatures is as follows (with average rank order in parenthesis): Chile (1.3), Uruguay (3), Mexico (3.7), Argentina (5.3), Venezuela (5.3), Ecuador (7), Colombia (7.3), Costa Rica (7.7), Peru (7.7), Bolivia (9.3), Brazil (10), and the Dominican Republic (10.3).

Ideally, we would have complemented this exercise with an analysis of the fourth space, the competitive space of party systems. As explained in Chapter 1, politicians cannot hope that the "program elasticity of votes" will be large enough to warrant a change in their programmatic appeals if a partisan dimension is not also a competitive dimension. As a consequence, the competitive space is of a dimensionality lower than or equal to that of the political space. In order to explore the competitive space in our twelve legislatures, we would need to analyze salience scores for all issues in the issue space, but the Salamanca surveys do not include such scores. Elsewhere in this volume, we investigate the relationship between ideological and partisan divides, on the one hand, and legislators' self-placement on a left-right scale, on the other, thus providing indirect evidence about the contents of the competition space. Unfortunately, a direct analysis of the structure of party competition in Latin America remains a task for future research. To support our findings, we have developed summary measures of the substance of ideological and partisan divides. We use these measures, along with other indices developed in the following chapters, as indicators of different aspects of programmatic party competition in Part I. In Web Appendix 2.1 (at www.cambridge.org/9780521114950), we develop indices that succinctly capture the simplicity of ideological and partisan spaces. As mentioned before, this exercise throws further light on the prospects of programmatic party competition in the region.

3

Left-Right Semantics as a Facilitator of Programmatic Structuration

Elizabeth J. Zechmeister

Ideological labels work like compass directions in politics; they provide a means by which citizens and other political actors orient themselves within a political arena. Ideally, they allow citizens to distinguish among political choices without requiring them to possess significantly high levels of information. Political elites aid this process by employing these labels to communicate party programs. For ideological labels to function as useful heuristic aids, there must be minimal variation around their meaning, and they must reference relevant dimensions of choice. By using the Salamanca survey of political elites to assess the symbolic and substantive significance of these labels in Latin America, this chapter contributes to our understanding of the left-right semantics in the region and, moreover, gives us insight into the programmatic structuration of these party systems.

The analyses in this chapter reveal several interesting tendencies. First, we find significant variance in the left-right stances taken by legislators across party systems, with some party systems leaning more toward the right (e.g., Bolivia), some toward the center (e.g., Chile), and some more toward the left (e.g., Uruguay). Second, there is variation in the substantive meaningfulness of left-right labels across left and right party families, with parties on the left associating relatively greater issue content with these labels. Third, our analyses reveal significant variation in the substantive meaningfulness of left-right semantics across party systems. Those countries marked by strong programmatic partisan dimensions in Chapter 2, particularly with respect to economic issues, are those in which left-right labels possess the greatest substantive meaning: Chile, Mexico, and Uruguay.

THE IMPORTANCE OF THE LEFT-RIGHT SEMANTICS

This chapter starts from the premise that citizens are information misers who, when possible, use "shortcuts" to make sense of the often complicated political arena while limiting the amount of time and energy spent on this task (e.g., Downs 1957; Sniderman, Brody, and Tetlock 1991; Hinich and Munger 1994; Popkin 1994). Ideological labels are one type of heuristic that citizens and political elites may use to discriminate easily and efficiently among parties, candidates, and issues. They are most effective when actors in a society use the terms in consistent manners and when they mark relevant dimensions of conflict.[1]

Much research demonstrates that in advanced industrialized countries ideological labels are frequently used by citizens to make political choices. In Europe, for example, voters' self-placements on left-right ideological scales are key determinants of party support and vote choice (e.g., Inglehart and Klingemann 1976; Fleury and Lewis-Beck 1993; Evans, Heath, and Lalljee 1996; Knutsen 1997). Comparisons within this region as well as others further reveal that the positions and parties with which ideological labels are linked vary across time and space and are not necessarily limited to a single dimension of conflict (see Bobbio 1996; Kitschelt and Hellemans 1990; Nathan and Shi 1996; Evans and Whitefield 1998). Less work has been done, however, on the political significance of left-right labels in Latin America and, consequently, what meanings they contain and to what extent these are shared within and across countries.[2]

What meanings might ideological labels hold? In Chapter 1 we noted that ideological labels may reference at least two components: symbolic and substantive. The symbolic component links the labels to political groups without necessarily also referencing the political stances of those entities.[3] The substantive component reflects the extent to which labels are linked to policy divides within a society.[4] A left-right label with significant substantive content allows one to predict a person's stance on a policy or a bundle of policies, such as those falling within the traditional economic state-market basket, simply by knowing her left-right self-placement. Theoretically, this

---

[1] Decision making using ideological heuristics is not at odds with making decisions directly on the basis of policy stances. As heuristic aids, substantively meaningful left-right labels can help individuals to discern the policy positions of relevant political actors.

[2] Cross-national studies do exist that use left-right indicators to examine ideological placement and cohesion across Latin American legislators; see, for example, work by Colomer and Escatel (2005), who use both mass and elite data to examine left-right placement in Latin America and work by Freidenberg, García, and Llamazares (2008). Missing from the literature are comprehensive, cross-national studies that specifically investigate the *meaning* of the left-right semantics in Latin America (but see Zechmeister 2006).

[3] In existing works, the groups referenced by this component typically are political parties, and thus this has also been conceptualized as a partisan component. However, in part to avoid confusion with the concept of partisan issue dimensions described in Chapter 2 and referenced throughout this chapter, we use the term "symbolic" rather than "partisan" to refer to this component of left-right semantics.

[4] Zechmeister (2006) argues that ideological semantics may also reference valence issues, in addition to policy stances; this aspect of the substantive component is not considered in this chapter.

content may be one or more of four types: latent or active general ideological dimensions (dividing actors but not necessarily parties) and latent or active partisan dimensions (breaking down along party lines).

The meanings assigned to the left-right labels within a given party system are important for at least two reasons. First, they mark lines of conflict in a society, whether they are new, latent, long-lasting, or dying out. Unpacking the meaning of the left-right semantics provides a snapshot of the political arena that can reveal where a country has come from and where it is headed. Second, the nature of the left-right semantics speaks to the heuristic aids that citizens have for making programmatic political decisions. Most studies argue that left-right labels are more accurate predictors of party membership than of issue orientations, though both symbolic and substantive components are present within advanced industrialized societies (Evans and Whitefield 1998; Inglehart and Klingemann 1976; Knutsen 1989; see also Huber 1989). If a symbolic (partisan) component dominates, then the utility of left-right labels for guiding programmatic vote choice in that country is diminished; the use of left and right would signal only a party name to voters. Where neither component is strong, left-right labels are devoid of utility in that they do not help structure the political system and, at the extreme, may confuse individuals confronted with competing understandings and usages of these terms.

As noted, for left-right labels to be most useful for programmatic structuration, political elites must use the terms in consistent ways that reference relevant dimensions of political choice. Specifically, they should organize themselves such that several conditions are met. First, political elites should exhibit agreement over the relative placement of their party on the left-right dimension; to the extent that politicians do not send clear signals about the specific location of their party in left-right terms, citizens will find it difficult to distinguish among parties on this potential programmatic dimension. Second, there must be a strong connection between the policy stances advocated by political elites and their use of left-right semantics. In other words, there must be substantive content to the left-right semantics, so that the terms convey information about programmatic alternatives; clearly, left-right labels are most useful when they are associated with active, competitive issue dimensions. Finally, there should be a strong overlap between the symbolic and substantive components; in this way, elites can use left-right labels to signal simultaneously their party affiliation and their party's programmatic stances on this abstract dimension of competition.

AN OVERVIEW OF THE LEFT-RIGHT SEMANTICS IN LATIN AMERICA

The primary data that we draw on in this chapter are the responses to surveys of Latin American legislators in our twelve countries and the specific subset of twenty-seven issue questions. Our dependent variables in this chapter are based on two additional survey questions, each asking respondents to indicate, on 10-point scales, their party's left-right placement and their own left-right self-placement.[5] Before proceeding to the more specific data analyses, we consider left-right tendencies across the party systems included in this analysis and examine the average placements on the left-right scale by party systems and parties. We first examine the distribution of self- and party placements across countries. Figure 3.1 contains graphs of the response frequencies for each country; only respondents from the main parties that we consider throughout this volume are included, and responses are weighted to reflect the actual representation of that party in congress at the time of the survey.[6] Both left-right party placements (LRPP) and left-right self-placements (LRSP) are included. Note that the left-right integer scale runs from 1 to 10, so that the exact center, 5.5, was not an option. Most respondents likely interpreted 5 as representing the middle of the scale. Some caution must be used when making comparisons across graphs, given that left-right semantics have different meanings across countries.

As the data show, for both variables the modal response is 5 in all countries except Bolivia (for both LRSP and LRPP) and Chile (for LRSP). In Bolivia, the modal response is 7 on left-right self-placement and 8 on left-right party placement. In this country, numerous responses fall on the right side of the scale, and the mean self- and party placements in Bolivia are 6.1 and 6.5, respectively, making this system the furthest to the right among all those considered here.[7] Colombia and Peru are also right-oriented party systems, with mean self- and party placements of 5.6 and 6.1 for Colombia and 5.7 and 5.9 for Peru. The Dominican Republic appears somewhat oriented toward the center-right, though its mean left-right self- and party placements are not far from the center (5.3 and 5.7, respectively). In contrast, other Latin American party systems are left-oriented. For example, Uruguay has very few legislators who place their party on the right, and none that choose locations in the extreme positions of 9 or 10; in the case of self-placement, we see that no one places themselves at 8, 9, or 10.

---

[5] The questions were asked in this order, but not back to back. One possible concern with our data is that legislators might censor themselves on the left-right continuum. To assess the degree to which this may have occurred in the data we use, we compared mean responses in our dataset to those in countries and parties for which there exist expert surveys conducted by Huber and Inglehart (1995) and Michael Coppedge (these data were supplied to the authors by Coppedge). While caution must be used because of the difference in timing of the surveys, the comparisons suggest that there is some censoring, particularly among parties of the right but also among some parties on the left. While these patterns are interesting, we do not make any correction for them. In this chapter we are interested in the meanings of the signals that elites are sending to citizens and other political actors. If there is a discrepancy between the use of left-right semantics in self-description and legislators' issue orientations, we will, and want to, measure the degree to which this clouds the meaning of left-right semantics in that country.

[6] Missing values are not recoded and therefore not represented in these graphs.

[7] These mean placements are weighted to reflect the proportion of seats each party held in congress at the time of the survey.

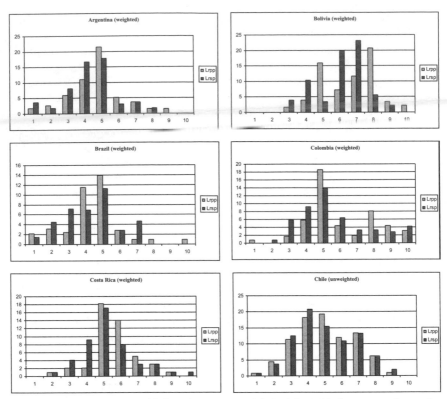

FIGURE 3.1. Frequency of left-right party and left-right self-placements in twelve countries.

Argentina and Brazil show a similar lean to the left. In Uruguay, Brazil, and Argentina, the average self-placement is 4.3; the average party placements are 4.5, 4.4, and 4.7, respectively. Venezuela shows a similar tendency, particularly with respect to self-placement (the mean is 4.5), though its mean party placement is overall slightly more centrist compared to these three countries (4.9). Despite the modal response in Chile being slightly to the left on self-placement, the average self- and party left-right placements in this country are more centrist (both are 5.0). Costa Rica (mean party placement is 5.2 and mean self-placement is 5.6), Ecuador (5.1 and 5.4), and Mexico (4.9 and 5.1) are likewise fairly centrist and balanced systems in terms of their left-right tendencies.

In every case except Chile (where the values are equal), the mean left-right self-placement is to the left of the mean party placement. Also noteworthy is the strong affinity for what was likely the perceived center of the scale, 5, across the cases. Not only is the center an ideologically less distinct position to occupy, but midscale answers may indicate uncertainty (Alvarez and Franklin 1994). Given this strong tendency toward the center, one

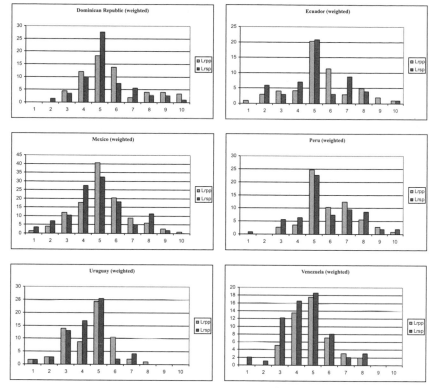

FIGURE 3.1 (*continued*)

might suspect that left-right labels do not have very significant symbolic or substantive meanings in Latin America.

Before turning to our examination of the substantive content of left-right semantics in Latin America, we examine the average left-right placements of legislators, by party, in each of the twelve countries to see if the ordering provided by these mean scores corresponds to scholars' typical expectations regarding the parties' and legislators' relationships to one another along a left-right scale. Table 3.1 presents the mean left-right party and self-placement scores of Latin American legislators, by each of the main parties for which we have sufficient data. The ordering of the mean party placements corresponds nearly exactly with common understandings of the left-right positioning of these parties.[8] The only clear exception to the strong correspondence between common understandings of the left-right placement of these parties and the data is the case of Venezuela. Here, the party placement

---

[8] Examining only the mean scores admittedly does not speak to the extent to which legislators from a given party agree on a particular mean score. This variation will, however, be taken into account in individual-level regression analyses later in this chapter.

TABLE 3.1. *Mean Left-Right Party and Self-Placements, Party Averages*

	LRPP	LRSP		LRPP	LRSP
Argentina			Ecuador		
FREPASO	3.50	3.45	Pachakutik	3.43	3.14
UCR	4.53	4.50	DP	4.50	4.25
PJ	5.24	4.62	PRE	4.57	4.36
Correlation[a]	.76		PSC	6.83	6.46
Bolivia			*Correlation*	.78	
CONDEPA	4.40	4.67	Mexico		
MIR	5.57	4.71	PRD	3.23	3.70
UCS	6.06	6.47	PRI	5.40	4.87
MNR	7.68	6.38	PAN	6.45	6.15
ADN	8.00	7.33	*Correlation*	.55	
Correlation	.76		Peru		
Brazil			APRA	4.14	4.29
PT	2.00	1.88	UPP	5.58	5.50
PSDB	4.11	4.22	C95/NM	6.27	5.98
PMDB	4.53	4.63	*Correlation*	.57	
PFL	5.75	5.09	Uruguay		
Correlation	.75		FA	2.96	3.04
Chile			PC	5.00	4.90
Socialista	2.62	2.92	PN	5.60	4.95
PPD	4.36	3.60	*Correlation*	.80	
PDC	4.42	4.52	Venezuela		
Renovación	6.48	6.70	MAS	3.67	4.13
UDI	6.81	6.45	AD	4.50	4.53
Correlation	0.89		Causa R	4.60	3.60
Costa Rica			CONVERG	4.71	4.11
PLN	5.00	4.38	COPEI	5.75	5.39
PUSC	6.22	6.17	*Correlation*	.37	
Correlation	.85				
Dominican Republic					
PLD	4.54	4.15			
PRD	5.10	5.00			
PRSC	6.63	6.05			
Correlation	.83				

Note: Missing values are dropped (from both summary stats and correlations) from this analysis, for which data are reported for main parties only. The number of missing values per country is overall relatively low. With respect to party placement, with one exception, the number of missing values ranges from 0 in Chile, Costa Rica, and the Dominican Republic to 6 in Argentina (the exception is Venezuela, where there are 19). With respect to self-placement, missing values range from 0 in Chile, Colombia, and the Dominican Republic to 7 in Ecuador (in this case Venezuela has only 5 missing values).

[a] This correlation statistic is based on individual-level data correlating each legislator's self- to party placements.

of the once-Marxist Causa R is slightly further to the center than the Acción Democrática, perhaps a result of Causa R's concerted efforts to portray itself as more centrist beginning in the 1980s (López-Maya 1997). Interestingly, the average left-right *self*-placement among Causa R members indicates that the party registers as the furthest left of the parties. This would appear to lend some credence to López-Maya's argument about the strategic centrist advertising of Causa R.

Most of the mean left-right self-placements of the parties mirror the legislators' mean party placements. In fact, the correlation between the two mean placements for all systems with more than two parties to analyze is at or above .95 (these correlation statistics are not presented in Table 3.1). Exceptions occur in Bolivia and Venezuela, where the correlations are .87 and .69, respectively. At the individual level, as shown in Table 3.1, nine of the party systems display a fairly high level of consistency across the two variables, with correlations at or above .75. The exceptions occur in Mexico and Peru, where at the individual level left-right self- and party placements are correlated at .55 and .57, respectively, and in Venezuela, where this statistic is only .37.

In sum, legislators in most of the parties and party systems we examine here perceive themselves ideologically in ways similar to how they perceive their parties and to how they are perceived by scholars. However, there appears a tendency for members of right-leaning parties to place themselves further toward the center than they place their parties. This is not necessarily the case among members of left-leaning parties, who appear almost equally likely to place themselves further toward the left as they are toward the center. This interocular observation is supported by additional analyses of the data in Table 3.1. To assess differences across left and right party families, two sets of "left" and "right" parties were created, the first based on the same scheme applied in the analysis shown later in Table 3.5 and the second based on the mean party placements in Table 3.1 where values 4.0 and below were coded "left" and values 6.0 and above were coded "right." An additional measure was then created to quantify the percentage of left and right parties, respectively, in which the mean self-placement falls more toward the center than the mean party placement. With the first coding of party families, the percentage of left parties for which self-placement falls more toward the center is 38 percent; the percentage of right parties is 78 percent. With the second coding of parties, these values are 57 and 82 percent, respectively. Thus, the results for left parties are not robust; we cannot easily conclude that left parties show a weak tendency to have members place themselves further to the left (away from the center) of their party placement (as the first coding suggests) nor a weak tendency to do the opposite (as the second coding suggests). In contrast, among right parties, there is a clear tendency regardless of the coding scheme for members to place themselves further toward the center compared to their party placement. Similar conclusions are reached if one analyzes the actual gap between party placement and self-placement. This tendency for right party members to place themselves further toward the center may help to explain the tendency seen in Figure 3.1 for self-placements to average out on the left of party placements. Of course, the analyses leave aside the substantial variation across parties (noting only a tendency, not a universal trait) and, as well, leave centrist parties unanalyzed.

THE SUBSTANTIVE MEANINGS OF THE LEFT-RIGHT SEMANTICS

The principal concern of this chapter is to gauge the substantive component of the left-right semantics, which captures the extent to which these labels represent issue divides or ideological dimensions and therefore the extent to which they enhance programmatic party system structuration. There are various ways to examine the nature and strength of the substantive component of left-right labels across countries. First, one might regress left-right placement on a common set of variables representing distinct policy questions (Huber 1989). However, to the extent that left-right labels represent issue orientations, they are most useful if they connote issue bundles or ideologies. Second, one might generate a common set of issue bundles and regress left-right placement for each country on these. The drawback to this approach is that the external designation of issue dimensions might underestimate the substantive meaningfulness of left-right labels if variables are included that lack relevance within a particular country context. Third, one might extract all significant ideological dimensions in each country and then regress left-right self-placement on these country-specific factors. This approach does not treat the political space in each country as homogeneous and therefore the possibility of finding a substantive component to left-right labels in each country is maximized. Cross-country comparisons can then be made by examining the amount of variance explained by each set of factors, as well as the type of factor that explains the most variance or exerts the greatest effect. This last approach is the one taken here.

In Chapter 2 we distinguished between ideological dimensions and partisan dimensions. As noted there, ideological dimensions divide legislators according to sets of preferences over policy issues regardless of party affiliation, whereas partisan dimensions refer to legislators' positions on issue clusters on which parties subscribe to contrasting policy preferences. In Chapter 2 ideological dimensions were detected via factor analysis and partisan dimensions via discriminant analysis. Here, we examine the role that each of these dimensions plays in the left-right semantics. There is no limit to the number of issue bundles that left-right labels might reflect, although the more nonoverlapping dimensions that are attached to the left-right semantics, the more muddled those terms may be to voters and politicians.

The dependent variable in this section is left-right self-placement. We use this rather than party placement because the survey questions used to create our independent variables ask for the individual legislator's personal policy preferences; the odds of detecting substantive content within the left-right semantics are increased by analyzing the relationship between self-placement on issue positions and self-placement on left-right scales. Further, this allows us later to add back into the analysis the symbolic component by using the mean left-right placement of the party as a predictor of left-right self-placement alongside the ideological variables. From this, we can detect the extent to which the symbolic component overlaps with the substantive component. Before turning to this analysis at the end of this chapter, however, we analyze the relationship between each type of substantive dimension and the left-right semantics.

Partisan Divides and the Left-Right Semantics

Because of their greater political relevance, we examine the relationship between partisan issue dimensions and left-right labels first. Table 3.2 reports the results of regressions of left-right self-placement on the discriminant functions from Chapter 2 for the eight countries in our study for which those functions capture relevant partisan divides. For the remaining four countries – Bolivia, Brazil, Colombia, and Peru – the discriminant analysis yielded factors that were substantively meaningless, that is, there is no clear partisan divide with which to perform a regression analysis. The results in Table 3.2 show that, in each of these eight countries, the left-right semantics are significantly related to a substantive partisan dimension. In the case of Chile and Mexico, both of which yielded two discriminant functions, only the first divide passes a traditional significance cutoff ($p \leq .10$).

In short, in most of the countries included in this study, left-right labels differentiate legislators on issue bundles that divide parties. In five of these cases (Argentina, Chile, Costa Rica, Mexico, and Uruguay), the partisan divide that is related to left-right semantics contains a bundle of economic issues, and in four out of these five countries (the exception is Costa Rica) those economic issues overlap with other issues, such as religion and law and order. This overlap suggests that the terms "left" and "right" can be used to signal an actor's position on more than one bundle of politically relevant issues; the fact that they are not orthogonal to each other means that the signals are clearer and less muddled than they would be if the dimensions did not overlap. In contrast to these cases where economic issues dominate, in the Dominican Republic, Ecuador, and Venezuela the relevant issues comprising the significant dimension are, respectively, law and order, rights and regime issues, and regime issues.

Ideological Divides and the Left-Right Semantics

One might protest that this analysis is too rigid a test of the substantive meaningfulness of the left-right semantics in Latin America. Left-right labels

TABLE 3.2. *Partisan Divides as Components of Left-Right Self-Placement: Country-by-Country OLS Regression Results*

Country, Variables	Coefficient	p-Value	Adjusted Regression R^2
Argentina (weighted n = 61)			
Constant	4.326	.000	
State-market, law & order, rights	−0.162	.028	.06
Chile (weighted n = 86)			
Constant	4.977	.000	
State-market, law & order, social issues, regime	0.527	.000	
Religiosity, social issues	0.089	.273	.53
Costa Rica (weighted n = 48)			
Constant	5.224	.000	
State-market, welfare	0.387	.000	.22
Dominican Republic (weighted n = 62)			
Constant	5.347	.000	
Law & order	−0.306	.004	.12
Ecuador (weighted n = 56)			
Constant	5.060	.000	
Rights, regime issues	−0.077	.504	.00
Mexico (weighted n = 119)			
Constant	4.922	.000	
State-market, welfare, religiosity, social issues	0.477	.000	
Law & order, rights	−0.152	.118	.29
Uruguay (weighted n = 69)			
Constant	4.315	.000	
State-market, welfare, FDI, religiosity, abortion choice, rights, regime	0.391	.000	.47
Venezuela (weighted n = 67)			
Constant	4.477	.000	
Regime issues	0.271	.003	.11

Note: Data from 1997 survey of Latin American legislators. Regressions are on discriminant functions reported in Chapter 2. Parties with less than six respondents are not included. Data are weighted to reflect the actual proportion of legislators per party in the legislature at the time of the survey. Missing values in the dependent variable are recoded to the mean of the respondent's party.

may carry meaning to political actors but in a more general way that is not necessarily linked to partisan divides. While not as useful to programmatic party competition, it is nevertheless worthwhile to investigate a more general content to the left-right semantics in Latin America. As an additional analysis, then, we regress left-right self-placement on the ideological factors reported in Chapter 2 for each country. In the analysis presented in Chapter 2, the factors that appear most frequently in each country are those containing either economic or religious variables. Other factors indicate positions on questions concerning law and order, authoritarianism or general regime design, and progressive or "postmodern" values (e.g., the importance of human rights and the environment). Several factors are not as easily classified and seem to be more a hodgepodge of variables that typically do not have high loadings (see Chapter 2).

Table 3.3 reports the results of a series of regressions of left-right self-placement on each country's set of general ideological dimensions. In the table, each factor is labeled to reflect the issue content of that factor. Most important, the results show that the left-right semantics correspond with one or more existing ideological dimensions in every country. In other words, left-right semantics have some substantive content across all the Latin American political systems considered in this study. With a few exceptions, this substantive content reflects either economic or religious stances.

The most important of these ideological dimensions is the economic one, some version of which is clearly related to left-right labels in ten of the countries (at p ≤ .10). Only in Argentina and in Ecuador is an economic factor not significant in its relationship to left-right placement, and in the Dominican Republic the economic aspect of this factor is fairly weak (reflecting just one variable, pro-IMF, among other noneconomic factors), though a more robust welfare-oriented factor nearly reaches statistical significance. This underlines the important point that significant economic dimensions are not always similar across countries but vary in terms of content and the strength of that content. In some countries, the economic dimension connected to left-right semantics comprises issues that relate most closely to social protectionism (e.g., the "welfare" factor in Mexico), to the proper role of the state in guiding the market (e.g., the "state-market" factor in Ecuador), and to issues of economic nationalism or regionalism (e.g., the "pro-FDI" factor in Brazil); in other countries, two of these factors (typically welfare and state-market stances) overlap. Nevertheless, whatever their specific content, left-right labels are related to economic issues in almost all Latin American countries.

The other important ideological dimension is the religious one, which is attached to the left-right semantics in nine out of the twelve countries. Again, the exact nature of this dimension is specific to each country. In Ecuador and Peru, the religious dimension comprises only attitudes toward church and religion. In the other seven cases, the religion factor appears significant alongside another set of issues: social issues (in Argentina, Chile, Mexico, and Uruguay), economic issues (in Colombia and Venezuela), or issues of rights (in Costa Rica).

In sum, with a few exceptions, the results show that traditional ideological dimensions are linked to left-right labels in Latin America. In most countries,

TABLE 3.3. *Ideological Divides as Components of Left-Right Self-Placement: Country-by-Country OLS Regression Results*

Country, Variables[a]	Coefficient	p-Value
Argentina (weighted n = 61)		
Constant	4.366	.000
1 Right state-market and welfare	0.158	.375
2 Left religious and social?	0.443	.015
3 Law & order over minority rights	0.117	.536
4 Law & order over the environment	−0.573	.003
5 FDI is good, especially US	0.299	.119
Adjusted R²		.20
Bolivia (weighted n = 69)		
Constant	6.074	.000
1 Right state-market, law & order	1.033	.000
2 Pro-labor, antienvironment, anti-IMF	−0.056	.653
3 Right religious and social, no housing	0.192	.127
4 Corruption always exists, right social	−0.471	.000
Adjusted R²		.57
Brazil (weighted n = 41)		
Constant	4.240	.000
1 Pro-dole, antirights, law & order	0.398	.110
2 Pro-FDI	0.664	.010
3 Right religious	0.343	.172
Adjusted R²		.18
Chile (weighted n = 86)		
Constant	5.023	.000
1 Right state-market & welfare, pro-rights, pro-democracy	1.111	.000
2 Right religious and social	0.742	.000
3 Pro-FDI, especially US and EU	−0.359	.016
Adjusted R²		.54
Colombia (weighted n = 49)		
Constant	5.636	.000
1 Right state-market and welfare	0.645	.028
2 Pro-FDI (US) and right religious	0.963	.001
3 Right law & order, antidivorce	−0.068	.818
4 Law & order over rights	−0.204	.498
Adjusted R²		.21
Costa Rica (weighted n = 48)		
Constant	5.224	.000
1 Right religious, antiminority rights	0.661	.003
2 Left state-market and welfare	0.600	.005
3 Pro-FDI	0.303	.145
4 Crime & corruption are problems, antidemocratic	0.255	.234
Adjusted R²		.28

Country, Variables[a]	Coefficient	p-Value
Dominican Republic (weighted n = 62)		
Constant	5.347	.000
1 Right welfare, corruption	0.287	.163
2 Antirights	−0.455	.028
3 Antilabor, pro-IMF, pro-choice	0.527	.014
4 Pro-FDI	0.129	.560
Adjusted R²		.14
Ecuador (weighted n = 56)		
Constant	5.062	.000
1 Pro-labor, soft on crime	−0.288	.243
2 Right religious	0.444	.071
3 Pro-FDI	0.079	.744
4 Elections not important	0.670	.009
5 Pro–social security, pro-environment	−0.193	.434
Adjusted R²		.12
Mexico (weighted n = 119)		
Constant	4.887	.000
1 Right welfare	0.464	.002
2 Right religious and social	0.889	.000
3 Justice does not work, antirights	−0.208	.181
Adjusted R²		.28
Peru (weighted n = 66)		
Constant	5.744	.000
1 Right state-market, pro-rights	0.229	.305
2 Pro-FDI, law & order	0.370	.104
3 Right religious	0.674	.005
Adjusted R²		.12
Uruguay (weighted n = 69)		
Constant	4.304	.000
1 Pro-FDI	0.552	.000
2 Violence over environmental rights	−0.227	.052
3 Left religious and social, anti-IMF	0.685	.000
4 Right welfare?	−0.367	.002
Adjusted R²		.53
Venezuela (weighted n = 67)		
Constant	4.678	.000
1 Right religious, antisubsidies	0.564	.001
2 Pro-dole, antirights	−0.360	.044
3 Pro-FDI (especially EU and LA)	0.213	.244
Adjusted R²		.17

Note: Data from 1997 survey of Latin American legislators. Main party respondents only. Regressions are on factors reported in Chapter 2. Missing values in the dependent variable are recoded to the mean of the respondent's party. Data are weighted to reflect the actual proportion of legislators per party in congress at the time of the survey.

[a] Policy content of substantive variables (factors) is based on an assessment of the variables that load highly on these factors; see Chapter 2.

TABLE 3.4. *Comparing the Ideological and Partisan Divides as Components of Left-Right Semantics*

	Strength of Partisan Divide	Strength of Ideological Divide
Chile	.53	.54
Uruguay	.47	.53
Mexico	.29	.28
Costa Rica	.22	.28
Dominican Republic	.12	.14
Venezuela	.11	.17
Argentina	.06	.20
Ecuador	.00	.12
Colombia	–	.21
Brazil	–	.18
Bolivia	–	.57
Peru	–	.12

Note: Data are taken from Tables 3.2 and 3.3.

being "left" means being secular, in favor of social redistribution to the poor, and protectionist or nationalist. The implication of some shared meaning across countries is important because it suggests that the terms "left" and "right" may have a reasonable breadth of carrying capacity across most countries in Latin America, even if they are not always linked to partisan dimensions of conflict.

Comparing the Strength of Substantive Components across Countries

How much do ideological and partisan dimensions contribute to the variance in left-right placements found within each country? To compare the strength of the substantive components of the left-right semantics, we use the R^2s from the regressions of left-right self-placement on the ideological and partisan dimensions reported in Tables 3.2 and 3.3. Low R^2s suggest that substantive divides explain very little of the variance found in legislators' left-right self-placements; the converse is true for high R^2s.

Our analyses, summarized by size in Table 3.4, show that there is significant variance in the strength of the substantive component, whether that is measured by general ideological dimensions or partisan dimensions. Data for the strength of the partisan divides indicate that Uruguay and Chile are the two countries where the left-right semantics are most strongly connected to issue bundles that follow party lines. Costa Rica and Mexico fall into an intermediate category, below these two. In contrast to these cases, despite the presence of partisan dimensions, left-right labels lack such meaning in the Dominican Republic, Venezuela, Argentina, and Ecuador. Data that capture the strength of the ideological dimension show that the regression R^2s range from a high of .57 in Bolivia to a low of .12 in Ecuador and Peru. The placement of Bolivia, along with Uruguay and Chile, in the highest range of values, is surprising; however, it should be recalled that Bolivia lacks any clear programmatic discriminant function that could then be associated with left-right semantics. Mexico, Costa Rica, and Colombia show relatively moderate levels of general substantive content and are trailed just slightly by Brazil. In the remaining five countries, the strength of the substantive component is weak.[9] The same countries make up the midrange and lowest rows in each column. In general, countries in which ideological dimensions are strongly associated with left-right labels are also those in which partisan dimensions are highly correlated with these terms. The correlation between these two sets of R^2s for those cases that have both is .97.[10]

The overall substantive content of the left-right semantics is relatively low in Latin America when compared to other regions of the world. This is true for comparisons not only with Western Europe, where the left-right semantics are often strongly related to issue stances (see Huber 1989),[11] but also with Eastern Europe. Analyses of postcommunist Eastern Europe that predict left-right party placements using factors tapping policy disagreements typically yield values on the high end, if not higher, than those values presented here for Latin America. Thus, for example, Kitschelt et al. (1999: chap. 7, table 7.5) report that the explained variance from such analyses is .75 for Czech Republic and .74 for Hungary, values that significantly exceed those for the highest-ranking Latin American countries. The authors also report moderately high values for Poland (.57) and Bulgaria (.55). Kitschelt and Smyth (2002) report a similar statistic for the case of Russia, where the explained variance from regression analysis of left-right party placement on issue factors is .40. Even this low value falls on the high side of findings in

---

[9] It might be surprising to some that Argentina is at the bottom in terms of the substantive meaning of ideological labels; however, Argentina has never had a strong left party. Moreover, results reported in other work (e.g., Zechmeister 2006) are consistent with this low finding with respect to substantive content.

[10] If we set the missing scores for countries that have no substantively meaningful discriminant function characterizing the strength of partisan divides equal to zero, then the correlation between the explained variance of factors and discriminant functions for respondents' left-right self placements is 0.63. The discrepancy is driven nearly entirely by the case of Bolivia; if dropped, the correlation is 0.94.

[11] Regression analyses in Huber (1989) do not provide data comparable to those presented here, as Huber regresses left-right placement on both issues stances and partisanship simultaneously; the explained variance of the issue stances alone is not presented. But Huber (1989) still makes a compelling argument that issues are strong predictors of the left-right semantics in the countries. Some scholars contend that the partisan component of the left-right semantics is stronger in Western Europe than the substantive component (e.g., Inglehart and Klingemann 1976), though still present; a comparison of the strengths of each component in Latin America is presented later in this chapter.

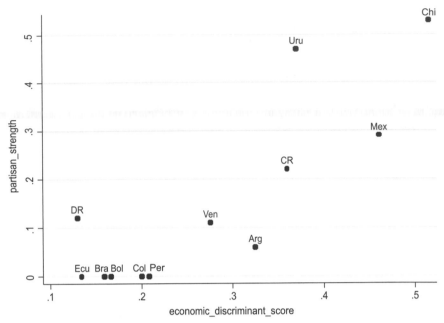

FIGURE 3.2. Comparing left-right substantive strength and economic function scores.

the Latin American cases, where only two countries – Chile and Uruguay – exceed 40 percent in both the analysis based on functions and that based on factors.[12]

The Strength of the Substantive Component Compared with Other Indicators of PPS

In Chapter 2 we found that substantive policy divides greatly vary in strength across Latin America. Figure 3.2 presents a scatterplot comparing the strength of the substantive component of the left-right semantics (as captured by the R^2s from the partisan divides regressions in Table 3.2) with the strength of the economic partisan divide found in Chapter 2. The graph shows a strong correspondence between these two indicators of programmatic party structuration. The correlation for all twelve countries is .85; and, if we leave aside the four countries that lack a substantively meaningful discriminant function (Bolivia, Brazil, Colombia, and Peru; these countries are assigned a value of zero in the graph), the correlation still remains high (r = .79). In Uruguay, Chile, and Mexico, we find clear divides between

---

[12] The issue questions used by these scholars are party placements, which could partly, but we think not entirely, explain the relatively higher correlations among left-right and issue stances found in these analyses.

party members on economic issues and a moderate to high level of substantive content assigned to the left-right semantics. We do find slightly lower levels of left-right substantive content in Mexico and slightly higher levels in Uruguay than one would predict on the basis of the strength of the economic partisan divide, but these differences are marginal. Occupying the intermediate space on the graph, we find Costa Rica, Venezuela, and Argentina – all of which have moderate to low values on each of the two variables. Finally, clustered in the bottom left-hand side of the graph we find those countries with very low values on both variables: Ecuador, Brazil, Bolivia, Colombia, and Peru. A possible outlier in this case is the Dominican Republic, which has a slightly higher value on the partisan strength left-right variable than one would predict on the basis of its discriminant function score; again, however, the degree to which the prediction is off is minimal. Overall, Figure 3.2 shows that where partisans distinguish themselves from each other with policy positions, their policy positions vis-à-vis other parties can also be mapped quite well in left-right terms.

PARTY FAMILIES AND THE LEFT-RIGHT SEMANTICS

A final way to examine the substantive meaning of the left-right semantics is to look across party families. The small number of legislators for most parties makes a within-country analysis of the different parties difficult to undertake when examining the relative size of the substantive component across party types. In this analysis, we pool the parties according to whether they are on the left or the right in terms of party families and run separate regressions of left-right placement on factors. In order to compare across party families, we now use general factors that are the same for each country. We also include legislators from small parties, as those parties tend to be noncentrist parties and therefore may be key contributors to the significance of the left-right semantics. We created three general, nonweighted indices using bundles of variables that appeared most often in the previous analyses: state-market and social protection, economic nationalism, and religion.[13]

We take two indicators as guides to code party families: the mean left-right party placement of the party (Table 3.1) and Coppedge's classification of the parties.[14] Table 3.5 shows the results of OLS regressions of left-right self-placement on each of the general factors for each party family type. As the table shows, both the economic issues factor and the religious

---

[13] The variables that compose these indices are the following: for economic policies – *don't control prices, don't sponsor jobs, don't provide houses, don't provide social security, don't give dole,* and *don't subsidize basics;* for economic nationalism – *US investment good, EU investment good,* and *LA investment good;* for religion – *I go to church, no abortion, no divorce, I'm very religious.*

[14] Coding details are contained in the notes to Table 3.5. For Coppedge's dataset, see http://www.nd.edu/~mcoppedg/crd/.

TABLE 3.5. *Comparing the Substantive Significance of Left-Right Semantics across Party Families*

	Left[a]		Right[b]	
	Coefficient	p-Value	Coefficient	p-Value
Constant	4.15	.000	6.64	.000
Economic policies	0.46	.066	0.11	.655
Economic nationalism	0.11	.310	0.36	.171
Religious issues	0.66	.053	0.11	.786
N	247		206	
Adjusted R²	.02		.00	

Note: Members of parties with less than seven members are included in these regressions. The independent variables are defined in the text.

[a] Parties are considered "left" if they are either an umbrella leftist group, have socialist or communist roots or leanings, have a progressive platform, or are considered social democratic. The designations are based on codings by Coppedge, their mean party placement in this chapter, and the authors' research. Left parties in this analysis include the following: Argentina – FREPASO; Bolivia – MBL, CONDEPA, MIR; Brazil – PSB, PCdoB, PT, PSDB; Chile – Socialista, PPD; Costa Rica – PLN; Dominican Republic – PLD, PRD; Ecuador – Pachakutik, ID; Mexico – PRD; Uruguay – FA, Nuevo Espacio; Venezuela – MAS, AD, Causa R. Interestingly, if social democratic parties are removed from the analysis, economic nationalism becomes significant and the other two drop below standard significance levels.

[b] Parties are considered "right" if they have authoritarian roots or leanings and/or conservative platforms. Parties are coded as "right" on the basis of their mean party placement in this chapter, Coppedge's codings, and authors' research. Right parties in this analysis are the following: Argentina – UCEDE; Bolivia – UCS, SyD, MNR, ADN; Brazil – PFL, PTB, PPB; Chile – UDI, RN; Colombia – PS; Dominican Republic – PRSC; Ecuador – PSC; Mexico – PAN; Peru – Renovac.

factor are significant predictors ($p < .10$) of left-right self-placement among leftist parties, whereas no factors are significant in the regression using rightist parties. In addition, the adjusted R^2 for the left parties regression is greater than zero (though not by much), while it is not for the right parties' regression.[15] Thus, it appears that left-right semantics, on average, are somewhat substantively more meaningful among left parties than they are among right parties. In particular, it is the left in Latin America that, on average, connects left-right semantics to religious and economic policy bundles. One potential reason for this could be a tendency among political elites to avoid in general using the term right, at least in some countries

[15] To check whether this poor result for the rightist parties was a result of the construction of the independent variables, we reran the regression using all the individual variables that constitute the three indices. The adjusted R^2 remained 0.00, and only one of the variables was significant (*don't subsidize basics*). Finally, it seemed possible that right parties might associate these terms with law-and-order type policies or authoritarian-democratic preferences. We created two additional nonweighted indices, each composed of four variables that represent these bundle types, and regressed left-right self-placement on these. The results were not significant, and the R^2 remained at 0.00.

(see Zechmeister 2006). We might expect this to be the case in countries with high income inequality or poverty (where conservative stances do not appeal to important segments of the population) or in countries that have experienced authoritarian military governments in recent memory. Power (2000) states that the elite in Brazil avoids the term "right" because of its association with economic conservatism and military rule. With some possible exceptions (e.g., where the term has been associated with domestic terrorist groups), the "left" may more frequently be associated with policies that have popular appeal. The more comfortable elites are using the terms, the easier it may be to coordinate around those labels.[16] To conclude, these results suggest that – at least with respect to the left-right component – it is parties on the left that are playing a relatively greater role in increasing programmatic party structuration. However, it is also important to note that the absolute size of this role may be only slightly greater than the role played by the right; the small difference between the R^2 statistics in Table 3.5 and, as well, the sensitivity of the left's results to party codings (see the note to Table 3.5) both speak to this.

COMPARING SYMBOLIC AND SUBSTANTIVE COMPONENTS OF LEFT-RIGHT SEMANTICS

In assessing the components of left-right semantics among elites in Latin America for each country, is the symbolic or substantive component larger and, perhaps more important, to what extent do these components overlap and so reduce the complexity of the political arena? To gain insight into answers to these questions, we add the symbolic component to the same regression model used to measure the substantive component and compare the two sets of results. We use the substantive component regressions found in Table 3.2 as our baseline because issue bundles that capture latent or active partisan dimensions should be those that allow left-right semantics to best facilitate programmatic party competition. The (potentially overlapping) symbolic component is captured by the mean position of each party in a system on the left-right dimension (see Table 3.1 for these mean values). These mean positions should be interpreted as the "true" positions of the parties (Inglehart and Klingemann 1976). Although they may include much of the substantive component already measured by the partisan issue dimension, they should also incorporate the symbolic component of left-right semantics; the amount of additional variance they explain when included in the model thus provides us with an indicator of the independent symbolic component.

---

[16] If elites on the left tend to use that term more frequently, this should facilitate coordination around a common placement on the left-right scale. Indeed, if we examine the standard deviations around the means presented in Table 3.1, we find that the average standard deviation is higher for right parties than for left parties.

A dominant strand of literature, led by Inglehart and Klingemann (1976), suggests that the symbolic component dominates over the substantive component in Western advanced industrialized countries (see also Butler and Stokes 1969; Inglehart and Sidjanski 1976; Klingemann 1979; Converse and Pierce 1986). However, Huber (1989) finds that the substantive component is significant among citizens of Western Europe and that, while the symbolic component is important, it is not always strong.[17] Because of these conflicting findings, prior research of Western European countries does not provide clear guidelines for forming expectations about the relative weight of each component within Latin American countries.

In order to discern the relative weight of each component, symbolic and substantive, within each country, we analyze the results of a step regression where we first report the influence of the partisan dimension(s) on left-right self-placement (the previously discussed Table 3.2) and then add in the mean left-right party placement. The relative independent strength of two components and the extent to which they overlap can be gauged by observing any changes in the size of the coefficients and the R^2s from the original model when the symbolic component is added in.[18]

Table 3.6 presents a summary of the results of the set of step regressions. In every country, including the mean left-right party placement reduces the size of the coefficient of the partisan dimension(s). However, the exact effect of this additional variable varies greatly. In three countries, the mean left-right party placement is not statistically significant: Argentina, the Dominican Republic, and Mexico (although, in the case of the Dominican Republic, it is close to a standard significance cutoff of $p \leq .10$, and including the mean left-right party placement renders the substantive component insignificant). The adjusted R^2 statistics for these three countries are essentially unaffected by the inclusion of the symbolic partisan component. Thus, in these cases, the symbolic and substantive components overlap to a significant degree. In Costa Rica, we see evidence of a similar strong correspondence between the symbolic and substantive partisan components. In this case, when the former is included in the model, the effect of the latter loses statistical significance. The absolute value of the correlations between the symbolic and substantive partisan components in these four countries reveals that it is between .83 and .87 for Argentina, the Dominican Republic, and Costa Rica and .72 for Mexico.

The symbolic and substantive partisan components are also highly correlated in Chile and in Uruguay (at levels of .82, for the first substantive

---

[17] Huber employs individual issues rather than ideologies or partisan issue dimensions in regressions of self-placement. The difference in technique should not greatly affect conclusions regarding the substantive component in each study.

[18] This method also allows us to test whether issue orientations have an indirect effect on left-right semantics through their impact on party choice (Knutsen 1997).

TABLE 3.6. *Step Regression, Adding Symbolic Partisan Component (LRPP) to Regression of Left-Right Self-Placement on Substantive Partisan Dimension(s)*

	Constant	Dimension 1	Dimension 2	LRPP	Adjusted R^2	Weighted N
Argentina	4.326***	−0.162**	–	–	.06	61
	2.490	−0.075	–	0.392	.06	61
Chile	4.977***	0.527***	0.089	–	.53	86
	1.581*	0.189*	0.032	0.679***	.59	86
Costa Rica	5.242***	0.387***	–	–	.22	48
	−3.517	−0.032	–	1.568**	.29	48
Dominican Republic	5.347***	−0.306**	–	–	.12	62
	1.780	−0.076	–	0.628	.14	62
Ecuador	5.060***	−0.077	–	–	.00	56
	−0.041	−0.032	–	0.953***	.47	56
Mexico	4.921***	0.477***	−0.152	–	.29	119
	3.794***	0.381***	−0.087	0.220	.30	119
Uruguay	4.315***	0.391***	–	–	.47	69
	2.377**	0.197*	–	0.427*	.49	69
Venezuela	4.477***	0.271**	–	–	.11	67
	1.902	0.210**	–	0.538**	.15	67

Note: * $p \leq .10$, ** $p \leq .05$, *** $p \leq .001$, two-tailed. Dimensions 1 and 2 refer to those indicated in Table 3.2. See the text for a more complete explanation of this table.

dimension in the case of Chile, and .89 for the case of Uruguay). In these cases, though, both the substantive partisan dimension and the symbolic component are significant, though the effect of the former is diminished by the inclusion of the latter. In somewhat of a contrast, the correlation in Venezuela is fairly low (.33); yet, looking across the two steps for these cases, one sees fairly similar effects as those indicated for Chile and Uruguay.

Ecuador stands out as a unique case; here there is no clear relationship between the substantive and symbolic components (correlation is −0.09). Ecuador is the only country for which the substantive dimension, even included on its own, does not have an effect. In contrast, as the results show, the symbolic component is significantly related to left-right self-placement. Thus, it appears that in Ecuador, left-right labels are tied to party labels but not to relevant policy dimensions. The utility of the left-right semantics for guiding programmatic party competition in Ecuador is limited; left-right labels may to some degree orient actors with respect to parties but not with respect to dimensions of programmatic party competition. In contrast, in the remaining seven cases examined here, to at least some degree left-right labels signal both party labels and relevant policy stances to political actors.

CONCLUSION

In some Latin American countries, citizens can rely on politicians' left-right self-placements as providing information that reflects on their personal and their parties' policy appeals, in others they cannot. As a comparison of the results in Chapter 2 to those presented here reveals, the ability of citizens to employ left-right self-placements as policy markers tends to be greatest in countries containing a strong partisan issue divide, particularly around economic issues, as identified in Chapter 2. These are, above all, Chile, Mexico, and Uruguay, followed at some distance by Bolivia and Costa Rica. Venezuela and Argentina constitute the lower bound of countries where programmatic issue positions of party politicians have anything to do with politicians' left-right self-placements. In the remaining five countries – Brazil, Colombia, the Dominican Republic, Ecuador, and Peru – neither the left-right semantics nor powerful discriminant functions with starkly featured programmatic policy content matter in the parties' games to shape their reputations. The greatest discrepancy between the strength of programmatic discriminant functions and the substantive policy content of the left-right semantics exists no doubt in the case of Bolivia – but only when the substantive component of left-right labels is measured according to general ideological divides (per Table 3.3). Overall, when the substantive component of the left-right semantics is derived from analyses of partisan divides, the strength of programmatic economic divides is a good predictor of the strength of the programmatic nature of the left-right semantics.

4

Political Representation in Latin America

Juan Pablo Luna and Elizabeth J. Zechmeister

In its modern manifestation, democracy is the process of channeling a great amount and variety of public opinion into a smaller, more homogeneous number of elected representatives charged with carrying out the plurality's preferences. This perspective is consistent with that of "responsible party government," in which voters (principals) choose among parties (agents) offering alternative policy packages (Adams 2001; Schmitt and Thomassen 1999; Converse and Pierce 1986; Dalton 1985). From such a perspective, perhaps the ultimate test of programmatic party structuration lies in the extent to which party elites and party supporters correspond across issue and ideological divides or, in other words, in the degree of representation that exists within the system. While in the previous two chapters we have explored the amounts of programmatic structure present in each case among partisan elites, in this chapter we explore how the different configurations we have described at the elite level relate to the levels of programmatic linkage between citizens and partisan elites. This is particularly relevant because in theory we could imagine party systems that have relatively high levels of programmatic structure at the elite level but which do not seek or simply are unable to structure programmatic ties to voters. If this scenario were to hold true, it would jeopardize the causal inferences we draw concerning programmatic structuration in coming chapters.

In this chapter, we combine elite and mass survey data to assess the nature and levels of programmatic representation in nine Latin American countries: Argentina, Bolivia, Brazil, Chile, Colombia, Costa Rica, Ecuador, Mexico, and Uruguay. On the basis of analyses of these data, we offer a measure of the extent to which political parties represent voters' policy preferences in these countries. First, we situate our study within the broader literature on political representation and briefly expand our argument on the importance of representation to the study of democratic quality. Second, we discuss our data and methods and, in particular, explain how we create our measure of political representation. Third, we present overall representation scores for each of the countries in our study and then representation scores by issue bundles. Fourth, we focus on elite-mass representation on a single issue, privatization, in order to examine some party-level details. Finally, we compare our key findings with other aspects of programmatic structuration detected in the preceding chapters.

THEORETICAL PERSPECTIVES ON POLITICAL REPRESENTATION

We define representation as the extent to which political parties and their constituents have consistently matching preferences over a set of relevant policy dimensions. This type of representation has been termed mandate or issue representation; it captures the degree of correspondence between parties and their constituents (Ranney 1962; Dalton 1985; Powell 1982, 1989; Converse and Pierce 1986; Iversen 1994a, 1994b; Thomassen 1994; Przeworski, Stokes, and Manin 1999; Schmitt and Thomassen 1999). Issue representation and "responsible party government" are, in many ways, coterminous. Two conditions are central to the notion of responsible party government: policy divergence among the parties contesting the election and policy voting on the part of the electorate (Adams 2001); issue representation obtains when these two conditions hold.[1]

The study of issue representation can be traced back to Miller and Stokes's "Constituency Influence in Congress" (1963). Comparing mass issue positions across different U.S. districts with the policy positions of each district's congressional representatives, Miller and Stokes assessed the degree of the public's control over Congress. Miller and Stokes stimulated several methodological and substantive criticisms, as well as a rich research tradition examining representation within and across democratic political systems. With

[1] A third condition of responsible party government arguably is policy stability on the part of the parties contesting the election (Adams 2001). We are aware that mandate or issue representation defined as correspondence between the policy preferences of a set of parties' electoral constituencies and the preferences of the parties' elites is not the most robust conception of representation, as it ignores the intertemporal dimension of representation that can be so vital for the functioning of democracy. Can those who vote for party i at time t still see themselves represented by that party at time $t + 1$, or has the representation of their preferences migrated to party j, or even no party at all? Conversely, can a party deliver policy results that voters endorse at time $t + 1$, although they previously disapproved of the policy means chosen by the party to attain those goals at time t? Scholars have termed this latter phenomenon "accountability representation," where the incumbent party selects policies unconstrained by party platforms or promises and voters act retrospectively, retaining the incumbent party only when that party or politician delivers good output (Alesina 1988; Przeworski et al. 1999; Stokes 1999). In both cases we are dealing with modes of intertemporal representation that lie at the heart of conceptions of accountability and responsiveness. Our data do not allow us to examine relations as complex as these. We can, however, establish whether there is a modicum of correspondence between principals and agents in a snapshot comparison at a single point in time. As we discuss later in this section, this type of representation still has significant implications for the nature of the democratic process.

respect to the former, Achen (1977; 1978) criticized the use of correlation coefficients alone to measure representation connections between elites and mass publics. Achen advocated instead the use of multiple measures in order to assess both the absolute distance between the positions of elites and masses ("proximity" and "centrality") and the extent to which our knowledge of each party's constituency positions allows the prediction of their party representatives. At about the same time, Weissberg (1978) showed that Miller and Stokes's measure of "dyadic" representation, which focused on the relationship between district constituencies and their congressional representatives, could significantly downplay situations of "collective" representation between the whole citizenry and the national legislature. Following this latter critique, the comparative research tradition on substantive representation has focused almost exclusively on political representation by national parties (instead of district partisan representatives).[2]

Miller and Stokes's article has been succeeded by several decades of work on political representation, most in the form of single case studies.[3] More recently, this research program witnessed what Powell (2001: 27) deemed an "explosion of comparative substantive representation studies," with the publication of a significant number of explicitly cross-national comparative analyses (Miller et al. 1999; Schmitt and Thomassen 1999; Kitschelt et al. 1999; Esaiasson and Heidar 2000; Powell 2000). All these studies focus on the quality of representation and its system-level determinants in Europe.

Interestingly, the nature of political representation has not received much scholarly attention in the focus on democratic quality in Latin America. Cross-national studies of representation as issue congruence outside of Europe's boundaries likely have been hindered by lack of data and by concern with other important research topics. O'Donnell's (1994) description of "delegative democracies" as regimes in which a neo-Hobbesian pattern of representation arises and Stokes's (1999; 2001) accounts of the "policy switches" pursued by, among others, Carlos Menem in Argentina and Alberto Fujimori in Peru are notable exceptions, and both highlight the importance of examining this subject in greater detail. Among the small group of exceptions are also important studies by Hagopian (1998), Moreno (1999), and Roberts (2000). In addition, a few single case studies of different parties or party systems have been performed across Latin America (e.g., Levitsky 2001; Mainwaring 1999; Coppedge 1996; González 1991; Hartlyn 1988). These studies provide important insights into the study of political representation in contemporary Latin America. However, their single-case focus limits the chances for cross-national generalization and analysis.

We believe that understanding the nature of representation and its determinants is critical to the study of democracy in Latin America. In the first

---

[2] See Powell (2001) for an excellent and more thorough review of this research tradition.
[3] See relevant references in Powell (2001).

place, and essentially by definition, representation affects the quality of democracy by ensuring that political elites' policy preferences reflect those of their voters. Such programmatic linking does not guarantee positive policy outcomes, of course, but it does typically facilitate such results. As Kitschelt et al. (1999) note, when elites and citizens are linked by ideological commitments, cycles of responsiveness and accountability are created. In the long run, such cycles are key to establishing a coherent and stable policy-making environment and long-standing institutional frameworks with the capacity to foster socioeconomic development (North 1990). Moreover, scholars have shown that the presence of ideologically committed and differentiated political parties affects the capacity of the subordinated classes to pursue their interests (Rueschemeyer, Huber, and Stephens 1992). Other things being equal, we should expect more progressive distributive outcomes in those party systems in which the main actors have ideological commitments that are structured and stable and which, at the same time, are the basis for both competition among parties and coherent and well-rooted links between the party and its constituency. In other words, political representation is not only a crucial determinant of the procedural quality of democracy in a given polity but also a significant factor capable of shaping its substantive yields.

If democratic consolidation is defined as a significant decrease in the probability of a reversal to an authoritarian system, then the degree of representation may also contribute to this aspect of a young democracy.[4] The relationships among regime durability or stability, representation, and democratic quality are subtle and hinge on the interaction between the former and a set of contextual factors such as the salience of distributive conflicts. As such, it is not necessarily the case that representation will always contribute to the longevity of democracy. In fact, some authors point to representation failures in the context of widespread poverty and inequality as making democracy faulty and therefore durable in current Latin America (Huber and Stephens 1999). According to this view, democracy is consolidated precisely as subordinated classes lack effective channels of political representation, thereby keeping elite interests secure and threat perception low.

Nevertheless, to the extent that representation fosters perceptions of regime legitimacy, a lack of representation may threaten democratic consolidation.[5] There is strong reason to believe that the level of representation affects citizen support for the system and therefore contributes to

---

[4] Mainwaring, O'Donnell, and Valenzuela (1992) state that transitional democracies are distinguished from consolidated ones according to the degree to which all actors commit to the rules of the game and, in a related manner, by the degree to which the permanence of democracy appears certain.

[5] Diamond (1996: 33) argues that democratic consolidation is "the process of achieving broad and deep legitimation such that all significant actors, at both the elite and mass levels, believe that the democratic regime is better for their society than any other realistic alternative they can imagine."

its durability. The shallower the connections between elites and the mass public, the less committed the mass public will be to the democratic regime and, at worst, the more open the public will be to an authoritarian reversal (Diamond 1996). Thus, while high levels of representation could potentially threaten a fragile democracy in which the masses possess strong redistributive concerns, countries in which this is a possibility would seem to be caught in a difficult situation: increasing representation may make the regime susceptible to democratic breakdown at the elite level; yet, if large numbers of citizens are underrepresented by parties, they may withdraw support from the regime, resort to unconventional forms of participation, or be increasingly open to nondemocratic forms of government. In either case, the recent breakdown of previously institutionalized party systems (e.g., Venezuela), the growing stress on parties and party leaders, and Latin Americans' increasing distrust in parties and elections suggest that the nature of representation is one of the most important fault lines undermining the quality, and potentially even the durability, of these young democracies (Hagopian 1998).

MEASURING POLITICAL REPRESENTATION

Data

To build our indicator of issue representation, we have to reduce an overwhelming amount of data into nine sets of system-level indicators of political representation. We rely on two sets of survey data: the Salamanca survey and the 1998 Latinobarometer survey of mass publics in most Latin American countries. A legislator's political affiliation is clearly indicated from his partisanship in congress. To capture party support among the masses, we use respondents' partisan vote choices (if an election were held that day).[6]

Case Selection

We analyze elite-mass issue congruence in and across the following nine Latin American countries: Argentina, Bolivia, Brazil, Chile, Colombia, Costa Rica, Ecuador, Mexico, and Uruguay. In order to include as many party systems as possible, we kept all cases for which we had data, with two exceptions. For the most part, while young democratic contexts are fluid, the temporal proximity of the surveys is close enough that we are confident we are capturing a stable snapshot of elite-mass representation in the two

---

[6] In the case of Argentina, the question included a single category for UCR and FREPASO, on account of their electoral alliance. While we cannot distinguish between preferences for these individual parties, the survey reflects the options presumed available to citizens at that time and this fact is therefore reflected in our measure of political representation.

years around this time period. However, two Latin American countries, Peru and Venezuela, experienced significant changes in their party systems during these two years. Parties that were very prominent in 1997 had virtually disappeared and lacked significant popular support in the 1998 mass survey; these were replaced by newly emergent parties and groups that were not represented in the 1997 elite survey. As a result, only a very small number of parties in those two countries satisfied our conditions to be included at both levels, yielding a very limited and nonrepresentative sample of the overall system; we therefore excluded these countries from our analyses. A third country covered by our legislators' surveys, the Dominican Republic, is not part of Latinobarometer and thus could not be included in our analysis. While the loss of these three countries is unfortunate, we are still left with a wide array of political systems to analyze.[7]

Another case selection issue concerns the parties that we examine. Not surprisingly, we sometimes had few or no respondents affiliated with small parties. In many of these cases, we have a small set of respondents for one survey (elite or mass) and none for the other survey (mass or elite). In such cases, we had no choice but to leave these parties out of our analysis. Among the remaining small parties, we exclude those with fewer than three respondents for the elite survey and fewer than fifteen respondents for the mass survey. By leaving these parties out, we limit the domain of our analysis to representation by main parties. Because the vast majority of voters express a preference for these parties, we believe we still adequately capture the overall level of representation in each party system. In Appendix 4.1 to this chapter, we list the parties on which we based our analyses, the parties we excluded, and the number of respondents from each survey for all parties.

A final, but also very relevant case selection decision concerns the treatment of those mass respondents who do not identify a party they would vote for if elections were held that week in their countries. On the one hand, the relative presence of nonpartisan identifiers could be thought as a proxy for mass alienation with political parties. If this presumption was true, the percentage of nonidentifiers should weight (negatively) in a given measure of voter-elite issue congruence. That is, the quality of representation should be less (and our index lower) in those systems where survey nonidentifiers represent potential voters who feel alienated from parties. On the other hand, it is possible that the percentage of nonidentifiers in a given survey relates to stochastic and contingent factors, such as the relative temporal proximity of elections or the country's economic mood. If this alternative view is correct, weighting our index on the basis of the relative presence of nonidentifiers would be misleading.

---

[7] The absence of these arguably less structured party systems should be kept in mind, as it could make our overall portrait of representation in Latin American party systems appear too optimistic.

While these are not entirely rival factors, we tend to favor the second view, particularly because variance in this variable did not seem to follow a theoretically discernible (and homogeneous across cases) pattern.[8] Nonetheless, it should be noted that by restricting our analysis in this way, we omit respondents who do not express any preference. Thus, our measure of programmatic representation is defined by a focus on main parties and on individuals who indicate a vote choice for one of these parties.

Matching Variables across Surveys

In order to evaluate elite-mass issue representation, we needed elite and mass survey datasets that contained a number of similar issue questions. A difficulty with any type of project that attempts to match two survey databases is that question wordings do not always correspond exactly. The surveys that we employ differ in the scope of policy dimensions that they cover and in the question wordings of variables that represent similar policy considerations. Nevertheless, both datasets did contain questions that we believe represent

---

[8] In the Latinobarometer data, for the nine countries we examine the percentage of nonrespondents ranges from a low of 21.5 percent in Mexico to a high of 69.5 in Costa Rica. For five of the countries, the percentage of nonrespondents is close to 50 (+/−5 percentage points). The remaining two countries, Brazil and Uruguay, both have nonresponse rates that round to 36. While one might be tempted to incorporate nonresponse rates into an indicator of representation, we are convinced that, because the surveys were conducted at different times in each country's electoral cycle, one cannot interpret these percentages as comparable indicators of political disconnect. Factors such as the timing of the most recent election and the nature of that campaign likely have a significant effect on the number of respondents willing to indicate a party preference. Not surprisingly, country-specific laws also influence this number. For example, we found that, using data from the IDEA.int Web site to code our nine countries as either having no compulsory voting, compulsory voting that is weakly enforced, or compulsory voting that is strongly enforced, the correlation between nonrespondents and compulsory voting is in the expected direction and at least moderately high (−.63). As another thought, we did consider that we might be able to capture the proportion of truly alienated citizens by measuring the percentage of nonrespondents to the vote choice question who also indicate (in response to another question) that they have little or no confidence in political parties. This "alienation" measure ranges from a low of 3 percent in Mexico to a high of 30 percent in Costa Rica. However, because this measure might also be subject to electoral cycles and other such factors, we did not incorporate it into our representation measure. Therefore, our representation measure should only be interpreted as capturing the degree of programmatic linking that exists between main party representatives and party supporters. Nevertheless, as such, our measure of representation does capture whether clear opportunities and examples of programmatic linkages exist in a country. As a final exploration into the issue of nonrespondents, we examined the correlation between our measures of representation (discussed later in the text and shown in Table 4.4) and the percentage of nonrespondents, and between representation and the percentage of alienated respondents. The correlation between percentage of nonrespondents and our "best case" representation score is only −.11, and −.13 for our "conservative" representation score. For alienated nonrespondents, the correlations are −.15 and −.16, respectively.

a total of five issue bundles, or potential ideological dimensions: economic (3 variables), foreign investment (2), religion (2), regime (2), and law and order or good governance (2).[9] These five policy areas represent a wide array of issues that are relevant to the countries in this project. Table 4.1 depicts our scheme for matching questions across the surveys according to our five issue bundles.[10]

Measuring Mandate Representation

A critical decision for our analysis was how exactly to measure representation. In any study, this decision substantially hinges on the conceptual definition of representation subscribed to by the researchers. In accord with our earlier discussion, we adhere to the "issue congruence" approach, which analyzes the correspondence between party electorates and their representatives across a set of salient policy dimensions (Powell 2001).[11]

In examining issue congruence among party elites and party electorates, two basic measures are of primary importance to us: the relative ordering of mean party positions and the presence of significant divides among these positions. First, we measure issue congruence by examining whether party elites and mass electorates are consistent in their relative stances on a given issue. That is, if arrayed on that single issue from left to right, do the party elites and party electorates "line up" in the same order? In other words, if the mean placements of party elites on an issue scale are such that party A is to the left of party B, and party C is to the right of party B (i.e., their order is A-B-C), do party supporters also place themselves, on average, in this same ordering?

[9] Our selection of issues and questions ranges from cases in which the questions match very closely to at least one case where, rather than match the specific policy, we are able to match only on policy orientation (*US Investment–Trade*, where the mass survey asks about trade with the United States and the elite survey asks about investment). In one case, *Privatization*, there was another alternative match available: pairing the mass survey questions with a question about privatizing public services. We elected not to use this question because in some countries the telecommunications industry and/or the electricity industry is under private control.

[10] In addition to analyses with these policy variables, we also have examined representation with respect to the general left-right dimension. Because left-right semantics do not necessarily reflect significant ideological divisions in every country (see Chapter 3) and because we are interested in representation along ideological or issue bundle lines, we do not focus on these results in the body of this chapter.

[11] As noted earlier, this approach to the study of representation is limited in that it does not consider policy output or other factors that matter significantly to intertemporal studies of representation. For example, we are also unable to examine whether the political elites follow or reflect citizens' preferences or engage in issue leadership (Miller and Stokes 1963; see also Hurley and Hill 2001 and Page and Shapiro 1983). For a discussion of the limitations of studies such as this one, which focus only on "comparative-static constellations of preferences," see Kitschelt (2002).

TABLE 4.1. *Matched Issues by Bundle*

Issue Bundle and Specific Issue	Variable in Mass Survey	Variable in Elite Survey
Economic		
Privatization	Two questions each asked whether the electricity and telephone industries, respectively, should be privatized. These were combined into a single 3-point variable where the highest value means most in favor of privatization.	Question asked about whether industries should be privatized. Recoded to 3-point scale where higher values mean in favor of privatization.
Job creation	Question asked whether it was important to create more jobs even if prices rise. The variable is dichotomous and coded so that the highest value means do not create more jobs.	Question asked whether the government should sponsor more job creation. It is coded on a 5-point scale where higher values mean government should not sponsor more job creation.
Unemployment insurance	Question asked whether the government should spend more or less on insurance against unemployment. The variable is dichotomous and coded so that the highest value means spend less.	Question asked whether the government should provide more unemployment insurance. The variable is coded on a 5-point scale where higher values mean provide less unemployment insurance.
Foreign investment		
U.S. investment– trade	Question asked about the importance of trade with the U.S. The variable is coded on a 4-point scale where the highest value means trade with the U.S. is very important.	Question asked the extent to which the country should (or should not) pursue economic investment and relations with the U.S. The variable is coded on a 5-point scale where higher values mean more in favor of establishing such links.
L.A. investment– regional integration	Question asked whether one favors economic integration in Latin America. The variable is coded on a 4-point scale where higher values mean more pro-integration.	Question asked the extent to which the country should (or should not) pursue economic investment and relations with Latin America. The variable is coded on a 5-point scale where higher values mean more in favor of establishing such links.
Religion		
Religious-secular	Question asked how devout a religious practitioner is the respondent. The variable is coded on a 4-point scale where the highest value means very devout.	Question asked how religious a practitioner is the respondent. The variable is coded on a 10-point scale where the highest value means very religious.

(continued)

TABLE 4.1 *(continued)*

Issue Bundle and Specific Issue	Variable in Mass Survey	Variable in Elite Survey
Attend church	Question asked how often the respondent attends church. The variable is coded on a 5-point scale where the highest value means more than once per week and the lowest value means never.	Question asked how often the respondent attends church. The variable is coded on a 4-point scale where the highest value means at least once per week and the lowest value means never.
Regime		
Guns or butter	Question asked if more or less money should be spent on defense and the armed forces. The dichotomous variable is coded so that the higher value means more.	Question asked if army budget should be transferred to social security. The 4-point variable is coded so that the highest value means the respondent disagrees.
Democratic order best	Question asked whether democracy is always preferable, sometimes an authoritarian government is necessary, or if it doesn't matter to the respondent. The 3-point variable is coded so that the highest value means an antidemocratic response, and the lowest value means a pro-democratic response.	Question asked whether democracy is the best system of government. The 4-point variable is coded so that the highest value means an antidemocratic response, and the lowest value means a pro-democratic response.
Law and order–good governance		
Public security	Question asked about spending on public security. The dichotomous variable is coded so that the high value means the respondent would prefer that his country spend more.	Two questions asked about a respondent's concern for the issue of security. The first asks if delinquency is a threat to democracy; the second asks if violence is a problem. The combined variable is coded so that higher values mean greater concern for security.
Corruption	Question asked how serious a problem corruption is in the respondent's country. The 4-point variable is coded so that the highest value means not at all serious.	Question asked if corruption is a problem that has always existed in the country. The 5-point variable is coded so that the highest value means the respondent agrees strongly.

Note: All variables were standardized into 0–1 scales. We attempted to match questions as closely as possible but were limited by the data. However, differences in exact question wording and in the scales are less relevant for our study because we do not compare exact stances on these issues across the mass and elite divide. Thus, at no point do we assert that a value on a variable in the mass survey can be directly compared to a value on its peer variable in the elite survey. The regression and correlation analyses do, however, take into account the relative mean positions of party voters or representatives in the two surveys measuring mandate representation.

Second, we analyze the data for the presence of policy divergence among the parties competing for election, and among party supporters. For our second measure, therefore, we ask for each issue: is there a significant divide among political elites by party, and is there a significant divide among party electorates? If elites do not offer clear and distinct alternatives, the potential for representation is very weak. Likewise, if party electorates do not differ significantly on a given issue, then levels of representation will be low.

Our initial step, then, consisted of measuring these two components (coherent ordering and significant divides) for our eleven issues, for each of the nine countries. We first measured the degree of coherence in the ordering of party supporters or members by the correlation between the mean placements of the party electorates and the mean placements of party legislators, on each issue.[12] We reduced the results of these correlation analyses into three categories: a strong positive correlation (r > .50), a weak correlation (−.50 < r < .50), and a strong negative correlation (r < −.50).[13] Second, in order to examine the strength of the divides among party elites and party electorates, we ran analysis of variance (ANOVA) tests using the means and standard deviations we obtained for each party, at each level and across each country and issue. ANOVA allows us to assess whether party means on each issue (and at each level) are significantly different in a given party system. The results yielded four potential categories for the second component (significant divide) for each issue: significant elite divide and significant mass divide; significant elite divide but no significant mass divide; no significant elite divide but significant mass divide; and, no significant elite nor mass divide.[14] In those cases in which we identified significant differences in the

[12] We followed Achen's (1977; 1978) methodological suggestions and the basics of Kitschelt et al.'s (1999) empirical strategy to analyze issue congruence between mass electorates and party leaders. As a result, we computed both correlation and regression coefficients in order to analyze how well voters' opinions predicted elites' programmatic predispositions for each country and for every issue. Given that the regression and correlation analysis results were highly consistent, here we rely primarily on the latter; we address regression results in the final section of the chapter. Tables available from the authors show each country's elite and mass positions (means and standard deviations), for each party, on each of the eleven issues we constructed for this analysis. The summary results of these analyses are presented in Web Appendix 4.2 at www.cambridge.org/9780521114950.

[13] Because we only had two parties in Colombia and Costa Rica, our analyses here were overdetermined and correlations could not be meaningfully computed. In these cases we instead check whether party elite and supporter mean issue positions were consistently ordered and assign a "correlation coefficient" greater than 0.5 when that occurs. When a crossing existed between elites' and citizens' positions, we considered the situation as one similar to those in which we obtained negative correlations lower than −.5. While not an ideal solution, we felt it was our best recourse for these two-party systems.

[14] It should be noted that our use of ANOVA analyses and Bonferroni tests is a departure from methods used by other scholars of representation. We hope that, by introducing this alternative methodology and identifying its utility, we contribute to the development of this aspect of the representation literature. To be more precise, this methodological

party system, we also used the Bonferroni post hoc test in order to identify which parties were responsible for the significant difference of means. For both of these latter tests, we used a significance cutoff of $p < .10$ because of the small sample sizes.

In synthesis, as a result of our preliminary analysis of the data, we acquired the following for each of the countries we examine: means and standard deviations corresponding to each party's electorate for eleven issues; and means and standard deviations corresponding to each party's elites for eleven issues. From these, we computed, first, correlation and regression results for each issue and country (coefficients, slopes, and intercepts); and, second, ANOVA results based on these means and standard deviations for each issue at each level. These provide measures of the two components of representation we identified previously: coherent ordering and significant divides.

Before moving on, it might be helpful to make this discussion more concrete by presenting a couple of examples of issues for which we constructed these two measures. The examples we have selected, privatization in the case of Chile and spending on public security in Ecuador, yield very different results on our measures. With respect to the former, we determined the average position, and the standard deviation around this position, of party elites and party supporters for each of the parties in our datasets. Our analysis at the elite level yielded the following means and standard deviations: PS (mean = 0.37, standard deviation = 0.26); PPD (0.52, 0.04); PDC (0.48, 0.18); UDI (0.84, 0.32); and RN (0.83, 0.23). At the mass level we found the following: PS (0.36, 0.38); PPD (0.36, 0.40); PDC (0.37, 0.41); UDI (0.48, 0.42); and RN (0.56, 0.45). To measure the degree of coherent ordering, we ran a correlation analysis in which the mean positions taken by party elite and party supporters were compared. The correlation between these values is .91. The strong positive result indicates to us that there is significant congruence in elite-mass ordering on this issue. To detect the presence of significant divides among the party elites and then also among the party supporters, we used ANOVA to detect differences in the mean values (based on these, the number of observations, and the standard deviations). The ANOVA results at the elite level confirm significant differences between the average positions taken by the PS, PPD, and PDC, on the one hand, and the

strategy allows one to answer the following questions: (1) How cohesive are party elites and masses on each particular issue? (2) How different are party positions on a given issue? (3) Therefore, how much polarization is there in the system around a specific issue and policy dimension? (4) Which parties are polarized on a given issue? (5) To what extent are the parties that were polarized at the mass level the same that are polarized at the elite level? ANOVA analyses help to answer questions 1, 2, and 3; the Bonferroni post hoc test to significant ANOVA results provides answers to questions 4 and 5. In this chapter most of our analyses are focused on the system as a whole; we use the Bonferroni test results in the final section to explore party-level results with respect to one issue, that of privatization.

UDI and the RN, on the other. At the mass level, the ANOVA results reveal significant divides between RN supporters and those of the three leftmost parties: the PS, PPD, and PDC. In sum, the two sets of results – the correlation statistic and the ANOVA analyses – tell us that, for the most part, party elites and party supporters are taking clear positions on the issue of privatization in Chile (in particular, those on the left take positions distinct from those on the right) and that elites and supporters link to each other on the basis of these positions, in a like order.

The case of spending on public security in Ecuador provides an example that looks essentially the opposite of what we find in Chile on the issue of privatization. In this case, our analyses of the average positions taken by party elites yielded the following: DP (mean = 0.65, standard deviation = 0.22); PRE (0.48, 0.29); and PSC (0.63, 0.24). At the mass level, we find the following: DP (0.78, 0.42); PRE (0.79, 0.41); and PSC (0.78, 0.42). The correlation between these sets of mean positions is −.99. Yet, if we look at the data in terms of whether these mean values are truly distinct, the ANOVA analyses reveal (not surprisingly, given these close values and high standard deviations) that in no case is there a significant divide at either the elite or mass level on this issue. In sum, in Ecuador, party elites and party supporters are not taking distinct stances, or linking to each other in expected ways, on the issue of spending on public security.

Generating System Representation Scores Based on Preliminary Analyses

The amount of information generated by the preceding analyses is unwieldy, and the individual results for each issue do not provide us with an understanding of the overall level of representation in each country. The relevant question is, what combination of results would indicate "good" or "bad" representation? In other words, what configurations of partisan elite and mass opinions (described as a function of correlation and ANOVA results) express failed, nonexistent, weak, or strong relationships of representation? In this section, we describe a scoring scheme to summarize information on levels of representation in each system.

The combination of our two measures (the three categories from the correlation analyses and the four categories that describe the nature of elite-mass divides) yields twelve classes that potentially describe each issue. The resulting 3 × 4 table is presented as Table 4.2. The numbers in parentheses in the upper-left corner of the cell serve an identification purpose. The remainder of the information in each cell will become clear as we proceed.

Our main concern is to assess the degree of representation indicated by each of the twelve cases in Table 4.2. We begin by recognizing that the upper-left and upper-right corners indicate the furthest extremes. That is, where there are clear, significant divides among elite and mass positions and a strong, positive correlation between the elite and mass mean positions, we

TABLE 4.2. *Representation Types, Scoring, and Distribution of Issues*

		Correlations between Elite and Mass Partisan Mean Positions		
		$r > .50; b > 1.00$	$-.50 < r < .50$	$r < -.50$
Significant differences within elite or mass partisan positions?	Y/Y	(1) Strong representation success Score = 2.0 N = 11	(5) Score = 0.0 N = 3	(9) Strong representation failure Score = −2.0 N = 1
	Y/N	(2) Weaker representation success Score = 1.5 N = 12	(6) Score = 0.0 N = 1	(10) Potential representation failure I Score = −1.0 N = 3
	N/Y	(3) Still weaker representation success Score = 1.0 N = 16	(7) Score = 0.0 N = 6	(11) Potential strong representation failure Score = −1.5 N = 2
	N/N	(4) Weakest representation Score = 0.5 N = 15	(8) Score = 0.0 N = 16	(12) Potential representation failure II Score = −0.5 N = 12

have a case of strong representation success (cell 1). Our previous example regarding elite-mass congruence on the issue of privatization in Chile is a case that meets the criteria for this cell. In contrast, where there are clear partisan divides among the elites and the masses and where there is a strong, negative correlation between the elite and mass mean positions, we have a case of strong representation failure (cell 9). In other words, party elites and party supporters are taking distinct stances, but party supporters are linking to party elites that hold positions exactly contrary to their own.

The first column in Table 4.2 includes cases of positive correlation between elite and mass mean party positions; we consider that each row down column 1 furnishes a progressively weaker case for representation. That is, if party elites and masses are arrayed in essentially the same order, but there is no significant divide among the masses, then this (cell 2) represents a slightly weaker case of issue representation than the case portrayed in cell 1. On the other hand, because we believe representation hinges significantly on clear signals sent by elites and because elites have higher levels of political sophistication and should otherwise be able to exhibit greater coherence on any given issue, representation is a bit weaker where there is a significant mass divide but no significant elite divide (cell 3). Finally, where elite and mass partisans are arrayed in a consistent ordering, but there are no significant divides registered among the party means for either group, we consider that there is only a very minimal level of representation (cell 4).

A rank order of the cells in column 2 is less straightforward (cells 5–8). On the one hand, if there are significant divides among elites and masses, but not a consistent ordering between the groups, this may indicate a state of flux in which the potential for strong representation exists. On the other hand, we cannot be certain of the direction the party system might take from this situation of inchoate representation – that is, whether it is likely to move toward strong representation success or failure. We are forced to admit that these cells represent ambiguous representation outcomes.

Finally, the third column is close to a mirror opposite of the first column. As already indicated, cell 9 shows a case of strong representation failure. Cell 12 is clearly a case of poor representation but less so than the cells above it because neither elites nor masses take significantly different stances on the issue. This cell might reflect issues that are simply not salient among voters or party elites. The example of public security spending in Ecuador, discussed in the preceding section, fits the criteria for this cell: party elites and supporters are arrayed "incorrectly," but neither set takes clear, distinct positions on the issue.

When comparing cells 10 and 11, we consider that a relatively worse case of representation occurs where there is a significant divide among the masses, but not among the elites, and a strong, negative correlation between elites and masses. Our rationale here is that it should be more difficult to detect a significant divide among the masses than among the elites – given the lower levels of political sophistication among the former – and, therefore, if there are clear partisan divides among the masses, but elites are arrayed in the wrong direction and not taking clear positions (cell 11), this then should be construed as a stronger case of representation failure than when there are partisan differences among the elites that are not reflected among the masses (cell 10).

To reflect our qualitative assessments about the success or failure of issue representation, we assign values ranging from -2.0 to 2.0 to each of the twelve classes in Table 4.2 (identified as "score"). Clearly, there is room for measurement error in translating qualitative judgments into quantitative indicators. To check the robustness of our results, we considered several other scoring systems. The different schemes all considered the first column as indicative of some (descending) level of representation success, and the last column to indicate different levels of representation failure. The alternative schemes differed mainly according to whether we assigned some nonzero value to the cells in the middle column or made slight changes to the lower three cells in the first and last columns. Table 4.2 shows the distribution of cases (issues pooled across countries) across the twelve cells. Most cases fall into the first column and the bottom row; relatively few cases fall into the first three cells of the second and third columns. Likely as a result of the distribution of cases, the alternative scoring schemes we attempted did not produce significantly different results.[15]

Each issue in our study received a score according to the system we developed (Web Appendix 4.2, at www.cambridge.org/9780521114950, to this chapter contains country tables). The final step in constructing a system-level representation indicator requires that we combine issue scores for each country. Once again, we tried several options in computing such summary scores and settled on two methods. First, we calculated average scores for each of our five issue bundles and added them to construct an indicator that emphasizes the importance of ideological dimensions to the concept of representation.[16] This first measure provides a "conservative" estimate of issue representation because it averages scores within an issue dimension. Second, we construct a "best case" scenario for each country, by noting only the highest scoring issue from each policy bundle and then adding these scores together for each country. Like our "conservative" measure, our "best case" measure theoretically ranges from −10 to 10. In the next section, we report and discuss the results of these two measures of representation for the nine countries in our study. We then disaggregate our measures to examine conservative and best-case scores for each of our five issue bundles.

REPRESENTATION SCORES

Table 4.3 presents the summary scores for each of the two methods we described in the previous section. As the table shows, levels of representation vary significantly across countries. The two sets of scores are fairly similar and highly correlated (Pearson's $\rho = .94$). In each case, the countries with

[15] Pairwise correlations among our alternative scoring schemes were always above 0.90.

[16] To do this, we computed a score for each policy dimension by adding up the representation scores obtained for each of the issues on a given bundle and dividing the sum by the number of issues in the basket. We thus constructed a standardized index of the quality of representation for that policy dimension in the range −2, 2. We then added up the results for each of the five dimensions to create a final representation score. The resulting score ranges theoretically from −10 to 10. The advantage of this technique over the alternative of simply adding up each individual variable is that we give less weight to the specific issue questions and more to the overall dimensions those questions represent. However, had we simply added up each variable, the results would not be significantly different from those discussed in the text.

TABLE 4.3. *Summary of Representation Scores*

Country	"Conservative" Score[a]	"Best Case" Score[b]
Chile	6.9	9.0
Uruguay	6.5	9.0
Argentina	4.5	6.5
Colombia	2.3	5.5
Brazil	1.6	3.5
Bolivia	1.5	1.5
Mexico	0.0	2.0
Costa Rica	−0.1	3.5
Ecuador	−0.1	1.5

[a] Sum of average scores for each policy dimension.
[b] Sum of highest score for each policy dimension.

the highest levels of representation are Chile and Uruguay, followed by Argentina. Perhaps surprisingly, Colombia yields a score in the intermediate range, while in the first column Costa Rica scores very low. The fact that Costa Rica assumes a relatively more intermediate slot in the second column (when only the highest ranking issue for each dimension is counted) shows that there are certain issues (if not issue bundles) on which there is at least a moderate level of issue congruence between party elites and voters in Costa Rica. Costa Rica might thus be thought of as providing a less robust type of representation, given that it shows moderate levels of representation on particular policies but not on coherent issue dimensions.[17] In contrast with Colombia and Costa Rica, Bolivia and Ecuador consistently display low levels of representation regardless of the scheme used. Brazil just edges out Bolivia on the "conservative" measure but moves a small distance away from Bolivia's low position in the "best case" scenario. Mexico also shows a relatively lower score within the conservative rank and is just slightly ahead of both Bolivia and Ecuador in the second column.

An obvious question at this point is what issues or issue dimensions are being represented most successfully in those instances in which we find moderate or high levels of representation? In our analysis of the country-specific 3 × 4 representation tables, we found that of the eleven issues that can be classified as "representation successes" (N = 11 in cell 1, Table 4.2), four are economic (both foreign investment–trade issues and domestic issues), four are religious, two are law-and-order issues, and one is a regime

---

[17] It should be kept in mind that the scores for Colombia and Costa Rica were generated in a slightly different fashion, given that the presence of only two parties in these systems prohibited analyzing mean positions via correlation analysis. We cannot rule out the possibility that the bluntness of our alternative approach has led us to overestimate the amount of representation in Colombia and perhaps underestimate it in the case of Costa Rica.

issue. While there has certainly been a general convergence on the left-right economic dimension in Latin America, it appears to us that – at least in some cases – elites are still offering distinct economic policy options to voters who in turn are linking to parties on those bases. To the extent that religious attitudes are well represented (i.e., appear in the cell 1), it is worth noting that they always appear together with other issues.

Interestingly, despite the salience of public security in Latin America, law-and-order issues are less successfully represented in the countries we examine here. A careful look at the nine country-specific representation tables (Web Appendix 4.2 at www.cambridge.org/9780521114950) reveals that it is much more likely to see a divide among mass partisans on corruption and public security issues than among the elites. Thus, not only are elites generally not taking distinct stances on these issues, but they are also not responding to partisan divides where they exist (the exception is Argentina, where the issue of public security is successfully represented).[18] A similar pattern occurs among regime issues: significant divides are more often found among the masses than among the elites, which could result from either more sophisticated levels of self-censoring among elites or true beliefs about the importance of upholding democratic procedures. On economic issues, in contrast, it is equally likely to find countries with a mass divide and no elite divide as it is to find countries with an elite divide but no mass divides. Clearly, elites in Latin America are less willing to take distinct stances on law-and-order and regime issues than on other issues. To the extent that regime issues are construed as referring to preferences over basic regime type, the lack of representation at the elite level (due to convergence among elites) may actually signal a positive development within the context of a young democracy – that is, a sign that elite players have accepted democracy as "the only game in town" (Przeworksi 1991). However, to the extent that these really represent stances on issues related to institutional design and practices within a democracy (i.e., policies on which we would expect actors in a healthy democracy to have divergent opinions), then our results (showing convergence among elites but not among the mass public) paint a less positive picture of representation. As our regime questions did not probe beyond an individual's preference over system type, we cannot assess whether either of these alternative interpretations has more merit than the other.

This discussion raises an important issue, namely, that it is possible that our system-level indicators of representation mask instances of good

---

[18] Survey data collected at the time of the data we analyze here help support our assertion that, not only was public security salient among the mass public, but there was also a demand for system-level responses to this issue. Thus, for example, in the *Expectations for Democracy Survey, 1998*, in which face-to-face interviews were conducted with national samples from Mexico, Costa Rica, and Chile, respondents were asked about the main task of democracy. Of those respondents in the pooled dataset, 31.3 percent selected "to combat crime"; this is a higher proportion than was received by any of the other options presented to respondents (see dataset provided within Camp 2001).

TABLE 4.4. *"Conservative" and "Best Case" Representation Scores by Issue Basket*

Country	General Economic		Foreign Investment		Religion		Law and Order		Regime	
	Cons.	Best	Cons.	Best	Cons.	Best	Cons.	Best	Cons.	Best
Argentina	1	2	0	0	1.3	1	1.5	2	0.8	1.5
Bolivia	0	0	1.5	1.5	0.3	0.5	0	0	−0.3	−0.5
Brazil	0.3	1	0.5	1	0.5	1	−0.25	0	0.5	0.5
Chile	1.7	2	1	1.5	2	2	0.75	1.5	1.5	2
Colombia	0.5	1.5	0	1	1	1.5	0.5	0.5	0.3	1
Costa Rica	0.7	1.5	0	0.5	−0.5	−0.5	0	1	−0.3	1
Ecuador	0.2	0.5	0.5	1	−1	−0.5	−0.5	−0.5	0.8	1
Mexico	−1	0	0	0	0.8	1.5	0.25	0.5	0	0
Uruguay	1	2	2	2	1.5	2	1	1	1	2
Average	0.49	1.17	0.61	0.94	0.64	0.94	0.36	0.67	0.47	0.94

representation on specific issue bundles. It may be objected that averaging scores across all five baskets underestimates the extent of representation on key dimensions by weighting all dimensions equally. To address this concern, we also examine each country's representation scores for each of the five individual issue bundles. Table 4.4 presents these scores, along with the average representation score achieved by all countries on each dimension.

An examination of Table 4.4 reveals that, to a significant degree, representation scores across issue bundles resemble average representation scores. If we examine Chile and Uruguay – the two countries with the highest general representation scores – we see that these countries score consistently high on each issue basket. Among the remaining seven countries, we do see some interesting differences across issue bundles. For example, Colombia and Argentina, which have relatively high average representation scores, are significantly below average on the foreign investment dimension. As noted previously, there are some issues on which Costa Rica's system obtains high representation scores. These are now reflected in better than average scores on the general economic issue bundle and the country's "best case" scores on both the law-and-order and regime dimensions. Bolivia, which scored relatively low on both the conservative and best-case general representation scores, shows relatively high scores (in fact, the second highest) on the foreign direct investment dimension. While representation levels are generally low in Mexico, the country does register higher than average representation scores on the religious dimension; of course, the fact that this dimension is not a salient competitive political dimension in Mexico makes the relatively higher showing in this column of less significance. Finally, Brazil and Ecuador show mostly poor representation scores across all issue bundles, though Ecuador shows at least moderate scores on the foreign policy and regime dimensions, and Brazil has moderate "best case" scores on foreign policy and religious issues.

The results for the individual issue baskets confirm our finding that programmatic political representation is highest in Chile and Uruguay and lowest in countries such as Bolivia and Ecuador. However, it is worth noting that the majority of the countries we examine here display at least moderately high to high levels of political representation on at least one of our eleven issues. It is also worth noting that average representation scores by issue basket are consistent with our previous discussion, which indicated that political elites and party supporters more often establish programmatic linkages over economic issues (particularly when one considers "best case" scores) and religious issues, as opposed to regime and, particularly, law-and-order issues.

A UNIVARIATE EXAMPLE: THE CASE OF PRIVATIZATION

In this final section we provide the reader with a closer look at the data by analyzing issue congruence and distinctiveness on a single issue across countries. Given the salience of the debate on privatization of state-owned enterprises in Latin America during the 1990s, and given the centrality of privatization within the economic competitive divide, we decided to center our exploration on this issue. With the exceptions of Brazil and Colombia, this is an economic issue that seems to show relatively good policy congruence across Latin American party systems. In other words, this issue seems to provide relatively good opportunities for citizen-elite programmatic linking in all countries. Tangentially, this issue-specific analysis will also allow us to identify individual political parties that are less representative of their constituents' policy preferences – at least on this particular issue – within each specific party system.

In addition to the correlation analyses we developed earlier, we also estimated linear regressions using voters' issue positions as predictors of the policy positions of their congressional representatives. Although they lack statistical significance, these regressions are used to summarize distinct geometric relationships that indicate different types of issue congruence.[19] Here we report R-squared (R^2) statistics (predictive capacity of citizen preferences' on elite programmatic stances), intercepts (consistent and distinctive ordering of partisan positions at each level), and slopes (absolute differences in the average positioning of elites and masses). Interestingly, in almost every case we obtain positive slopes. Although this could be alternatively blamed on question-wording bias, we think it is reasonable to state that on average Latin American citizens tend to prefer lesser degrees of privatization than their congressional representatives. We also report Bonferroni matrices for

---

[19] See Kitschelt et al. (1999) for a detailed discussion. Powell (2004b) discusses alternative methodological strategies to measure issue congruence.

elites and citizens in order to identify individual parties that hold significantly different positions on the privatization issue. Web Appendix 4.3 (at www.cambridge.org/9780521114950) reproduces the graphs and related tables.

In general, the results are consistent with our overall representation scores. In both Ecuador and Bolivia, we observe small levels of issue congruence signaled by important crossings in the graph, as well as negative slope coefficients. Meanwhile, whereas in Ecuador the mean positions of both elites and citizens do not significantly differ, in Bolivia we found significant Bonferroni coefficients only between the voters of the MNR and the UCS. In Bolivia, while the congressional representatives of the MNR hold a similar position to that of their voters, the opposite holds for the UCS. In short, we conclude that most, though not all, political parties in these systems tend to misrepresent their voters' preferences on privatization.

In Mexico, in spite of a predominant centripetal pattern of competition, significant differences in party positions are observed among elites and masses; with the exception of the PRD, the parties are consistently aligned at both levels. Surprisingly, perhaps, PRD voters tend to prefer relatively more privatization than their peers in the PRI and the PAN. The PRD's relative inconsistency explains the reduced R^2 and the negative slope coefficient we report.

The graph obtained for Brazil and also the regression results are similar to the ones just described in the Mexican case. On the one hand, voters (except for those of the PSDB) present more statist views than their congressional representatives. Meanwhile, the PT and the PSDB are the parties for which we observe a higher degree of congruence between both levels, as the leaders of both the PMDB and the PFL lay more to the right than their voters. Finally, as in Bolivia, we observe significant differences at the mass level only among PT, PSDB, and PMDB voters.

The traditional two-party systems in our sample (Costa Rica and Colombia) present intermediate levels in terms of our aggregate scores and display similar patterns of representation regarding the issue of privatization. Although significant differences at the elite level are found in Costa Rica (along with a greater absolute difference between both levels as a result of relatively higher degrees of statism in the electorate), in both systems the electorates (and the elites in Colombia) sit very close together. Nevertheless, the relative ordering of parties across levels is consistent in both cases.

In Argentina, in turn, our regression is overdetermined because the electorates of the Alianza and the PJ share the same mean position. Although we fail to obtain significant ANOVA results at the elite level (a consequence of relatively high levels of internal inconsistency), the corresponding graph in Web Appendix 4.3 suggests that the leaders of the PJ are less representative of the mean preferences of their electorate than those of the UCR and the FREPASO.

Finally, the two cases that obtained the greater congruence levels in our index (Chile and Uruguay) also present the highest R^2 statistics, as well as positive regression coefficients. Be this as it may, Uruguay shows lower levels of consistency resulting from NE's inconsistent placement, as its voters are relatively less statist than its leaders. Meanwhile, the three major parties in the system are consistently aligned on the privatization issue, and significant differences exist between the leaders and voters of FA and those of the traditional parties (PC and PN). Meanwhile, the Chilean system displays the best congruence pattern as reflected by an R^2 of .84 and a positive slope coefficient. Indeed, issue congruence would have been even greater had we considered the two electoral alliances – Concertación (PS, PDC, and PPD) and Alianza (UDI and RN) – that currently compete in Chilean politics. Although we find greater levels of polarization at the elite level, the Bonferroni results suggest that issue preferences of voters and leaders of both electoral coalitions are clearly distinct and consistent. In spite of this, it is also clear that the leaders of UDI and RN are less representative of the views of their voters, at least with respect to the issue of privatization.

CONCLUSION: REPRESENTATION SCORES COMPARED TO OTHER INDICATORS OF PPS

We continue to uncover significant heterogeneity among Latin American countries regarding the degree to which they demonstrate attributes of programmatic party structuration. The analyses in this chapter show that party elites in some countries truly represent the interests of their party supporters. Not surprisingly, we find the highest levels of representation in Chile and Uruguay – countries with strong histories of party competition, institutionalization, and socioeconomic development. On the other end of the representation scale, we are also not surprised to find Ecuador with the lowest levels when it comes to this aspect of programmatic party structuration: Ecuador consistently falls short across all our measures thus far (see Chapters 2 and 3). If we consider the "best case" scenario index, Bolivia obtains the same (low) ranking as that of Ecuador. Although it would be premature to claim that the index developed in this chapter has such a predictive power, it is interesting to note that both Ecuador and Bolivia underwent deep party system crises a few years after our measurement was taken. Indeed, the countries that we now retrospectively diagnose as showing the lowest levels of issue congruence in the region subsequently went through a significant "crisis of political representation," as characterized by Mainwaring, Bejarano, and Pizarro (2006). One harbinger of the emergence of antiparty, populist politics in these countries, then, may have been the comparatively low levels of representation, as measured by elite-mass (in)congruence on issue positions.

Beyond this speculation, in this concluding section, we pause to compare our measure of representation with the components of programmatic

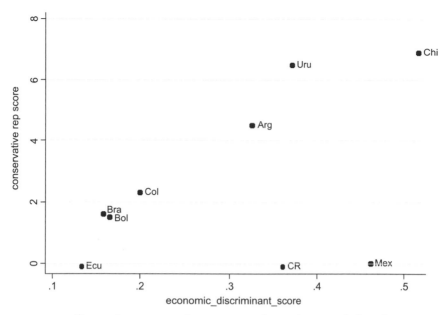

FIGURE 4.1. Comparing conservative representation and economic function scores.

party structuration that we examined in Chapters 2 and 3. Figures 4.1 and 4.2 display scatterplots that show the extent to which our conservative representation scores correspond to values on the economic partisan divide measure (Chapter 2) and the symbolic partisan left-right measure (Chapter 3). Because of our reduced sample, only nine observations appear in Figures 4.1 and 4.2. Later in this volume, we examine in more detail two particular dimensions of representation: religion and economics. For now, as a broad brush, we make our comparisons with the general conservative representation score.

The first fact to note is that there is a moderately high level of correspondence among our measures. For the nine countries examined in this chapter, the correlation between the conservative representation and the economic partisan divide scores (Figure 4.1) is .46. Yet there are two clear outliers: Costa Rica and Mexico. Removing these momentarily from the analysis, we find a correlation of .96 for the remaining seven countries. In Chile, we find high scores on both. In Uruguay, we find a high score on representation and a fairly high score on the economic partisan divide measure. Argentina is our intermediate case, with moderate scores on both. Finally, we find that partisans in Brazil, Bolivia, Colombia, and Ecuador tend not to be very distinguishable on the basis of economic policy stances, nor does there exist anything beyond low-to-moderate levels of representation in these countries – that is, these four cases score low on both measures.

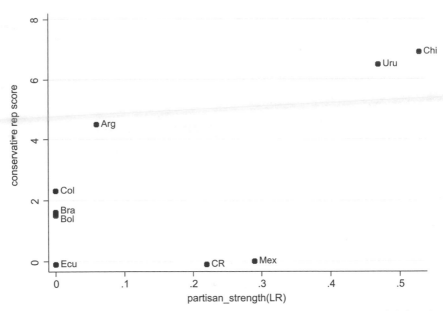

FIGURE 4.2. Comparing conservative representation and partisan strength left-right scores.

We find a similar story in Figure 4.2. Here, the correlation for all nine countries is 0.62 (but when Costa Rica and Mexico are excluded from the analysis, that statistic bounces up to 0.90). At both extremes of the distribution, the results we obtain in our study of elite-mass congruence are largely collinear with those discussed in Chapter 3 on the left-right semantics and are therefore reassuring. In particular, Chile and Uruguay obtain once again the most positive appraisals, while Colombia, Brazil, and especially Ecuador and Bolivia gravitate toward the bottom end of our representation index. Three cases present relevant discrepancies that are theoretically interesting and that allow us to complement (and weight more appropriately) previous results according to the scope of mass-elite issue congruence. First, although we find low levels of left-right structure in Argentina (a legacy of the historical trajectory of the party system and a particular result of the characteristics of the PJ as a highly influential catchall party), in this chapter we find intermediate levels of issue congruence between parties and elites. Second, and to the contrary, Mexico and Costa Rica score lower in terms of our index of mass-elite congruence than what we could have expected on the basis of our previous measures.

The case of Mexico (undergoing at the time of our data a transition to democracy that could cause economic and governance issues to have different salience levels for elites and masses) provides an interesting illustration. While left-right structure at the elite level is relatively high and seems to be driven by programmatic stances related to economic issues, such structure does not seem to help in providing efficient programmatic linkages to voters, who at that time, might have related to parties on the basis of issue stances that dealt with the political transition process (or, possibly, on the basis of nonprogrammatic linkages). Moreover, parties were, and have been, attempting to reach out to supporters of different ideological stripes (in particular, the PRI and the PAN; on the latter, see Magaloni and Moreno 2003; Moreno 2003). And, party supporters themselves have frequently displayed quite divergent opinions on key issues (see Estévez and Magaloni 2000), making it difficult to detect significant divides within this group. Thus, even though elites in Mexico show moderate levels of division on economic policy stances, this relatively limited divergence when also combined with wide variation among party supporters is not sufficient to translate into even correspondingly moderate levels of representation.

Turning to consider the case of Costa Rica, one potential reason for low representation scores may lie in recent developments within its party system. While portions of the party system have collapsed under the brunt of corruption scandals, there were earlier signs of voter discontent. According to Lehoucq (2005), electoral rules specific to the system "bred centrism to the point of alienating large chunks of voters," and, by the 1990s, citizens frustrated by the consequent lack of representation commonly complained that "the PLN and PUSC were mirroring each other."[20] More specifically, the implementation of (gradual) neoliberal reforms under the leadership of the social-democratic PLN in Costa Rica might have contributed to programmatic diffuseness in the system, as the party that crafted the country's "welfare state" contributed to its dismantling.[21] Although we found relatively high levels of congruence for some economic issues (privatization and job creation), we also observed partisan crossings in others (unemployment insurance). Furthermore, we seldom found significant differences along these issues, and even the few significant differences did not appear simultaneously at both levels.[22]

---

[20] The decay of the system is also seen in a substantial increase in independents and a decline in turnout (Lehoucq 2005). It may also provide an explanation for the high level of nonrespondents to the question about voter preference, which was discussed in note 8.

[21] Seligson (2002) argues that declining democratic legitimacy observed in the system is part of the same phenomenon.

[22] Why would Colombia retain a higher score than Costa Rica, despite having only two parties in the analysis? One possibility is that party system fragmentation in the 1990s, following the introduction of the 1991 constitution, has helped pull parties and their adherents somewhat away from the center. Interestingly, Costa Rica's party system has also begun to fragment in more recent times; it remains to be seen, then, if fragmentation will increase representation as new political groups (e.g., the PLN splinter group, Citizen Action Party, which won 25 percent of the vote in the 2002 legislative elections) present citizens with more appealing platforms (on the fragmentation of the two-party system, see Lehoucq 2005).

APPENDIX 4.1. *Parties Included (bold font) in and Excluded from Analysis*

	Elite N	Mass N		Elite N	Mass N
Argentina			Colombia		
FREPASO	11	296[a]	P Liberal	41	338
UCR	19		P Conserv	14	160
PJ	24	222	Independent	0	83
UCEDE	3	0	Costa Rica		
ACCION	0	31	**PLN**	25	150
Bolivia			**PUSC**	23	112
MBL	4	6	Fuerza Dem	0	43
CONDEPA	6	12	Ecuador		
MIR	7	91	Pachakutik	8	11
UCS	17	70	ID	3	100
SyD	3	0	**DP**	10	151
MNR	23	114	**PRE**	14	163
ADN	9	95	FRA	3	3
NFR	0	8	**PSC**	24	175
IU	0	8	PUN	0	4
Brazil			PL	0	10
PSB	4	4	CFP	0	4
PT	9	283	APRE	0	1
PcdoB	3	3	MPD	0	13
PSDB	10	118	PSFA	0	1
PMDB	16	121	NP	0	19
PFL	12	49	Mexico		
PTB	3	10	**PRD**	23	268
PPB	6	8	**PRI**	64	333
PV	0	3	**PAN**	35	271
PSC	0	1	PT	0	27
PRONA	0	4	PCD	0	3
PL	0	2	PVEM	0	40
PDT	0	26	Uruguay		
PSTU	0	2	**Frente Amplio**	25	306
PPS	0	2	**Nuevo Espacio**	4	29
Chile			**PC**	22	227
Socialista	13	95	**PN**	22	221
PPD	11	111			
PDC	31	214			
UDI	12	91			
RenoNacl	23	71			
PRSD	0	3			
UCCP	0	11			
PHV	0	4			
PC	0	30			

[a]FREPASO and UCR partisans combined.

5

Ideological Cohesion of Political Parties
in Latin America

Kirk A. Hawkins and Scott Morgenstern

While it is common to talk about political parties as unitary actors, parties generally harbor members with disparate opinions on important issues. In this chapter we describe and explain the varying level of ideological cohesion – the degree to which party members agree on political issues – in Latin America.

Cohesion is an important indicator of the nature of a party and, by extension, relations between that party and other political actors in the system. Foremost, cohesion affects the chain of relations between voters, parties, and legislators. If parties are cohesive, then voters can focus their attention on national party platforms and campaigns, safely assuming that the parties' local representatives will support the same objectives. This conception excites scholars concerned with the personal vote or party "nationalization." (APSA 1950; Cain, Ferejohn, and Fiorina 1987; Morgenstern and Swindle 2005). Party cohesion also influences interparty negotiations by determining whether some or all of a party's members are potential coalition members for particular parties or the executive. Within a party, cohesion helps determine the willingness of backbenchers to entrust their party leaders with delegated authority (a defining trait of conditional party government; Aldrich and Rohde 2001). It also influences the party's ideological placement. Cohesion, then, is a defining factor in explaining patterns of legislative activity.

In this chapter we focus on cohesion as an indicator and facilitator of programmatic structuration. From the perspective of the politician, if the party operates in a system characterized by a programmatic mode of linkage – that is, if the party's electoral success depends primarily on the provision of policies – then the politician will be able to factor his or her policy preferences into the decision of which party to join. Thus, in a programmatic party system, a self-selection of party members takes place that results in higher cohesion. Likewise, from the perspective of voters, party cohesion helps individuals assess the credibility of a party's programmatic positions. Voters confront the possibility of opportunistic behavior by their politicians under conditions of information asymmetry. If the party they are considering lacks the institutional mechanisms or the attachment to a charismatic leader that can generate discipline, the ideological cohesion of its members makes it more likely to act on commitments made ex-ante in an electoral campaign. In other words, as Schattschneider (1942) argued, cohesive parties facilitate responsible partisan government.

The goal of our chapter is to describe and compare the levels of cohesion across countries and individual parties, as well as across different issues, by exploring a variety of indicators drawn from the University of Salamanca's Parliamentary Elites survey. We find that Latin American parties are not very cohesive – there are few issues that generate even a moderate level of agreement among the members of any given party. Still, we show some important distinctions both across borders and among parties within particular countries. The patterns of variance that emerge generally match those found in the preceding descriptive chapters. We offer a few tentative explanatory notes here, but leave the primary explanation of the trends for Chapter 6.

MEASURING COHESION

In order to measure the cohesion of a given party, we examine its legislators' responses to questions in the Salamanca survey. Because we take agreement on these questions to indicate cohesion, we operationalize cohesion as the standard deviation of the responses. A low standard deviation, therefore, implies high levels of cohesion and vice versa.[1]

While any issues theoretically could be pertinent to measuring cohesion, cohesion is irrelevant for issues that do not actually divide the parties. We thus rely on twenty of the twenty-seven survey questions used elsewhere in this volume. These are the twenty that correspond to the four main issue

---

[1] The design and execution of some of the survey questions create potential problems in using the standard deviation as an indicator of cohesion. Specifically, some of the questions use categorical or nonordinal scales, several questions have very few (less than 5) response categories, and some of the parties have a small number of respondents (meaning that, if just one or two members do not give the same response as the others, the standard deviation of the party's response increases greatly). As a robustness check, we developed a second indicator of cohesion that we call the modal percent. The formula for calculating this statistic is:

$$\text{model percent} = 1 - ((n_{\text{mode}}/n_{\text{total}}) * (k/k - 1) - 1/(k - 1))$$

where k is the number of categories in the response scale and n is the number of responses or observations. Very simply, the modal percent indicates the percent of respondents in any party that choose the modal response, adjusted for the number of possible responses; in addition, we reverse the scale to make it more compatible with the standard deviation. The correlation between standard deviation and modal response in our sample is usually more than .75. Because the overall results using both measures are similar, in this chapter we present data that reflects the standard deviation method of measuring cohesion.

divides found in Chapter 2: economic policy (v49, v50, v64, v65, v69, v70, v71, and v72), regime (v11, v15, v26, and v32), economic nationalism (v54, v57, v59, and v61), and religion (v210, v235, v236, and v240). We also make use of the two questions (Chapter 3) used to gauge left-right placement (v132 and v234). In order to enhance comparability across questions, we have rescaled all survey questions that have interval- or ordinal-level scales to fit a standard scale from -1 to 1. Consequently, the values for cohesion range from 0 to 1, with 0 indicating perfect cohesion and 1 complete diffuseness. In this chapter we do not impute missing values because of the tendency this will have of biasing the standard deviations.[2]

By themselves, however, our cohesion measures may be biased or inefficient if the policy issues to which the party members are responding do not represent relevant political divisions. First, if an issue is so uncontroversial that all respondents in all parties agree on it, then the resulting high cohesion is not particularly puzzling and will give a false impression about the overall degree of cohesion in certain parties. For example, the survey shows that Argentine parties are highly cohesive around the question of whether the military played a positive role in the decades of the 1970s and 1980s, but the parties are all in strong agreement that the military's role was a negative one – the military role is thus a valence issue, and the presence of high cohesion is uninteresting. Second, parties could show low or high cohesion on issues that lack current relevance to their country's politics; including such issues could bias our data or simply add noise. For example, issues regarding church-state relations were divisive in many Latin American countries in the late nineteenth and early twentieth centuries. These may still leave traces in opinion divides that would serve as useful predictors of party membership and generate high cohesion, but for the most part these issues are no longer politically relevant. Using them as indicators of cohesion would be misleading. In short, in order to describe cohesion meaningfully, we ideally want to consider issues on which the parties in a polity are significantly divided and that are salient for the political debate and the parties' efforts to attract voters.

Unfortunately, as noted in the introduction to Part I, the survey fails to include a set of questions that ask respondents to gauge the salience of the particular issues included in our analysis. We know that economic issues writ broadly tend to be seen as more important, especially when compared with regime issues, but many of the survey questions lack a corresponding

---

[2] If we replace missing values with averages from across the entire set of countries, we will tend to increase the apparent cohesion of moderate parties and decrease the apparent cohesion of extreme parties; if, on the other hand, we use the Amelia technique, we will increase the apparent cohesion of all parties. These biases are not as pernicious in other chapters because of the analytical techniques they use, and so it is more appropriate for them to impute missing values.

measure of salience. While bearing these results in mind, we employ two correctives that attempt to reduce the potential biases just noted. First, we calculate the divisiveness of each issue-question and use the two or four most divisive questions in each issue basket for calculating cohesion. We calculate divisiveness by performing an analysis of variance (ANOVA) on each survey question, using the respondent's party as the grouping variable, and then reporting the p-value associated with the F-test. We consider as divisive any question with a p-value of .10 or lower. Although imperfect, this technique does allow us to nearly eliminate the first source of error that results from including valence issues, and it lets us tap into issues that are more likely to be relevant for political competition.[3]

Table 5.1 indicates the total number of divisive issues in each country for each basket of questions. Aside from left-right placements, which are highly divisive in almost all twelve countries (the partial exception is Argentina), the variance across countries and issue areas is dramatic. Although a few countries are divisive over few if any issues (Colombia, Brazil, Ecuador, Peru, and the Dominican Republic), most countries are divisive over several questions and at least two substantive issue areas, especially economic policy and religion. Web Appendix 5.1 (at www.cambridge.org/9780521114950) provides the actual p-values for all variables in each country. On economic policy, eight countries divide on the issues of privatization (v49 and v50) and price controls (v64), seven divide on whether the government should provide unemployment insurance (v71), and six divide on whether the government should provide employment opportunities and subsidies for basic products (v65 and v72). Only three countries are divided over the issues of government housing (v69) and social security (v70), suggesting either that there is considerable agreement on these issues already or that they are simply not politically relevant. Religion and regime issues generate somewhat less divisiveness, with party systems in seven countries dividing on abortion (v235) and whether legislators from different parties consider themselves very religious (v240), and party systems in eight countries dividing over the effectiveness of the judicial system (v32). Questions on economic nationalism generate little overall divisiveness, but the issue area is particularly

---

[3] We recognize, following Sani and Sartori (1983) that not all issues on which the parties disagree are politically active. Thus, we cannot eliminate our second source of error. Furthermore, because ANOVA estimates take into account the within-party variance, our technique for estimating divisiveness probably gives a premium to issues with high cohesion and may introduce its own upward bias. Nevertheless, the low cohesion we actually find should help offset these concerns.

An obvious alternative to using ANOVA to gauge divisiveness is to measure the difference in party means for each issue. We initially considered this technique but found it even more inadequate. It cannot easily cope with multiparty systems (which difference in means do we consider?), and it does not adjust for the number of respondents that underlies each party mean. It also fails to provide a precise statistic for correcting standard deviations in party systems that lack any absolutely divisive issues.

TABLE 5.1. *Divisive Issues*

Country	Left-Right Semantics (2 possible)	Economic Policy (8 possible)	Religion (4 possible)	Regime (4 possible)	Economic Nationalism (4 possible)	Total (issue questions only)
Uruguay	2	7	4	2	4	17
Chile	2	7	4	4	1	16
Mexico	2	8	4	1	0	13
Venezuela	2	5	3	3	1	12
Argentina	1	6	2	2	0	10
Bolivia	2	3	1	2	2	8
Costa Rica	2	5	1	1	1	8
Colombia	2	1	3	0	1	5
Brazil	2	2	0	2	0	4
Ecuador	2	1	0	1	2	4
Peru	2	2	0	2	0	4
Dominican Republic	2	2	1	0	0	3
TOTAL (% POSSIBLE)	23 (95.8)	49 (51.0)	23 (47.9)	19 (39.6)	12 (25.0)	126 (47.7)

Note: Divisive issues defined as issues for which the F-test of the ANOVA generates a p-value of .10 or less.

divisive in Uruguay. The fact that economic policy is the most divisive issue area (again, outside of left-right semantics) correlates with the findings in Chapter 2, which indicate that most programmatic structuration occurs around this set of issues; it also confirms the limited information we gleaned from the survey's module of salience measures. Because of this tendency, we focus on economic policy issues for much of the rest of this chapter while still providing results for other issue areas.

Unfortunately, some countries lack even a minimum number of divisive issues in each issue basket (e.g., Brazil, Colombia, the Dominican Republic, Ecuador, and Peru). We therefore make a second correction to the cohesion measures. In all countries we rely on the survey questions that showed the highest level of divisiveness, but in order to give more weight to the questions that yield distinctions among the parties, we increase the original standard deviation by a factor based on the p-value from the ANOVA, specifically, $1 + \text{p-value}$. Thus, survey questions that were very divisive (and have low p-values in the ANOVA) are left largely unchanged, while less-divisive questions (which have non-negligible p-values) are slightly increased. In practice, this results in a set of values that are slightly higher than the original figures but still close to the original mathematical limits of the standard deviation (± 1). Because this is a crude correction that necessarily incorporates some arbitrariness, we report both the original and corrected versions of our cohesion indicators throughout the chapter.[4]

DESCRIBING SYSTEM COHESION

Left-Right Placement

We begin our description by looking at cohesion on left-right placement. Unlike the survey questions on specific issues, which we consider next, questions on left-right placement have the virtue of being highly comparable with data on cohesion from Kitschelt et al.'s (1999) study of programmatic structuration in Eastern Europe, which also asks respondents in those countries about their parties' left-right placement. Because of this, the data on left-right cohesion provide us with a benchmark for assessing the

---

[4] Specifically, the size of the multiplier is somewhat arbitrary, as there is no mathematical reason why it should be $1 + \text{p-value}$ instead of, say, $1 + 2^*\text{p-value}$ or $1 + .5^*\text{p-value}$. That said, we selected a multiplier that would produce figures with meaningful cardinality. A smaller multiplier than $1 + \text{p-value}$ would produce penalties too small to make any difference in the original figures, and a larger multiplier would generate actual values well outside the mathematical limits imposed by the numerical scale of the survey questions. As a check, we performed all of the analyses in this chapter using an alternative method of penalizing low values of divisiveness – one that essentially assigned parties a standard deviation or modal percent of 1.00 on any issue where they were not divisive – and achieved very similar results. Those results are available from the authors.

TABLE 5.2. *Average Cohesion on Left-Right Placement*
(standard deviation only)

Country	Party Placement	Self-Placement
Latin America		
Argentina	0.32	0.35
Bolivia	0.23	0.23
Brazil	0.26	0.27
Chile	0.24	0.25
Colombia	0.41	0.43
Costa Rica	0.26	0.30
Dominican Republic	0.37	0.33
Ecuador	0.29	0.28
Mexico	0.24	0.34
Peru	0.24	0.38
Uruguay	0.18	0.20
Venezuela	0.24	0.32
Average	0.27	0.31
Correlation	0.70	
Eastern Europe		
Bulgaria	0.38	–
Czech Republic	0.33	–
Hungary	0.22	–
Poland	0.34	–
Average	0.34	–

cohesion of Latin American party systems in more absolute terms. As noted in Chapter 3, respondents were asked to indicate the left-right placement of both themselves and their party, and we report the results for both of these questions. Because all countries but Argentina have a high level of divisiveness on both of these questions (and, in Argentina, the exception is borderline), we do not provide any corrected values of cohesion.

Table 5.2 displays country-level results for both of these questions on left-right placement and compares them with data from Kitschelt et al. (1999). Both sets of results are averages of the individual parties in each system, although in our results each party's cohesion is weighted according to its share of seats in the legislature when the survey was administered. Our country-level pattern correlates at a moderately high level with the indicator of left-right substantive content devised in Chapter 3 ($r = -.60$, $p < .04$ for party placement; $r = -.68$, $p < .02$ for self-placement), suggesting that the countries with the most meaningful understandings of left and right are also those with the highest levels of cohesion – a result that supports the reliability of our indicators.

As the data indicate, cohesion on left-right placement in Latin American party systems is relatively high and, in particular, is very close to levels in Eastern Europe. The average standard deviations for party placement and self-placement (0.27 and 0.31, respectively) show that more than two-thirds of respondents locate themselves in the same one-third of the left-right scale as fellow party members. The average standard deviation for the party placement variable is not statistically distinguishable from that for Eastern Europe; a two-tailed difference of means test is significant only at the p < .32 level. Of course, we know from Chapter 3 that some portion of this cohesion reflects agreement about mere labels and not substance, so we must qualify these findings somewhat. Yet overall these data give us some initial optimism that, similar to the Eastern European party systems, the Latin American party systems distinguish themselves on the basis of programmatic issues.

There is some variance across our indicators. Although our two measures of left-right cohesion produce very similar results (the self- and party placement cohesion results are correlated at 0.70), cohesion tends to be higher on party placement than on self-placement. The difference of means between these two indicators is significant at the p < .07 level (two-tailed test). This result suggests that either parties really do aggregate the preferences of roughly similar groups of politicians into tightly bundled packages or (more pessimistically) that Latin American legislators use the terms "left" and "right" differently when they apply it to themselves than when they apply it to their parties. Without additional data, however, we cannot say much more about what causes this difference.

There is also important variance across countries within the region. On one end of the scale is Uruguay, where the parties' standard deviation scores (0.18–0.20) are much lower than any of the countries in the East European sample. This contrasts with the Colombian parties, whose scores (0.41–0.43) are higher than any of the East European countries. Yet we should not overstate this cross-national variance. Most of the countries in Latin America are very close to the regional average, and, as we demonstrate in this chapter, the differences among countries on this measure are less than the difference between average regional cohesion on left-right placement and average regional cohesion on specific issues. Indeed, the least cohesive country on left-right placement in Latin America (Colombia) is about as cohesive as the most cohesive countries on specific issues (Bolivia and Chile).

Issue Placement

This picture of high cohesion with moderate variance changes dramatically when we consider cohesion on specific issues. As noted, we consider cohesion on the issues in each country that manifest the greatest divisiveness, as indicated in Table 5.1, and we provide two sets of figures: one a straightforward average of the standard deviation on each of these most divisive questions, and the other a "corrected" average that adjusts each standard deviation according to the level of divisiveness of the issue, using a factor

TABLE 5.3. *Average Cohesion, Most Divisive Issues (uncorrected standard deviation)*

Country	All Questions	Economic Policy	Regime	Economic Nationalism	Religion
Argentina	0.47	0.46	0.37	0.53	0.53
Bolivia	0.39	0.42	0.33	0.47	0.29
Brazil	0.56	0.54	0.43	0.68	0.60
Chile	0.39	0.46	0.26	0.40	0.36
Colombia	0.49	0.51	0.35	0.53	0.56
Costa Rica	0.49	0.54	0.38	0.43	0.56
Dominican Republic	0.45	0.52	0.23	0.49	0.46
Ecuador	0.53	0.57	0.43	0.49	0.61
Mexico	0.55	0.50	0.61	0.60	0.54
Peru	0.51	0.49	0.57	0.39	0.62
Uruguay	0.41	0.46	0.20	0.49	0.44
Venezuela	0.44	0.46	0.32	0.44	0.51
Average	0.47	0.49	0.38	0.50	0.51

(1 + p-value) derived from our ANOVA. For economic issues, we calculate the average cohesion of all parties in a country on the four most divisive issues; for the issue baskets concerning political regime, economic nationalism, and religion, where we have fewer policy items to work with, we calculate national averages of party cohesion on the two most divisive issues. For each country, the average standard deviation for any survey question is calculated by taking the arithmetic mean of the standard deviation for all parties in that country on these two or four questions, weighted by each party's share of seats in the lower house of the legislature (using the same weights found in Web Appendix E at www.cambridge.org/9780521114950). Because different issues divide the parties in different countries, the particular questions used to calculate the average cohesion for each country may vary.

Tables 5.3 and 5.4 present these national averages of issue cohesion. Using either the initial or the corrected version of our indicators, the main result is clearly a lack of strong cohesion for any country. For all issues except regime, the standard deviation rarely drops below 0.4, suggesting that typically about two-thirds of party members are more than half the scale apart from each other, or that less than half of any party's members agree on the same response. This result is especially surprising given the data on issue cohesion in Eastern Europe from Kitschelt et al., as well as additional data on the Russian party system reported in Kitschelt and Smyth (2002). These other studies estimate average issue cohesion scores of around a standard deviation of 0.35 for Eastern and Central Europe (grand mean over all issues) and a standard deviation of 0.45 for Russia (grand mean over two different surveys), figures in the same league as their cohesion on left-right placement.

TABLE 5.4. *Average Cohesion, Most Divisive Issues (corrected standard deviation)*

Country	All Questions	Economic Policy	Regime	Economic Nationalism	Religion
Argentina	0.51	0.47	0.37	0.67	0.55
Bolivia	0.41	0.45	0.35	0.48	0.31
Brazil	0.67	0.60	0.45	1.01	0.71
Chile	0.40	0.46	0.26	0.44	0.36
Colombia	0.55	0.56	0.46	0.61	0.58
Costa Rica	0.52	0.54	0.41	0.49	0.64
Dominican Republic	0.52	0.56	0.28	0.69	0.49
Ecuador	0.60	0.62	0.52	0.51	0.74
Mexico	0.62	0.50	0.80	0.76	0.54
Peru	0.63	0.57	0.60	0.51	0.93
Uruguay	0.41	0.46	0.21	0.49	0.44
Venezuela	0.45	0.47	0.32	0.48	0.51
Average	0.53	0.52	0.42	0.60	0.57

Of course, the East European studies are not perfectly comparable with ours on this indicator because they use somewhat different questions and because they measure party placement rather than self-placement. However, even if we adjusted our Latin American data to account for the possible difference between party placement and self-placement scores, the average, overall cohesion in Latin America (between standard deviations of 0.41 and 0.46 if we adjust for low divisiveness) would still be as low as that of the least cohesive party systems in Central and Eastern Europe, party systems regarded as only weakly programmatic.[5] Only Uruguay's, Chile's, and Bolivia's party systems would begin to approach the levels of cohesion seen in Eastern Europe (roughly, standard deviations between 0.34 and 0.36). Thus, our data on specific issues do not support our findings on left-right placement and instead suggest that party systems in the region have very low levels of issue cohesion. If we used this metric alone, we would be forced to reach very pessimistic conclusions about the region's programmatic structuration.

There is of course some variance within this general finding of low cohesion. As mentioned, Chile, Uruguay, and (somewhat surprisingly) Bolivia are countries with relatively higher levels of cohesion, followed by Argentina and Venezuela; Costa Rica and Mexico have increasingly lower levels; and Ecuador, Brazil, the Dominican Republic, Peru, and Colombia all have

[5] The adjustment is made using the ratio of average, country-level, left-right self- and party placement found in Table 5.2, or .27/.31. This adjustment is admittedly somewhat problematic because the difference of means between these two left-right cohesion indicators was only marginally statistically significant.

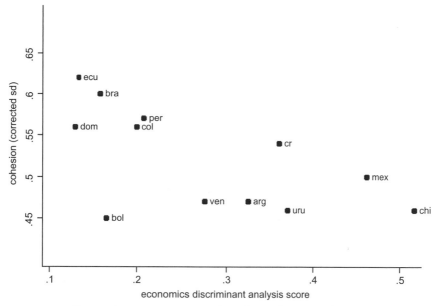

FIGURE 5.1. Comparing average economic policy cohesion and economic partisan divides.

extremely low levels of cohesion, especially after we correct for their lack of divisiveness. This pattern roughly matches what we saw in the analysis of left-right cohesion.

This variance is also consistent with the findings in Chapters 2 through 4. The following paragraphs compare the indicators from these chapters with our results for issue cohesion. Specifically, we inspect our cases with an eye to the question of where the national values of issue cohesion diverge from the countries' relative strength of partisan divides on the same dimensions, as reported in Chapter 2, Table 2.6; the substantive content of left-right semantics, as reported in Chapter 3, Table 3.2; and the representativeness of the party system, as reported in Chapter 4, Table 4.3. For the sake of simplicity, we consider only the results on economic policy, our most divisive issue basket, and we use only the corrected values of cohesion as these figures are arguably more meaningful than the uncorrected values.

Partisan Divides

Figure 5.1 is a scatterplot juxtaposing our country cohesion averages on economic policy issues (corrected) with the scores for partisan structuring of issue divides as found in Chapter 2 (Table 2.6). The resulting correlation is moderately high ($r = -.61$, $p < .04$) and allows us to distinguish three groups of countries. First, there are countries that are highly to moderately structured in terms of both relative average party cohesion and political partisan divides on economic issues. These include Chile and possibly Mexico, Uruguay, Costa Rica, Argentina, and Venezuela. Specifically, Chile consistently scores high on programmatic divides and has comparatively high cohesion, while Mexico, Uruguay, Costa Rica, Argentina, and Venezuela (in roughly that order) score in the middle range on these two attributes.

Second, in five other cases we have consistently low programmatic structuration on both the party cohesion and partisan divides dimensions – at least after controlling for possible overestimates of their cohesion. These five countries are Brazil, Peru, the Dominican Republic, Ecuador, and Colombia.

Finally, there is one difficult case where partisan divides and average cohesion measures clearly fail to match up, even after correcting for the lack of divisive issues: Bolivia has much higher cohesion than its weak partisan divides would have led us to expect. This discrepancy can possibly be explained by examining the idiosyncrasies of its domestic politics. First of all, most of the major Bolivian parties covered by our survey data in the late 1990s were characterized by extraordinarily high levels of personalism. This applies to the three traditional parties (MNR, ADN, and MIR), as well as the UCS, the newcomer thriving in the 1990s (cf. Gamarra 1996: 78). Second, all three established parties had at one time or another participated in electing a president and supporting neoliberal policies in the 1980s and 1990s and had migrated to the "right" side of the political spectrum (see Chapter 3), leaving a big gap in the political representations of their electoral constituencies (see Chapter 4); thus, the cohesion in Bolivia tends to be of a valence type, even though the party system passes our threshold of divisiveness on several questions. The combination of tightly knit internal organization and personalist control plus repositioning into a limited range on economic policy issues appears to result in a situation where minor programmatic differences on the economic dimension are not all that discernible (see Chapter 2, and the x-axis of Figures 5.1 and 5.2), and yet parties are still relatively cohesive on these issues. The fact that this discrepancy is repeated across the next two comparisons suggests that the level of cohesion is a misleading indicator of programmatic structuration for the Bolivian party system.

Substantive Content of Left-Right Semantics

Figure 5.2 compares the country-level cohesion on economic issues (corrected) to levels of substantive or partisan content in left-right semantics found in Table 3.2. The correlation is moderate but in the expected direction ($r = -.54$, $p < .07$).[6] We again see roughly three groups emerge, although a

---

[6] This correlation and the accompanying figure (Figure 5.2) are somewhat misleading in that the analysis in Chapter 3 finds that there is almost no economic content to left-right placement in Venezuela and Ecuador; rather, left-right labels in these two countries are associated with

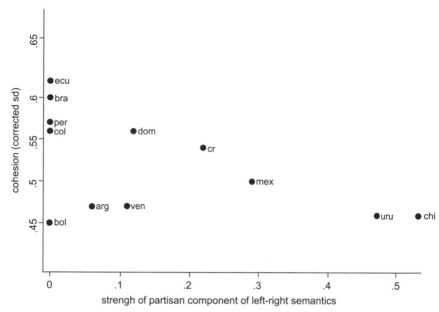

FIGURE 5.2. Comparing average economic policy cohesion and partisan left-right scores.

few countries shift positions. First, in the moderate to high category, Chile and now Uruguay show the highest levels of programmatic structuration on these dimensions, with relatively high cohesion and a strong substantive component to their understandings of the terms "left" and "right." Costa Rica and Mexico are again moderate cases of programmatic structuration. In contrast, Venezuela and Argentina are no longer in this intermediate category because the substantive content of their left-right semantics is lower than we would expect given their levels of cohesion.

In the second category, the Dominican Republic, Brazil, Peru, Ecuador, and Colombia again manifest low levels of programmatic structuration on both indicators after we adjust for their lack of divisive issues. In the third category, Bolivia and now Venezuela and Argentina stand out. Their substantive left-right content is very low, given their relatively high or moderate levels of cohesion and the correlation of this cohesion with the moderate strength of their economic partisan divides discussed in the previous section, at least for the latter two countries. The earlier explanation given for the divergence of cohesion and partisan divides in Bolivia may explain the divergence here also. In contrast, the other two divergences may indicate

human rights and regime issues. If we take this into account and set the figure for substantive left-right content in these two countries at 0, then the correlation drops slightly to r = −.51 (p < .09).

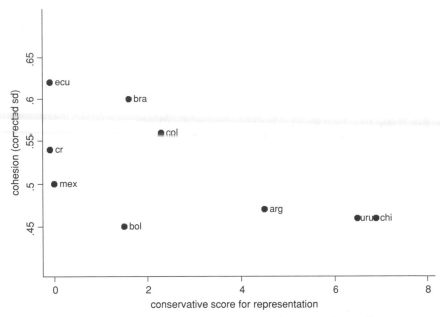

FIGURE 5.3. Comparing average economic policy cohesion and overall voter representation scores.

idiosyncratic results of the left-right measurement. In particular, Venezuela's low left-right substantive content may result from the presence of a peculiar New Left party (Causa R) emphasizing participatory democracy and rejecting traditional notions of left and right. This is evidenced by its odd placement in Table 3.1 at the center of the left-right spectrum (see also Buxton 2001 and López-Maya 1997). In Argentina, additional research on left-right semantics by Zechmeister (2006) suggests that the concepts of left and right are in fact very weak in this country, having been obfuscated by the presence of a strong populist party (the PJ) that occupies much of the electoral space normally filled by the traditional left.

Issue Representation

Finally, we compare the cohesion scores on economic issues with the scores for issue representation found in Table 4.3. Data are presented in Figure 5.3, which for simplicity compares the corrected values of cohesion with only the conservative representation scores. The lack of data on issue representation for three of our twelve countries (the Dominican Republic, Peru, and Venezuela) presents us with a handicap as we try to make this comparison. In addition, the representation scores take into account a reduced set of survey questions (eleven overall, and only three of the original eight economic policy questions) from all four issue baskets. Thus, this comparison must be considered much more tentative, and we forgo presenting any correlation coefficients (which, in any case, are not statistically significant).

As before, we can divide the countries into three categories. In the first category, that of moderate to high cohesion and issue representation, we again find Chile and Uruguay (with relatively high cohesion and high representation) and also Argentina (moderate cohesion and moderate representation). In the second category, that of low cohesion and low issue representation, we have Brazil, Colombia, and Ecuador. The placement of these countries is very similar to those found in the previous two comparisons.

In the third, odd category, we again have Bolivia but now also Costa Rica and Mexico. In all three of these cases, the levels of cohesion are much higher than we would expect given their relatively low levels of issue representation. The divergence of cohesion and partisan divides in Bolivia fits the pattern we have already seen in the previous scatterplots. In the case of Costa Rica and Mexico, the reasons for the divergence are not as clear. The most obvious explanation focuses on the peculiarities of their economic policy reforms over the past two decades. In these two countries, the traditional governing parties (the PLN and PRI) have both proved willing to embrace neoliberal reforms when in office in the 1980s and 1990s in spite of their earlier commitments to social policy. Thus, these parties are moderately cohesive on economic issues but lie far to the right of their constituents' preferences. This explanation is supported if we compare the representation scores with our cohesion averages for other issue baskets (regime, economic nationalism, and religion); in all of these other cases, Costa Rica and Mexico are no longer outliers, while Bolivia remains one. That said, we would expect similar divergence in the case of Argentina, where the PJ also engaged in neoliberal reforms during the 1990s that went against the party's traditional center-left stance. While we do find some divergence, the country's level of issue representation falls largely in line with its cohesion.

At the country level, our results for left-right cohesion are high and comparable with levels in postcommunist countries, but levels of issue cohesion are much lower in Latin America. Patterns of variance are similar to those for other indicators from previous chapters, especially after we correct for the lack of divisive issues in some countries. Because cohesion is the one indicator for which we are able to engage in direct comparison with a study from a different region, the implications are serious: low absolute levels of issue cohesion suggest that levels on the other indicators of programmatic structuration that we measured in previous chapters are similarly low in comparison with postcommunist countries. Although this and previous chapters point out important variance – typically, Chile and Uruguay (moderate programmatic structuration) versus the others (low or very low) – this within-region variance may be moderate when compared with the variance across Latin America and other regions. Of course, the results for left-right cohesion are at odds with this negative assessment, as they suggest that the programmatic structuration of party systems in Latin America is actually comparable to that of other party systems in regions of moderate or low democratic experience. The difference between these two indicators of cohesion – left-right placement versus issues – is hard to resolve. However, because our data on issue cohesion draw from a much larger number of questions and are based on specific ideas rather than vague ideological labels, we tend to place more stock in this result and remain somewhat pessimistic about the overall programmatic qualities of party systems in Latin America.

COHESION II: PATTERNS AT THE LEVEL OF INDIVIDUAL PARTIES

Unlike in other chapters, the indicator of programmatic party structuration that we explore – ideological cohesion – can easily be disaggregated to the level of individual parties; in fact, our country-level indicators are derived from party averages. An analysis of this party-level data is especially useful because it provides us with an opportunity to examine the party-level foundations of this element of programmatic party system structuration.

While there seems to be only moderate or low cohesion at the level of party systems in Latin America, as we step down the ladder of abstraction and consider the cohesion of individual parties we begin to see higher levels of cohesion and greater patterns of variance. These patterns of variance suggest both country- and party-level factors that may help explain patterns of cohesion and thus programmatic structuration in Latin America. Because later chapters engage in a more focused study of the causes of programmatic structuration across countries, we emphasize here only a few of the most evident party-level factors and abstain from a comprehensive multivariate analysis.

Left-Right Placement

As in the previous section, we start with cohesion of left-right placement in order to provide a benchmark for comparison. Party-level cohesion (an average of self- and party placement) is found in Table 5.5 along with a few other indicators that will be discussed later, with parties ranked according to their scores. A complete set of numerical data on the standard deviation for all parties on all questions can be found in Web Appendix D (at www.cambridge.org/9780521114950). As we look at individual parties, the previous country-level pattern of high cohesion of left-right self- and party placement is in many ways repeated. Only three of the forty-one parties have an average standard deviation greater than 0.40 (the PC and PL in Colombia, and the PRSC in the Dominican Republic), while three parties actually have average standard deviations of less than 0.20 (the PC in Uruguay, and LCR and MAS in Venezuela).

TABLE 5.5. *Cohesion on Left-Right Placement, by Party*
(standard deviation)

Party	Country	N	Average of Self- and Party Placement Scores
LCR	Venezuela	13	0.15
PC	Uruguay	22	0.18
MAS	Venezuela	8	0.19
PSDB	Brazil	10	0.20
PDC	Chile	31	0.20
FA	Uruguay	25	0.20
UCS	Bolivia	17	0.20
PS	Chile	13	0.21
AD	Venezuela	18	0.22
APRA	Peru	7	0.22
UPP	Peru	12	0.22
PRD	Mexico	23	0.23
PRI	Mexico	64	0.24
MIR	Bolivia	7	0.24
PMDB	Brazil	16	0.24
RN	Chile	23	0.26
PN	Uruguay	22	0.26
COPEI	Venezuela	18	0.26
PT	Brazil	9	0.27
PUSC	Costa Rica	23	0.27
ADN	Bolivia	9	0.27
PPD	Chile	11	0.28
PLD	Dominican Republic	13	0.28
MNR	Bolivia	23	0.28
CONDEPA	Bolivia	6	0.28
PRE	Ecuador	14	0.28
FREPASO	Argentina	11	0.30
DP	Ecuador	10	0.30
PK	Ecuador	8	0.31
PLN	Costa Rica	25	0.32
UCR	Argentina	19	0.33
PSC	Ecuador	24	0.34
PAN	Mexico	35	0.34
C95	Peru	52	0.34
UDI	Chile	11	0.35
PRD	Dominican Republic	29	0.35
PJ	Argentina	24	0.36
PFL	Brazil	12	0.36
Convergencia	Venezuela	9	0.38
PC	Colombia	14	0.40
PRSC	Dominican Republic	19	0.41
PL	Colombia	41	0.44
Average			0.28

Some of the high levels of cohesion we find at this level of analysis are probably the result of country-level factors such as long-term trends in party-system development or short-term factors such as electoral rules; an ANOVA of this data using the country as the grouping variable produces an F-test significant at the $p < .006$ level and an adjusted R^2 of .37. However, there is obviously considerable variance that cannot be explained merely by the average country tendency, suggesting that we must also consider the level of individual parties. Several party-level causes suggest themselves just by eyeballing the results in Table 5.5; most of these are repeated with greater force in the analysis of party-level issue cohesion below.[7] For example, the overall average of these unweighted party-level standard deviations (0.28) is slightly lower than the weighted country-level averages back in Table 5.2 (about 0.29), an indication that the larger parties are somewhat less cohesive and that cohesion is inversely related to the electoral strength of parties; this difference, however, is significant at only the $p < .31$ level (one-tailed t-test). If we consider a slightly different measure of electoral strength, the average size of the party's legislative cohort over the previous twenty years (lower chamber only), this modest difference is repeated. The parties in the top half of the list have an average of 23 percent of the seats in the chamber, while parties in the bottom half have 25 percent; this difference is significant at the $p < .36$ level (one-tailed t-test). Likewise, the parties with the highest cohesion tend to have less governing experience; about 57 percent of the parties in the upper half of the table have held the presidency at some time in their history, versus 62 percent of those in the bottom half; this difference is also significant at only the $p < .38$ level (one-tailed t-test). Another, stronger pattern we find which reaffirms some of the results in Chapter 3 is that parties of the left tend to be more cohesive than parties of the right ($r = .40$, $p < .01$ for party placement, and $r = .25$, $p < .10$ for self-placement). This pattern may reflect the unique meanings of "left" and "right" in the region, where "right" is often a pejorative associated with the historical legacy of inequality and oligarchic politics; or it may reflect the relatively greater levels of development of leftist ideologies in the region. Although interesting in its own right, this phenomenon has less relevance to a general study of cohesion and is discussed at greater length in Chapter 3. Finally, there is some tendency for more extremist parties to be more cohesive; that is, while parties on the left tend to be more cohesive than parties on the right, the most cohesive parties within this group are also the most extreme. The correlation is only $r = -.20$ ($p < .20$) for party placement, but $r = -.40$ ($p < .01$) for self-placement, where extremism is measured as the absolute distance of the party from the center of the scale. This pattern may

---

[7] The fact that these causal patterns for party-level cohesion are generally stronger when we examine issue cohesion suggests again that a portion of the left-right placement scores captures identity markers rather than programmatic substance.

be a result of the nature of the party (extremist parties also tend to be newer, less experienced at government, and less concerned about appealing to the median voter) or it may simply be a statistical artifact (a party would lose its statistical extremist position if some members diverged from that extreme).

Issue Cohesion

Table 5.6 provides similar, party-level cohesion data for substantive issues (corrected values), with parties ranked according to their average overall cohesion. The numbers here are averages over the four issue baskets, divisive issues only, with economic policy weighted twice as heavily.

Not surprisingly, individual party cohesion on issues is much lower than cohesion of left-right placement, reaffirming our earlier country-level results. Parties generally have a standard deviation of 0.45 or greater, and the difference of means between party-level cohesion on left-right placement and party-level cohesion on issues is statistically significant at the $p < .000$ level (one-tailed t-test). Yet there is again considerable variance across parties. If we consider data on specific issues and issue bundles (see Web Appendix D at www.cambridge.org/9780521114950) half of the parties have a cohesion of a standard deviation of 0.40 or less on at least one issue bundle (usually the regime divide), and several parties reach a high level of cohesion on more than one issue: FREPASO and UCR in Argentina; ADN and CONDEPA in Bolivia; the PC in Uruguay; UDI, the PDC, the PPD, and the PS in Chile; and Convergencia and AD in Venezuela.

System-level factors are important predictors of this variance; an ANOVA of these scores with country as the grouping variable produces an F-test significant at the $p < .000$ level and an adjusted R^2 of .70. Yet party-level predictors also matter, and we see repeated some of the same correlates mentioned previously for cohesion on left-right placement. In fact, the associations here are generally stronger. As was true with left-right cohesion, the average overall cohesion across individual parties is slightly lower than the weighted country-level averages (0.50 versus 0.52, with the difference of means now significant at the $p < .20$ level using a one-tailed t-test), reaffirming that high cohesion is associated with a lack of electoral strength or governing experience. Likewise, cohesion on issues tends to be much higher among leftist parties. The party-level correlation between cohesion on economic issues and average ideological placement is $r = .39$ ($p < .01$) if we consider left-right self-placement and $r = .44$ ($p < .004$) for left-right party placement. The positive value shows that cohesion is highest at the lower, leftist end of the scale. And extremism, measured here as the average distance of the party from the center of the scale on the most divisive economic issues, is again mildly associated with cohesion. The correlation is $r = -.24$ (at $p < .12$), the negative sign showing that more extreme parties tend to have smaller standard deviations.

TABLE 5.6. *Cohesion on Divisive Issues, by Party (corrected standard deviation)*

Party	Country	N	Average across All Issues
FREPASO	Argentina	11	0.28
Pachakutik	Ecuador	8	0.29
ADN	Bolivia	9	0.33
PPD	Chile	11	0.34
UDI	Chile	11	0.38
UCR	Argentina	19	0.39
Convergencia	Venezuela	9	0.39
PC	Uruguay	22	0.39
PT	Brazil	9	0.39
MAS	Venezuela	8	0.40
LCR	Venezuela	13	0.43
PRD	Mexico	23	0.43
FA	Uruguay	25	0.43
PDC-Ch	Chile	31	0.46
DP	Ecuador	10	0.46
AD	Venezuela	18	0.46
APRA	Peru	7	0.46
PLN	Costa Rica	25	0.47
MIR	Bolivia	7	0.47
PS	Chile	13	0.50
UCS	Bolivia	17	0.50
MNR	Bolivia	23	0.50
PRI	Mexico	64	0.51
PL	Colombia	41	0.52
RN	Chile	23	0.53
CONDEPA	Bolivia	6	0.53
UPP	Peru	12	0.55
PN	Uruguay	22	0.56
PJ	Argentina	24	0.57
PAN	Mexico	35	0.57
COPEI	Venezuela	18	0.58
C95	Peru	52	0.58
PSDB	Brazil	10	0.58
PRSC	Dominican Republic	19	0.60
PLD	Dominican Republic	13	0.60
PRE	Ecuador	14	0.60
PRD	Dominican Republic	29	0.60
PUSC	Costa Rica	23	0.62
PFL	Brazil	12	0.63
PSC	Colombia	14	0.66
PMDB	Brazil	16	0.68
PSC	Ecuador	24	0.81
Average			0.50

Of these different correlates, however, the strongest seem to be size and governing experience. About 52 percent of the parties in the top half of the list have ever won control of the presidency, while 67 percent of the parties in the bottom have this experience; this difference is significant at the $p < .18$ level (one-tailed t-test). In fact, of the ten parties with average cohesion of 0.40 or better, only three have held the presidency (UCR in Argentina, PC in Uruguay, and Convergencia in Venezuela), and one of these (Convergencia) had only a small contingency in the legislature and had been in power for just one or two years. In contrast, of the nine parties with cohesion of 0.60 or worse, all but two (the PRD in the Dominican Republic and the PFL in Brazil) have held the presidency at least once and sometimes more often. Similar results prevail if we consider the average size of each party's legislative cohort over the past twenty years (lower chamber only). Parties in the upper half of the list average around 20 percent of seats in the chamber, whereas parties in the lower half average around 28 percent of seats; this difference is significant at the $p < .03$ level (one-tailed t-test).

While we can only speculate here, two causal mechanisms could link size and government experience with cohesion. On the one hand, cohesion may be somewhat endogenous: large size and governing experience reflect a prior decision by many of these parties to moderate their ideology and create a more cross-class appeal; low cohesion precedes winning control of government. This story is familiar in the more programmatic context of West European party systems (Kirchheimer 1966). On the other hand (and perhaps at the same time), governing experience may cause low cohesion. In the clientelistic environment that characterizes many of these party systems, control of the executive branch offers opportunities for parties to capture rents that can be used to further their electoral ambitions. This tactic may increase their strength in the legislature and consolidate political control, but it will also tend to have a corrupting influence on the party and attract opportunistic candidates while driving away ideological purists. We can see additional evidence for this association between governing experience and cohesion by moving beyond absolute levels of cohesion and considering relative cohesion of specific parties within each country. Table 5.7 indicates the most and least cohesive parties within each country on each question of our most divisive issue bundle, economic policy. To better highlight these patterns, we take into account not only the original questions used to calculate the average but any other question in that issue bundle that has a divisiveness score of less than $p < .10$; the fraction of the total number of questions is indicated in parentheses after each party name. In one instance where no party is clearly the most or least cohesive in at least half the cases, the category is labeled as indeterminate.

In spite of the low overall issue cohesion we have identified, the results indicate strong patterns within almost all of these countries, with at least one party being consistently more cohesive than others in that system. This

TABLE 5.7. *Most and Least Cohesive Parties*

| Country | Economic Policy[a] | |
	Most	Least
Argentina	FREPASO (4/6)	PJ (5/6)
Bolivia	ADN (2/4)	CONDEPA (2/4)
Brazil	PT (3/4)	Indeterminate
Chile	UDI (4/7)	PDC (4/7)
Colombia	PL (4/4)	PSC (4/4)
Costa Rica	PLN (4/5)	PUSC (4/5)
Dominican Republic	PRD (2/4)	PLD (2/4)
Ecuador	Pachakutik (4/4)	PSC (3/4)
Mexico	PRD (7/8)	PRI/PAN (4/8)
Peru	APRA (2/4)	C95 (2/4)
Uruguay	FA (4/7)	PN (6/7)
Venezuela	LCR (3/5)	COPEI (3/5)

[a] Numbers in parentheses indicate the fraction of total issues over which the party was the most cohesive (column 1) or the least cohesive (column 2).

fact alone means that some party-level factors may be at work in shaping cohesion, masked perhaps by low or high average levels of cohesion in that country. However, the more striking pattern that emerges is that the most cohesive parties in most of these countries are those that had never achieved control of the presidency or a majority of the legislative seats at the time of this survey. FREPASO in Argentina, ADN in Bolivia, the PT in Brazil, UDI in Chile, the PRD[8] in the Dominican Republic, Pachakutik in Ecuador, the PRD in Mexico, and the Frente Amplio in Uruguay all fall into this category (the exceptions are the PL in Colombia, the PLN in Costa Rica, and APRA in Peru, parties with low levels of cohesion in absolute terms). Likewise, nearly all of the least cohesive parties are ones with experience in the presidency and/or considerable strength in the legislature, including the PJ in Argentina, the PSDB in Brazil, the PDC in Chile, the PLD in the Dominican Republic, the PSC in Ecuador, the PRI in Mexico, Cambio'95 in Peru, and the PN in Uruguay; the exceptions here are CONDEPA in Bolivia and Causa R in Venezuela. This finding reaffirms the idea that electoral strength and/or governing experience have a negative effect on party cohesion.

In short, patterns of cohesion at the level of individual parties tend to match what we find at the country level, but with some revealing differences that hint at the presence of both system- and party-level causes. Party-level

[8] Although founded in 1939, the PRD held the presidency only once before the survey was administered, for a brief period in 1963 under Juan Bosch; it finally won the presidency again in 2000.

cohesion remains stronger for left-right placement than for issues, where it is generally very weak; thus, judging only on the basis of issue cohesion, we would still have to conclude that most Latin American party systems are only weakly programmatic. Even in the case of issue cohesion, however, there are a handful of parties with noticeably higher cohesion than their party systems, levels that place them in the same league as parties in Eastern Europe analyzed by Kitschelt et al. (1999); thus, some parties stand out as potentially quite programmatic and seem less affected by the broader system. Likewise, the average cohesion at this level of analysis is higher than the country averages for both left-right and issue cohesion, where larger parties are weighted more heavily; this fact indicates that electorally successful parties are less cohesive. Finally, an examination of relative cohesion on economic policy issues within each party system finds that the most and least cohesive parties are not only fairly consistently ranked but are nearly always those without or with (respectively) governing experience. This result again suggests an important party-level determinant of cohesion, although the precise causal mechanisms cannot be explored systematically in this volume, which generally focuses on the level of party systems.

CONCLUSION

Our study of ideological cohesion in Latin America supports and advances the descriptive findings of previous chapters. We find that patterns in country-level cohesion are similar to the patterns in partisan issue divides, left-right semantics, and representativeness outlined in Chapters 2 through 4.[9] Countries such as Uruguay and Chile stand out as more programmatically structured on all the dimensions we consider; others, such as Ecuador and Colombia, stand out as very poorly structured; and the remaining countries fall somewhere in between.

Our analysis also makes an important descriptive contribution to these previous chapters. We are able to compare the cohesion of Latin American party systems directly with the cohesion of party systems in other regions, specifically Eastern Europe. This comparison gives us a much better sense of where Latin American countries stand not only relative to each other but also in absolute terms. The results of this comparison are fairly negative. While cohesion on left-right placement is high across both Latin America and Eastern Europe, cohesion on issues is much lower in Latin America. Even after making multiple corrections, only three Latin American countries (Chile, Uruguay, and Bolivia) come close to achieving the levels of

---

[9] At least with regard to partisan divides, this is not surprising, as our discriminant analysis of parties' issue cohesion (Chapter 2) employs the same observations and the same variance among respondents (though not among party means) on which we also draw here in Chapter 5.

cohesion found in the most programmatic countries of Eastern Europe, and the other Latin American countries fall farther behind. This suggests that the intraregional differences in programmatic structuration that we find and repeatedly confirm in this volume are more than matched by variance between Latin America and other regions. This conclusion is necessarily tentative, as it is based on only one major point of comparison, but it also suggests a cautionary note as we shift to the explanatory chapters in Part II.

CAUSES AND CORRELATES OF PROGRAMMATIC PARTY SYSTEM STRUCTURATION

Explaining Cross-National Diversity

Where do national profiles of programmatic party system structuration come from? What are their correlates and consequences and what are their potential implications for the future of democracy in the region, particularly given that we can see a decade beyond our point of observation in the late 1990s and consider intervening developments? Part II is devoted to these causal questions, whereas the conclusion takes up more speculative themes concerning the subsequent development of Latin American politics after the turn of the millennium. Chapters 6 and 7 deal with the long-term and short-term developments that might have influenced economic PPS, the most powerful issue dimension in Latin American party systems insofar as they have any programmatic structuration. In Chapter 8, we take up religion and regime as further programmatic dimensions that make a difference in some of our countries.

Long-term causal mechanisms turn out to be decisive in accounting for the rise and tenacity of economic and religious programmatic alignments, whereas regime divides are driven by recent episodes of authoritarianism or manifest performance failures of current democracy. Nevertheless, exceptionally sharp and prolonged economic decline since the 1980s also erodes established economic PPS, at least within the subgroup of countries with favorable long-term conditions for economic PPS. Our analysis, however, suggests that neither good nor bad performance builds up economic PPS in countries with inauspicious long-term dispositions to programmatic party competition.

One further finding merits early notice. The most powerful forces that best explain patterns of economic PPS across the entire group of Latin American countries fail to account well for the largest country in the continent, Brazil. In our 1997–98 data analysis, Brazil displays much less economic PPS than our explanatory account would predict on the basis of both long-term or short-term political and economic features. The case of Brazil stubbornly refuses to comply with any general explanatory account adequate to cover just about all the other cases. Brazil specialists would invoke its electoral rules and federalism to account for weak programmatic structuring (cf. Mainwaring 1999; Ames 2001; Samuels 2003). But institutionalist explanations cannot account for cross-national variation in PPS in our entire sample of countries under investigation. Possibilities we explore are that our PPS measure does not pick up critical features of programmatic structuration in Brazil or that we measured Brazilian PPS "too early" just when it was caught up in the gradual rise from a low PPS equilibrium prevailing until the early 1990s to a higher PPS equilibrium more recently (Lyne 2008).

Chapter 9 makes an effort to explore political and economic correlates, if not consequences, of contrasting practices of democratic accountability and party competition. We intend this chapter to persuade the reader that measuring and accounting for economic PPS cross-nationally is not an idiosyncratic exercise but an enterprise that sheds light on many facets of democratic political quality. Countries with persistently intense economic PPS tend to display less corruption, more effective governance, and higher levels of public support for democracy. This relationship is not explained by better economic performance in high PPS countries per se. Economic PPS is a meaningful tracer, if not a cause, of important features of democratic quality that many citizens, politicians, and scholars care about.

Before we embark on our long journey of probing into causes and consequences of economic, religious, and regime PPS, let us clarify the conceptualization of dependent variables. We develop summary scores of economic and religious PPS, each of which draws on key elements elaborated in previous chapters. Let us elaborate here only on economic PPS as the most important variable. Party systems are structured programmatically around economic issues, if the economic partisan divide is articulated (Table 2.6), if politicians place parties on a formal left-right dimension according to the parties' scores on the economic-distributive partisan divide (Table 3.2), if parties represent their constituencies on economic issues (Table 4.3), and if the average diffuseness of parties on economic policy issues in a polity is relatively modest (Table 5.4).

In creating an index, we first rescored all values on a standardized scale that measures a country's distance from the cohort mean as a multiple of the standard deviation in the sample. Second, so as not to make extreme values too influential, we score values within half a standard deviation of a cohort mean value as zero (0), lower values as minus one (−1), and higher values as plus one (+1). We then summarize these coarse scores to derive an index of economic PPS. We actually calculate four different indices. The smallest index includes only economic partisan divides and policy content of parties' left-right placements, as listed in columns 1, 2, and 5.1 of Table II.1. These two variables may be most important for voters to distinguish political parties.

TABLE 11.1. *Diversity of Programmatic Structuration in Twelve Latin American Countries: Economic Distribution and Governance*

| | (1) Economic Partisan Divide (Table 2.6) | | (2) Economic Policy Content of Parties'/Left-Right Placements (Table 3.2) | | (3) Economic Issue Congruence Voters Legislators: Conservative Score (Table 4.3) | | (4) Economic Policy Average Party Issue Diffuseness (relative values: sign inversed) (Table 5.4) | | (5) Economic PPS: Indices of Programmatic Partisan Structuration Based on These Attributes from Columns | | | | Standard Deviation of Relative Attribute Scores |
	Absolute	Relative	Absolute	Relative	Absolute	Relative	Absolute	Relative	PPS-1 (5.1) I+2	PPS-2 (5.2) I+2+3	PPS-3 (5.3) I+2+4	PPS-4 (5.4) I+2+3+4	
Chile	Strong (1) .516	+1.83	Strong (1) .53	+2.00	Strong (1) 1.67	+1.59	Strong (1) .46	+1.00	+2	+3	+4	+4	.44
Uruguay	Strong (1) .371	+.73	Strong (1) .47	+1.70	Strong (1) 1.0	+.69	Strong (1) .46	+1.00	+2	+3	+4	+4	.47
Costa Rica	Strong (1) .361	+.65	Medium (o) .22	+.45	Medium (o) .67	+.25	Medium (o) .54	+.33	+1	+1	+1	+1	.17
Mexico	Strong (1) .461	+1.41	Strong (1) .29	+.80	Weak (−1) −1.0	−1.97	Medium (o) .50	+.33	+2	+1	+1	+2	1.48
Argentina	Medium (o) .325	+.37	Medium (o) .06	−.30	Strong (1) 1.00	+.69	Strong (1) .47	+.83	0	+1	0	+2	.50
Venezuela	Medium (o) .276	.00	Weak (−1) .11 (oo)	−.65	No data		Strong (1) .47	+.83	−1	−1	0	0	.74
Dominican Republic	Weak (−1) .130	−1.11	Weak (−1) .12 (oo)	−.65	No data		Weak (−1) .56	−.67	−2	−2	−3	−3	.26
Colombia	Weak (−1) .200	−.58	Weak (−1) .00	−.65	Medium (o) .50	+.03	Weak (−1) .56	−.67	−2	−2	−3	−3	.34
Peru	Weak (−1) .208	−.52	Weak (−1) .00	−.65	No data		Weak (−1) .57	−0.83	−2	−2	−3	−3	.16
Brazil	Weak (−1) .159	−.89	Weak (−1) .00	−.65	Medium (o) .33	−.20	Weak (−1) .60	−1.33	−2	−2	−3	−3	.47
Ecuador	Weak (−1) .135	−1.08	Weak (−1) .00	−.65	Medium (o) .17	−.41	Weak (−1) .62	−1.67	−2	−2	−3	−3	.55
Bolivia	Weak (−1) .166	−.84	Weak (−1) .00	−.65	Weak (−1) .0	−.64	Strong (+1) .45	+1.17	−2	−3	−1	−2	.94
Mean absolute score	.276		.13		.48		.57		−.50	−.42	−.42	−.33	
Standard deviation	.131		.20		.75		.06		1.78	2.11	2.68	2.84	

We then add the economic issue congruence between voters and partisan legislatures in index 5.2. The difficulty here is that we have data on only nine of our twelve countries and had to score the missing cases as "medium" or zero. This may actually work slightly to the detriment of our hypotheses in the empirical analysis. The final attribute we include is the average programmatic diffuseness of parties on economic issues, calculated in Chapter 5. Intraparty cohesiveness is probably one of the hardest achievements of politicians to accomplish and for investigators to measure. We showed that constructing this variable is difficult and numerous assumptions have to be made. The variable generates one severe outlier (Bolivia) for which we offered a plausible ad hoc explanation in Chapter 5. Cross-national differences on this variable are therefore not as sharply articulated as on the partisan divide and left-right semantics variables. We create one index that includes average diffuseness but excludes representation because of the missing values. We create a further index with all four variables included. Table II.1 presents all the relevant raw and standardized scores of our four original variables that go into various indices of economic PPS, as constructed in columns 5.1 through 5.4.

Altogether we have four different ways to calculate our economic PPS index. In our analysis of the causes of lesser or greater programmatic structuration around economic issues, however, the choice of index does not substantially affect our results. In the following chapters, we primarily display economic PPS index 5.2., that is, the one that excludes the diffuseness variable.

How meaningful is our PPS index, in its multiple variants, given that it reports just a snapshot of data at a single point in time in the late 1990s? What if we had measured PPS for 1985 or, for that matter, for 2007 instead? Would we have generated similar results? Or, if not, what qualifies the 1997–98 results as representative and relevant for an analysis of Latin American party systems over a longer period of time?

Before answering these questions, let us remind the reader what, in our theoretical perspective, is the critical measure of PPS we should aim for. The hard challenge for party builders is to establish democratic political accountability through programmatic partisan appeals and policy-based voting for the long haul. It may also be only this type of durable accountability that "pays off" in ways that affect democratic stability and even the political economy, as we explore in Chapter 9. In the short run, there may always be occasional "blips" and "surges" of programmatic competition, but they remain inconsequential, unless sustained for a longer period of time. The critical question, then, concerns the conditions and processes that effect the "lock-in" of programmatic party competition: is it momentous long-term shifts in capacities, opportunities, and political(-economic) stakes that build up cumulatively in a country, or do politicians and voters respond to short-term incentives to build programmatic competition and then are able to lock in this mode of democratic accountability even in the absence of new durable capacities, opportunities, and stakes?

In inspecting our observations of PPS for each case against this theoretical background, we therefore need to determine whether our data of 1997–98 reflect a long-term lock-in of patterns of party competition or just a purely singular and highly volatile score that would have been very different had we measured PPS ten or twenty years earlier, or even ten years later. On the basis of a careful reading of case study narratives about all of our Latin American party systems, we argue that (1) countries and parties that our data analysis scores as high PPS tend to have displayed that attribute of party competition consistently for some time (since the 1980s at the latest, but often starting at a much earlier point in time, even if democracy was punctuated by spells of authoritarianism since then), while (2) countries our data analysis scores as low PPS would have consistently scored that way, had we taken similar measurements at other points in time, even if punctuated by a few instances of short, intermittent, and fleeting surges of programmatic partisan appeals.

In justifying this assessment, let us focus on countries where this judgment may be most contentious. The literature would provide little ammunition to consider Chile anything but a country with comparatively strong programmatic party competition, albeit such practices were also usually supplemented by clientelistic mechanisms of political exchange. Costa Rica and Argentina approximate a somewhat weaker mix of PPS, combined with powerful clientelistic politics throughout much of their post–World War II histories of democratic elections. Mexico's dominant party system is a somewhat harder case, but its ubiquitous clientelism was always supplemented by programmatic differences between the ruling party and the opposition parties, particularly the PAN. If we move on to a country with a lower-intermediate level of programmatic politics in the late 1990s, Venezuela, our measure appears to reflect the realities of predominantly clientelistic partisan politics at least since the Pact of Punto Fijo in 1958 when redemocratization put an end to the Pérez Jiménez dictatorship. Venezuela for a long time had a highly institutionalized party system, but this institutionalization tended not to be grounded in programmatic competition. At the other extreme of countries where we measure nonprogrammatic democratic partisan politics in the late 1990s – Colombia, the Dominican Republic, and Ecuador – the case study literature gives us every reason to consider our scores as representative for the general democratic practice of partisan politicians over a number of decades.

Beyond these countries where generalization of our PPS scores for longer periods of time is indisputable, four cases are contentious and require closer examination: Bolivia, Brazil, Peru, and Uruguay. Do our data deliver exceptional scores in the late 1990s? Would Uruguay have come in with much lower PPS scores had we measured at a different time? And are our low scores measured in the late 1990s for Bolivia, Brazil, and Peru unrepresentative of the practice of politicians against the historical record of party competition in these countries?

In Uruguay's case, there is little reason to doubt its scoring as a comparatively high PPS polity in the Latin American context, certainly for the time period since the early 1970s but, most likely, also in the very long run. For example, Uruguay went through a period of intensely programmatic politics in the first decades of the twentieth century under both the presidency of the older Batlle (1903–7 and 1911–15) and that of his nephew Luis Batlle in the late 1940s, in which the Colorados' dominant faction enacted economic and social policies that favored organized labor (Gillespie 1986: 174). At this point, however, one could also argue that factions rather than parties were the main embodiment of programmatic competition. Moreover, one must remember that the Colorados was essentially a hegemonic party until 1958, which suggests that whatever programmatic alternation existed in the party system was mostly the product of the rise and decline of different factions within this party. What may be historically contentious is the practice of Uruguayan party competition in the 1950s and 1960s. Blancos and Colorados were always internally factionalized, reinforced by the Uruguayan electoral system. In those decades, the two major old parties were doubtlessly less programmatically contoured than earlier in the twentieth century, and a new programmatic competitor appeared only in 1971. With the rise of the Frente Amplio since 1971, but especially after military rule, programmatic competition in Uruguay became starkly articulated, albeit running primarily between the two "old" parties, on one side, and the Frente Amplio, on the other (Luna 2007).

Nevertheless, there are at least two reasons not to underestimate programmatic politics in Uruguay even in the middle decades of the twentieth century. First, conflicts about economic-distributive politics repeatedly erupted into interparty rather than intraparty competition, particularly when it came to the expansion or defense of the Uruguayan welfare state under deteriorating domestic economic conditions (Haggard and Kaufman 2008: 88), a policy area that plays a crucial role in our explanation of levels of programmatic competition in the next chapter of our study. Thus, throughout the twentieth century and up to the rise of the Frente Amplio, the tensions around which programmatic politics appeared in Uruguay related to the rise of ISI. Second, while the two major parties were deeply factionalized, with clientelistic and personalistic divides structuring factions, they maintained intraparty discipline in the legislature and voted along partisan lines. As Gonzalez (1995: 144) notes, while the two major Uruguayan parties had a catchall character due to the diversification of their factions, legislative coalition building never crossed partisan lines. Even if interparty programmatic differences were vague and minute, party labels did not entirely lose their informational value to voters responding to programmatic cues.

As already noted, in Brazil we observe a low level of democratic account-ability through programmatic politics in 1998, a judgment that is consistent with the dominant mainstream interpretation of Brazilian democracy (e.g., Ames 2001). Programmatic structuring of party competition appears to have been low throughout Brazil's first major democratic era (1946–64) as well as during the initial phase of political liberalization and democratization in the 1980s and early 1990s. But it may underestimate programmatic structuring with the rise of the Workers' Party (PT), the crystallization of center-left social democratic parties with mildly redistributive penchants (especially PSDB and PMDB, but also PSB and PDT and a few small splinter parties), and the reconfiguration of the older clientelistic parties around a more right-wing, market-liberal agenda led by the PFL and the PP. Since the mid-1990s, both increasing party discipline in legislative voting in the Brazilian congress and a declining willingness of legislators to switch party affiliations suggest a durable change in Brazilian partisan competition that puts a premium on greater programmatic profile, credibility, and drive to enact programmatic proposals into law (cf. Lyne 2008). Brazil is thus clearly a hard case that may have been in a long-term transition toward a more programmatic party system for now already a decade and a half, but one that our data analysis did not fully pick up. We therefore examine, in each instance where we attempt to explain patterns of party competition across Latin America, how recoding the Brazilian experience would affect our descriptive or causal inferences.

Our late 1990s scores in the final two cases – Bolivia and Peru – look again broadly representative of the experience of these countries during extended periods of time. In the twentieth century, each country produced only a single durable and more or less institutionalized party, MNR in Bolivia and APRA in Peru. In both instances, these parties started with vague populist-nationalist appeals, and either with a dose of sympathies toward European national socialism or fascism, as exhibited by MNR in Bolivia (cf. Gamarra and Malloy 1995: 401–3), or at least with a penchant for antidemocratic and intransigent tactics, as attested by APRA in Peru (McClintock 1989: 342). Both parties were led over very long time periods by charismatic figures that proved to be highly flexible in terms of their programmatic stances and tactical alliances. It should also be noted for our analysis in Chapter 6 that in moments of greatest triumph neither the Bolivian MNR during the 1952 revolution nor the Peruvian APRA during Alan García's presidency more than thirty years later made much effort to advance the claims of unionized wage earners. Instead, they tended to deprive organized labor of electoral strength, as Whitehead (1986: 53–54) or Gamarra and Malloy (1995: 403) would characterize the Bolivian MNR in its revolutionary episode, or governed without and against an internally splintered leftist partisan sector, as well as leftist internal party opposition, in the case of Peru's García. Overall, it would be inadequate to characterize the two best institutionalized parties in Bolivia and Peru, MNR and APRA, let alone their respective fields of competitors as programmatic parties engaged in a programmatic electoral contest.

We set aside here the programmatic and highly ideological surge experienced in countries such as Bolivia, Ecuador, Peru, and Venezuela since the early 2000s. As we argue in our Conclusion, sudden programmatic competition and even polarization may in fact be directly associated with weak patterns of programmatic competition until recently. And it is as yet an open question whether these novel efforts to crystallize programmatic alternatives in these countries will lead to durable programmatic competition in the future or to a new clientelistic politics configured around hegemonic parties that capture the state, or even an abolition of electoral competition altogether.

Given the very small number of cases available for purely cross-sectional comparison, let us finally add a word about the rather crude statistical method of data analysis employed through much, but not all, of the explanatory part of our book. With an N of twelve, we cannot seriously push quantitative-statistical reasoning beyond simple univariate frequency tables and bivariate correlations, and those only for illustrative purposes. Regardless of whether a significance test is meaningful, if we deal with cases covering more than 90 percent of the population found in the universe, with a dataset of only twelve observations, a single large measurement error may lead to entirely erroneous conclusions. This has two implications. First, it is desirable to substantiate our conclusion with independent measures of the causal process involved or with independent measures of different aspects of a hypothesized causal process. Second, we do not attach much credibility to weak correlations, whether statistically significant or not. After checking for the substantive size of effects that can also be gleaned from the distribution of values on the causal variables, we have confidence only in correlations that are at least stronger than $|.60|$ or, even better, $|.70|$. With weaker associations, a simple recoding of two of twelve cases – or, in the extreme, even a single case – could lead to entirely different conclusions. For this reason, we have confidence only in very robust patterns of association. It is more important to appraise whether stipulated relations reflect a plausible causal story that is consistent with a logic of political partisan mobilization.

The small number of cases and the purely cross-sectional nature of the data also make it hazardous to go from contemporaneous statistical correlation to causal-sequential claims. Because endogeneity problems are ubiquitous, it is important to establish a clear timeline along which potential causal effects had the opportunity to kick in. Placing the evidence from a single point in time in a broader dynamic context is something we can ground exclusively in our reading of the qualitative case study literature dealing with individual Latin American countries.

6

Long-Term Influences on the Structuring of Latin American Party Systems

Herbert Kitschelt, Kirk A. Hawkins, Juan Pablo Luna,
Guillermo Rosas, and Elizabeth J. Zechmeister

Programmatic party systems develop during extended periods of adaptive political learning, catalyzed by historical episodes in which momentous societal conflicts crystallize around alternative modes of political-economic domination. When large constituencies and their political representatives struggle for the adoption of far-reaching political-economic arrangements, and when they have the opportunity to play electoral politics repeatedly, then advocates of change and their antagonists may coordinate around rival programmatic party visions. These alternatives become progressively more structured through a process of building lasting party organizations and by locking in social and economic policies and institutions that bind electoral constituencies to specific partisan alternatives. The development of such divides may extend over decades, even though it may erupt in profound economic and political crises and violent domestic or external conflicts.

In this chapter, we probe into the historical origins of late twentieth-century Latin American programmatic party structuration (PPS), which we claim is rooted in early episodes of democratic competition and fierce struggles over the governance of each country's political economy. From this perspective the formation of programmatic party competition is a long-term process. Novel socioeconomic and political challenges may trigger a process of learning how to mobilize politically that ultimately results in a sustained configuration of programmatic partisan alternatives. Once actors have constructed partisan divides and dimensions of competition, such alignments may erode under the impact of changing political-economic circumstances that lead to the emergence of new groups and alignments of economic, political, and cultural interests not reflected in the existing political party system. Costs incurred in the construction of programmatic citizen-politician linkages are "sunk," as it were, but produce consequences for long periods to come. Hence, party systems may reflect the "stickiness" of political alignments even decades after the original political-economic conditions that gave rise to the dominant partisan alternatives have disappeared. In part, this stickiness is due to the high transaction costs new challengers have to incur in order to enter competitive politics successfully and build the name recognition, reputation, and organization that allow them to rally citizens to their cause. In part, this stickiness is also due to the capacity of strategic politicians in the established parties to modify their programmatic appeals and thus to preempt, or at least delay, the entry of new partisan alternatives. Even in these instances, however, processes of learning and unlearning of patterns of programmatic party competition may never quite translate into the stable arrangement that Lipset and Rokkan (1967) metaphorically captured with the notion of "frozen" cleavages.[1]

In this chapter, we attempt to identify and – less conclusively – to disentangle conditions affecting long-term learning of programmatic party competition in Latin America.[2] Complementary or counteracting short-term processes are analyzed in Chapter 7. We begin with the simple hypothesis that economic development (resulting in greater affluence and education in a changing work force) enhances *capacities* for collective political action, including programmatic party formation. We then move on to consider the *opportunities* citizens and politicians had across Latin American countries to engage in iterative games of electoral competition that might facilitate the emergence of programmatic parties. The data suggest that countries with early economic development and opportunities for competition over extended periods of time eventually created more programmatic partisan competition. But what were the substantive mechanisms and "stakes" that organized and then kept alive programmatic competition? We argue that the critical link is the entrenchment of comparatively encompassing social policies protecting urban wage earners much more so than general strategies of import-substituting industrialization (ISI) per se. Only where socioeconomic development, political mobilization, and democratic party competition favored the development of moderately encompassing social policies within an ISI framework was programmatic party competition around economic-distributive issues locked in.

CAPACITIES FOR PARTY SYSTEM STRUCTURATION: EARLY ECONOMIC DEVELOPMENT

Economic resources may help political actors overcome collective action problems and learn to construct more powerful vehicles of political mobilization (net of demands, stakes, and deprivations) and of opportunities

---

[1] Actually, the literature around Lipset and Rokkan's original statement, more than Lipset and Rokkan's own text, created the image of permanent "freezing" of European partisan cleavages as a foil against which to study party system change.

[2] For a conceptualization of long-term causality through chains and cumulative processes, see Pierson (2003; 2004).

presented by democratic civil rights and political freedoms. Rising affluence makes it less costly for challengers to organize and more costly for dictators to enforce exclusion – or for prospective dictators to expect high returns from authoritarian rule. Once democracy is in place, it tends to persist at higher levels of development (cf. Przeworski et al. 2000). For our purposes, it is irrelevant to determine whether that link between development and democracy is mediated by patterns of inequality that may have made authoritarian rulers more accepting of democratic party competition (Boix 2003; Boix and Stokes 2003).

Interestingly, when cross-national comparison is confined to Latin American polities, with levels of development ranging from wretched poverty (e.g., Bolivia) to the upper-middle tier of affluence (Argentina, Uruguay, Chile), economic development predicts neither transitions to nor durability of democratic regimes (cf. Mainwaring and Pérez-Liñán 2003). The same problem may beset explanations of democracy by inequality, as highly unequal countries, such as Chile, accumulated some of the most lasting runs of democratic party competition. Even if the fundamental effects of development and inequality on political democratization do not surface in a comparison of middle-income Latin American countries, does greater affluence, especially under conditions of democracy ("opportunity"), lead politicians and voters to converge on programmatic party competition? And does it matter for the emergence of economic PPS in electoral competition that countries have been relatively affluent for a comparatively long period of time, so that political entrepreneurs have had plenty of time to overcome collective action problems? Of course, if countries must enjoy a period of many decades of relative affluence to produce high levels of programmatic party competition, and if we in fact observe such democracies in action, intervening causal mechanisms must be sought out that can account for the tenacity of programmatic competition and its reproduction over time.

Table 6.1 lists per capita GDP estimates for three time points in the twentieth century. The earliest is for 1928 after a long run of export-led, trade-based economic growth in some Latin American countries that was terminated by the Great Depression of the 1930s. The second is in 1960 after a decade of uneven economic recovery from the aftermath of World War II. In most Latin American countries, postwar growth was associated with vigorous ISI development strategies, although some of the most ISI-committed countries already showed relatively poor economic performance (Argentina, Chile, and Uruguay). The third time point is 1980, during the twilight years of ISI development strategies after two oil crises, the effects of which were partly buffered by high external debt taken on during the 1970s that later triggered the Latin American debt crisis and the widespread misery of the "lost decade" in the 1980s.

While most Latin American countries in a global comparative analysis would count as "middle income," there is considerable diversity among them

TABLE 6.1. *Relative per Capita Income across Latin America, 1928–1980*

	Per Capita GDP		
	1928[a]	1960	1980
Argentina	+1.39	+1.00	+.74
Bolivia	No data (−1.46)	−1.24	−1.68
Brazil	−.79	.62	+.25
Chile	+1.02	+.68	+.21
Colombia	−.84	−1.02	−1.01
Costa Rica	−.51	−.19	+.05
Dominican Republic	No data (−.95)	−.93	−.98
Ecuador	No data (−.91)	−.97	−.84
Mexico	−.33	−.03	+.63
Peru	−.81	−.02	−.43
Uruguay	+1.51	+1.27	+1.08
Venezuela	−.63	+2.00	+1.89
Average	313 (1970 $)	918 (1980 $)	1,510 (1980 $)
Standard deviation	185 (59.1% of mean)	431 (46.9% of mean)	560 (37.1% of mean)
Economic partisan divide (correlation)	.58* (N = 9)	.58**	.56*
Economic policy content of parties' left-right placement (correlation)	.72** (N = 9)	.43	.39
Representation: Economic policy issue congruence of parties' voters and legislators (correlation)	.58 (N = 7)	.53 (N = 9)	.23 (N = 9)
Average diffuseness of parties on economic policy issues (correlation)	−.53* (N = 9)	−.59**	−.40
PPS-2 index of economic programmatic structuration (Table II.1, column 5.2) (correlation)	.83*** (N = 9) .88***	.64*	.61*

Note: Income expressed in units of standard deviation from the unweighted mean per capita gross domestic income of all Latin American countries in each of the three years (1928; 1960; 1980). Unless otherwise noted, N = 12 for each correlation. $p \leq .10$; **$p \leq .05$; ***$p \leq .01$.
[a] For the three countries for which we have no 1928 data, we show in parentheses the average across their 1960 and 1980 values.
Sources: Bulmer-Thomas (1994: 444), for 1928 in 1970 $; Swift (1978: 157–58), for 1960 and 1980 in 1980 $.

even within a contiguous geographic space – for example, among Argentina, Bolivia, and Chile. Moreover, they also changed relative positions over time, with some countries growing faster than others. Consider, for example, Chile, Brazil, and Venezuela. From 1928 to 1980, Chile fell relative to the mean affluence in our twelve-country sample from a very high score to the intermediate range. Conversely, Brazil lingered among the subset of poor countries in 1928 and 1960, but made it into the middle range of Latin American affluence in the subsequent twenty years. Venezuela, finally, started out as an extremely poor country before it exploited its oil deposits. By 1960, it was Latin America's richest country, only to see its position erode slightly until 1980 and much more thereafter.

As can be seen easily from our 1960 and 1980 figures, the three countries for which we have no 1928 data are not randomly distributed across the spectrum of affluence in the later years. In fact, Bolivia, the Dominican Republic, and Ecuador are the three countries near the bottom of the twelve-country rank order in both 1960 and 1980. For 1928, we therefore assign to these countries the average of their 1960 and 1980 relative (standardized) per capita scores (in parentheses in Table 6.1).

From 1928 to 1980, the variation in per capita GDP across Latin America diminished a bit, but it then increased again in the more recent past from 1980 to 1998, as we discuss in Chapter 7. Overall, Argentina and Uruguay, among the comparatively affluent countries, and Bolivia, Colombia, the Dominican Republic, and Ecuador, among the relatively poor countries, stayed in the same tier, but the other half-dozen polities moved up or down substantially over time. If we find stronger associations between economic development at earlier points in time and economic PPS at the end of the twentieth century, this pattern would suggest long time horizons of learning programmatic partisan competition. If a country's relative position of affluence in 1980, however, is a better predictor of PPS in 1997–98 than its affluence in 1928 or 1960, maybe political learning of specific modes of party competition can be achieved within little more than a decade. This would apply with even greater force if patterns of PPS were more closely associated with circumstances in the 1990s than with earlier times, a point we examine in the next chapter.

The lower four rows of Table 6.1 provide correlations between the economic PPS index and individual measures of economic PPS, on the one hand, and the per capita income figures (for 1928 for nine of twelve countries, and then with imputed estimated values for the missing cases) on the other. The overall pattern consistently shows some correlation between economic affluence and programmatic party structuration, but on closer inspection these relations are in many instances quite frail. Overall, economic PPS is predicted best by the oldest, most remote figures for GDP level but less so by 1960 and 1980 GDP levels. This observation applies to both the individual components of PPS and the overall index.[3] It is most pronounced when we fill in the three missing GDP figures for Bolivia, the Dominican Republic, and Ecuador with the plausible guesses suggested in Table 6.1. In this case, the correlation between 1997–98 economic PPS and 1928 per capita GDP is an impressive +.88. The one outlier in 1928 is Costa Rica, with a below average level of affluence but a moderately high 1997–98 economic PPS score. Economic PPS at the end of the millennium is better predicted by affluence at an early time in political development than at later points in time. Countries that rise in the economic ranks late do not "catch up" in terms of programmatic party competition (Brazil, Venezuela), and countries whose relative affluence declined over time tenaciously preserved their high levels of economic PPS (Chile and Uruguay and, to a lesser extent, Argentina).

It is obvious that affluence, even affluence with a lag of many decades before 1997–98, does not by itself give us a convincing account of economic PPS formation. There is no apparent causal story to support the high association between early (1928) economic development and programmatic party competition seventy years later. What is missing is a mechanism, or a set of mechanisms, that explains how and why greater affluence at a comparatively early point in the twentieth century may have more to do with 1997–98 PPS scores than later affluence in the 1960s or 1970s. In short, it appears to be the case that countries with early economic development generated higher programmatic party structuration in the late twentieth century, even if they could not sustain their relative material advantage terribly well over subsequent decades. But how is it that the distant economic past affects the political near present?

It is necessary to identify plausible intervening causal processes of strategic interaction among politicians and voters that act as "causal chains" (Pierson 2004) bridging the big temporal gap manifest in Table 6.1. The intervening causal stories that we suggest here concern the *opportunities* actors created or seized upon to articulate political divides configured around salient *political-economic stakes* that instigated political conflict throughout much of the twentieth century.

OPPORTUNITIES FOR MOBILIZING PROGRAMMATIC PARTISAN ALTERNATIVES

The opportunity for citizens and politicians to accumulate experience with electoral competition is central to a long-term learning model of programmatic competition. If political entrepreneurs have the option to participate

---

[3] Unless otherwise noted, references to PPS are to the PPS-2 index of economic programmatic structuration (Table II.1, column 5.2). Results would be essentially the same had we employed the other PPS indices described in part II of this book.

in party competition round after round, they are more likely to make investments in programmatic principal-agent linkages. Of course, this may presuppose that politicians and citizens also have the resources and the political stakes that make it worth their while to engage in programmatic competition. Opportunities to experience democratic competition thus help to fill in as causal mechanisms between early economic development and later PPS levels of competition. Development helps to "lock in" democracy for extended periods of time. Durable democracy, in turn, facilitates the creation of programmatic citizen-politician linkages.

Empirically, it is not entirely obvious how the number of rounds with open, competitive democratic elections in a polity should be counted. Do elections need to be fully competitive to contribute to the political learning experience of politicians and electoral constituencies? Which time frames are critical to corroborate the long-term learning model? Are elections fought on a level playing field among the competitors with full civic and political rights (in the sense of Dahl 1989) the only ones that contribute to the experience and the incentives of politicians to invest in programmatic partisan politics? Or should we count less demanding settings – for example, hegemonic party regimes that permit a modicum of opposition activity and bottom-up civil mobilization in interest groups – as meaningful learning experiences that facilitate the eventual emergence of programmatic party competition? What is at stake here is not just various options to operationalize democracy empirically (cf. Munck and Verkuilen 2002) but also the treatment of "hybrid" regimes not easily captured by simple regime classifications (cf. Levitsky and Way 2002). Given the challenges of scoring hybrid regimes, of course, substantive conclusions can be drawn only if they withstand the test of alternative concept operationalizations.

It may well be the case that programmatic party formation may be triggered by less than perfect competition in a hybrid regime with semi-authoritarian conditions of limited civic and political rights. The constitutional monarchy of imperial Germany (1871–1918), without accountability of the executive to the legislature, provides an example. Despite this lack of accountability, voters and politicians had plenty of opportunities before the advent of Weimar democracy to gather experience with interparty competition and craft citizen-politician linkages that involved overwhelmingly programmatic ties.

With these considerations in mind, let us propose three different measures to gauge the opportunities for learning programmatic party competition in Latin America. We start with a baseline count of years with partial or full democratic competition in each country between 1945 and 1998. Next we consider a measure of electoral contestation that weights democratic competition according to finer distinctions. Then we restrict the time frame of democratic experiences relevant for long-term learning by excluding recent years of democratic practice in order to capture the long-term experience in the post–World War II period as critical for the formation of programmatic partisan alternatives.

For the first and most inclusive measure, we rely on Mainwaring et al.'s (2001: 49) scores of democracy in our twelve Latin American countries to build a baseline estimate for the duration of democracy, 1945–98. Mainwaring et al. count the number of years in which countries had electoral democracies that made possible the replacement of government executives. Furthermore, they identify "semi-democracies" with restricted contestation and distinguish them from dictatorships without open electoral contests. We create an index of cumulative political experience with democratic political competition by assigning full unit scores (1.0) to a country for each year in which unrestricted democracy prevailed, half scores (0.5) for country-years with semidemocratic conditions, and zero scores for years of dictatorship. Country values for 1945–98 therefore range from continuous dictatorship (score 0) to continuous, durable democracy (score 54.0). Table 6.2 reports the relevant scores for our twelve countries. Using 1945 as a cutoff point discounts the experience of countries with democratic or semidemocratic conditions in the first half of the twentieth century, such as Argentina, Chile, Colombia, Costa Rica, and Uruguay. It turns out, however, that including the pre-1945 democratic experience of these countries only marginally improves our ability to account for their later economic PPS levels (results not reported).

Experience with democratic contestation over the entire post-1945 period until 1998 – or even including the first half of the twentieth century – is, by itself, only very feebly related to later profiles of PPS, as the correlations indicate. By the same token, an alternative index of political contestation and participation inspired by Rueschemeyer et al.'s (1992: 162) characterization of Latin American democracies does not improve the explanatory power of semidemocratic or fully democratic partisan contestation for PPS much (results not shown here). This may be due to two factors. First, Mexico is scored continuously as a dictatorship until the late 1980s (column 1: only 6.5 weighted years per contestation). While not permitting open contestation to replace the executive, Mexico nevertheless tolerated opposition parties that were permitted to contest elections and gain a modicum of state and national legislative seats. In order to address the theoretical question of experience with electoral contestation, Mexico must at least be scored as a semi-authoritarian country for much of the post–World War II period.

Second, the timing of experience with electoral contestation may matter in at least two regards for our theoretical question. In the case of polities with discontinuous regimes, displaying intermittent democracy, at least some of the experience should have been gathered early in the post-1945 period, so as to make the process of intermittent electoral party competition more drawn out than if all the experiences were bunched together in the most recent episode of democracy. This may bring a further political-economic consideration into play. Maybe electoral contestation was

TABLE 6.2. *Opportunities: Experience with Electoral Competition (in years, weighted)*

	Duration of Democracy, 1945–98	Electoral Contestation, 1945–73
Argentina	24.5	6.0
Bolivia	21.0	4.0
Brazil	32.0	17.0
Chile	37.0	28.0
Colombia	30.5	9.0
Costa Rica	52.0	25.5
Dominican Republic	24.0	3.5
Ecuador	35.0	14.0
Mexico	6.5	14.0
Peru	18.0	9.5
Uruguay	42.0	27.0
Venezuela	42.5	17.5
Average (standard deviation)	30.4 (12.4)	14.6 (8.7)
Economic partisan divide (correlation)	.10	.65**
Economic policy content of parties' left-right placement (correlation)	.24	.77***
Representation: Economic policy issue congruence of parties' voters and legislators (correlation)	.68** (N = 9)	.47 (N = 9)
Average diffuseness of parties on economic policy issues (correlation)	−.01	−.19
Economic PPS-2 Index (Table II.1, column 5.2) (correlation)	.30	.73**

Note: Unless otherwise noted, N = 12 for each correlation. * p ≤ .10; ** p ≤ .05; *** p ≤ .01.

Sources: Column 1: calculated from Mainwaring et al. (2001: 49); column 2: calculated from Mainwaring et al. (2001: 49), with revision for Mexico.

particularly important for the long-term development of PPS when it coincided with a critical period of political-economic restructuring that featured big "stakes" of societal reorganization dividing political camps. Clearly, the post–World War II global economic reconstruction era was critical for a number of Latin American countries to bring about new political-economic and social policy strategies loosely assembled under the intellectual umbrella of import-substituting industrialization.

Before directly addressing the significance of political "stakes" for the development of PPS, let us consider an index of electoral contestation that corrects Mexico's score and that confines the years under consideration to the 1945–73 window of post–World War II recovery (Table 6.2). This measure indeed shows a much stronger correlation with different features of PPS in the late 1990s than the crude 1945–98 democracy measure. Furthermore, and with the exception of Argentina, this alternative measure suggests that the chances that political actors could gather experiences with electoral contestation in the post–World War II period were substantially better in those countries where economic development proceeded early in the twentieth century than in the less developed countries, thus suggesting a causal link between early development of capacities and later emergence of political opportunities. Of course, more fine-grained analysis would have to establish that the urban, more affluent, and educated citizens in the early developers were indeed also the ones who pushed hardest for a democratic regime shift, a claim that still needs to be substantiated elsewhere.

Let us advance two hypotheses about mechanisms that individually or jointly can account for the correlation between electoral contestation in this critical period and PPS at the end of the twentieth century. First, strong PPS comes about only where *capacities* for electoral mobilization, roughly measured by per capita incomes, and *opportunities* for party construction, as measured by episodes of electoral contestation, coincide. Second, the influence of capacities and opportunities on programmatic party system contestation is large only if it works through the construction of political stakes that divide mobilized constituencies into rival political camps configured around alternative conceptions of public policy and political economy. If voters find that their life chances depend on highly salient state policies, then politicians will find it easier to build programmatic partisan alternatives rather than to target voters through clientelistic exchanges. We now explore the first hypothesis and postpone discussion of the second hypothesis until the next section.

Given our small number of cases and thus an inherent inability to work with interaction scores, in Table 6.3 we have simply summed up each country's 1928 relative GDP score, expressed as a standard deviation from the group mean,[4] and its 1945–73 relative score on exposure to electoral contestation. This joint index reflects the cumulative strength of resource capabilities and political opportunities for the emergence of high PPS in the long run. The two components of the index are actually not very highly correlated ($r = .49$). In other words, the fact that countries were comparatively

---

[4] The mean and standard deviations are calculated based on the nine countries for which data are available. As explained earlier, for the missing cases, additional scores were assigned based on their relative affluence in later time periods. Whether or not these missing cases are included, however, makes no difference for the patterns of results reported here.

TABLE 6.3. *The Cumulative Effect of Capacities and Democratic Experiences on PPS*

	Cumulative Capacities and Electoral Experiences (sum of standard deviations)
Argentina	+.40
Bolivia	−2.68
Brazil	−.51
Chile	+2.56
Colombia	−1.48
Costa Rica	+.71
Dominican Republic	−2.23
Ecuador	−.98
Mexico	−.40
Peru	−1.40
Uruguay	+2.94
Venezuela	−.30
Economic partisan divide (correlation)	.78***
Economic policy content of parties' left-right placement (correlation)	.86***
Representation: Economic policy issue congruence of parties' voters and legislators (correlation)	.65* (N = 9)
Average diffuseness of parties on economic policy issues (correlation)	−.42
Economic PPS-2 Index (Table II.1, column 5.2) (correlation)	.93***

Note: Unless otherwise noted, N = 12 for each correlation. * $p \leq .10$; ** $p \leq .05$; *** $p \leq .01$.

wealthy before World War II does not give them an exceptional advantage in developing opportunities for electoral contestation in the postwar era.

The cumulative measure correlates with PPS at .92 in the subset of nine countries for which we have 1928 GDP data and at .93 in our full set of twelve countries when we impute 1928 GDP data for the three missing cases.[5] While the small number of observations makes it impossible to test for interaction effects, the fact that our PPS index (as well as its separate components) correlates more highly with our joint capacity-plus-opportunities-for-contestation index than with either the separate capacity or the opportunities indicators suggests that a combination of both is particularly conducive to making politicians and voters coordinate around programmatic linkages. This analysis, however, does not answer the question

[5] Instead of a cumulative index, of course, we could run a regression with PPS as dependent variable and both 1928 GDP and electoral contestation as independent variables. Given the small number of observations, we do not display this regression here, although it does yield significant effects for both independent variables.

as to what the "stuff" of politics is that makes programmatic alternatives durable, once capacities and opportunities are in place. In other words, what are the symbolic or material distributive "stakes" that mobilize people around partisan alternatives in pursuit of conflicting policy visions favored by identifiable electoral constituencies?

THE STAKES OF PROGRAMMATIC PARTISAN CONFLICT

Let us consider now the political-economic stakes that may have informed Latin American programmatic party system formation in the twentieth century. All Latin American countries sooner or later saw themselves confronted with the challenge to move beyond economies centered primarily on an agrarian and natural resource base, sometimes supplemented by mineral extracting industries, toward industrial and service-based urban economies with a large wage-earning labor force. In the aftermath of the Great Depression that undercut the raw materials–based export economies, urban business and labor constituencies moved toward ISI with a combination of tariffs on imports, an overvalued currency to purchase industrial imports cheaply that could not be locally manufactured, and a variety of state-led efforts to hasten the development of manufacturing industries. But while political parties representing broad urban social groups may have initially pushed on programmatic grounds for the strategic reorganization of the political economy toward ISI in order to benefit large electoral constituencies, ISI policy implementation enabled governing parties to allocate resources in particularistic ways to individuals and small groups of constituents. These included public-sector jobs, preferential access to foreign currency, and the award of export licenses or access to imports on favorable terms. A deeply state interventionist political economy thus promoted clientelistic politics associated with a fragmentation of the electorate into rent-seeking groups as much as or more so than programmatic partisan competition.

The growing proportion of urban wage laborers, however, also triggered the increasing mobilization of labor movements whose members and leaders demanded social policies to protect citizens from the vagaries of labor markets through social security, health care, and unemployment insurance. Contingent upon the level of electoral enfranchisement and effective party competition, policy schemes emerged from the political struggle more or less inclusive and more or less generous to urban electorates. Segura-Ubiergo (2007: chap. 2) distinguishes two policy paths that led some countries in Latin America to relatively more inclusive and universalistic social policies. The first path is exemplified by only a single country, Costa Rica. It combines intermediate levels of development, trade openness, democracy, and left labor and agrarian smallholder mobilization as engines of strong social policy innovation in the 1940s through 1970s. The second path is predicated on above-average economic development (by Latin American standards) and

ISI-induced trade barriers. Under these circumstances, politics would yield more inclusive social policies if it was based on open democratic competition or if a labor movement was strongly mobilized. Both conditions prevailed in Chile and Uruguay. In Uruguay, the struggle for social policy goes back to the beginning of the twentieth century and in Chile to the 1920s and 1930s. In Argentina, from the early twentieth century onward, industrial unions mobilized strongly, but much of the post–World War II period from 1955 until well into the 1980s saw little open electoral party competition. As a further variant of the second pathway, Segura-Ubiergo includes Brazil as a case of above-average social policy extension. But this may be inappropriate. As shown here, Brazil's social policy commitment fell far short of that in the other four countries with comparatively strong social policy commitments. Moreover, also on the causal side, Brazil does not quite match any of the conditions identified for these four countries. Until the 1970s, Brazil was comparatively poor and did not have a powerful labor movement. What social policy was introduced early came about as preemptive reform under the Vargas dictatorship. There is little indication that democracy in the 1940s through early 1960s was anything but clientelistic (cf. Lyne 2007).[6]

While splitting Latin America into polities with weak and strong social policy may be too simple, Segura-Ubiergo's (2007) Boolean analysis identifies important conditions that contribute to social policy innovation in the region. Higher economic development, economic closure, the presence of democracy, and a strong labor movement no doubt pressing for protectionist ISI policies created a constellation of political forces that promoted social policy. These variables directly relate to those we have identified as supporting programmatic party competition around economic distributive issues, namely the early development of economic capacities and opportunities for political mobilization that are favored by the presence of democracy or at least a modicum of civil rights that allows for the growth of interest groups, movements, and political parties. Social policy becomes the "stuff" of political conflict, where civil and political rights permit the rise of political interest groups under conditions of economic development with growing industrialization and urbanization (see also Haggard and Kaufman 2008).

Where the conditions that promote the salience of struggles about social policies were absent, politicians typically produced minimalist and particularistic social policy reforms that targeted only narrowly defined beneficiaries

---

[6] Segura-Ubiergo (2007: 30) scores Brazil as a high social spender based on averaging social expenditures from 1973 to 2000. This masks the fact that, in contrast to the other four high social policy spenders, Brazil developed its high expenditure pattern only in the 1980s and 1990s but not during the postwar era of democracy. Given the profound changes in Brazil's social policy, it is inadequate to conceptualize the dependent variable of the analysis as average spending from 1973 to 2000. Moreover, the classification of Brazil as a high spender seemingly disproves the link between social policy expansion and urbanization or industrialization as well as mobilization of labor movements.

in a clientelist fashion. Pension schemes limited to government employees are a prominent example. Where such social policies prevailed, there was little fertile ground for the programmatic configuration of party systems around economic distributive issues. The state played too small a role in the everyday well-being of broad categories of citizens to mobilize them around social policy alternatives.

ISI and Programmatic Party Competition

Let us first consider whether the general prevalence of import-substituting industrialization, induced either by an urban coalition of business and labor or by state-building authoritarian elites, gave rise to political alignments that support programmatic party competition, or whether it took the development of more encompassing social policies to generate PPS around economic distributive issues. On the basis of Segura-Ubiergo's (2007) analysis, not all countries with vigorous ISI policies exhibited the other conditions that fueled demand and supply of social policy. Conversely, Costa Rica illustrates that strong ISI may not be a necessary precondition for a more encompassing social policy, provided the polity witnessed sustained and strong political mobilization for redistribution and democratic politics.

It is difficult to find appropriate cross-national measures to gauge the extent to which policy makers adopted ISI policies. Ideally, we would observe how governments intervened in the allocation of capital, labor, and commodities in the economy to promote industrialization as well as how they controlled the flow of goods and capital across borders during the heyday of the ISI development model.

An especially important aspect of ISI economies was the expansion of public enterprise in the 1950s, 1960s, and still in the 1970s, whether in primary commodities (mining, oil, gas), infrastructure and utilities (transport, communication, energy), or manufacturing. In a competitive situation, democratically elected politicians may be particularly attentive to the demands of a strong publicly owned, subsidized, or regulated enterprise sector. In times of good economic performance, such enterprises may become the troughs for feeding clientelistic benefits (jobs, contracts) to electoral constituencies. In bad times, the closure or privatization of state-supported enterprises becomes a focal point for intense political controversy with companies or sectors organizing in defense of their interests. As suggested earlier, the ISI-based logic of political governance in the economy may not clearly sustain programmatic party competition but instead promote the entrenchment of clientelistic politics.

Roberts (2002) was the first to collect data on the magnitude of public enterprise in Latin American economies, tracked by the share of the public sector in total business investment in the peak year in the 1970s, that is,

TABLE 6.4. *Indicators of Import-Substituting Industrialization and Programmatic Party Systems*

	Share of Total Investment in Public Enterprises, Peak 1970–80 (in percent)	Trade Openness 1970 (index of obstacles to disincentives)	Index of Market Liberalism	
			1970	1985
Argentina	20.7	.546	.569	.617
Bolivia	40.9	.644	.471	.445
Brazil	22.8	.493	.543	.492
Chile	20.0	.126	.347	.671
Colombia	10.3	.635	.421	.578
Costa Rica	19.6	.511	.548	.494
Dominican Republic	12.2	.380	.376	.446
Ecuador	n.d.	.516	.504	.556
Mexico	29.4	.714	.531	.578
Peru	22.1	.561	.482	.394
Uruguay	18.3	.000	.390	.815
Venezuela	36.3	.506	.443	.456
Average	23.0	.469	.469	.545
(standard deviation)	(9.3)	(.21)	(.074)	(.118)
Economic PPS-2 Index (Table II.l, column 5.2) (correlation)	−.20	−.64*	−.17	.78***

* $p \leq .10$; ** $p \leq .05$; *** $p \leq .01$.

during the final decade of ISI economic policies in most Latin American countries (except Chile). Roberts's data are displayed in the first column of Table 6.4. As can be seen, the strength of state-run public enterprises does not relate to economic PPS at all. This could be the case for two not mutually exclusive reasons. First, strong ISI policy intervention does not support programmatic party competition because it generates many opportunities for clientelistic exchange. Second, as explained in the literature on the "resource curse" (Ross 2001), intervention is particularly likely where state revenues rely on natural resource extraction, such as in Bolivia, Mexico, Peru, Venezuela, and to a lesser extent Chile. Thus, it is no wonder that this measure of ISI does not relate to programmatic PPS.

A crude index of industrialization that would take natural resource exporters out of the picture, however, does not fare better as predictor of later PPS. Roberts (2002: 16) measures the peak score of each country's manufacturing share of GDP between 1970 and 1980, and we compare these data with our index of economic PPS (calculation not shown here).

Industrialization, net of political regime and social policy developments, appears to have little effect on PPS in Latin American countries.[7]

Trade restrictions can serve as another tracer of ISI policies in the region. Again, they can derive from a programmatic call for the protection of whole factors and sectors of the economy from international competition. But in practice, the benefits of protectionism may be tailored to the interests of individual or small groups of businesses and fuel clientelistic politics. Raw figures on the magnitude of foreign trade relative to GDP are not terribly meaningful to gauge the protectionism of economic policy, as country size and natural resource endowment affect the trade pattern net of trade policies (tariffs, regulatory constraints on imports or exports).[8] To track ISI policies in the realm of trade and capital flows, the only measure of efforts to restrict the open flow of resources has been constructed by Morley, Machado, and Pettinato (1999: table A2 and A4) for the period of 1970 to 1995, albeit in the full knowledge of major sources of measurement error in the data (ibid., pp. 10–11). The data reported for trade in Table 6.4 (column 2) suggest that there is a moderately strong negative relationship between economic PPS in the late 1990s and the trade openness of Latin American countries in 1970 (but not with capital account liberalization or other measures of market liberalism calculated by Morley et al. 1999, as shown in Table 6.4, column 3). As we show later in this chapter, this relationship is likely to be mediated by social policy. Politicians who pushed for more encompassing social policy coverage in the 1950s and 1960s also promoted external protectionism to prevent downward pressures on wage levels through foreign exposure to competition. This dual arrangement created the "stakes" of the economic distributive struggle in these polities and locked in programmatic party competition for many decades.

Before we return to this topic through a closer examination of social policy, let us consider Morley et al.'s (1999) general economic liberalization index that covers the liberalization of banking, taxation, and privatization, in addition to trade and external capital account, as a general measure of ISI strategy. The 1970 liberalization scores for the twelve Latin American countries show virtually no association with their patterns of party competition almost thirty years later, but by 1985 there is a rather strong relationship: countries with greater market liberalization, as opposed to government-controlled ISI economies, also tended to possess stronger economic-programmatic party competition in 1997–98. Among them are

---

[7] This conclusion would also be derived from employing Gwynne's (1985: 36–37) data of manufacturing production and growth in Latin America at different points in time.

[8] Segura-Ubiergo (2007: 35) calculates the ratio of imports and exports to GDP to gauge the foreign economic exposure of Latin American polities. This measure may be adequate to determine whether social policy responds to trade exposure but not to determine the prevalence of import-substituting industrialization imposing an active restriction of trade and capital flows.

the three most affluent Latin American countries behind Venezuela in the 1970s: Argentina, Chile, and Uruguay. All of them had authoritarian regimes that preserved or sharply boosted levels of market liberalization,[9] as well as (by regional standards) quite generous, inclusive social policies for the urban economic sector when dictators took over against a backdrop of relative economic decline and intensifying distributive struggles in the 1960s. Economic liberalization and some social policy retrenchment in the 1970s and 1980s under dictatorship only tended to reinforce economic alignments in partisan politics as dictatorships fell.

One cause and consequence of ISI strategies in the 1950s and 1960s were strong working-class movements, manifested by labor unions in raw materials extraction, especially mining, and manufacturing. There is little systematic, reliable, and valid quantitative information about the mobilization of labor in Latin America. Against these odds, Roberts (2002) collected information that attempts to identify the highest levels of union enrollment and centralization among unions in each country. Table 6.5 summarizes the relative size of membership and the centralization-coordination of union organizations in a single value of labor mobilization. Roberts employs this index together with several other measures of ISI to construct a dummy variable that separates "labor mobilizing" from "elitist" party systems. Table 6.5 also presents Roberts's composite index, which captures how vigorously countries embraced ISI development strategies, and a judgmental score of the strength of Latin American labor unions primarily derived from Rueschemeyer et al.'s (1992) comparative-historical analysis, supplemented by Hartlyn (1998), Isaacs (1996), and Korzeniewicz (2000).

Table 6.5 delivers a clear message. The strength of labor movements, taken by itself, is not a determinant of programmatic party competition. But maybe there is a more complex, contingent relationship between labor mobilization, social policy, and programmatic competition. On the one hand, Bolivia and Peru were comparatively poor and agrarian countries with strong labor movements concentrated only in mining and natural-resource-extracting enclaves. This isolation may have prevented them from contributing to the formation of party systems with high PPS. As discussed earlier, the only semi-institutionalized parties in these countries, the Bolivian MNR and the Peruvian APRA, always had a vague programmatic profile and often tenuous, if not strained, relations with the labor movement. On the other hand, there were wealthier countries with labor movements that had substantial support in the metropolitan manufacturing or service sectors, albeit sometimes in addition to a natural resource core. This applies particularly to Argentina, Chile, Uruguay, and possibly Costa Rica, if we follow

[9] For Uruguay, however, many experts believe that the 1985 level of liberalization vastly overstates what was actually accomplished. Even removing Uruguay, however, would preserve much of the relationship of liberal reform and PPS.

TABLE 6.5. *Labor Strength and Economic PPS*

	Index of Labor Union Strength, peak year (density and concentration)	Labor Mobilizing versus Elitist Party Systems	Strength of Labor
Argentina	3.21	1	1
Bolivia	.91	1	1
Brazil	−1.26	1	0
Chile	.77	1	1
Colombia	−2.64	0	0
Costa Rica	−2.07	0	1
Dominican Republic	−1.93	0	0
Ecuador	−1.18	0	0
Mexico	1.57	1	0
Peru	.93	1	1
Uruguay	.56	0	1
Venezuela	1.06	1	1
Average	.006	.58	.58
(standard deviation)	(1.77)	(.58)	(.51)
Economic PPS-2 Index (Table II.1, column 5.2)			
(correlation)	.37	−.01	.41

Note: Unless otherwise noted, N = 12 for each correlation. * $p \leq .10$; ** $p \leq .05$; *** $p \leq .01$.
Sources: Column 1: Roberts (2002), data on peak trade union density (as percentage of the labor force) and union organizational concentration (low, medium, high). Index adds the standardized differences on each measure from the Latin American mean; column 2: Roberts (2002: 16), judgmental classification; labor mobilizing polities = 1; column 3: coded on the basis of the verbal characterization of cases in Rueschemeyer et al. (1992: 181–94, 234–36). Judgments for Ecuador and the Dominican Republic based on Hartlyn (1998) and Isaacs (1996).

Rueschemeyer et al.'s (1992) scoring. In these countries, sectoral union support was more broad-based, though urban centered, and placed social policy demands high on the list of political issues. In most rural areas, by contrast, labor could be marginalized by repression or bought off through particularistic, clientelistic arrangements. Venezuela is a special case: though relatively affluent and urban, it was almost wholly dependent on its petroleum industry rather than urban-based manufacturing and services. The resulting rentier economy fueled clientelism and undercut programmatic party competition.

Overall, then, direct and indirect measures of ISI development strategies do not provide strong mechanisms and predictions of programmatic party competition. There is no reason to presume, either theoretically or empirically, that state-interventionist ISI development strategies should result in a higher programmatic structuring of party competition in twentieth-century

Latin American politics. The effect of labor mobilization on programmatic party competition is conditional on economic development, civil-political freedoms, and, most important, the development of the welfare state as a proximate cause of building and sustaining distributive economic conflict in the arena of party competition.

Social Policy Development and Programmatic Party Competition

Research on the development of Latin American welfare states is still in its early stages, although most recently big steps forward have occurred (see Brown and Hunter 1999; Kaufman and Segura-Ubiergo 2001; Segura-Ubiergo 2007; Haggard and Kaufman 2008). We lack detailed comparative datasets specifying parameters of Latin American social policy schemes on coverage rates of the population, generosity of benefits (income replacement rates), eligibility criteria to qualify for benefits, and contribution and benefit schemes for different social policy programs. Investigations covering Organisation for Economic Co-operation and Development (OECD) welfare states generate such detailed data but have invariably found that the inclusiveness, universalism, and redistributive effect of social policies are robustly associated with fiscal public social policy expenditures.[10] Assuming the same to be true in Latin America, we rely here on Latin American social policy expenditure figures assembled by Kaufman and Segura-Ubiergo (2001) and updated and corrected by Evelyne Huber and John Stephens.[11]

The mechanisms through which social policies promote and are reinforced by programmatic party system development are twofold. First, inclusive social policies define costs and benefits of social risk protection in terms of broad categories of electoral constituencies. They remove from politicians the option to target benefits to individual voters or small groups of loyal voters, thus constraining, if not removing, their opportunities to build clientelistic linkages. The presence of universalistic social policies indicates the dominance of parties with a strong programmatic appeal over collective goods provision. Popular demands for such policies, in turn, are stimulated by political and economic developments we have already identified as historical antecedents of economic PPS: development and electoral contestation. Higher affluence reduces the value citizens attribute to clientelistic, targeted benefits and makes them more aware of the opportunity costs of such goods. Particularly under conditions of intense electoral competition, party politicians will stop pursuing clientelistic linkage strategies as affluence increases (Kitschelt and Wilkinson 2007).

---

[10] In cross-national analysis, for example, Esping-Andersen's (1990) index of policy decommodification, which calculates eligibility and benefit entitlements, tends to be correlated with public-sector social policy expenditure at rates of better than .90 in most instances.

[11] We thank these scholars for sharing their data with us.

Second, once in place, inclusive social policy schemes create and maintain their own constituencies and generate broad-based support, which democratic politicians might seize to build their partisan representational strategies. Because social policy benefits are significant for large constituencies, conflicts over welfare state retrenchment become highly salient as a major bone of contention in interparty programmatic competition, particularly in Latin America when governments tried to dismantle ISI strategies. It is easier for repressive regimes, such as Chile under Pinochet, to engineer such cuts. Where social policies went far enough to affect most citizens' economic risk exposure in a fundamental way, contestation about social policy is likely to remain a main source of partisan alignments even after an authoritarian interlude with policy retrenchment.

The only data on Latin American welfare states consistently available are social expenditure figures, for our set of countries from 1973 onward, except for Colombia, where the time series starts only in 1984. Because in most countries (except Argentina, the Dominican Republic, and Peru) social policy expenditures in the early 1980s were somewhat higher than in the early 1970s, we assign Colombia's 1984 expenditures to fill the missing value for its 1973 expenditure.[12] The year 1973 quite likely is near the high watermark of ISI development policies, just a handful of years before the onset of the Latin American debt crisis that contributed to the unraveling of a state-led industrialization strategy. In Table 6.6, we display total social policy expenditure figures for four time points altogether – 1973, 1983, 1993, and the last available year of data that in most, but not all, cases coincides with the year of the Latin American legislators' survey (1997). Higher expenditures do not necessarily mean a more egalitarian society. They may indicate only that the urban sector of formal wage earners in manufacturing and services is comprehensively covered. This creates moderately inclusive welfare states in the more urbanized countries. In more agrarian countries, however, such as Brazil in the 1960s through 1980s, even an intermediate level of social expenditure may indicate only that a small, privileged urban sector, often consisting mostly of civil servants, benefits from social policy, whereas the vast mass of the population does not. Welfare states in Latin America therefore may often be actively redistributive toward the better-off (cf. Rudra 2008).

The data reveal that the earliest measure of social policy expenditure in 1973 shows a better "fit" with our measures of economic PPS than later figures for 1983 and after. Social policy expenditure in 1973, in turn, is closely related to economic development in an earlier age that tended to fuel the rise of urban social movements demanding state policies of social

---

[12] Given that Colombia has preciously little programmatic party system structuration, this move slightly biases our data against our hypothesis, namely to find a relationship between Colombia's low social expenditure in the 1970s and the absence of PPS in the 1990s.

TABLE 6.6. *Social Policy Expenditures and Economic PPS*

	Social Policy Expenditure as Percent of GDP			
	1973	1983	1993	Latest before 1998
Argentina	11.4	9.1	13.0	13.6 (1997)
Bolivia	3.3	4.8 (1984)	9.3	11.3 (1997) HS
Brazil	7.8	10.5	13.2	13.9 (1997)
Chile	13.9	19.9	11.8 HS	12.0 (1997) HS
Colombia	6.4 (1984) HS	6.4 (1984) HS	4.6 HS	6.6 (1997) HS
Costa Rica	10.7	13.3 HS	13.1 HS	14.3 (1997) HS
Dominican Republic	5.3	4.5 HS	4.3	5.2 (1997)
Ecuador	4.1	5.1	4.7	4.9 (1994)
Mexico	5.6	5.6	7.6	7.1 (1997)
Peru	5.3	4.1	4.5 (1986)	4.5 (1986)
Uruguay	13.5	16.4	22.4 HS	22.7 HS
Venezuela	7.2	9.0	7.8 HS 1986	7.1 (1999) HS
Average (standard deviation)	7.9 (3.5)	9.1 (5.1)	9.7 (5.4)	10.3 (5.4)
Economic partisan divide (correlation)	.71***	.69***	.47	.41
Economic policy content of parties' left-right placement (correlation)	.76***	.82***	.64**	.59**
Representation: Economic policy issue congruence of parties' voters and legislators (correlation)	.80*** (N = 9)	.79*** (N = 9)	.48 (N = 9)	.50 (N = 9)
Average diffuseness of parties on economic policy issues (correlation)	−0.45	−0.43	−0.48	−0.47
Economic PPS-2 (Table II.1, column 5.2) (correlation)	.88***	.82***	.70***	.63**

Note: Unless otherwise noted, N = 12 for each correlation. * p ≤ .10; ** p ≤ .05; *** p ≤ .01.

Sources: Kaufman and Segura-Ubiergo (2001), supplemented by Evelyne Huber and John Stephens's dataset (indicated by HS).

protection (r = .86), as well as to opportunities for democratic party competition in the post–World War II era (1945–73) (r = .73). These findings are
roughly consistent with Segura-Ubiergo's analysis of causes of social policy
expansion in Latin America. Democracy and social mobilization of urban
interests are powerful forces advancing social policy. After 1973, and particularly since the Latin American debt crisis in the early 1980s, the pattern
has changed somewhat. In some of the countries with expansive policies in
an earlier era, fiscal retrenchment took place as ISI policies were disman-
tled (Argentina, 1973–83; Chile, 1983–93; Costa Rica, 1983–93; and, from
a lower level, Venezuela, 1983–94). In others, such as Bolivia and Brazil,
where weak industrial unionism and clientelistic democracy or authoritarian
politics provided little boost for social policy until the 1970s, social policy
expenditures expanded from a low base in subsequent decades. Nevertheless, only in countries that experienced sustained mobilization in favor of
inclusive social policies in the 1950s and 1960s did party systems exhibit a
pronounced alignment around economic-distributive issues after 1990.

It would require detailed process-tracing case studies to demonstrate that
the data pattern conveyed in Table 6.6 is not simply one of correlation but
of causation. Where social expenditures remained comparatively low, welfare states served only narrow special interests primarily located in the civil
service and a few privileged ISI industrial sectors.[13] This suited clientelistic
parties well. Countries with high social policy expenditures, by contrast,
exhibit a politics of distributive partisan conflict with rather stark polarization in the 1960s and 1970s, which carried over into conflicts about the
defense, retrenchment, and reform of welfare states in the 1980s, 1990s,
and beyond. Military dictatorships in Argentina, Chile, and Uruguay were
important vehicles to experiment with a partial dismantling of the welfare
state, an objective that juntas apparently attained more thoroughly in Chile
than in Argentina or Uruguay. This polarization set the agenda for democratic party competition later when the military retreated to the barracks.
Among strong social policy spenders, Costa Rica is the only country that
witnessed an incremental expansion of social policy and did not go through
an authoritarian episode in the 1970s or 1980s.

A clear outlier for our explanation is Mexico, with moderately high programmatic party competition in the late 1990s but a very small welfare state
throughout its twentieth-century history. Here a hegemonic ruling party
built a sophisticated system of clientelistic compensation and market regulation (e.g., of employment, landownership, access to capital) that may in part
have served as a substitute for the protection of wage labor from market
risks through social policy as practiced in other countries. Not by accident,

---

[13] In contrast to Segura-Ubiergo's (2007) characterization of Brazil as a generous welfare
spender, this narrow client-oriented social policy appears to have been dominant in Brazilian
social policy as well.

the underdog opposition party PAN identified itself partly in programmatic market-liberal terms against this legacy.

In Venezuela, relatively low social policy expenditures combined with weak programmatic partisan alignments around economic-distributive issues. Although this relationship confirms the hypothesized pattern, the case commands special attention. Given its resource and rent-based economy and the poverty of the country's largely agrarian economy, social mobilization in general and working-class mobilization in particular remained weak in the 1930s through 1950s, even as Venezuela became Latin America's most wealthy polity measured by per capita GDP. After elite negotiations restored democracy in 1958, the oil-based rentier economy enabled the two leading parties, AD and COPEI, to establish a duopoly based on the ample opportunities offered by the resource extractive economy to dispense a bounty of pork and clientelistic inducements. The oil regime and the two-party cartel enabled politicians to avoid programmatic competition that might have committed them to welfare state expansion. In light of these developments, it is unlikely that our descriptive finding of relatively weak programmatic party competition around economic-distributive issues in Venezuela in 1998 is simply an accident of measuring at the moment of party system collapse. It is more likely that nonprogrammatic, clientelistic politics began to dominate Venezuela shortly after its redemocratization in 1958 and displaced whatever modicum of programmatic competition might have been initially present (cf. Coppedge 1994). The centrality of clientelistic strategies in a rentier economy, in turn, is one major reason for the inability of the traditional parties to confront the changing international conditions of economic competitiveness and the crises of economic performance and political governance, a failure that ultimately resulted in the collapse of the Venezuelan party system.

Let us close this discussion of long-term political-economic conditions for programmatic party competition around economic-distributive issues in Latin America by (re)considering two factors that theoretical analyses have identified as potential causes of weak social policy development – namely, an open economy and ethnocultural pluralism. If entrenched social policy promotes and sustains high economic-distributive PPS, but trade and ethnic pluralism undermine social policy, then trade and ethnic pluralism should be correlated with, and at least indirectly causally related to, programmatic party system structuration.

The data bear out this expectation. There is a moderately negative association between trade openness in 1970 and economic PPS in our twelve Latin American countries ($r = -.64$). But trade is more strongly related to social policy expenditure in 1973 ($r = -.74$),[14] which, in turn, is almost perfectly

---

[14] This association is statistically confirmed with a more powerful time-series cross-sectional analysis by Segura-Ubiergo (2007: chap. 3).

related to economic PPS in 1997–98 (r = .88). Considering the historical timeline of political mobilization, trade restriction, and social policy development, it is likely that strong urban political party mobilization in favor of ISI policies precipitated both external trade closure and the emergence of comparatively encompassing social policies. Both trade restrictions and social policies, in turn, reinforced and perpetuated high economic PPS in the party system. Once party economic alignments and social policies are entrenched in a polity and become highly salient for voters and politicians alike, they have a tendency to become self-perpetuating until a new era of dislocations occurs. Key actors have a strong stake in the social policy status quo.

In less-developed countries that compete primarily on the cheapness of wage labor, greater trade openness reduces the degrees of freedom for politicians to institute social policy contributions and benefits. Conversely, where external trade relations can be restricted, Latin American politics has delivered more generous and encompassing social policy. Trade is thus an indirect negative contributor to programmatic partisan competition around economic-distributive issues, mediated by social policy expenditure.

The relationship between ethnocultural pluralism and economic PPS is even more striking but depends on the measure of pluralism we choose. Theory holds that in ethnically divided countries the dominant ethnic group will favor *less* supply of public goods that accrue to all members of society the *greater* is the proportion of minorities in the population (Alesina, Baquir, and Easterly 1999). Ethnic groups try to limit the provision of social policy benefits to their own ethnicity. Members of ethnic groups accept redistribution within their own group but not beyond its boundaries. Compatible with this argument, theories of clientelism hold that ethnic divisions facilitate clientelism because ethnic networks permit easier monitoring of the exchange between targeted material goods and vote in favor of the clientelist party (Kitschelt and Wilkinson 2007). The consummation of clientelistic exchanges, in turn, reduces the attractiveness of programmatic competition for politicians operating under conditions of resource constraints. Finally, the presence of greater ethnic divisions usually implies a smaller share of immigrants from Western Europe in the eighteenth and nineteenth centuries. Following the logic laid out by Acemoglu, Johnson, and Robinson (2001), if immigrants were the main initiators of investment in market-sustaining institutions of governance, a smaller proportion of immigrants might lead to less investment in public institutions, such as those that enforce property rights and facilitate market exchange. This ultimately results in lower growth.

Inspecting the evidence for our twelve Latin American countries, these hypotheses are broadly borne out (Table 6.7). It all depends, however, on the appropriate measure of ethnic pluralism. If we stick to an old but widely used index of ethnolinguistic fractionalization (ELF), statistical relations are

TABLE 6.7. *Measures of Ethnic Fractionalization and Programmatic Competition*

	Ethnolinguistic Fractionalization		
	Standard	Annett 2001	Alesina et al. 2003
Chile	.14	.43	.17
Uruguay	.20	.26	.25
Argentina	.31	.41	.26
Costa Rica	.07	.24	.24
Mexico	.30	.59	.54
Venezuela	.11	.54	.50
Dominican Republic	.04	.46	.43
Brazil	.07	.64	.54
Colombia	.06	.67	.60
Ecuador	.53	.66	.66
Peru	.59	.66	.66
Bolivia	.68	.71	.74
Mean and standard deviation (in parentheses)	.26 (.23)	.52 (.16)	.47 (.19)
Correlation with 1928 GDP	−.23	−.68*	−.81**
Correlation with 1980 GDP	−.40	−.48	−.52
Correlation with 1998 GDP	−.42	−.57	
Correlation with electoral contestation, 1945–73	−.39	−.60*	−.62*
Correlation with cumulative capacity and opportunity for mobilization	−.36	−.75**	−.83**
Correlation with social policy expenditure, 1973	−.47	−.81**	−.93***
Correlation with economic PPS-2	−.33	−.78**	−.86***

Note: Unless otherwise noted, N = 12 for each correlation. * $p \leq .10$; ** $p \leq .05$; *** $p \leq .01$.
Source: Data reported in Birnir and Van Cott (2007) from Annett (2001) and Alesina et al. (2003)

in the expected direction but are too weak to suggest a causal relationship (column 1). But the traditional ELF measure does not pick up racial and other nonlinguistic cultural group markers. Two recent indices of cultural pluralism that have incorporated this additional information confirm theoretical expectations of the ethnic politics literature in a spectacular fashion (Table 6.7, columns 2 and 3). More pluralist ethnocultural polities in Latin America have been substantially poorer, particularly when we compare 1928 income figures. Multicultural societies also enjoyed less electoral contestation since 1945 and a significantly lower level of social policy protection in 1973 (r = −.93, using Alesina's ethnocultural fractionalization measure). If we posit that ethnocultural pluralism is an exogenous variable in Latin America, at least when we consider the twentieth century, then there

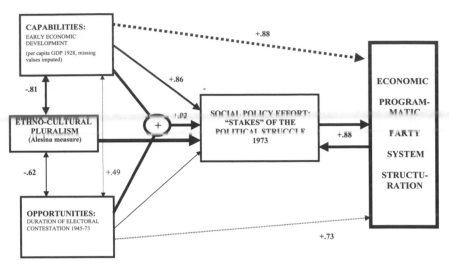

FIGURE 6.1. Long-term capabilities, opportunities, and stakes shaping programmatic party system structuration.

is a plausible causal link running from high cultural pluralism to less programmatic structuring of party systems and less social policy effort. Once this pattern has been locked in, it perpetuates low programmatic structuring of party competition.

As a final step let us visualize the simple, but powerful relations among capacities, opportunities, and "stakes" in party systems as interrelated forces that promote durable patterns of programmatic party competition (Figure 6.1). Ethnoculturally fragmented polities were poorer from the early twentieth century onward and also developed fewer opportunities for electoral contestation. Higher development, particularly in interaction with opportunities for electoral contestation, and ethnocultural homogeneity promote political mobilization that translates into more encompassing social policies by the early 1970s. Social policy, in turn, constitutes the "stakes" that keep programmatic party system structuration around economic-distributive issues, particularly in an era of economic liberalization, when all sorts of institutions and arrangements originating in the ISI era of Latin American development come under siege. The figure shows bivariate associations larger than .60, with a few exceptions, and includes broken lines for strong statistical associations without intervening causal mechanisms, that is, those between early capabilities and post–World War II electoral contestation, on one hand, and economic PPS, on the other.

Given the small number of cases and the high collinearity among variables, there is no statistical way to demonstrate causality in the way postulated in Figure 6.1. But ontological and narrative-historical considerations make this a plausible argument. Ontologically, causes require temporal precedence, temporal and spatial proximity to consequences, and the capacity to specify and measure mechanisms, here understood as logics of strategic interaction that historical collective actors are likely to have chosen in bringing about the observed consequences (social policies, party system structuration). In a narrative-historical perspective, accounts of political development in countries with more encompassing social policies point to the mechanisms of economic development and political mobilization that we think explain the persistence of economic-distributive programmatic party system structuration (cf. Collier and Collier 1991; Segura-Ubiergo 2007).

Let us finally emphasize the presence of a hard case, Brazil. While weak economic development and high ethnocultural pluralism are consistent with the observation of weak economic PPS at the end of the millennium, Brazil's intermediate, albeit not high, level of social policy effort in the 1970s and its post–World War II opportunities for democratic competition would have pointed toward a stronger articulation of programmatic political alignments.

PARTY SYSTEM INSTITUTIONALIZATION AND ECONOMIC PPS?

Mainwaring and Scully (1995) developed a widely cited and frequently modified index of party system institutionalization in Latin America. Following Huntington's (1968: 12) famous phrase that institutionalization involves a "process by which organizations and procedures acquire value and stability," an important component of Mainwaring and Scully's operationalization of the concept for parties has to do with the average age of parties and the prominence of older parties in Latin American party systems. But what creates different levels of institutionalization and what consequences may it have? These are salient questions intimated in Mainwaring and Scully's study but not explicitly analyzed by them. Moreover, for us the question is how institutionalization relates to economic PPS as the most important divide within the Latin American countries that have any programmatic competition.

There is a clear relationship between party system institutionalization and programmatic structuring of party systems, but also a key difference. Politicians who have more time to hone relations with constituencies and build experienced party organizations are more likely to develop programmatic appeals and compete against other parties on the strength of their programmatic reputations. Conversely, voters are able to discern parties' positions better, the longer such competitors have been around. Institutionalization thus goes hand in hand with programmatic competition. But not all institutionalization is programmatic. Politicians can also develop stable machines around clientelistic relations of exchange, and at least the Colombian party system that we have shown to be almost entirely devoid of programmatic content and the weakly programmatic Venezuelan party system both demonstrate this possibility well.

TABLE 6.8. *Party System Institutionalization and Economic PPS*

	Party System Institutionalization	
	Original Mainwaring-Scully Index	Revised Index: Electoral Incorporation
Argentina	9.0	4.5
Bolivia	5.0	3.0
Brazil	5.0	3.0
Chile	11.5	6.0
Colombia	10.5	2.5
Costa Rica	11.5	6.0
Dominican Republic	No data	2.5
Ecuador	5.0	3.0
Mexico	8.5	4.5
Peru	4.5	2.5
Uruguay	11.5	5.5
Venezuela	10.5	5.5
Average (standard deviation)	8.4 (2.96)	4.0 (1.44)
Economic partisan divide (correlation)	.71*** (N = 11)	.83***
Economic policy content of parties' left-right placement (correlation)	.64* (N = 11)	.74**
Representation: Economic policy issue congruence of parties' voters and legislators (correlation)	.53 (N = 9)	.47 (N = 9)
Average diffuseness of parties on economic policy issues (correlation)	−.51 (N = 11)	−.61**
Economic PPS-2 Index (Table II.1, column 5.2) (correlation)	.75** (N = 11)	.85***

Note: Unless otherwise noted, N = 12 for each correlation. * p ≤ .10; ** p ≤ .05; *** p ≤ .01.
Sources: See text. Scores in columns (1) and (2) calculated from Mainwaring and Scully (1995) and supplemented by score of the Dominican Republic.

Without Colombia and Venezuela, the same variables that account for high economic PPS also explain Mainwaring and Scully's institutionalization index – namely, early economic development, ample opportunities for electoral competition, and later the development of more encompassing social policies. As a consequence, the institutionalization index is also robustly associated with the components of programmatic party competition and especially with the economic PPS index (Table 6.8). And it may not be an accident that in Colombia and Venezuela, where institutionalization scores are high but conditions that antedate high institutionalization elsewhere are weaker or absent, party systems unraveled in the 1990s and after. We revisit this issue in our conclusion. In Colombia the persistence of oligarchy and disenfranchisement, punctuated by civil war, and in Venezuela the oil rentier economy from the 1930s onward created favorable conditions for durable party machines to arise with only weak programmatic content but a great capacity to channel resources to strategic constituencies controlled by national two-party cartels.

CONCLUSION

Programmatic divisions may not be strong anywhere in Latin America by global standards, but they vary dramatically within the region. Most parties have deployed clientelistic techniques of constituency building, but the extent to which such practices have been supplemented or displaced by programmatic appeals differs across countries. Long-term processes of political mobilization based on economic capabilities, regime opportunities, and political-economic stakes that allow politicians and voters to organize around programs do a good explanatory job in accounting for cross-national patterns of party competition in our twelve Latin American countries in the late 1990s. This is the main message of the chapter. The causal chain is rather complicated and long, but Occam's razor would be unhelpful in our quest to reconstruct the mechanisms that contribute to these patterns of party competition. Cutting off distant causes that are tightly linked to later developments that serve as proximate causes might create the illusion of easy malleability of party systems. And distant causes sometimes provide parsimonious predictions of ultimate outcomes (e.g., 1928 per capita GDP), but they do not identify the empirical mechanisms that account for the production of the ultimate outcome. We have therefore worked our way through a chain of causation that includes opportunities for electoral contestation experienced by each Latin American country between World War II and the peak of the ISI development strategy at the time of the first world oil crisis in the mid-1970s, and social policy achievements that may constitute focal points for political conflict that are quite diverse across nations.

Nevertheless, none of the parties covered here has relied exclusively on programmatic politics. As we suggested with regard to the political-economic dynamic of ISI development strategies, even political parties that initially led the drive to establish new political-economic regimes and policies to provide broad collective or club goods have over time developed clientelistic practices governed by party machines that at least partially displace the parties' programmatic profiles. This trajectory is certainly borne out by historical accounts of the Argentinean Peronists (Gibson 1997; Levitsky 2003: chap. 2), the two main Venezuelan competitors between 1958 and the mid-1990s (Coppedge 1994, 1996; Kornblith and Levine 1995), the Mexican ruling PRI (Bruhn 1997; Craig and Cornelius 1995; Fox 1994; Dresser 1996), or the Costa Rican parties (Gudmundson 1996; Yashar 1995).

The Uruguayan case is historically more complicated. Here an oligarchical faction tried to establish its supremacy through electoral incorporation of the urban masses and by granting social policy reform as early as the beginning of the twentieth century. But even then the established parties and party factions never abandoned their clientelistic practices and actually reinvigorated them upon reaching an accommodation on the status quo of social policy (cf. Biles 1975; Gillespie and González 1989; González 1995; Rial 1996). It was the steady downward pressure on social policy due to weak economic performance in the 1950s and 1960s that created the ground for a New Left confronting the established clientelistic parties.

Because of data constraints, our comparison had to leave out several small Central American countries (El Salvador, Guatemala, Honduras, Nicaragua, and Panama). In these cases, Mahoney (2001) lays out long-term chains of causal mechanisms that in some instances led to fundamental distributive struggles about new "stakes" of political-economic development. While such countries experienced these struggles several decades later than comparable conflicts in most of the Southern Cone, their conflicts may have generated a similar momentum to entrench programmatic alignments. At least in El Salvador and Nicaragua, the protracted struggles among military and civilian political camps about land reform and economic redistribution created the potential for crystallizing programmatic partisan alignments under conditions of democratic contestation. Rival elites certainly had the time to build up programmatic reputations. If they locked them in through social policy and income redistribution, they were likely to last for some time.

Before we declare ourselves satisfied with an explanation of economic partisan divides that relies on a causal chain leading from economic development through opportunities for political contestation and welfare state deployment, let us appreciate its limitations. For each country, Table 6.9 presents actual and predicted economic PPS-2 values, based on knowing the countries' cumulative effects of economic capacities and electoral experiences or their social policy expenditures in 1973. The PPS scale has a range of six units (-3 to $+3$) and a median of slightly less than zero ($-.40$), together with a rather large standard deviation of 2.1. In a number of countries, the discrepancy between *predicted* and *actual* economic PPS value is small ($|<1.06|$, one-half of one standard deviation), with some countries exhibiting discrepancies between one-third and one-half standard deviation on one out of two PPS measures (Argentina, Colombia, Dominican Republic, Ecuador, Venezuela). Two countries, however, emerge as consistent and stubborn outliers. In 1997–98 Brazil had substantially less PPS than we would have predicted on the basis of all long-term influences on programmatic party structuration. Predictors would place the country almost two units higher on PPS than is actually observed, almost one standard deviation

TABLE 6.9. *Predictive Power of Long-Term Determinants of Economic PPS-2*

	Actual Value of Economic PPS-2 (Table II.1)	Cumulative Effect of Capacities (1928) and Electoral Experiences (1945–73) (Table 6.3)		Stakes of the Political Struggle: Social Policy Expenditures (1973) (Table 6.6)	
		Expected Value	Studentized Residual	Expected Value	Studentized Residual
Argentina	+1.0	0.36	+.84	1.40	−.40
Bolivia	−3.0	−3.16	+.22	−2.77	−.24
Brazil	−2.0	−.68	*−1.99*	−.46	*−1.71*
Chile	+3.0	2.83	+.25	2.68	+.36
Colombia	−2.0	−1.78	−.28	−1.18	−.83
Costa Rica	+1.0	.72	+.37	1.04	−.04
Dominican Republic	−2.0	−2.64	+.90	−1.74	−.26
Ecuador	−2.0	−1.22	*−1.05*	−2.36	−.37
Mexico	+1.0	*−.55*	**+2.56**	*−1.59*	**+4.73**
Peru	−2.0	−1.70	−.40	−1.74	−.26
Uruguay	+3.0	3.27	−.41	2.48	+.49
Venezuela	−1.0	−.44	−.72	−.76	−.23

Note: Discrepancy between predicted and actual value of PPS-2: scores italicized: discrepancy >|1.05|, that is, one-half standard deviation of economic PPS (sd = 2.11), but < |2.10|; scores italicized and in boldface: discrepancy > |2.10|. Actual scores shown as too high (+) or too low (−).

above the observed value. Our second case, Mexico, is an even more extreme outlier, but in a direction opposite to that of Brazil. Mexico displays much higher PPS than would have been predicted by long-term determinants of economic PPS. In the case of early economic development and experience with electoral contestation (cumulative capacities or opportunities), this discrepancy looks less extreme than that regarding the social policy effort in 1973, where the actual Mexican policy predicts an economic PPS value at the opposite end of its actual location. Clearly, our theoretical model does not provide an adequate explanation for Mexico's programmatic party system structuration.

The top ad hoc explanation for the failure of the theory to predict PPS in Mexico and Brazil may be measurement error of programmatic structuring. Maybe Brazilian party appeals are more programmatically coherent than is evidenced by the survey response pattern, whereas the inverse applies to Mexico. Beyond measurement error, however, there may be *functional equivalents* for an encompassing urban welfare state in place. For example, in Mexico, protection of the labor force through land tenure patterns (the *ejido* system) and labor legislation until the 1980s, as well as public and quasi-public employment in an oil rentier economy, may have provided such a functional equivalent. Social policy expenditure figures may therefore understate somewhat the effective level of social protection enjoyed by citizens in Mexico.

Conversely, Brazil might have a longer run of democracy than is compatible with its economic PPS-2 record, but the poverty of the country up to the 1950s and even 1960s, paired with continuing deep economic disparities and combined with electoral institutions that undercut incentives for strong programmatic party competition among coherent teams of politicians running under distinct partisan labels, may contribute to its outlier status. Also, given the high concentration of benefits on a narrow stratum of white-collar civil servants and white-collar workers more generally, simple expenditure measures may overstate the reach of the Brazilian welfare state. These ad hoc explanations point to systematic variables that in the short run may shape party system competition in the 1990s, such as prevailing democratic institutions and patterns of affluence and inequality. The next chapter purports to explore such mechanisms more systematically in a comparison of the entire cohort of Latin American democracies.

Short-term explanations can trump our long-term explanations if several conditions are met. First, rival explanations should account for the "anomalies" found in the long-term model, namely, Brazil and Mexico. Second, they should explain a wide range of observable PPS scores in other countries that are reasonably covered by the long-term explanation. And, finally, the relevant short-term variables should not be causally endogenous to the long-term conditions and associated mechanisms we have identified in this chapter.

7

Democratic Politics and Political Economy since the 1980s

Transforming the Programmatic Structure of Latin American Party Systems?

Herbert Kitschelt, Kirk A. Hawkins, Juan Pablo Luna, Guillermo Rosas, and Elizabeth J. Zechmeister

Even a cursory review of Latin American history since the 1970s reveals that the subcontinent has undergone fundamental, if not traumatic, economic and political change over the course of the past quarter century. Such momentous shocks and prolonged periods of social dislocation in the recent past may account better for the programmatic profile of party systems evidenced by our twelve Latin American countries in 1997–98 than can older political-economic patterns of party system building and long-term political experiences.

Given the power of long-term causal factors to account for party system structuration in the 1990s, it is an uphill battle, methodologically and empirically, to establish that recent developments in Latin America – economic growth, political economy, political regime change, and the design of democratic institutions – have left their mark on patterns of partisan accountability and citizen-politician linkage in the democratic process. Statistically, recent causes will be collinear with powerful predictors based on the past (e.g., 1973 social policy expenditure) and, in substantive terms, possibly endogenous to such prior developments. Moreover, before they are fully articulated, new partisan alignments may need more time to gestate than the brief period running from the "lost decade" to the late 1990s.

The lower the chance that any recent political-economic or institutional developments accounting for party system programmatic alignment in Latin America are endogenous to prior conditions, the stronger the claim that party systems are malleable in light of relatively short-term developments outside a long-term causal chain of determination.[1] More concretely, short-term causal explanations gain particular leverage if they account for what

---

[1] For a discussion of short-term and long-term causality with respect to causal chains, see Pierson (2003).

long-term explanations discard as "outliers" – that is, the relative strength of economic PPS in Mexico (too high) and in Brazil (too low).

Temporally proximate explanations of party system alignments may also be contingent rather than either completely exogenous or endogenous to temporally more remote causes. Short-term causes may operate on outcomes contingent upon certain prior conditions that "select" cases into a subset displaying a distinctive short-term dynamic. Here, the causal efficacy of short-term factors surfaces only within subsets of countries that share common long-term features. For example, economic dislocations of the 1980s and government responses to such dislocations may erode PPS only where there was significant structuration beforehand, or it may boost programmatic crystallization only where these conditions were previously absent.

In this chapter, we examine *economic capacities* and argue that the level of a country's economic development in the late 1990s is not a plausible explanation of economic PPS. Then we investigate whether short-term democratic institutions and political regime trajectories in the 1970s–80s shape economic PPS, but here again we arrive at an ultimately negative conclusion. Even in purely correlational terms, democratic institutions show weak association with cross-national variation in economic PPS. There is little reason to consider institutions as explanations of economic partisan competition, a surprising finding given scholarly investment in the study of the impact of electoral rules on party system formats. Next, in what is the heart of this chapter, we explore how the political economic "stakes" commanding popular attention in Latin American countries may have shaped patterns of programmatic party system structuration throughout the region in recent years. In a successively more subtle exploration, we consider how Latin American economic performance in the 1980s and 1990s, the governing parties' effective economic policy choices, and the match between politicians' appeals and actual policies in light of economic crises affect programmatic partisan alignments.

Our analysis assembles a modicum of quantitative and qualitative circumstantial evidence in favor of the proposition that an *interaction of both long-term and short-term conditions in fact does shape PPS.* Where prior conditions for higher economic PPS were relatively favorable – and presumably PPS evolved whenever political regimes permitted open party competition – a combination of economic crisis and dismantling of the prevailing economic development strategy based on import-substituting industrialization (ISI) *weakened* programmatic party competition. In countries that enjoyed long-term predispositions toward programmatic party competition, bad economic performance in the 1990s or policy switches by ostensibly populist leaders who enacted neoliberal reform against the desires of their constituents (which tended to follow bad economic performance in the 1980s) eroded the effectiveness of programmatic appeals. In this set of countries, programmatic competition weakened where economic performance was bleak in the 1990s or governments acted against preelectoral commitments. However, no such contingent relation can be found in the other group of Latin American countries, that is, those with weak prior conditions for the development of PPS. Neither good nor bad economic conditions nor the strategies parties and governments employed to cope with such conditions made a difference for the emergence of programmatic party competition in these other countries, at least as measured in 1998. The forces of destruction thus outweigh those of construction: bad economic performance can discredit existing parties and make them embrace strategies that undercut programmatic party competition and erode their electoral alignments, but good performance does not boost the generation of new party alignments with programmatic and institutionalized parties where prior conditions have not been conducive to such an outcome.

The Latin American countries with long-term prior conditions (economic capacities, electoral opportunities, political-economic stakes) that, on average, promise higher economic PPS scores in 1998 than in the rest of the comparison set are Argentina, Chile, Costa Rica, Mexico, Uruguay, and Venezuela. As our outlier analysis indicated (Table 6.9), Mexico is a marginal case, possibly disqualified from inclusion in this group by low social policy development in 1973, provided we do not make ad hoc allowance for certain functional equivalents of social insurance systems (land tenure and employment contracts, distributive consequences of a rentier oil economy). Conversely, Brazil is a marginal case on the opposite side of the divide, as its long-term conditions suggest at least an intermediate level of economic PPS in the late 1990s, not the observed low level. Its poor early per capita GDP (1928) (Table 6.1) and the heavy concentration of its moderately developed social policy benefits on a comparatively small group of civil servants, however, are likely factors that disqualify Brazil. Whereas the exclusion of Mexico from the subset of countries with at least moderately favorable conditions for economic PPS does not affect the contingent relationship between long-term prior conditions and the impact of short-term economic crisis, the inclusion of Brazil would weaken, if not undermine, the claims advanced by our analysis. Hence, our findings in this chapter are more tentative and suggestive than conclusive.

CURRENT CAPACITIES AND RESOURCES FOR PROGRAMMATIC PARTY COMPETITION

In Chapter 6, we noted that the oldest indicator of economic capabilities, measured crudely as a country's per capita GDP in 1928, is most closely associated with 1997–98 economic PPS, but that such data offer little to build a causal mechanism of how affluence at an early stage would translate

TABLE 7.1. *Current Affluence, Human Development, and Economic PPS*

	Per Capita GDP 1998[a]	Human Development (Index 1998)
Argentina	12.0 (+2.11)	.837
Bolivia	2.3 (−1.48)	.643
Brazil	6.6 (+.11)	.747
Chile	8.8 (+.93)	.826
Colombia	6.0 (−.14)	.764
Costa Rica	6.0 (−.11)	.797
Dominican Republic	4.6 (−.63)	.729
Ecuador	3.0 (−1.22)	.722
Mexico	7.7 (+.52)	.784
Peru	4.3 (−.74)	.737
Uruguay	8.6 (+.85)	.825
Venezuela	5.8 (−.19)	.770
Mean	6.3	.765
Standard deviation	2.7 (42.9% of mean)	.055
Economic PPS-2 index	.76***	.86***
Economic partisan divide	.67**	.75***
Policy content of parties' left-right placements	.52*	.64**
Representation: Economic policy issue congruence of parties' voters and legislators (correlation)	.44	.52
Average diffuseness of parties on economic policy issues (correlation)	−.40	−.30
1928 per capita GDP (Table 6.2)	.86***	.91***
1973 social policy expenditures (Table 6.6)	.79***	.86***
1980 per capita GDP (Table 6.2)	.64**	.71***

[a] In $1,000; standardized measures in parentheses.

* p ≤ .10; ** p ≤ .05; *** p ≤ .01.

Sources: World Bank Indicators (online); United Nations, *Human Development Report, 2000,* table 1.

into patterns of democratic partisan mobilization a number of decades later. If we now inspect 1998 GDP per capita figures in Table 7.1, affluence in the late 1990s is also closely associated with PPS and to some lesser degree with its individual components. Moreover, if we choose the United Nations' Human Development Index (HDI) for 1998 as our measure of capabilities, and thus factor in quality-of-life aspects such as mortality, morbidity, health care, and education, its relationship to economic PPS is even closer. This would lead us to infer a simple developmental hypothesis: increasing human capabilities translates into more programmatic structuring of party systems.

But matters are not that straightforward. An inspection of the last three rows of Table 7.1 reveals how heavily endogenous both the per capita GDP values for 1998 and, even more so, the HDI scores are to long-term determinants of programmatic party competition. This is particularly true for 1973 social policy expenditures. What is the causal story behind these simple correlations? As argued at the end of the preceding chapter, early affluence and cumulative opportunities for democratic political contestation "locked in" certain distributive patterns of social policy by the 1960s. Where these policies yielded substantial levels of social expenditure benefiting broad popular strata, they created electoral constituencies crystallized around political-economic stakes that have perpetuated programmatic partisan divides. In prominent cases, these partisan divides even deepened into regime divides wherever repressive military dictatorships countered a challenge from the left to intensify economic redistribution (Chile and Uruguay and, to a lesser extent, Argentina).

The causal arrow between the 1970s and the 1990s then may work through several paths. First, in these countries the strong programmatic political polarization around distributive issues in the 1960s and 1970s often prompted repressive military regimes to dismantle many of the ISI regulatory schemes. As may be recalled from the previous chapter (Table 6.4), authoritarian governments in Argentina, Chile, and Uruguay implemented considerable structural market liberalization from the early 1970s until the mid-1980s and obtained higher structural liberalization scores than any of the other twelve countries by 1985. These reforms were contentious, even where economically successful, and created the climate in which a programmatic dimension of competition around economics would resurface with subsequent democratization.

Second, the existing stock of higher investment in social infrastructure in countries with long-term dispositions to develop strong PPS scores in the 1990s did not simply disappear under authoritarian or democratic governments in the 1980s and 1990s, even where fierce retrenchment of social policies occurred (e.g., Chile), and may have had some beneficial economic effects. Also, more generous social policy may have boosted the wealthier countries' Human Development Index scores for 1998 that are closely linked to social expenditure. Both social policy expenditures and HDI scores, in turn, are more closely related to cross-national patterns of economic PPS than simple affluence or development scores captured by per capita GDP. Social policies mattered by producing more entrenched programmatic party competition while also boosting quality of life.

In our small-N comparison, we can probe into the endogeneity or independence of current economic capacities from long-term political economic conditions by examining outlier patterns. If the short-term 1998 per capita GDP correlation with economic PPS accounts for cases that were left as outliers in our analysis of long-term causes of party system structuration and, vice versa, if the latter account for outliers left by the former, we could identify some modest complementarity and independence of the two causal strands in spite of their substantial collinearity. In Table 6.9 we showed that Brazil and Mexico are outliers not well explained by long-term determinants of economic PPS. In Table 7.2, we compare the residuals that result from regressing national economic PPS scores alternatively on 1998 per capita GDP or on social policy expenditures in 1973 as the "proximate" long-term cause of economic PPS.[2] In each instance, we subtract the predicted economic PPS score from the actual value. A positive difference shows that the actual value is higher than the independent variable would predict, and a negative sign indicates that the independent variable predicts too high a value. We should recall that the PPS scale ranges from -3 to $+3$, with values for the twelve countries varying with a standard deviation of 2.11. Thus, a divergence smaller than roughly $|0.7|$ signals a very tight fit between prediction and actual value,[3] one smaller than $|1.4|$ a reasonable fit, and difference scores higher than this level a rather poor fit, although none of the residuals in our analysis are extreme (say, greater than half the entire scale of the variable). Table 7.2 indicates that, compared to social expenditures in 1973, the 1998 per capita GDP is a much better predictor of economic PPS in Mexico; growing economic resources and the decline of agriculture appear to have encouraged and facilitated political mobilization around questions of economic distribution that begin to structure the party system. But the same relationship does not apply to Brazil. Greater economic development in 1998 here does not associate with greater economic PPS. For Brazil, both long-term and short-term explanations of economic PPS that work elsewhere fare poorly.

Current 1998 per capita GDP, however, fails to account for economic PPS not only in Brazil but also in a number of other instances where long-term factors have provided plausible explanations (Argentina, Chile, and Uruguay and, to a lesser extent, Costa Rica and Colombia). Thus, overall, current development constitutes a less convincing explanation of programmatic party system structuration than long-term economic capacities, political opportunities, and political-economic stakes.

---

[2] Because outlying observations exert disproportionate influence on the slope of the regression line, Table 7.2 reports studentized residuals as more appropriate estimates of prediction error.

[3] The value of 0.7 is equivalent to one-third of the standard variation of roughly 2.02 to 2.16, contingent upon the number of cases.

TABLE 7.2. *Errors in Predicting Economic PPS-2: Unexplained Variance of Long-Term and Short-Term Determinants (studentized residuals)*

Long-term determinants of economic PPS-2:	1998 per Capita GDP as Determinant of Economic PPS-2 (r = .76)				
	Actual Value Much Lower Than Predictions		Predictions and Actual Values Close	Actual Value Much Higher Than Predictions	
	x < -1.4	-1.4 < x < -0.7	-0.7 < x < +0.7	0.7 < x < 1.4	x > 1.4
Social policy 1973 (r = .88)					
Actual values much lower than predictions					
x < -1.4		Brazil (-1.71/-1.33) Colombia (-.83/-1.02)			
-1.4 < x < -0.7					
Predictions and actual values close					
-0.7 < x < +0.7		Argentina (-.40/-2.29)	Bolivia (-.24/-.16) Dominican Republic (-.26/-.40) Ecuador (-.37/+.29) Peru (-.26/-.28) Venezuela(-.23/-.20)	Costa Rica (-.04/+1.19)	Chile (-.36/+1.58) Uruguay (+.59/+1.69)
Actual values much higher than predictions					
+0.7 < x < +1.4			Mexico (+4.72/+.42)		
x > +1.4					

Note: Parentheses contain studentized residuals from OLS regressions of social policy 1973 (first number) and of 1998 per capita GDP (second number) on economic PPS-2.

215

OPPORTUNITIES TO ENACT PROGRAMMATIC PARTY COMPETITION

Authoritarian Disruptions of Democracy

Short-term causal mechanisms that affect the opportunities for politicians and citizens to craft programmatic linkages have to do with the rules and conditions under which they play the game of party competition. How many rounds have they played? With a long number of recent rounds, observers should detect higher PPS scores. How often have their rounds of party competition been interrupted by authoritarian relapses? Such disruptions force politicians and voters to relearn experiences made in previous rounds of democratic competition after the end of an authoritarian episode. They hence impede the coordination of citizens and politicians around programmatic appeals.

Intensity of repression may also affect subsequent programmatic party system structuration. Extremely repressive authoritarian regimes may physically eliminate democratic politicians and thus make it harder to relearn the lessons of programmatic party competition after the transition to democracy. Moreover, they remake political-economic relations so fundamentally that it might take considerable time to crystallize economic group interests and reconstitute programmatic alternatives in a subsequent spell of democracy (e.g., after a very long period of communism). Moderately repressive regimes, by contrast, may stimulate postauthoritarian programmatic competition. Such regimes tend to divide and polarize the citizenry through political-economic change without physically liquidating the opposition. And mildly repressive regimes may instead dilute postauthoritarian PPS upon resumption of democratic politics, because the authoritarian regime barely touched economic governance and redistribution.

In most of our twelve Latin American countries, democracy was (re)-installed between 1978 and 1990. The only countries with a continuous record of free democratic elections going back before 1978 are Costa Rica, Venezuela, and – more arguably – Colombia. By 1998 democratic polities had thus seen anywhere between three and seven uninterrupted rounds of national presidential and legislative elections. But there is no pattern that would link the length of this run to economic PPS. Polities with medium or high PPS scores have both short and long runs of competitive elections (Chile and Mexico versus Costa Rica and Venezuela), while low PPS scores also coincide with short and long runs of democratic elections (Dominican Republic and Brazil versus Bolivia, Colombia, and Ecuador). In a similar vein, the number of authoritarian interruptions from World War II until the 1990s or the repressiveness of the military dictatorships of the 1960s and 1970s fail to account for patterns of PPS.

Authoritarian regimes in Latin America also differed in setting up strategies of mobilization through political parties or nonpartisan associations that would later constitute focal rallying points for their former supporters after returning to democracy. Working from comparative studies of military rule in Latin America (Rouquié 1987) or from studies of civil-military relations following a period of dictatorship (Fitch 1998), one may identify Bolivia, Brazil, and Uruguay as countries in which military rulers made vigorous efforts to build civilian vehicles of partisan mobilization. Chile under Pinochet was another regime where such objectives were pursued systematically, not through deliberate strengthening of a political party but through support of *gremialismo*. In that country, efforts to mobilize the population in support of the regime bypassed established parties in favor of the *gremialista* movement of Jaime Guzmán, thus channeling social opposition to Allende into support for the dictatorship, and eventually providing the backbone of UDI after the transition (Pollack 1997). Mexico is a unique case in Latin America with its encompassing civilian hegemonic party that permitted lopsided competition and cultivated a rhetoric of distributive politics, which is likely to have prompted oppositional politicians to stake out programmatic stances on distributive politics of their own.

In the remaining cases – Argentina, Dominican Republic, Ecuador, and Peru – it is not the civilian organizational capabilities of political parties associated with the authoritarian regime that shape economic PPS after dictators depart but the political-economic stakes that *precede* the advent of dictatorship. Thus, neither the intensity, length, nor even the mobilizational capacity of authoritarian regimes seems to be associated in a direct or interactive manner with patterns of PPS after the authoritarian interludes.

Institutional Incentives for Programmatic Coordination

Students of party competition often treat formal democratic institutions as providers of incentives for politicians to engage in more or less competition around programmatic alternatives with partisan labels. A prominent example is Barry Ames's (1995; 2001) analysis of Brazilian electoral laws and party politics. Ames shows how the Brazilian electoral law personalizes party competition and provides disincentives for programmatic party formation. His analysis is also borne out by our own empirical data for 1997–98, which finds lower programmatic competition in Brazil than we predicted on the basis of our long-term causal analysis. But does the argument that electoral system incentives and the relationship between legislatures and the executive shape programmatic party competition hold for our entire cohort of twelve Latin American polities?

Because this question impinges on the validity of influential institutionalist theorizing, we treat it in some detail, although we cannot empirically confirm institutionalist arguments. It is important for institutionalists to see how we derive our negative results in order to launch a defense and counterattack. Institutional incentives that have been tipped to be most likely to promote or subvert programmatic party competition (cf. Harmel and Janda 1982), net of long-term causal influences of development, democratic experience, and political-economic distributive arrangements, involve (1) the devolution of public jurisdictions to subnational legislatures and executives, (2) the professionalization and governance of the civil service, (3) electoral laws, and (4) the relation between legislature and executives in presidential or parliamentary systems.

With regard to *territorial (de)centralization*, neither refined measures of multilevel political governance and fiscal allocation that are available for only some of our countries (cf. Rodden 2004; Treisman 2002) nor a crude federalism dummy bears out a clear relationship to economic PPS. Five of the twelve Latin American countries have federal arrangements, such that popularly elected subnational governments have substantial policy jurisdictions (Argentina, Brazil, Colombia, Mexico, and Venezuela).[4] Detailed empirical research has shown that federalism – at least in Argentina (Levitsky 2003) and Brazil (Mainwaring 1999; Ames 2001: 18–23; Samuels 2004) – contributes to programmatic incoherence in political parties. Also, when the Mexican PRI's authoritarian control over the states relaxed, federalism permitted great diversity in the modes of party competition across states (Magaloni, Díaz-Cayeros, and Estevez 2007). Nevertheless, when we inspect economic PPS scores across federal and nonfederal polities, we fail to detect a systematic pattern of association. Across the subset of federal countries, such scores can be above average (Argentina, Mexico), average (Venezuela), or below average (Brazil, Colombia). The same applies to the subset of formally centralized polities. If we focus exclusively on the six countries with high long-term dispositions toward PPS, we do find that centralized countries (Costa Rica, Chile, and Uruguay) tend to have higher PPS scores than federalist countries (Argentina, Mexico, and Venezuela) ($r = .75$; $N = 6$). We run, however, into the usual endogeneity problems.[5]

With regard to the *professionalization of the civil service*, highly professional, rule-bound, and institutionalized public administrations should undermine the opportunities to exploit the state apparatus for the purposes

---

[4] For a score of Latin American federalism, see Wibbels (2005: 84–85). Treisman (2002: 32) does not include Colombia, but our assessment here does not hinge on the inclusion or exclusion of this country.

[5] Taking the subsample of the six cases with strong or intermediate economic PPS values, the federalism dummy is strongly correlated with electoral contestation 1945–73 (Table 6.2) (−0.89) as well as with 1973 social policy expenditures (−0.76), but not early development (−0.29). This, in fact, may suggest a rather different, temporally ancient, historical dynamic: even where economic development was relatively high early on, the decentralization of political power around geographically dispersed, subnational cliques hindered both democratic contestation as well as social policy stakes. Federalism is not a recent entrant into the causal chain toward greater or lesser programmatic competition but a very early entrant into this causal chain.

of clientelistic patronage network building (Shefter 1994). At least indirectly, disincentives for clientelistic politics may nurture politicians' disposition to embrace programmatic politics. Unfortunately, we lack data that would capture the state of affairs in the civil service in our twelve Latin American countries in the mid-1990s not too long before our reading of programmatic party competition. There is, however, a very recent and thorough assessment of civil service capacities from 2004 to 2005 (Stein and Tommasi 2005: 33; Stein et al. 2006: 65–76, 149–50). If we assume that civil service practices are "sticky," something that is plausible based on the thorough description of civil service practices by Stein et al. (2006), and therefore that the cross-national differences among civil service measured in 2004–5 also reflect cross-national relations in the late 1990s, we can employ the temporally posterior measure as a "predictor" of earlier programmatic party structuration. The fit, it turns out, is quite weak ($r = .50$). Some countries with strong civil development patterns exhibit low PPS (Brazil, Colombia), while countries with very high PPS have only moderately strong civil services (Chile, Uruguay).

Let us therefore turn to *electoral systems*, a subject with a vast literature that deals mostly with the impact of rules on the "format" or fragmentation of the party system, with individual parties considered as unitary actors (cf. Taagepera and Shugart 1989; Lijphart 1995; Cox 1997; Jones 1995, 1997; Shugart and Wattenberg 2001). For the analysis of the programmatic cohesiveness of parties and the programmatic structuration of party systems, Carey and Shugart's (1995) work on incentives to cultivate a personal vote provides the best theoretical inspiration. These authors demonstrate that in legislative elections the district size and the ballot format – in conjunction with the parties' choice of procedures for candidate nominations – interact in shaping the propensity of parties to generate either coherent teams of politicians or personality-centered politics. Single-member districts (SMD) restrict intraparty competition among candidates, provided the party as corporate entity has control over the nomination process. But such districts still provide individual candidates with enough incentives to show responsiveness to local district constituencies rather than to court favor with the national party. In large multimember district elections, candidates will be partisan team players and promote party cohesiveness, *provided* they run on "closed" lists and the party controls the nominations process. Although internal party unity ("discipline") is not the same as programmatic party competition, it constitutes one factor that increases the probability of high PPS values.

For Latin American parties, we develop a summary index of institutional incentives for party cohesion, based on ballot type, district magnitude, and intraparty competition over nominations for electoral office. High scores signal strong incentives for party cohesion. The reported scores are based on the prevailing electoral systems employed in lower house elections up to

TABLE 7.3. *Institutional Rules of Democratic Governance I: Electoral Laws*

Group 1 (favorable conditions, medium-high PPS) and Group 2 (unfavorable conditions, low PPS)	Electoral Rules: Incentives for Programmatic Structuration	
	Legislative Elections (around 1996)	Presidential Elections (around 1996)
1.1. Argentina	3	2
1.2. Chile	1	3
1.3. Costa Rica	3	2
1.4. Mexico	2	1
1.5. Uruguay	1	3
1.6. Venezuela	2	1
2.1. Bolivia	2	3
2.2. Brazil	0	3
2.3. Colombia	0	3
2.4. Dominican Republic	3	3
2.5. Ecuador	3	3
2.6. Peru	0	1
Mean	1.67	2.33
Standard deviation	1.23	.89
Correlation with PPS-2 (N = 12)	.08	−.06

* p ≤ .10; ** p ≤ .05; *** p ≤ .01.

Sources: Column 1: judgmental index, see chapter 5 by Hawkins and Morgenstern in this volume; values reversed so that high scores indicate strong incentives for party cohesion; column 2: Payne et al. (2002: 73); plurality election = 1; run-off with reduced threshold = 2; majority runoff = 3.

1998; since then, for example, the electoral systems of Ecuador and Peru have changed fundamentally.[6] Data are reported in Table 7.3, column 1. We expect that multimember district elections with closed lists and firm party control over the nominations process generate the most favorable conditions for programmatic structuration. Surprisingly, however, our data exhibit no evidence that these associations are in fact borne out. This holds true even if we restrict the sample to the six polities with background conditions (capacity, opportunity, stakes) that should moderately or strongly predispose them to programmatic politics.

Table 7.3 also provides a separate measure of electoral incentives in presidential elections that is not directly equivalent to the measure for lower house elections. We distinguish plurality elections (= 1), two-round runoff majoritarian elections with reduced threshold in the first round (= 2), and simple majority runoff systems (= 3). We could spell out linear, curvilinear,

---

[6] For changes in Latin American electoral systems since 1985, see the inventory in Payne et al. (2002: 111–15).

or complex contingent logics (the last based on the presence or absence of prior favorable conditions for strong economic PPS) according to which these institutions should give rise to greater or lesser programmatic party cohesion. Again, though, we fail to confirm any of these arguments.

Perhaps the *rules that govern the powers and the interplay of legislatures and independently elected executives (presidents),* especially insofar as law making is concerned, have consequences for the programmatic structuration of party systems. Parliamentary systems foster a greater cohesion of parties, as chief executives rely on continuous majority support in the legislature. At the opposite end are presidential systems with strong legislative and executive powers where the individual officeholder may try to govern by divide-and-rule tactics and without relying on any one party in the legislature and even trying to "disorganize" the cohesiveness of recalcitrant parties, especially where the president does not have direct control of a majority party (cf. Mainwaring and Shugart 1997; Cox and Morgenstern 2002). Presidents with weak legislative and executive powers are in between.

Given the small number of cases we are dealing with, we cannot test all conceivable configurations of the institutional rules that may affect programmatic party competition. We thus are compelled to resort to a rough-and-ready comparison. Empirically, we rely on Shugart and Carey's (1992) measure of proactive and reactive presidential legislative powers around 1990–91, an updated measure for 1996 (Mainwaring and Shugart 1997: 432), and yet another update for 2000 (Payne et al. 2002) in order to track the capacity and dispositions of presidents to disorganize (or prevent from organizing) cohesive legislative parties (Table 7.4). We reverse indices where needed so that high scores indicate weak presidential powers that should create strong incentives for cohesive programmatic parties. Because the metric varies from measure to measure, we also provide standardized scores for presidential legislative powers at each point in time to highlight intertemporal changes in actual presidential power or measurement error. Presidential powers in 1990–91 are indeed only modestly correlated with those in 1996 ($r = +.30$) and 2000 ($r = +.30$), but the scores for the latter two years are closely associated ($r = +.78$). This discrepancy is probably not the result of measurement error, but of historical shifts in presidential power in a number of Latin American democracies in the first half of the 1990s. For example, presidents in Peru, Ecuador, and Venezuela expanded their legislative leverage.

As already indicated, whether presidents actually attempt to disorganize cohesive parties depends not only on their legislative powers but also on their partisan powers in the legislature – that is, their capacity to control powerful electoral parties as presidential vehicles, sometimes combined with strategic opportunities to craft a reliable majority coalition around a party directly under presidential control. In order to tap the component of partisan powers, we rely on a judgmental rank ordering of presidents' partisan powers offered

TABLE 7.4. *Institutional Rules of Democratic Governance II: Powers of the Presidency*

Group 1 (favorable conditions, medium-high PPS) and Group 2 (unfavorable conditions, low PPS)	Legislative Powers of the Presidency: Incentives for Programmatic Structuration			Partisan Powers of the Presidency
	1990–91: Inversed Values, High Value = Weak Powers	1996: Inversed Ranks, High Value = Weak Powers	Around 2000: Inversed Values, High Value = Weak Powers	
1.1. Argentina	7 (+.56)	4 (−1.28)	7 (+.34)	3 (+.54)
1.2. Chile	4 (−.51)	4 (−1.28)	12 (−.92)	1 (−1.31)
1.3. Costa Rica	8 (+.92)	1 (+1.28)	2.5 (+1.47)	3 (+.54)
1.4. Mexico	4 (−.51)	1 (+1.28)	2.5 (+1.47)	4 (+1.46)
1.5. Uruguay	3 (−.86)	2 (+.43)	6.5 (+.46)	3 (+.54)
1.6. Venezuela	9 (+1.27)	1 (+1.28)	7 (+.34)	3 (+.54)
2.1. Bolivia	7 (+.56)	2 (+.43)	5 (+.84)	2 (−.39)
2.2. Brazil	0 (−1.93)	3 (−.43)	11 (−.67)	1 (−1.31)
2.3. Colombia	4 (−.51)	3 (−.43)	11 (−.67)	2 (−.39)
2.4. Dominican Republic	7 (+.56)	2 (+.43)	8 (+.08)	4 (+1.46)
2.5. Ecuador	3 (−.86)	4 (−1.28)	14.5 (−1.55)	1 (−1.31)
2.6. Peru	9 (+1.27)	3 (−.43)	13 (−1.18)	2 (−.39)
Mean	5.42	1.50	6.67	2.42
Standard deviation	2.81	1.17	3.97	1.08
Correlation with PPS-2				
All countries (N = 12)	−.14	−0.02	−0.30	.20
Group 1 only (N = 6)[a]	−.84**	.51	.39	−.50

* $p \leq .10$; ** $p \leq .05$; *** $p \leq .01$.

[a] Countries with both intermediate to favorable dispositions to develop high PPS scores and actual PPS scores $> = 0$ (on a −3 to +3 scale).

Sources: Column 1: Shugart and Carey (1992: 155), 1991 reforms in Argentina and Colombia included. Inversed values 9-x so that high scores = weak powers = strong incentive for party cohesion; columns 2 and 4: Mainwaring and Shugart (1997: 432); inversed values 4-x so that high scores = weak powers = strong incentives for party cohesion; column 3: Payne et al. (2002: 202); inversed values 5-x so that high scores mean weak powers conducive to strong party cohesion.

by Mainwaring and Shugart (1997: 432).[7] Empirically, there is a rather impressive negative correlation between a president's partisan (1996) and institutional legislative (1996) powers in Latin America (r = −.68). Whether by institutional design of rational, calculating constitutional assemblies or not, where great legislative powers are conferred on presidencies, they wield weak partisan powers.

The causality might run either way: weak parties may have delegated strong powers to the presidential office (Shugart 1998); or the very presence of such presidential powers may have weakened the parties and undercut presidential control of political parties in the legislative process.

Be that as it may, the results in Tables 7.3 and 7.4 show that institutional measures of Latin American democracies tell us little about cross-national patterns of programmatic competitiveness. The correlations between economic PPS and our various measures of presidential powers are ultimately weak and statistically insignificant. This negative result applies to the legislative powers of the presidency as well as the partisan powers of the office. The only partial exception is that among countries with better prospects for high economic PPS, strong presidential legislative powers in 1990 actually appear to undermine programmatic cohesiveness of parties. Overall, these results cast doubt on the thesis that executive-legislative relations shape programmatic competition.

Do the institutional constraints of democratic party competition look so weak because there are many intervening variables that may suppress institutional effects? Or did politicians and voters not yet have the time to coordinate around best equilibrium strategies? Overall, the political experiences and resources of actors appear to overwhelm any constraints and opportunities that institutions provide to shape party competition. The conclusion we draw from this exercise is that less weight should be attributed to institutionalist arguments in the causal analysis of collective action and, more specifically, party systems. In understanding patterns of principal-agent accountability and linkage building, such as the extent of PPS across Latin American party systems, it may be more important to identify how individual and collective actors control and appropriate tangible resources in the process of democratic competition.

ECONOMIC STAKES OF POLITICAL COMPETITION SINCE THE "LOST DECADE" IN LATIN AMERICAN POLITICS

Let us finally turn to the substance of political-economic struggles ("stakes") as a catalyst for programmatic party competition. Does the erosion of the old ISI development strategy weaken programmatic competition in countries

---

[7] A slightly modified version of the same analysis can be found in Payne et al. (2002: 216), table 8.10.

where it was high and possibly strengthen such competition in countries that had little programmatic competition in the past?

Our analysis proceeds in two steps. First, we explore whether policy reforms and political economic outcomes – measured in terms of per capita economic growth since 1980 – leave a direct imprint on patterns of party system structuration in the late 1990s. Next, we examine whether the relationship between parties' competitive stances before elections and their economic policy choices after elections (policy switches, "surprise," or "betrayal") affected the development of programmatic party structuration in Latin American democracies. At each step, we explore a direct, linear effect of each mechanism on partisan politics, as well as a contingent effect that applies only to subgroups of countries with either strong or weak preconditions to develop programmatic competition.

The main finding of our analysis is that changing political-economic stakes affect programmatic competition only in the group of countries with good long-term prospects to develop high economic PPS. If their economic performance is weak, or their governments act against preelectoral commitments, programmatic party competition vanishes. But, conversely, economic conditions and government actions do not affect the economic PPS scores of countries with inauspicious long-term conditions for programmatic competition until the 1980s. New political-economic developments could dismantle existing programmatic party competition but not build up new instances. Whether this still applies a decade later, given the rise of populist parties, belongs in our more speculative concluding chapter.

Economic Performance and Economic Policy Making

According to an assessment based loosely on the retrospective economic voting literature, enormous economic dislocations, surfacing in high inflation rates, unemployment, declining incomes, and the shift of employment across economic sectors, should undercut established programmatic alignments and prepare the way for new alignments. A contingency theory would argue that, in countries where high programmatic structuration crystallized around past political-economic development strategies originating in the ISI era, PPS scores are likely to erode following a downward spiral of economic performance, before citizens and politicians can rebuild political programs around new alignments supporting novel political-economic strategies of economic governance, property rights, and state intervention or liberal laissez faire in order to stimulate economic growth. By contrast, in polities that never had high PPS scores, such dislocations may stimulate politicians to engage in competition around political economic alternatives, particularly if economic performance is bad.

We have explored these hypotheses with an extraordinary range of economic variables signaling economic dislocations and strain. They cover macroeconomic bread-and-butter variables such as per capita GDP growth (and contraction), unemployment rates, and consumer price inflation, but also the external balance of accounts, trade deficits, and net external debts. On the basis of the World Bank's (2003) report on income distribution and poverty in Latin America, we also examined levels and rates of wage inequality ratios, Gini coefficients, and absolute levels of poverty (less than two dollars per day) at different points in time within Latin America. Other data included the development of real wages since 1980 (cf. Roberts 2002: 18) and the change in UNESCO's Human Development Index over time. In most of our explorations, we came up empty-handed; thus, for the sake of brevity, we do not refer further to some of these explorations.

For the sake of argument, let us revert to one of the crudest measures of all – the development of national per capita GDP from 1980 to 1997, around the time when we measure economic PPS – as a best-case scenario that captures whatever insight we could gain from political economic developments (Table 7.5). In order to visualize contingent effects of economic performance and politicians' economic policy choices on patterns of party competition, our displays here and in subsequent tables once again partition our Latin American countries into a set of six polities with moderately or strongly favorable long-term dispositions to develop high PPS and another six countries where our analysis in Chapter 6 showed this not to be the case.

In the "lost decade" of the 1980s, per capita GDP fell dramatically in most countries, but the spread of performance across Latin America is substantial, as shown in column 1 of Table 7.5, where we express GDP at the end of 1989 as a percentage of GDP at the beginning of 1980 (standard deviation = 16.6). In some instances, such as Argentina, Bolivia, Peru, and Venezuela, the income decline was catastrophic, associated also with sharply escalating inequality and impoverishment of large parts of the population. In the 1990s, incomes moderately recovered at an average rate of 2 percent per year, but this average masks great disparities of performance. Over the entire eighteen-year period, the central Andes region (Bolivia, Ecuador, Peru, and Venezuela) registered tremendous decline, while some countries substantially improved their standard of living (Chile, Dominican Republic, and Uruguay).

Do macroeconomic fortunes over the past two decades of the twentieth century correlate with – and possibly cause – differential levels of programmatic structuration in Latin American democracies by 1997–98? Bivariate correlations in Table 7.5 provide some clues. Among the set of six countries with better long-term conditions for programmatic party competition, better economic performance in the 1980–97 period is invariably associated with higher PPS. This case does not rest on but is strengthened by Venezuela, a country with moderate conduciveness to strong programmatic competition but dreadful economic performance since 1980. Among countries with inauspicious prior conditions for economic PPS, no relationship between economic performance and programmatic competition can be

TABLE 7.5. *Economic Policy Reforms and Economic Outcomes, 1980–1997*

Group 1 (favorable conditions, medium-high PPS) and Group 2 (unfavorable conditions, low PPS)	Change in per Capita GDP, 1980–89 (1980 = 100)	Index of Structural Market Liberalization				
		1990–97	1980–97	1985	1995	Change 1985–95
1.1. Argentina	78	132	103	.617	.888	.271
1.2. Chile	98	164	162	.671	.843	.172
1.3. Costa Rica	89	117	104	.494	.847	.353
1.4. Mexico	97	112	109	.578	.807	.229
1.5. Uruguay	97	136	132	.815	.891	.076
1.6. Venezuela	77	108	83	.456	.667	.211
2.1. Bolivia	78	112	87	.445	.816	.371
2.2. Brazil	114	104	119	.492	.855	.313
2.3. Colombia	114	116	132	.578	.792	.214
2.4. Dominican Republic	121	128	154	.446	.862	.416
2.5. Ecuador	91	103	94	.556	.801	.245
2.6. Peru	79	114	90	.394	.845	.451
Mean	95.1	120.5	113.9	.545	.842	.277
Standard deviation	15.4	17.3	25.9	.118	.09	.108
Correlations with PPS-2						
All countries (N = 12)	−.08	.72*	.41	.78***	.3*	−.65*
Group 1 only (N = 6)[a]	.78**	.82**	.92**	.87**	.7*	−.52

[a] For definition, see Table 7.4. * p ≤ .10; ** p ≤ .05; *** p ≤ .01.

Sources: Columns 1–3: calculated from Heston, Summers, and Aten (2006); columns 4–6: Morley et al. (1999).

detected. Where more affluent countries with more democratic experience and more comprehensive social policies perform relatively well economically in the 1980s and 1990s, they build or preserve economic PPS in 1997–98. But where such conditions are weak, good or bad economic performance makes little difference for politicians' propensity to engage in programmatic party competition.

One mechanism that might bring about this result has to do with the propensity to embark on economic liberalization. Economic PPS in the party system could be undermined wherever economic liberalization proceeded at a fast rate from a low level once ISI strategies became patently unviable. Market liberalization is never popular with large voting majorities, because it creates uncertainty about people's future income flows, and losers might at least initially outnumber winners, at least in all situations but a dire crisis (Weyland 2005). Politicians might conceal their intentions and activities to avoid electoral backlash in the run-up to elections. Conversely, in countries where distributive politics was divisive from at least the 1960s or 1970s onward, the decline of ISI development success gave market liberal conservatives their chance to implement reforms.

As data in Table 7.5 show, the Inter-American Development Bank (IDB) index of structural economic liberalization in 1985 was higher in countries with higher scores of economic PPS in 1997–98. Economic reform was put on the agenda of salient issues early on only in countries where economic divides were entrenched and there were organized forces that promoted reform. In other countries, politics was simply not organized around economic policy alternatives and leaders delayed reform. But these countries then caught up with the early liberalizers, as the crisis of the 1980s sent governments scrambling for policy alternatives to the status quo and to embrace market liberalization. While the table shows persistent leadership in economic liberalization in the country group with higher levels of economic PPS, the low-PPS reform laggards eventually caught up. They had to reform faster from a lower status quo of market institutions. Economic liberalization in the 1985–95 time frame, therefore, is associated with low-PPS countries that started late. This logic does not displace long-term causes as determinants of economic PPS but employs short-term causal mechanisms as intermediate steps to fill in the temporal gap between the 1970s, when economic stakes in social policy had set up programmatic policy alternatives in some countries, and the late 1990s, when we observed programmatic competition. By 1995 all countries in our cohort have converged on very high levels of market liberalism (Table 7.5), with the notable exception of Venezuela. The standard deviation of liberalization scores falls by half from 1985 to 1995, and even lower if Venezuela were not a dramatic outlier. Nevertheless, countries with high PPS that were the trailblazers in market reform from 1970 to 1985 kept those positions, so that even in 1995 the countries with the most clearly articulated economic-distributive political competition were also those that had higher market liberalization.

Promises and Policies: Does Consistency in Parties' Economic Policy Commitments Matter for Programmatic Party Competition?

Government initiatives to liberalize trade, capital flows, and domestic markets for goods, labor, and capital created anxieties among many citizens in Latin America. It is easier for actors and bystanders to identify losers of economic liberalization, whereas uncertainty shrouds the future winners of economic reform. Because losers are more identifiable and therefore more easily mobilized, politicians have incentives to stay away from strong demands for economic reform, provided the economy is not already in a desperate free fall (Weyland 2002). If politicians, however, run on a nonreform "populist" platform of economic continuity and state intervention and then deliver massive market-liberal reforms after emerging victorious from national elections ("policy switching"), voters begin to discount the sincerity of their policy commitments. Voters will no longer bring prospective assessments of parties' declared policy positions to bear on their electoral choice. Politicians, in turn, may strategically obfuscate questions of policy and issue multiple, ambiguous, and varied, if not contradictory, policy messages, even when they run under a single partisan label. Moreover, politicians may attract voters by providing targeted clientelistic side payments, particularly in tight electoral contests, rather than holding out collective and large-group club goods. Our hypothesis, therefore, is that policy switching undermines programmatic party system structuration. In group 1 – countries with higher prior conditions and performance records indicating that strong economic PPS scores can indeed be achieved – the loss of PPS because of policy switching is likely to be painful, whereas in low-PPS countries, voters may already discount whatever policy commitments are made by politicians.

On the basis of Stokes's (2001) narrative and scoring practices, let us identify elected presidents in our twelve countries between 1980 and 1998 that switched from a populist policy appeal before elections to economic liberalization policies after electoral victory. We already know which countries resisted economic liberalization up to the mid-1980s from Table 7.5 (column 4). Let us now develop an additional indicator of "economic policy populism" that identifies governments whose constituent parties both ex ante advertised and ex post implemented heterodox-populist policies of fiscal reflation, easy monetary conditions, trade protection, expansionary public employment, and high public-sector deficits in order to create employment and growth. Drawing on Stokes's (2001) narrative and scoring practice, Table 7.6 identifies presidential governments between 1980 and 1998 by their ex ante policy appeals and the ex post policies they delivered.

TABLE 7.6. *Populist Heterodoxy or Market-Liberal Orthodoxy? Initial Appeal and Policies of Latin American Governments, 1980–1998*

	Appeal of Economic Populism: Security-Oriented Campaign and Electoral Rhetoric	Appeal of Economic Liberalism: Efficiency-Oriented Rhetoric
Actual policies consistent with preelection commitments	Argentina 83–89 (Alfonsín) Peru 85–90 (Garcia) Bolivia 82–85 (Siles) Uruguay 85–90 (Sanguinetti) Colombia 86–90 (Barco) Venezuela 83–88 (Lusinchi) Colombia 94–98 (Samper) Costa Rica 86–90 (Árias) Dominican Republic 86–90 (Balaguer) Dominican Republic 94–98 (Balaguer)	Bolivia 85–89 (Estenssoro) Colombia 90–94 (Gaviria) Brazil 85–90 (Sarney) Costa Rica 90–94 (Calderón) Brazil 90–92 (Collor) Brazil 92–95 (Franco) Ecuador 84–88 (Febrés) Chile 80–90 (Pinochet) Mexico 82–98 (various) Chile 90–94 (Aylwin) Uruguay 90–94 (Lacalle) Chile 94–98 (Frei)
Actual policies inconsistent with preelection commitments	Argentina 89–94 (Menem) Bolivia 89–94 (Paz) Costa Rica 94–98 (Figueres) Dominican Republic 82–86 (Blanco) Ecuador 88–92 (Borja) Ecuador 92–96 (Durán) Peru 90–95 (Fujimori) Venezuela 88–92 (Pérez) Venezuela 92–97 (Caldera)	

Sources: Coded from Stokes (2001).

TABLE 7.7. *Economic Policy Approach of Governments in the 1990s*

Group 1 (favorable conditions, medium-high PPS) and Group 2 (unfavorable conditions, low PPS)	Heterodox Economic Policies in the 1980s[a]	"Policy Switching"[b]	"Policy Betrayal"[c]
1.1. Argentina	5	1	1.16
1.2. Chile	0	0	.14
1.3. Costa Rica	4	1	1.55
1.4. Mexico	0	0	.61
1.5. Uruguay	5	0	.54
1.6. Venezuela	5	1	1.08
2.1. Bolivia	4	1	2.15
2.2. Brazil	0	0	.49
2.3. Colombia	4	0	3.27
2.4. Dominican Republic	4	1	No data
2.5. Ecuador	0	1	1.34
2.6. Peru	5	1	4.04
Mean	3.0	.58	1.56
Standard deviation	2.26	.51	1.22
Correlations with PPS-2			
All countries (N = 12)	−.08	−.43	−.60**
Group 1 only (N = 6)[d]	−.34	−.73*	−.54

[a] Number of years with governing parties enacting populism consistently.
[b] Shifting from populist preelection stance to market-liberal government policy.
[c] The magnitude of "surprise" in legislative parties' structural economic liberalization.
[d] For definition, see Table 7.4. * $p \leq .10$; ** $p \leq .05$; *** $p \leq .01$.

Sources: Columns 1 and 2: coded from Stokes (2001); column 3: own calculations (see text and contact Guillermo Rosas).

Governments listed in the top left are consistently populist governments with heterodox economic policies.

Our second indicator is also based on Stokes's description and covers "policy switchers" among partisan governments. We first follow Stokes's practice to assign a dummy value to policy-switching administrations. Table 7.7 identifies these governments in the lower left quadrant. This information yields the scoring of column 2 in Table 7.7. In order to validate our crude judgmental dummy variable of policy switching and provide more insight into the conditions under which citizens and politicians may abandon programmatic politics, we developed a second measure of partisan governments' "betrayal" of electoral constituencies. This indicator is the residual of an OLS pooled cross-section time-series regression in which each country's annual index of economic liberalization from 1986 to 1995 is regressed on a number of variables that citizens can conceivably take into account when anticipating governments' economic policies. The average residuals for each country that emerge from this regression are a measure of "surprise" that citizens experience when they register actual economic policy. We focus only on the surprise residual of governments that deliver more market liberalization than citizens could expect on the basis of the predictor variables. This measure is based on methods and data for eleven of our countries discussed in Johnson and Crisp (2002), but unfortunately it requires us to drop the Dominican Republic from our sample. The independent variables in the regression are the lagged economic liberalization index, economic growth and inflation as economic controls, and an indicator of the ideological "center of gravity" in the legislature based on Michael Coppedge's expert scoring of left-right party ideologies weighted by party seat share.[8] Citizens expect less reform where the legislature has a more "leftist" center of gravity. The rationale for including economic controls is the expectation that politicians and voters will not necessarily think that a leftist government's turn to the right is a betrayal if economic conditions are dire. Needless to say, the lagged variable is the most powerful predictor of present policy output.[9] We also experimented with weighting residuals more heavily if they occurred in years closer to 1997–98, when PPS scores were observed, than in years that were further back in the past, but the difference between scores was negligible. Column 3 of Table 7.7 reports aggregate "betrayal" or "surprise" residuals for each country. It is interesting and rewarding that our sophisticated measure of "switching" correlates strongly with Stokes's original dummy variable (r = .88).

At least for group 1 countries, heterodox economic policies in the 1980s did indeed subsequently foster both policy switching between the late 1980s and mid-1990s (r = .69) and greater cumulative constituency betrayal by governing parties between 1986 and 1995 (r = .65). Table 7.7 shows that our switching and betrayal measures are robustly related to economic PPS scores *at least within the group of countries where prior conditions for high PPS scores based on long-term dispositions, institutionalization, and achieved values are encouraging.* Wherever governments inflicted economic policy switching and "citizen betrayal," economic PPS scores ended up lower in 1998 than in countries where policy making remained more consistent with expectations.

Our exploration suggests that at least in the subset of countries where conditions for strong economic PPS were favorable, the presence or absence of voter betrayal in recent governments makes a net difference. Concretely, policy switching and voter betrayal by governments in Argentina, Costa Rica, and Venezuela are in part responsible for these countries' lower PPS

---

[8] Alternatively, we worked with a presidential ideology dummy (leftist = 1), but the legislative center-of-gravity variable performed much better in predicting economic liberalization.

[9] The OLS model employs panel-corrected standard errors. More detail about the regression and the construction of the residuals can be obtained from Guillermo Rosas.

score in 1997–98, when set against predictions based on historical conditions (affluence, democratic experience, welfare state) and the scores of Chile, Mexico, and Uruguay.

In countries with inauspicious conditions for strong economic PPS, policy-switching governments and bad economic performance can hardly undermine already weak programmatic structuration. Yet in these cases the reverse process cannot be observed either – namely, that better economic performance paired with partisan governments that stick to their promises would boost PPS. It appears to be easier to lose the quality of programmatic party competition after it has been built up through cumulative, long-term processes of political-economic regime building than to build it up again in the short run after the "lost decade" of Latin American development.

CONCLUSION

In this chapter, we have attempted to challenge the claim that long-term conditions shape the extent of programmatic structuring around economic distribution in Latin America. The only new explanation building on recent causal mechanisms that could account for our set of countries moderately well is the level of economic wealth and human development in the late 1990s. Yet even this account offers a far less precise explanation of the cross-national economic PPS profiles than long-term conditions, leaves more cases underexplained, and is heavily endogenous to long-term mechanisms. The prominence of long-term mechanisms in our account is certainly at odds with the predilections of most current epistemologists in the social sciences, who place a premium on short-term causal mechanisms that are proximate to the explained effects, even though there are dissenters who would concur with the importance of long-term causal chains (Pierson 2004).

Nevertheless, at least for the subgroup of six countries with more or less promising long-term conditions promoting high economic PPS – early development, more democratic-competitive experience, and a more encompassing welfare state – we have suggested a short-term causal dynamic that fleshes out mechanisms that link earlier conditions for economic PPS with later observed delivery of programmatic party competition in 1998. Our analysis is hampered, however, by the small number of countries in which these relations are expected to prevail and the problem of drawing boundaries between cases that warrant inclusion in the group of Latin American polities with at least moderately favorable conditions for higher PPS, or marginal cases where the decision to include is analytically murky (Brazil and Mexico).

Against the backdrop of this qualification, let us in this conclusion schematically represent bivariate associations between conditions and processes that shape levels of economic PPS within the subset of Latin American countries with at least moderately promising long-term prior conditions

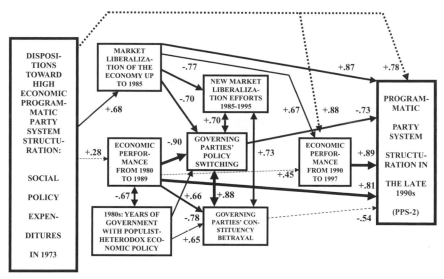

FIGURE 7.1. Relations among determinants of programmatic party system structuration (includes only countries with at least moderately favorable long-term predispositions toward strong PPS, N = 6).

conducive to higher PPS. Figure 7.1 organizes the variables along a historical timeline as a way to construct a plausible chain of causal relations that suggest why some countries with strong prior conditions for programmatic party competition – that is, the presence of import-substituting industrialization with a fairly generous welfare state, at least for those working in the urban formal economic sectors – still display comparatively robust economic programmatic competition in the late 1990s (Figure 7.1 shows only bivariate associations larger than 0.60, with a couple of exceptions, with broken lines indicating either weak linkages or statistical correlations mediated by causal mechanisms specified by solid lines). Obviously, the number of observations and the statistical means to relate them are clearly inadequate for the task. Consider Figure 7.1 therefore as a purely heuristic device to stimulate further discussion.

First, countries with strong prior conditions for economic PPS tended to liberalize their economies early, often under the impact of authoritarian regimes (Argentina, Chile, Uruguay, but also Mexico under De la Madrid). More resolute dismantling of ISI economic institutions and extension of market liberalism then coincides with better subsequent economic performance in the 1990s as well as higher economic PPS in the party system in 1997–98. The reforms crystallized political alternatives around controversies pertaining to economic reform. Moreover, successful economic liberalization made citizens believe in the sincerity of programmatic partisan government. But there is a second dynamic that works through the nature of partisan governments in the 1980s and is affiliated with economic performance in the "lost decade" directly. Where economic performance was worse in the 1980s and governments implemented heterodox reforms, political leaders tended to engage in fiscally expansionary economic policies, two associated and probably causally intertwined developments. As a consequence, partisan governments adopted economic market reforms only belatedly (market liberalization efforts in 1985–95) when compared to the reform leaders. Moreover, because such policy innovations had to be adopted under democratic rather than authoritarian conditions, they often occurred only through a sharp about-face and break with the governing party's preelection populist promises ("policy switching") that abandoned prior policy commitments in favor of liberal market retrenchment after elections and "betrayed" some of the governing party's constituencies in that process. This deceptive conduct by politicians undercut popular confidence in democratic party competition and made voters (and politicians) discount whatever programmatic statements parties issued before elections. This logic was at work most prominently in Venezuela (1988–98) but also in Argentina and Costa Rica. Policy switching and constituency betrayal undermined programmatic party competition.

None of these sets of mechanisms can be uncovered within the subset of Latin American democracies that had weak long-term prior conditions for programmatic party competition around economic issues or in the entire set of twelve countries. Where there was little disposition to embrace programmatic competition to begin with, party competition was nonprogrammatic in 1997–98 (and presumably had been such in the preceding decades as well, given these countries' background conditions), regardless of variation in trajectories of market liberalization, governing parties' policy switching, and voter betrayal in the 1980s and 1990s. Where there were weak political-economic foundations for programmatic party system competition, the "lost decade" and its aftermath in the 1990s did not instantly create them. Even partisan governments that abstained from policy switching and engaged only in moderate economic liberalization did not boost programmatic party competition. It is difficult to build new patterns of programmatic party competition where none existed but easier to destroy what already is in place, when politicians engage in policy switching and governing parties are perceived as delivering bad economic performance.

Long-term explanations of economic PPS in the late 1990s encountered two serious outliers, Mexico with more programmatic party competition than predicted on the basis of historical conditions, and Brazil with much less economic PPS than one might have expected, given its almost twenty-year democratic experience until the 1964 coup and the comparatively advanced state of its economy in the 1980s and 1990s.

Mexico's outlier status may well be resolved if we take short-term mechanisms into account. While its historical prior conditions were not so favorable for strong PPS, by the 1990s Mexico had reached a comparatively high level of economic development and urbanization as well as a substantial share of skilled industrial and white-collar employees. Such conditions are likely to have created constituencies whose members demanded some measure of greater programmatic accountability, prompting the parties to engage in strategies of "product differentiation," offering programmatic and clientelistic appeals to different electoral target constituencies (cf. Magaloni et al. 2007). Moreover, what may have actually helped Mexico's PPS score most is the implementation of a consistent market-liberal government policy that crystallized a sharp opposition around the newly evolving PRD, often with former activists from the ruling party defecting to one of the new parties.

This leaves us with Brazil, the other stark outlier reported in Table 7.2. The table showed Brazil to have a much lower economic PPS score in 1998 than both long-term predictors of PPS propensity and short-term economic affluence would have led us to expect. Admittedly, the Brazilian party system may be patterned by programmatic differences between the PT and the center-right parties, especially around presidential elections that the surveys do not reflect.[10] But with regard to programmatic competition in the legislature, hardly any of the mechanisms discussed in this chapter help to resolve the Brazilian puzzle. Brazil had a mediocre economic performance and liberalization record since 1980, but not one that would place it at the bottom of the class (Table 7.5). True, Brazilian electoral institutions to select legislators predispose the polity against programmatic partisan competition, but the same does not apply to its presidential election rules. Its constitutional rules governing presidential powers and the interplay between executive, legislative, and political parties are only mildly unfavorable to strong programmatic competition (Table 7.4). Brazilian governments also abstained from vote switching and policy betrayal (Table 7.7) and earned a highly respectable index score of responsible partisan governance (Table 7.7). Brazil may be exemplary for a class of cases for which the very failure of short-term predictions of stronger economic PPS may, in the long run, actually help bring about programmatic partisan competition.

Overall, our analysis of short-term mechanisms to shape programmatic party competition has been partially successful as a contingency theory according to which economic partisan policy and economic performance do make a difference for patterns of programmatic party competition, *provided* conditions for economic PPS were promising, on the basis of the countries long-term trajectory. We return to this theme in the concluding chapter.

---

[10] We thank an anonymous reviewer for making this point.

8

Programmatic Structuration around Religion and Political Regime

Kirk A. Hawkins, Herbert Kitschelt, and Iván Llamazares

In Latin American countries at the turn of the twenty-first century, programmatic party structuration over economic-distributive issues is clearly more important and more starkly articulated than other forms of PPS. For this reason, the two preceding chapters have been devoted to accounting for cross-national diversity in patterns of political accountability that involve economics. But a number of countries also display programmatic structuration over religion and political regime form. In this chapter, we try to make sense of the diversity of religious and regime PPS by employing a similar logic as in the analysis of economic PPS.

First, we probe long-term determinants of political learning. Are religious and regime PPS more pronounced where general resource endowments and opportunities to engage in partisan competition have enabled politicians and citizens to construct programmatic partisan divides more easily over long periods of time? If strong capabilities and opportunities have developed gradually, have correspondingly high "stakes" of political conflict over religion or regime become the decisive catalysts to trigger the formation of durable partisan divides within a polity? Second, we probe into more recent conditions conducive to partisan mobilization around religion or regime that have arisen during the so-called Third Wave of political democratization in Latin America. Are there specific political and economic experiences or cultural developments in the recent practice of political rule across Latin America that have induced citizens and politicians to coordinate around regime or religion-based programmatic party divides?

We show in this chapter that indeed religious partisan divides can be satisfactorily explained within a template that focuses on long-term determinants. It took early capabilities and opportunities for political mobilization in conjunction with high-profile "stakes" – in this instance, the intense nineteenth- and early twentieth-century conflicts over the role of the Roman Catholic Church in the political order – to trigger the formation of religious partisan divides. Such partisan divides not only are a consequence of antecedent economic developments that shook up agrarian oligarchies but also depend heavily on differences in the timing and intensity of the church-state conflict across Latin America.

Our causal account of the emergence of religious programmatic divides does not, however, explain the presence and relative strength of Christian political parties with explicitly religious labels. In Latin American polities, "Christian Democratic" parties do not necessarily represent the Catholic pole of a religious programmatic divide. Parties with formally secular labels may also play that role. Moreover, Christian Democratic parties do not necessarily even flourish in those countries that have the strongest religious divides. Parties with Christian Democratic labels require a different explanation, one that draws on an account of strategic interaction among parties as well as fairly recent economic and political experiences that encouraged politicians to found parties with religious labels. The presence of a strong religious partisan divide anchored in deep-seated church-state conflicts is neither a necessary nor a sufficient condition for the presence of electorally successful Christian Democratic parties.

Turning from religious to regime divides, a parallel argument that focuses on the development of a long-term interplay of capabilities, opportunities, and "stakes" of conflict in the process of democratic competition does not account well for the intensity of regime-based PPS. In order to make sense of the pattern in regime divides, recent and current political developments take center stage. Two very different kinds of polities evidence high-profile political regime divides. These are either democracies in which the authoritarian experience of the past is not yet so far removed to render it entirely irrelevant, or democracies with severe, current performance problems and intensive group conflicts that are difficult to accommodate under existing democratic governance. In most cases, these configurations are tied to longer-term trajectories of economic and democratic development, but the effect of short-term factors clearly predominates in explaining regime PPS.

The feeble and indirect role of long-term factors in the articulation of partisan regime divides may be due to the transitory nature of these divides. Where political actors had experienced nondemocratic regime alternatives in the past, followed by a longer period of democratic governance, the passions surrounding justifications for alternatives to democracy may be close to extinguished. Dictatorship becomes a historical phenomenon that elicits some nostalgic sentiments for and against. Only recent authoritarian experiences and novel concerns about the prospective operational workability of democracy fuel regime divides. Thus, regime divides have causal genealogies in Latin American party systems that set them apart from economic-distributive or even religious divides.

THE RELIGIOUS DIVIDE AND CHRISTIAN DEMOCRACY

Let us first capture the main empirical features of the religious divide in Latin American politics in order to highlight the puzzles that require tackling. Table 8.1 organizes the twelve Latin American countries in the order in which they rank on the strength of an *index of religious PPS, a measure directly analogous to the variants* we developed for gauging the degree of economic PPS in Chapters 6 and 7; this measure is found in column 5. The component indicators for this index are found in the preceding columns and are constructed exactly or approximately like those for economic PPS. These indicators essentially draw from four questions in the survey that get at religious attitudes, including the respondents' frequency of church attendance (v210), their stances on abortion (v235) and divorce (v236), and how religious they consider themselves (v240).

The first of these components is the *religious partisan divide*, as calculated from the results of the discriminant analysis presented originally in Table 2.6 (column 1). Mexico exhibits the strongest religious partisan divide, followed closely by Chile. At a large distance, this top duo is trailed by Uruguay, whose religious partisan divide is in turn much stronger than that of all the other countries in the big field with weak to nonexistent religious divides. The strength of the religious partisan divide correlates robustly with the *representativeness of the parties* on religious issues calculated in Chapter 4 (column 2 in Table 8.1). Parties tend to line up more clearly with their constituencies' religious predilections where religious partisan divides are stronger (correlation between columns 1 and 2 in Table 8.1: r = .60; N = 9).

When constructing economic PPS, we employed the predictive power of legislators' economic issue positions for their parties' left-right placement to capture the programmatic "left-right" semantic of political discourse in a country. We cannot perform a similar calculation for religion, as religious issues show up too rarely and weakly in the discriminant functions that divide parties in Latin American countries. Instead, we employ the ideological religious divide among legislators, independent of their party affiliation, as a predictor of politicians' left-right self-placements (column 3, Table 8.1). Such ideological divides can predict left-right self-placements in a number of countries. Moreover, these coefficients correlate robustly with the strength of religious partisan divides (correlation between columns 1 and 3: r = .68).

Our final and most demanding descriptive measure of programmatic party structuration, developed in Chapter 5, is the average internal cohesion of parties on religious issues in each country. Given the weakness of religious items in most party systems' discriminant functions, for simple mathematical reasons it is only to be expected – and confirmed by our data – that Latin American parties are generally diffuse on religious issues. Nevertheless, there is a modest negative association (r = − .35) between the

TABLE 8.1. *Religious Partisan Structuration in Latin American Politics*

	Strength of the Religious Partisan Divide	Religious Representativeness of the Parties	Religious Opinion Factor as Predictor of Legislators' Left-Right Self-Placement	Average Diffuseness of Political Parties on Religious Issues	Index of Religious Programmatic Party Structuration[a]	Strength of Christian Democratic Parties[b]
Chile	.581	2.0	.74***	.36	3	23.0 (PDC, 1997)
Uruguay	.443	1.5	.69***	.44	3	0
Mexico	.658	0.8	.89***	.54	2	26.6 (PAN, 1997)
Colombia	.283	1.0	.96***	.58	1	0
Argentina	.245	1.3	.44*	.55	1	0
Venezuela	.200	No data	.55	.51	0	12.3 (COPEI, 1998)
Brazil	.198	0.5	.34	.71	−1	0
Costa Rica	.208	−0.5	.66***	.64	−1	47.0 (PUSC, 1998)
Ecuador	.210	−1.0	.44*	.74	−1	28.6 (DP, 1998)
Peru	.153	No data	.67**	.93	−1	0
Bolivia	.188	0.3	.19	.31	−2	0
Dominican Republic	.028	No data	.00	.49	−2	0
Average (standard deviation)	.283 (.184)	.66 (.96)	.55 (.28)	.57 (.17)	.17 (1.80)	11.6 (16.1)
Correlation with the economic partisan divide	.85***	.59*	.61*	−.36	.81***	.45
Correlation with economic PPS	.72**	58*	.47	−.35	.83***	.35

[a] On variables reported in columns 1–3; countries receive a score +1 (−1), if their values are > 0.5 (< −0.5) standard deviations above (below) the country mean. Column 5 summarizes the scores over all three columns.

[b] Percentage of vote in the last lower house legislative election before 1998.

* p < .10; ** p < .01; *** p < .001.

Sources: Column 1: Table 2.6; column 2: conservative score, Table 4.4; column 3: coefficients, Table 3.3; column 4: standard deviations, Table 5.4; column 5: religious PPS-2: based on columns 1 + 2 + 3.

strength of a country's religious partisan divide and the average cohesion of parties on religious issues.

Just as with respect to economic-distributive issues, we then construct a single *index of religious PPS* that may combine two, three, or four of the components of religious party system structuration. Again, we settle here on an index that excludes the measure of programmatic diffuseness and combines only the other three attributes in the index, based on the same scoring rules employed in constructing the economic PPS index. Where a country's value is more than half a standard deviation above or below the cohort mean on a variable, it obtains a positive or negative unit score (± 1) on that dimension. The index is the summary of these scores derived from columns 1–3 in Table 8.1 and is reported in column 5. The index ranges from -3 to $+3$.

The index of religious PPS, interestingly enough, is not related to the strength of Christian Democratic parties in Latin America ($r = .16$). Partisan label and active promotion of a religious programmatic agenda are different. Furthermore, the representation of religious constituencies in Latin America is not necessarily the most clear-cut in polities with Christian Democratic parties. Consider the cases of Costa Rica and Ecuador, where there are religious parties, but where the party system does not represent religious electoral constituencies in any systematic and consistent fashion. Both countries have strong Christian Democratic parties but report negative partisan representation on these issues. We thus have two different objects of explanation here: the strength of a religious divide in partisan politics, regardless of whether it is represented by religious parties; and the strength and distribution of Christian Democratic parties.

Table 8.1 provides correlations between the different indicators and indices of religious programmatic politics and select indicators of economic-distributive divides. The message is that religious and economic-distributive divides reinforce each other, with the leftist redistributive economic positions (and parties) teaming up with secular positions on the religious divide. The robust correlation between economic and religious programmatic divides suggests that it may be possible to explain religious divides in similar terms to economic divides. It turns out, however, that this is true only in a very limited way.

Explaining Religious PPS

In Chapter 6, we constructed a causal chain linking economic PPS to early economic development (1928 per capita GDP), political experience with electoral contestation (electoral contestation, 1945–73), the cumulative effect of development and experience with contestation, and the rise of narrowly particularistic or somewhat more inclusive welfare states covering at least most of those employed in the formal urban manufacturing

TABLE 8.2. *Long-Term Determinants of Religious Partisan Divides*

	Religious Partisan Divides	Representativeness of Political Parties on Religious Issues	Index of Religious Programmatic Party Structuration
Capacities			
Per capita GDP 1928	.43 (N = 9); .53*	.69* (N = 7); .70* (N = 9)	73* (N = 9); .80**
Per capita GDP 1960	.33	.65* (N = 9)	.58*
Opportunities			
Electoral contestation 1945–73	.53*	.18 (N = 9)	.56*
1928 capacity + 1945–73 contestation	.62*	.53 (N = 9)	.80**
Political-economic stakes			
Social policy expenditure as % of GDP 1973	.44	.62* (N = 9)	.70**

Note: Unless otherwise indicated, N = 12 for each correlation. * p < .10; ** p < .01; *** p < .001.

Sources: Religious partisan divide, representativeness of political parties on religious issues, and index of religious PPS: Table 8.1, columns 1, 2, and 5. All other variables, see Tables 6.1 through 6.6.

and service economy in the context of import-substituting industrialization (ISI) development strategies. When we look at religious PPS, however, such an explanation is less powerful. The correlation between religious PPS and the long- and short-term factors highlighted in Chapter 6 is only moderate. Table 8.2 compares these long-term determinants with religious PPS. While there is a pattern of relations similar to what we found in Chapter 6, it is really only early economic development and later the political economy of social policy that relate to religious partisan structuration in a decisive way.

Moreover, it deserves careful consideration to determine *why* these long-term conditions should be related to religious PPS. We suggest that religious PPS in Latin America is the result of a different but analogous set of long-term factors as those we explored in the study of economic PPS in Chapter 6. First, the strength of religious PPS does depend on the presence of factors similar to those that facilitated the subsequent emergence of an economic divide – namely, relatively high early economic development and experience with electoral contestation. These conditions provide citizens and politicians with general capacities and opportunities to build programmatic partisan alternatives.

Second, however, and preceding the political-economic divides of the twentieth century that fed into the economic-distributive issues of ISI strategies and social policy, the ongoing presence of a religious divide also depends on the timing and intensity of an early church-state conflict, a long process of sometimes violent policy reform that unfolded throughout the latter half of the nineteenth and the early twentieth centuries. The church-state conflict about the scope of religious or secular state authority over citizens' family affairs, socialization, and cultural freedoms furnishes the substantive policy "stakes" that inspired the formation of religious partisan divides. In the emergence of the economic partisan divide, the equivalent stake was the struggle over social policy. The stakes of the religious struggle emerge already in an oligarchical period when few capacities and opportunities were present to articulate the conflict within an arena of party competition. But where the struggle was sufficiently intense and the timing of its initial settlement in favor of secular authorities was closer to periods of electoral contestation and conditions of greater development in the twentieth century, it became a cause for the subsequent formation of partisan alternatives and persisted as a salient political divide.

In the formation of economic partisan divides, however, the struggle about the "stakes" of ISI development strategies and especially its distributive implications for social policy expansion occurred much later relative to the emergence of capacities and opportunities for programmatic party structuration. In fact, in some ways the earlier assertion of secular-urban "liberal" forces in church-state conflicts may have cleared the way for later political-economic innovation, particularly the differential expansion of social policy. This may account for the high correlation we find between the strength of religious and economic PPS at the end of the twentieth century. We have to leave an investigation of the interaction between Latin American development strategies of economic and social policy and church-state conflicts to future studies. Let us here first characterize the church-state conflicts in Latin America and then return to the causal story concerning the rise of religious PPS.

Church-State Conflicts

As in Europe, the process of state building after the wars of independence in Latin America eventually led to attempts at limiting control of the church over key institutions, such as regulation of cemeteries; civil registries for births, marriages, and deaths; compulsory tithes; control over education; *fueros* or separate courts for clergy and other "corporations" dealing with civil and criminal matters; and constitutional provisions allowing freedom of religion. The secular or anticlerical stance initially manifested itself primarily in liberal and radical parties, while the interests of the church were usually defended by conservative and confessional parties. Eventually the liberalizing groups reached some kind of accommodation with the church and its defenders, typically by the 1890s, and often after very divisive or violent political conflict. In most cases the church was forced to accept the secularizing reforms, although in a few instances it maintained significant privileges (Mecham 1966: 255; Lynch 1986).[1]

The conflict over church and state was formative for many Latin American party systems (Scully 1992; Middlebrook 2000). While some conservative and liberal parties could also trace their roots to conflicts over other early aspects of what Lipset and Rokkan (1967) call the "national revolution," in particular center-periphery conflicts over federalism, as well as rural-urban divides associated with the earliest stages of the industrial revolution (Gibson 1996), in most Latin American countries the first legally organized parties, especially conservative ones, were a product of the ideological competition over the appropriate role of the church in a modern state.

In this volume we do not systematically explore the distant causes of the church-state conflict in Latin America, as we consider this beyond the scope of our analysis; however, one of the attributes of that conflict that makes it a particularly compelling independent variable for explaining religious PPS at the end of the twentieth century is the fact that its causes seem diverse and largely unrelated to the level of early economic development or the institutional strength of the church (a factor often mentioned in the literature on church and state in Latin America).[2] Some of the countries where the church-state conflict was most severe had a comparatively weak, resource-poor church (such as Chile and Ecuador), while other countries with a strong institutional presence of the church had only minor conflicts (such as Peru). Furthermore, the conflict seems to be uncorrelated with levels of democracy and development in earlier periods. Years of democratic experience and per capita GDP at the end of the nineteenth century have little relationship to the strength of the conflict. Thus, the church-state conflict is a potentially exogenous, independent cause of religious PPS.

The church-state conflict varied in two ways that could affect the strength of subsequent religious PPS in Latin America. First, it varied in intensity, or the degree to which church-state issues affected alignments of politicians and parties. In some countries the conflict was insignificant or even nonexistent,

---

[1] We are reluctant to call this a "separation of church and state," as in most cases it was less a separation of the kind institutionalized in the United States than it was a subjection of certain church functions to state control, as in most of Europe. Thus, at the same time that some of these secularizing reforms were being pursued in Latin America, many governments also sought and exercised patronage rights, or control over naming of prelates in exchange for financial and legal support for the church.

[2] There are no quantitative studies of the origins of the church-state conflict in Latin America. However, qualitative, multicountry studies emphasize that the conflict arose out of a complex combination of domestic developments and international factors and was shaped by both the ideological considerations and the interests of the actors engaged in these struggles (Lynch 1986; Mecham 1966; Safford 1985).

either because such reforms were never attempted or were attempted only in a limited way, or because they simply failed to galvanize public opinion or become a source of debate. By contrast, in other countries the public and the parties divided over the issue of secularizing reforms and sometimes even engaged in violent conflict. We presume that countries with more intense conflicts would be more likely to have strong religious PPS later in the twentieth century.

Second, the conflict varied in its timing. While most conflicts played themselves out between the 1870s and 1890s, the peak period of anticlerical legislation, a few conflicts were resolved much earlier, during the 1850s, and several others went unresolved until much later, during the first half of the twentieth century. Presumably, a delayed, intense church-state conflict would produce a stronger religious partisan divide at the end of the twentieth century than a conflict of similar intensity that occurred relatively early in the nineteenth century.[3]

The combination of these factors yields a potential scale of church-state conflict shown in Table 8.3 that ranges from 0 (none) to 3 (high). Because this is the first time that any attempt has been made to quantitatively measure the level of church-state conflict in Latin American countries, we briefly discuss each of these countries and categories. Most of our coding decisions are based on the country studies in the classic volume by Mecham (1966), but we have also drawn on additional sources for each country.

LOW OR NO INTENSITY – EARLY RESOLUTION (BOLIVIA, DOMINICAN REPUBLIC, PERU). In this first category of countries there was simply never any significant politicization of the church-state issue, usually because traditional Catholicism remained strong or liberalism was almost entirely absent from national politics. Laws separating church and state (e.g., public education, control over cemeteries, marriage and divorce laws) were gradually introduced during the 150 years after independence but without significant partisan conflict. Rights of patronage were maintained during this period, but in a way that was usually very favorable to the clergy. In Peru after independence, the government made the Catholic Church a "state" church (supported by public funds, with tithes and the *fueros* abolished, and the government essentially exercising patronage), although it eventually allowed some degree of religious tolerance. Unlike in countries such as Mexico, there

---

[3] The church-state conflict also varied in a third way, in terms of outcome. That is, in some countries the resulting settlement disproportionately favored one side of the conflict (e.g., liberal forces in Mexico or the church in Colombia), while in others it was a more neutral outcome favoring neither side (e.g., Brazil, where disestablishment was complete but not punitive). Although probably a more analogous indicator of "stakes," this aspect of the church-state conflict seems to be fairly highly correlated with the intensity and timing that we measure here and is somewhat less tractable to code; moreover, preliminary measures that we considered yielded very similar results to the present analysis. Thus, we opted to focus on the intensity and timing of the conflict.

TABLE 8.3. *Levels of Church-State Conflict: Timing and Intensity of Conflict*

	Intensity of Conflict	
	Low/None	Medium/High
Timing of conflict		
Early resolution (before 1870s)	0 Bolivia Peru Dominican Republic	1
Intermediate resolution (1870–90)	1 Brazil Costa Rica Argentina	2 Venezuela
Late resolution (after 1890)	2 Uruguay	3 Chile Colombia Mexico Ecuador

Sources: Argentina: Mecham 1966, Alonso 2000, Rock 1975; Bolivia: Mecham 1966; Brazil: Mecham 1966, Lynch 1986, Thornton 1973; Chile: Mecham 1966, B. Smith 1982; Colombia: Mecham 1966, Abel 1987, González G. 1977; Costa Rica: Mecham 1966, Campos Salas 2000, Salazar Mora and Salazar Mora 1991; Dominican Republic: Mecham 1966; Ecuador: Mecham 1966, Larrea 1954; Mexico: Mecham 1966, Loaeza 2003; Peru: Mecham 1966, Pike 1967; Uruguay: Mecham 1966, Hawkins 2003; Venezuela: Mecham 1966, Rodríguez Iturbe 1968.

was no expropriation of church property, and the state remained friendly to the church. Although liberals made some initial attempts at anticlerical reforms during a brief period of rule after independence, conservatives regained control by 1860 and passed a constitution that satisfied both sides on the issue of church-state relations. After 1860, the church-state issue "was essentially removed from Peruvian politics" (Pike 1967: 36). In Bolivia also, the government effectively exercised patronage until the 1960s and, as in Peru, never experienced a significant period of politicized anticlerical reform. Anticlerical laws were enacted after liberals came to power in 1899, arousing a vocal response from the hierarchy, but the conservative opposition was no longer effective, and Catholics never organized a partisan alternative. When new parties came to power after 1920, their programs were built around issues besides those of church and state (Klein 1969; Barnadas 1987). In the Dominican Republic, relations between the church and state were also generally favorable to the church, to the point that one of the most effective presidents of the nineteenth century was a priest and eventual archbishop, Arturo Meriño, who was allied with the liberals. In any case, the century after independence was a time of great political upheaval, and opportunities for a coherent program of anticlerical reform were limited to mild efforts in the area of public education. Under the dictatorship of Rafael Trujillo in the twentieth century, the church was given considerable support from the government (albeit conditional on its support for the regime) and successfully negotiated a Concordat in 1954. The clergy did experience some persecution during Trujillo's last years after it began to oppose his regime, but this persecution was short lived and the Concordat remained unchanged after Trujillo's death (Wipfler 2001; Lluberes 1998).

LOW INTENSITY – INTERMEDIATE RESOLUTION (ARGENTINA, BRAZIL, COSTA RICA). Although the timing of the church-state conflict in Argentina, Brazil, and Costa Rica is similar to that in Venezuela, playing itself out by the early 1890s, the intensity was clearly much lower and failed to divide many of the politicians or the electorate. In Argentina, the state retained the rights of patronage in the Constitution of 1853 while avoiding too close a relationship with the church. There was no real church-state conflict until the 1880s, when the administrations of Julio Roca and Miguel Juárez Celmán successively passed secular education and marriage laws. These aroused a pro-Catholic reaction but never in large enough numbers to create a significant, politicized debate that could leave an imprint on the party system, such as the system was at the time (Lynch 1986: 167–68). The chief lay spokesman for the pro-Catholic side, the scholar Manuel Estrada, did found a small, short-lived clerical party, Catholic Action; this and other pro-Catholic groups joined with the coalition of forces that supported the Civic Union, the parent organization to the Radical Civic Union, in 1889 and participated in the revolt against Juárez Celmán (Auza 1966; Alonso 2000: 48, 55, 57). However, subsequent schisms within the Civic Union led Estrada's group of clerical supporters to leave the party and support the candidacy of Roque Sáenz Peña in 1892 (Alonso 2000: 93). Those pro-Catholic groups that remained in the new Radical Civic Union carried little weight, especially as the party evolved over the next two decades and focused on issues of democratization and middle-class access to state resources (Rock 1975).

In Brazil, the continuance of the Bragança monarchy made independence easy for the clergy, and the clergy was noted for supporting state control over the church. Many of the clerics were liberals and Masons. However, this relationship became more difficult as the monarchy exercised increasing control over the church and as Freemasonry in Brazil began to assume a more anti-Catholic form (Thornton 1973). A national controversy over state control of the church emerged in 1872 when two bishops ordered all Masons expelled from the religious fraternities, invoking papal bulls that had not been approved by the crown; although the controversy was officially resolved a few years later, liberals in the government began pressing for anticlerical legislation (Lynch 1986: 564). When the monarchy ended in 1889, the republicans included provisions in the new constitution that formally disestablished the church but allowed it to enjoy its own juridical identity and hold property, thereby creating a legal separation of church and state much like that in the United States. Both sides peacefully accepted the new arrangement.

In Costa Rica there was a minor, short-lived conflict between the clergy and the state in the 1880s, but it was one that largely failed to divide political elites. In 1883, about a decade after liberals assumed power, the president of Costa Rica issued a decree that forbade the entry of new Jesuits into Costa Rica; after initially trying to stay clear of the conflict, the bishop became involved and was deported along with the Jesuits in 1884. The government subsequently revoked the 1852 Concordat, secularized the cemeteries, and prohibited the establishment of monasteries. However, the acting bishop restored relations with the government, and when the president died in 1886, the regular bishop was able to return. The clergy continued to resent the liberal laws and in 1891 created a clerical party, the Catholic Union, that comprised largely the clergy and peasant voters. This party participated in the municipal elections that year and in the presidential election of 1893, but it encountered significant resistance from the elite and was outlawed by constitutional amendment in 1895. This was the last time the church fought openly against the liberals and the secularizing laws (Campos Salas 2000: 62–72, 75–82; Salazar Mora and Salazar Mora 1991: 21–23).

MEDIUM TO HIGH INTENSITY – INTERMEDIATE RESOLUTION (VENE-ZUELA). In Venezuela, the most significant anticlerical reforms were carried out by the liberal President Antonio Guzmán Blanco, a classic "growth and progress" dictator in the 1870s and 1880s. After assuming power shortly after the end of the Federal War, a long conflict that pitted conservative against liberal caudillos, Guzmán Blanco reimposed anticlerical laws established by earlier liberal governments and attempted a variety of other radical reforms, including an ill-fated effort to create a national church. The church in Venezuela was relatively weak and its supporters were few (particularly as a result of the conservatives' losses in the Federal War); and it was eventually forced to accept most of these reforms. Subsequent caudillos encouraged a rapprochement with the church but without reversing many of the laws or allowing the church to criticize the laws or the government (Rodríguez Iturbe 1968; Lynch 1986: 578–79).

LOW INTENSITY – LATE RESOLUTION (URUGUAY). Uruguay is one of the more difficult cases to code. Formal separation of church and state was finally enacted with the new constitution of 1919 and was part of the secularizing program of President José Batlle y Ordóñez and his faction in the Colorado Party. This project of secularization was more extreme than that attempted in any other Latin American country; any mention of religion or deity was eliminated from most public institutions. However, the separation was a long time in the making and not strongly contested by the National Party. Although generally pro-clerical, the National Party's support was so lukewarm that defenders of the church felt compelled to found a new party, the Civic Union, in 1911; this largely confessional party played only a small role in politics before it was transformed into the Christian Democratic Party in the early 1960s.[4] Thus, despite the extreme nature of Batllista secularization, we count this as a case of only moderate but fairly recent church-state conflict.

MEDIUM OR HIGH INTENSITY – LATE RESOLUTION (CHILE, COLOMBIA, ECUADOR, MEXICO). In this last group of countries, the church-state conflict was prolonged or even renewed until well into the twentieth century and was a principal dimension of partisan conflict. Mexico started out much like the other countries mentioned previously, experiencing a "classic" conflict rooted in the victory of liberals over the conservatives, initially in the 1850s and again, after the French intervention, in the 1860s. However, the modernizing liberal dictator, Porfirio Díaz, ceased observing the anticlerical laws and forged a new alliance with the old conservative interests and the church. This sowed the seeds for a new church-state conflict after the revolution, as the postrevolutionary leadership sought to reimpose the old liberal laws. When the new laws governing church-state relations in the 1917 constitution were finally enforced in the 1920s, the clergy and many lay members rebelled. This conflict was resolved only in the late 1930s when the church reached a friendly understanding with the government of Lázaro Cárdenas, and even then lay opposition continued in the form of the National Action Party (PAN), founded in 1939.[5]

In Colombia also, beginning in the 1850s radical elements in the Liberal Party attempted to subject the church to complete state control, eventually denying it the right to hold property. These laws provoked violent conflicts between the liberals and conservatives in both the 1870s and the 1880s, with

---

4 The Uruguayan Christian Democratic Party was strongly influenced by student groups seeking a distinctly Catholic response to radical leftism and the challenges of modernization in the postwar period. It initially had considerable popularity and was a key founding member of the Frente Amplio (FA) in 1971. However, during and after the military government (1973–83) it temporarily distanced itself from the FA. Conflicts over these strategic decisions, together with the death of the party's most popular leader, disaffected many of the party members and undermined its electoral strength. Today the party is a minority faction of the FA. Thus, in a very indirect way the radical secularization program of Batlle y Ordóñez did help shape the Uruguayan party system today, but the presence of openly Christian Democratic or pro-Catholic elements is currently very limited and, as with Christian Democracy elsewhere in Latin America, can be traced primarily to Catholic responses to class-based issues rather than early conflicts over the boundaries between church and state. For more information on this history, see Hawkins (2003).

5 Loaeza (2003) emphasizes that the PAN was not initially a confessional party but that it quickly became so under the influence of its largely pro-Catholic leadership.

the conservatives eventually triumphing and establishing a constitution and Concordat in the mid-1880s that reversed many of the liberal reforms and ensured a privileged position for the church for several decades (González G. 1977). As the years passed, the church-state conflict retained great popular appeal, especially in rural areas. Conservative leaders during the 1930s and 1940s repeatedly raised the issue and used it as a tool for mobilizing voters, a tactic that helped precipitate La Violencia, a bloody civil war that took more than 200,000 lives, and for a time gave it the feel of a religious war. The church-state conflict was effectively resolved only with the dictatorship of Gustavo Rojas Pinilla in 1953 and the subsequent compromise between the Liberal Party and Conservative Party that produced the National Front in 1958 (Abel 1987).

In Chile, the conflict was also politically divisive but more gradual and less violent. According to Scully (1992), the liberal reforms were the most important ideological divide in Chile for much of the latter half of the nineteenth century and the key issue that prompted the formation of the first regularly organized political parties in the 1850s. Because Catholic roots ran deep and the conservatives were well organized, the liberal and more especially radical parties chose to pursue their secularizing platform in a more piecemeal fashion. Anticlerical laws were passed throughout the latter half of the nineteenth century, and it was not until the Radical Party won the presidency in 1920 that its leaders attempted the final, complete separation of church and state, which they achieved peacefully and formalized in the constitution of 1925 (B. Smith 1982: chap. 3).

In Ecuador, the conflict was postponed. Gabriel García Moreno and his successors from the Conservative Party ran the country from 1860 until 1895, instituting a profoundly Catholic government that staunchly defended itself from liberal reforms. Thus, unlike most of Latin America, Ecuador did not really experience any significant separation of church and state until after the Radical Liberal Party ousted the Conservatives and came to power in 1895. Most of these anticlerical laws were passed during the following decade. Conflicts over the reforms were frequently violent, but by the end of Liberal Party rule in 1925 the reforms were essentially permanent. In 1937 a new modus vivendi between the government and the papacy formalized this arrangement (Larrea 1954).

ADDITIONAL CHURCH-STATE CONFLICTS. A few Latin American countries experienced additional, short-lived conflicts between the church and particular governments in the middle of the twentieth century, such as Argentina during the last year of Perón's first government (ca. 1955) and the Dominican Republic during the last years of the Trujillo government. However, we have not included these in our coding because they failed to seriously question the legal relationship between the Catholic Church and the state. Rather, the conflicts seem to have been driven by personal issues, the government's flagrant abuses of human rights, or competition with leftist-populist groups for the hearts and minds of the poor that was associated with the emerging class cleavage. The church's involvement in these conflicts was often inconsistent, as it was in both Argentina and the Dominican Republic, where the hierarchy initially supported the regime.[6]

It is important to note that church-state conflicts in the second half of the nineteenth and the first half of the twentieth century are not endogenous to economic development or conditions of electoral contestation. It was not the rise of urban economic sectors with formal labor markets in commercial and government services that triggered a confrontation with the church, as education gained increasing importance for human capital formation and as urban settings fostered attitudes of individualism and tolerance for cultural diversity. Data for economic development in 1900, as measured by the Oxford Latin American Economic History Database (http://oxlad. qeh.ox.ac.uk/) and the Polity IV historical time series of political regime (Polity IV Project 2007), do not correlate with the profile of state-church conflicts at this early age.[7]

Accounting for Late Twentieth-Century Religious Partisan Divides
While a powerful church-state conflict could generate initial partisan divides in the nineteenth and early twentieth centuries, this was clearly insufficient to generate lasting programmatic structuration around religious issues a century later. Akin to programmatic structuration around economic issues, religious PPS thrived only if politicians had the opportunity to build programmatic alternatives through a sufficient number of rounds of democratic competition to make the construction of programmatic parties a cost-effective strategy for political elites ("opportunity") and could count on at least moderately educated electorates whose members could grasp, if not read, programmatic appeals and overcome collective action problems inherent in their relationship with their political representatives ("capacity"),

---

[6] Another well-known encounter between church and state during this period, the extraordinary alliance between the Catholic Church, Communist Party, and the Calderonista government in Costa Rica from 1940 to 1948, simply cannot be characterized as a period of conflict. The church's involvement was largely limited to the government's program of socioeconomic reforms and was, obviously, a case of cooperation. The subsequent 1948 revolution did not result in any negative reaction to the church, partly because the Figueres faction had also supported the socioeconomic reforms and partly because the church remained a neutral player during the conflict. The new constitution of 1949 essentially left church-state relations unchanged from those established in the 1871 constitution (Campos Salas 2000).

[7] Specifically, we use the total number of years of the Democracy indicator from the Polity IV database from independence to 1900 as our measure of "opportunity," and we use per capita GDP in 1900 as our measure for "capacity." We then standardize each country's score as the number of standard deviations from the regional mean and sum the two components – capacity + opportunity – to achieve a single measure. Very rough extrapolations of GDP in 1900 are made for countries that lack data this far back, namely, Bolivia (earliest data 1945), Costa Rica (1920), and the Dominican Republic (1945).

TABLE 8.4. *Interaction of Church-State Conflict with Development plus Opportunity for Contestation*

	Level of Church-State Conflict	Long-Term Dispositions Leading to Economic PPS (capacity + opportunity) Rescaled	Interacted Score (column 1 x column 2)
Argentina	1	0.57	0.57
Bolivia	0	0.05	0.00
Brazil	1	0.42	0.42
Chile	3	0.93	2.78
Colombia	3	0.25	0.76
Costa Rica	1	0.62	0.62
Dominican Republic	0	0.13	0.00
Ecuador	3	0.35	1.06
Mexico	3	0.43	1.30
Peru	0	0.27	0.00
Uruguay	2	1.00	1.99
Venezuela	2	0.45	0.90
Average (standard deviation)			0.87 (.84)

Sources: Column 1: Table 8.3; column 2: Table 6.3.

a condition that depended heavily on the level of economic development. Where these conditions persisted through the twentieth century, they facilitated not only the emergence of economic PPS but, wherever preceded by earlier church-state conflicts, the persistence of strong religious PPS as well.

If this argument is correct, then we should find that the historical format (timing and intensity) of the church-state conflict together and in interaction with general conditions of capacity and opportunity for programmatic electoral contestation should account for the relative strength of religious PPS in the late twentieth century. Ideally, the main causal force should be the interaction between both conditions, such that late and intense religious conflicts foster strong religious PPS only if capacities or opportunities are favorable as well. In Table 8.4 we report the interaction between church-state conflict (from Table 8.3) with the measures of cumulative economic capacity and democratic opportunity from Chapter 6, but rescaled between 0 and 1 (Table 6.3). The resulting scale attaches a harsh penalty to countries with low long-term propensity for PPS, which we feel is appropriate, because the lack of conditions to perpetuate the church-state divide should severely attenuate the presence of this divide over the subsequent decades. For countries with high capacity and opportunity (Chile and Uruguay), the effect is to leave the original church-state conflict score the same; for countries with

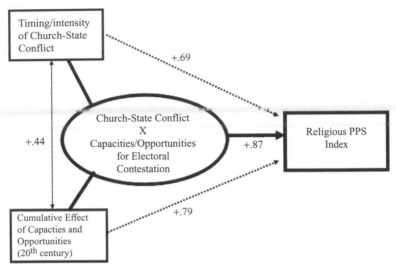

FIGURE 8.1. Causes of religious PPS. *Sources:* Combined index of religious PPS: Table 8.1, column 5; church-state conflict score: Table 8.3; cumulative effect of capacities and opportunities (twentieth century): Table 6.3; interaction of church-state conflict score and long-term disposition towards economic PPS: Table 8.4. Unless otherwise indicated, $N = 12$.

intermediate capacity and opportunity (basically Argentina, Brazil, Costa Rica, Mexico, and Venezuela), the effect is to halve their church-state score, and for countries with very low capacity and opportunity (in particular, Bolivia), the resulting interaction is basically zero. This interaction tends to add greater variance to the scores of countries with stronger church-state conflicts, especially Mexico, Colombia, and Ecuador.

The timing and intensity of church-state conflict is only weakly correlated with the general capacities and opportunities for programmatic democratic competition in Latin American politics ($r = .44$). Nevertheless, with only twelve cases, it is impossible to sort out precisely whether these two variables separately or in interaction shape the religious PPS at the end of the twentieth century.[8] Figure 8.1 therefore presents only crude bivariate correlations akin to Figure 6.1 to capture the logic of the argument. As earlier, the figure includes broken lines for strong statistical associations without intervening causal mechanisms, and solid lines for associations between intervening variables and outcomes. As can be seen, religious divides in programmatic politics occur wherever church-state conflicts were late and intense ($r = .69$)

---

[8] As a further check, we considered a multivariate regression with all three variables included: the original indicators for the church-state conflict and the long-term cumulative capacities and opportunities, plus the interaction term. The interaction term trumps the other two variables, but the small number of cases leaves us with standard errors too large to bother reporting the results here.

and in economic and institutional settings that nurtured politicians' and voters' efforts to bring about programmatic competition ($r = .79$). That is, each of these conditions seems to have some independent effect on religious PPS. But the religious divides especially occur both when the country has experienced early, intense conflicts *and* where democratic opportunities and economic conditions made their continuance feasible ($r = .87$) – it is their interaction that matters most. This strong correlation is robust; even when we eliminate our most extreme case, Chile, it remains high and statistically significant ($r = .84$, $p < .001$). Together, this evidence strongly suggests that a set of long-term causal processes analogous to what we discussed in previous chapters is at work in sustaining this alternative, historically distant source of programmatic party structuration. Just as with economic PPS, patterns of religious PPS depend on the early occurrence of specific issue conflicts that can create the stakes for electoral competition, as well as on a set of electoral opportunities and material capacities for political organization that can allow these stakes to become crystallized in parties and party systems. Given the greater historical distance involved here, this case provides nice confirmation of our theory.

Explaining Christian Democratic Parties

We can now draw a distinction between the general mobilization of religious partisan divides and the specific expression of such divides in Christian Democratic (Catholic) parties in Latin America. Table 8.5 depicts the intensity of religious programmatic structuration on the horizontal axis and, on the vertical axis, our measure of the interaction between the church-state conflict and the cumulative index of capacities and opportunities to develop programmatic party competition during the twentieth century. Italicized country entries have electorally substantial Christian Democratic parties at the time of our legislators' surveys. If there were a strong relationship between religious PPS and the incidence of electorally successful Christian Democratic parties, we would find all of these italicized countries clustered in the lower right cells of the table. What we actually discover, however, is that there is essentially no such relationship. There are Christian Democratic parties across the entire spectrum of church-state conflict ($r = .29$). In fact, there is at least one country with favorable conditions for religious PPS and strong religious partisan divides in which a Christian Democratic party is all but absent (Uruguay).

Why does Christian Democratic party strength not map directly onto religious PPS in Latin American party systems? First, in a number of countries, protagonists of the Catholic Church in the "old" religious conflicts have origins that go back long before the Christian Democratic label was invented. They constituted a combination of socioeconomic and church interests that ran under different, conservative partisan labels. Where church-state conflicts were less vibrant, it was harder to construct a conservative (and

TABLE 8.5. *Christian Democratic Parties and Religious Partisan Divides*

	Summary Index of Religious PPS				
Interaction church-state conflict × capacities/opportunities for electoral contestation	Low < –1.5	Medium Low –1.5–1	Medium –0.5 – +0.5	Medium High 1–1.5	High > 1.5
Weak: < .45	Bolivia (0/–2) Dom. Rep. (0/–2)	Brazil (.42/–1) Peru (0/–1)			
Medium: .45–1.29	*Ecuador* (1.06/–1)	*Costa Rica* (.62/–1)	*Venezuela* (.9/0)	*Argentina* (.57/1) Colombia (0/1)	
Strong: > 1.29					*Mexico* (1.3/2) *Uruguay* (1.99/3) *Chile* (3/11)

Note: Countries with Christian Democratic parties italicized.
Sources: Summary index of religious PPS: Table 8.1, column 5; interaction church-state conflict × capacities/opportunities for electoral contestation: Table 8.4

254

potentially antidemocratic) partisan camp (Middlebrook 2000). By contrast, Christian Democratic parties in Latin America tended to respond to processes of economic development (e.g., urbanization, industrialization) and the decisions over state-sponsored industrial promotion that came to the fore in the second third of the twentieth century. Unlike in much of Western Europe, Christian Democrats were not a response to the earlier church-state conflict, which instead either reinforced existing conservative parties or occasionally gave rise to short-lived confessional parties. Unlike the protagonists of the Catholic Church in the "old" religious conflicts, Christian Democratic parties in many countries adopted decisively reformist stances. Christian Democracy was a rallying cry for a "third way" between socialist statist development strategies and market liberalism (Williams 1967; Mainwaring and Scully 2003). In addition to broad background conditions such as urbanization, the duration of democratic competition, or the presence of electoral laws conducive to the entry of new competitors, it is thus rather specific opportunities for defining electoral stakes that account for the success or failure of separate Christian Democratic partisan labels. Distinct Christian Democratic parties are likely to flourish and become anchors of the religious programmatic divide only where they are not "crowded out" by other entrenched parties already occupying a centrist reform position in the economic-distributive issue space (Hawkins 2003). Second, net of such constellations of capacities, opportunities, and political-economic "stakes," the political effort to create genuinely Christian Democratic programs to promote a reformist socioeconomic reorganization of capitalist economies in Latin America could proceed only when young Latin American intellectuals were exposed to the social teaching of the Catholic Church in European and Latin American universities (Hawkins 2003).

All of these conditions – incipient modernization, strategic opportunities on the field of party competition, and ideational opportunities to define Christian "stakes" in the process of socioeconomic development and reform – were met in Chile, Costa Rica, and Venezuela. Between the 1930s and 1950s in all three polities, powerful new populist and even socialist political forces pushed socioeconomic reform and democratization against elements of an old oligarchic ruling class entrenched inside or outside partisan politics. Today's Christian Democratic parties or their predecessors in Costa Rica and Venezuela positioned themselves both as counterweights to the forces of radical change (the PLN and AD, respectively) and as agents of evolutionary reform against the defenders of an oligarchic status quo.[9]

---

[9] While Christian Democracy in Costa Rica and Venezuela had relatively rightist stances on economic issues by the 1980s, all of these parties had centrist or reform orientations when they first entered the political scene. In the case of Christian Democracy in Costa Rica, one made more complex by the successive iterations of this party that appeared over the course of the twentieth century, important antecedents to the PUSC were strongly influenced by the

A negative case where Christian Democracy did not make significant inroads confirms the same logic. Uruguay certainly had favorable background conditions for the rise of Christian Democracy (level of urbanization and development; experience with party competition and openness of the electoral system) early on, but it did not proceed to host a powerful Christian Democracy. In Uruguay in the early twentieth century, it was the Batlle faction of the Colorado Party (one of the previously oligarchical parties) that pushed for socioeconomic reforms and electoral inclusion and thus averted the political polarization occurring in the three contrasting cases listed previously. Furthermore, because of lack of interest among clerics, university students were not significantly exposed to the Catholic Church's social teachings until well after the Second World War. Thus, major Uruguayan social reforms preceded the spread of ideas from the international Christian Democratic movement to Latin America by several decades.

Mexico also raises issues of timing for the emergence of Christian Democracy, albeit for the opposite reasons as in the Uruguayan case. An explicitly Catholic party – the PAN – emerged in the early 1940s in opposition to the secularizing reforms of the ruling PRI and its precursors. How can we explain the success of this party, given the relative lack of strong background conditions such as urbanization, industrialization, and democratic competition? Here, the Mexican revolution and its aftermath of institution building and policy reform seem to play a key role. This process, which extended through much of the second, third, and fourth decades of the twentieth century, led to a more radical displacement of the oligarchical ruling class and its cultural manifestation, the Catholic Church hierarchy, as in the three reference cases in which eventually centrist or center-left Christian Democratic parties emerged (Costa Rica, Chile, and Venezuela). In Mexico, the assault of the PRI and its predecessors on the Catholic Church and its oligarchical supporters pushed the emerging Catholic party into a defensive position and toward identification with antirevolutionary interests. From the late 1930s through the 1980s, it developed not so much as a social reformist but as a conservative party in economic-distributive terms that defended private property and called for the acceleration of market liberalization. The party remained outside the Christian Democratic International until 1998 and over long stretches of its history had only a tenuous association with Christian Democracy (Mainwaring and Scully 2003: 33). In a number of respects, it is more steeped in the tradition of pre-1930 market-liberal variant of

---

Catholic social doctrine, above all the Reformist Party of the politician-priest Jorge Volio and later the center-left coalition of Rafael Angel Calderón Guardia, which included progressive Catholic groups led by the archbishop of San José, Victor M. Sanabría (Salazar Mora and Salazar Mora 1991). In Venezuela, COPEI had a progressive bent in its early years that represented the influence of the Jesuit priest Manuel Aguirre, a mentor to party founder Rafael Caldera (Hawkins 2003). Bear in mind that the AD against which COPEI competed in the 1940s was much more left-populist than after the transition to democracy in 1958.

politically conservative parties intertwined with oligarchical rule that also happened to support the Catholic Church hierarchy in cultural and institutional respects. Of course, since the advent of economic liberalization and ultimately political democratization in Mexico in the mid-1980s under the leadership of the PRI, the position of the PAN has become much more complicated, as either the leadership or the average PRI voter became as market liberal and almost as supportive of religious cultural positions as those of the PAN, and as PAN supporters became highly diversified internally under the impact of the temporarily crosscutting regime divide (cf. Magaloni and Moreno 2003; Greene 2007).[10]

Going beyond the four countries with durable and electorally robust Christian Democratic parties in the 1980s and 1990s, all the other Latin American countries in our set of twelve had structural conditions inhibiting the development of powerful Christian Democratic parties, even without considering the strategic options confronting potential partisan entrepreneurs and the timing of the exposure of young intellectuals to new Catholic social doctrines. Several of these countries were extremely poor and agrarian throughout the era of the "Christian Democratic moment" from the 1930s to the 1960s. Until the 1960s or even the 1970s and beyond, countries such as the Dominican Republic, Bolivia, Peru, Colombia, and Brazil to a considerable extent lacked the social engines of Christian Democratic growth. Christian Democratic support in these countries could not draw on sufficient numbers of emerging urban middle-class voters, and the church remained close to the agrarian oligarchy.

Some countries obviously were moderately affluent and had seen the balance shift toward urban areas well before 1960, but still did not experience the rise of Christian Democracy. In these instances, the lack of continuous democratic competition may be the crucial factor. Argentina did not enjoy a prolonged era of democratic electoral competitive politics from 1930 until well into the 1980s. Only after relations between Perón and the Catholic Church worsened in the early 1950s did the alienation of the church from the regime trigger the growth of a Christian Democratic partisan alternative, and by then the Peronists had already captured much of the electoral space that successful Christian Democratic parties in other countries relied upon. In a similar vein, the 1964 military coup in Brazil cut off whatever favorable opportunities might have emerged for the growth of Christian Democracy against the backdrop of Brazil's accelerating and broadening socioeconomic transformation beyond the established metropolitan centers.

---

[10] In the election of the first non-PRI president Vicente Fox, the PAN candidate, the PRI performed distinctly better among more religiously devout voters, whereas religious practice was not a predictor of the PAN's vote (cf. Magaloni and Moreno 2003: 268). PRI supporters, not PAN supporters, tended to be the most conservative on moral issues (ibid.: p. 262).

If economic mobilization and group struggle is the baseline for Christian Democratic partisan mobilization, the Ecuadorean Christian Democracy that peaked at the time of our legislators' survey with 28.6 percent of the vote in the 1998 national legislative elections appears to be a strange outlier. In Ecuador, neither the broad background context of socioeconomic development and democratic practice nor the specific strategic and ideational conditions facilitating the entry of a new party were conducive to sustaining a durable and powerful Christian Democratic party. It is therefore not all that surprising that the 1998 election result so favorable to Christian Democracy turned out to be an idiosyncratic extreme outlier, preceded by modest support for Christian Democracy and followed by a virtual collapse of the party in the new millennium.

Thus, Christian Democratic parties in Latin America typically experienced electoral success only at a particular historical juncture of political-economic mobilization when substantial electoral constituencies became available that did not endorse more radical populist or socialist strategies of political-economic transformation, but also did not rally around successors to the old oligarchic parties (Mainwaring and Scully 2003). Within this general setting, party success then depends on the existence of other competing parties with a "centrist" electoral appeal and the timing of the Christian Democratic effort (Hawkins 2003). Many Latin American countries missed the "Christian democratic moment" in history simply because they did not acquire one or several of the conditions and were not exposed to strategic settings conducive to the growth of new parties with Christian Democratic labels.

However, we emphasize that the presence of a pronounced religious partisan division does not stand or fall with the presence of electorally attractive Christian Democratic parties. Christian Democratic parties constitute a narrower phenomenon than that of religious divides in partisan competition. Catholic-clerical positions may articulate themselves in formally nonreligious conservative and new right parties. In fact, as recent cases such as Chile's RN and UDI and even Mexico's PRI demonstrate, parties unaffiliated with transnational federations such as the Christian Democrat Organization of America and the Centrist Democrat International may end up with electorates more distinctly supporting Catholic policy positions than the competitors running under the Christian Democratic label.

Short-Term Correlates of Religious PPS

So far, we have been preoccupied with long-term societal, political regime, strategic, and ideational forces that contribute to the articulation of religious partisan divides in general and Christian Democratic parties in particular. But are there also short-term conditions that may affect the articulation of religion on the plane of party competition?

Religion is clearly not a set of issues currently dividing parties in our sample of countries, and it is difficult to earmark short-term processes that might have boosted the importance of religious conflict in partisan politics. Liberation theology began to rise in the 1960s and fed into the tail end of the surge of Christian Democratic parties we have already considered. The competition between the Catholic Church and a myriad of Protestant and other non-Catholic Christian denominations has become increasingly intense, but these new religious challengers generally steer clear of the partisan arena. Furthermore, while the issues associated with the church-state conflict may be largely settled in Latin America, newer issues that tap into religious ties – such as "family values" or the various issues associated with the shift toward postmaterialist culture (Inglehart and Welzel 2005) – are just beginning to enter the political agenda in the region. Unfortunately, we lack any measure of the changing salience of these issues in Latin America in the mid-1990s and so we cannot test for their effects on religious PPS.[11]

This leaves us with short-term economic and institutional variables we have already considered in our chapter about the economic-distributive divide. Because causal conditions that give rise to religious and economic PPS partially overlap, it is no surprise that the correlations between such developments and religious PPS turn out to be very similar to what we found concerning economic PPS. As shown in Table 8.6, stronger religious divides prevail in more affluent Latin American countries with recent harsh authoritarian regime experiences and early market liberalization. These countries also tended to enjoy better economic performance in the last decades of the twentieth century and more responsible partisan governments that avoided manifest policy switching and voter betrayal, once dictatorships had given way to electoral democracies. As in the case of economic PPS, all of these short-term predictors of religious PPS, however, are heavily endogenous to earlier economic development, opportunities for political contestation, and political-economic development strategies that set the stage for the events of the 1980s and 1990s. Not all that much new can be learned, therefore, from a scrutiny of short-term developments.

POLITICAL REGIME DIVIDES AFTER THE THIRD WAVE OF DEMOCRATIZATION

Given existing research on Latin American authoritarian rule and democratization in the 1970s and 1980s (O'Donnell, Schmitter, and Whitehead 1986; Diamond, Linz, and Lipset 1989; Hagopian and Mainwaring 2005) and on public opinion in the early to mid-1990s (Moreno 1999), we

---

[11] The World Values Survey covers too few Latin American countries in the decade preceding the Salamanca survey, and the Latinobarometer has broader regional coverage but too short of a time series.

TABLE 8.6. *Short-Term Determinants of Religious PPS*

Determinants	Index of Religious PPS
Capacities	
Per capita GDP 1998	.73**
Opportunities	
Repressiveness of political regime after 1975	.50*
Legislative election rules (around 1996)	−.26
Presidential election rules (around 1996)	−.04
Political economic stakes	
Change in market liberalization of economic transactions 1985–95	−.84***
Social policy expenditure as % of GDP 1997 or latest before that	.45
Growth of per capita GDP 1980–97	.70**
Responsible partisan government[a]	
Economic policy switching 1985–95	−.70** (−.89*; N = 6)
Governing parties' economic policy betrayal	−.44 (−.75*; N = 6)

[a] Correlations for countries with (moderately) favorable economic PPS dispositions only (N = 6; Argentina, Chile, Costa Rica, Mexico, Uruguay, Venezuela). * p < .10; ** p < .01; *** p < .001.

Sources: Religious PPS: Table 8.1, column 5; all other variables: see Tables 6.6 and 7.1 through 7.8. Number of observations is N = 12 unless otherwise indicated.

anticipated fairly strong regime divides in at least some countries in the region. But regime divides turn out to be feeble even in cases where they were pronounced in the not-too-distant past. This conforms with Moreno's (1999) general proposition that the salience and sharp electoral partisan contour of the regime divide in Latin America may wane rapidly, as democracies persist over time.

Nevertheless, modest regime divides are present in several countries in our sample, giving us at least a faint pattern of variation that invites analysis and contrasts with the more persistent divides that we have examined until now. While some of these cases of moderate regime divides (Argentina, Chile, Uruguay) neatly conform to our expectations that past authoritarian experiences would influence present programmatic structuration around regime issues, others (Ecuador, Peru, Venezuela) defy this argument by manifesting pronounced regime divides against the backdrop of lasting democracy or mild dictatorships. The same phenomenon – regime divide – appears to result from different causal chains. We find that similar logics explain these apparently different outcomes. In some countries the regime divides are "retrospective" against the backdrop of a recent harsh authoritarian past, whereas in others they are "prospective," indicating a mounting restlessness about democratic polities caught up in performance crises and deep distributive conflicts that may not even be expressed by the dominant parties.

In either case, it is short-term factors – rather than long-term endowments, configurations of resource control, or institutional commitments – that shape the articulation of partisan regime divides.

Dimensions and Configurations of the Political Regime Divide

The three questions in the Latin American legislators' survey that best capture regime evaluations ask respondents to take a position on the assertion that "democracy is always the best system" (v11), that "elections are always the best way to express political preferences" (v15), and that "without political parties there can be no democracy" (v26). A fourth indicator may also tap regime issues in the survey. It asks respondents to assess whether "justice does not work" in their own country (v32).

Unlike economic-distributive and religious programmatic structuration, we cannot produce a complete index of regime PPS because we are missing crucial data. While we do have complete information about the regime partisan divide for all twelve countries, the weak articulation of regime issues in factor and discriminant analyses makes it impossible to assess their influence on left-right self- and party placements in ways parallel to the other issue baskets. And we have data for only nine countries gauging the representativeness of the parties' positions on the regime divide for each of their electoral constituencies. We therefore have to make do with the partisan *regime divide* as our main indicator of regime PPS and employ supplementary evidence from other sources

Table 8.7 lists the strength of the partisan regime divide across the twelve Latin American countries. It measures the relative weight of regime views in discriminant functions that indicate how parties distinguish themselves from each other in Latin America (Table 2.6). It also reports for nine countries the index of party system representativeness, as developed in Chapter 4. Reassuringly, where polities have a strong articulation of the partisan regime divide, parties also tend to be more representative of different opinions about political regime in their electoral constituencies (correlation between columns 1 and 2: r = .84).

The third column of Table 8.7 produces scores for each country measuring the strength of regime ideological divides among legislators, regardless of their party affiliations, by averaging the factor loadings (principal components) on regime issues reported in Chapter 2. Of course, given the technical limitations of factor analysis, this procedure yields indicators that are only very roughly comparable across countries or even types of issue divides in the same country. The average ideological factor loadings (column 3) and discriminant function loadings on regime issues (column 1) correlate with each other only modestly (r = .50). This may indicate that opinion divides, captured by the factors, do not always translate into partisan divides, signaled by discriminant functions.

TABLE 8.7. *Regime in Latin American Partisan Politics*

	Strength of the Regime Partisan Divide	Representativeness of the Parties on the Regime Divide	Ideological Divides over Regime among Latin American Legislators	Average Diffuseness of Parties on Regime Issues
Chile	.490	1.5	.37	.28
Venezuela	.388	No data	.35	.32
Uruguay	.348	1.0	.26	.21
Ecuador	.320	0.8	.32	.52
Peru	.285	No data	.29	.60
Argentina	.250	0.8	.25	.37
Dominican Republic	.195	No data	.32	.28
Mexico	.195	0.0	.21	.80
Bolivia	.163	−0.3	.28	.35
Colombia	.123	0.3	.23	.46
Brazil	.093	0.5	.39	.45
Costa Rica	.085	−0.3	.33	.41
Average (sd)	.245 (.126)	0.48 (.61)	.32 (.095)	.42 (.16)
Correlation with economic divide	.42	.30	.31	.02
Correlation with economic PPS	.46	.45	.32	−.32

* p < .10; ** p < .01; *** p < .001.

Sources: Column 1: Table 2.6; column 2: conservative score, Table 4.4; column 3: factor analysis (average factor weights), Tables 2.1 and 2.3; column 4: standard deviations, Table 5.4.

Finally, Table 8.7 provides scores measuring the average cohesiveness of parties on regime issues. Earlier, we found that the cohesiveness of parties on economic-distributive issues was fairly low. Diffuseness on economic issues reaches a high cross-national average of .52 (on an underlying scale ranging from −1.0 to +1.0) with a low standard deviation of .06 (see Table II.1). With regard to the regime divide, the data in column 4 show exactly the reverse pattern. The diffuseness of parties over regime questions is fairly low in absolute terms; moreover, there is a higher standard deviation in the set of national average values for parties' cohesiveness over regime, reflecting the fact that in some countries (Uruguay, Chile, Venezuela, Bolivia, and Argentina) the programmatic cohesiveness over regime questions is much stronger than anything witnessed in the realm of economic issues. That said, this measure still does not correlate highly with our other indicators; the average diffuseness on regime issues (column 4) has only a weak correlation with the strength of the partisan regime divide (r = −.33), although the result is in the expected direction.

TABLE 8.8. *Average Disagreement among Legislators on Three Democratic Regime Issues in the Population*

Country	Regime Disagreement
Peru	.73
Colombia	.66
Mexico	.66
Ecuador	.66
Venezuela	.59
Chile	.52
Bolivia	.49
Dominican Republic	.46
Argentina	.46
Brazil	.43
Uruguay	.38
Costa Rica	.35

Note: Average standard deviations on questions v11 (democracy not always best), v15 (elections not always best), and v26 (parties necessary) among all respondents within each country. The scales on each question run from 1 to 4.

Retrospective versus Prospective Political Regime Divides

To avoid a protracted discussion, we immediately admit that there are no interesting linear relationships between these indicators of political regime divides and the kinds of long-term and short-term explanatory variables we have considered for economic-distributive and religious PPS. We therefore do not bother with presenting and interpreting reams of weak correlations. Instead, as a preliminary step to a more meaningful explanation, let us bring in one additional indicator of PPS that we have not explored in any of our previous analyses: the extent of overall disagreement among legislators on political regime issues.

Discriminant and factor analyses reduce patterns of covariation among many variables to a few latent dimensions but do not allow us to gauge the depth or intensity of these dimensions. To measure this level of overall disagreement, we calculate a fairly primitive indicator, the average standard deviations of responses across all legislators in each of our twelve Latin American countries to the three questions that most directly measure attitudes toward democratic regime (v11, v15, v26). The range of responses on each variable runs on a 4-point scale from 1 (full agreement) to 4 (full disagreement). Table 8.8 presents the average of standard deviations of all legislators responding to these three questions in our twelve countries.

Because the modal response to each of the three questions turns out to be full endorsement of democracy (score 1), the magnitude of the standard deviations reflects the extent to which at least some respondents in a country

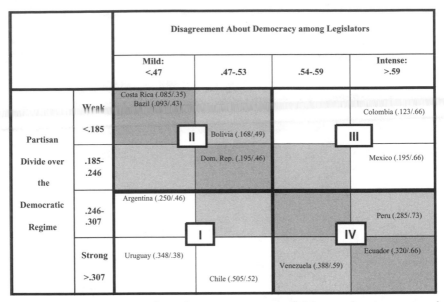

FIGURE 8.2. Disagreement about democracy among politicians and regime-centered partisan divides. *Sources:* Table 4.2 (disagreement about democracy) and Table 3.7 (partisan strength scores for the political regime dimension).

do not endorse the superiority of democratic over authoritarian practices. For example, if ten people evaluate democracy on a 4-point scale and seven choose 1 (= fully approve), but three choose 3 (= somewhat disapprove), the standard deviation would be 0.97, greater than anything reported in Table 8.8. Thus, there is overwhelming support for democracy everywhere, but at the margins there is more disagreement over democracy in Colombia, Ecuador, Mexico, or Peru than in Uruguay or Costa Rica. This descriptive finding, of course, could in part be a result of legislators' self-censorship. But given that self-censorship works probably everywhere, and particularly in countries where respondents may have reasons to oppose democracy, the cross-national variation of standard deviations on regime issues still conveys the relative strength of underlying political partisan divides across our set.

Let us now compare the level of overall disagreement over regime issues with our best indicator of political regime structuration, the strength of the regime partisan divide. Figure 8.2 shows that the intensity of disagreement among legislators over democracy, captured by the standard deviations in Table 8.8, and the regime partisan divides reported in column 1 of Table 8.7 hardly correlate at all ($r = .21$). If partisan divides over democracy as the desirable regime form occurred where deep overall disagreements existed, then our twelve Latin American countries would be located in the fields of Figure 8.2 shaded in dark or at least light gray. But this is the case for barely half of them. Some countries reveal pronounced partisan divides over the superiority of democracy *without* also having major disagreements among the entire group of legislators (quadrant I). Here, respondents just about agree on democracy as the best form of government, and whatever residual disagreements they have tend to run along partisan lines (Argentina, Uruguay, and Chile). Conversely, in some other countries the elites express relatively intense disagreement about the merits of democracy, but these disagreements do not translate into structured partisan regime divides (quadrant III: Colombia and Mexico). In line with the initial expectation about the correlation between elite disagreement about democracy and regime partisanship, we find some countries where both are low (quadrant II: Brazil, Costa Rica, Bolivia, and the Dominican Republic) and others where both overall disagreement and partisan divides on regime issues are comparatively high (quadrant IV: Ecuador, Peru, and Venezuela).

At the fuzzy borderline between a purely descriptive grouping of countries and a "proximate" causal explanation, we suggest that this comparison reveals two different types or patterns of (relatively) strong regime divides. In some instances, the presence of a regime divide appears to be more a matter of the past, encased in the memories of politicians and associated with party labels, but not a currently divisive issue. The regime divide is a retrospective one. In others, the regime divide is marked by higher overall levels of disagreement among legislators, indicating an ongoing or growing concern. It is current and prospective.[12]

Quadrant I incorporates the retrospective cases of Argentina, Chile, and Uruguay. All went through harsh authoritarian episodes that began in the mid-1970s and lasted until the early, mid-, or late 1980s. These severe "bureaucratic authoritarian" regimes ventured to dismantle preexisting modes of political association (parties, labor unions) and even to physically liquidate the most radical opponents of the existing social order. Given the critical economic conditions and ideological polarization that prevailed just before the military coups, as well as the policy and institutional changes made under the ensuing authoritarian regimes, some politicians may be tempted to defend these past authoritarian practices even though they endorse democracy without reservations by the late 1990s. The regime divide is a matter of retrospective assessment, not of current or prospective evaluation of democracy. Parties enshrine alternative views of the dictatorial past without organizing supporters around alternative visions of a future with or without democracy.

Quadrant IV encompasses the prospective cases, where there is a congruence between serious disagreements about democracy among individual

---

[12] To be clear, all of these survey questions ask about *current* regime preferences. The divide here is "retrospective" in the sense that it seems to respond to past experiences and is likely on the wane, not in the sense that it asks about what regime the respondents actually preferred in the past; that said, we think it likely that current attitudes reflect past preferences.

politicians and strong partisan divides. At the time of our survey, these countries were caught up in manifest crises of governance with coups and coup attempts revealing that members of the political elite were willing to sidestep democratic procedures, if not abandon democracy entirely. Our 1997–98 data reflect the constitutional crisis in Ecuador that unfolded with the removal of President Abdalá Bucaram in 1997. The data may even anticipate an exacerbating political-economic crisis that ultimately pinnacled in the military coup ousting President Mahuad in early 2000 and interfered with a program of market liberalizing reform, presumably in order to reassert the military's already vast role in the economy (cf. Diamint 2003: 57). In Peru, our data capture the aftermath of Alberto Fujimori's *autogolpe* (cf. Stokes 1996) and the advent of his struggle with the legislature about the constitutionality of running for a third presidential term (Degregori 2003). Finally, in Venezuela the survey was conducted in the run-up to an election completing the comprehensive disintegration of the institutionalized parties that had governed the country from 1958 to 1993. Our data mirror the last years of the presidency of Rafael Caldera, who won office as a result of a personalistic electoral campaign after leaving one of the two established parties, COPEI, which he had dominated for decades. By 1998, both established parties, AD and COPEI, were fading, as was Caldera's new quasi-partisan vehicle, Convergencia. The rise of a new leftist-populist movement crystallized by Lieutenant Colonel Hugo Chávez, the leader of the 1992 coup against then incumbent president Pérez, was just around the corner (Coppedge 1996; 2003; 2005). Both AD and COPEI were marred by the perception of record corruption and ineptitude that accelerated their decline from the late 1980s onward (cf. Coppedge 2003: 177).[13]

Where disagreements about democracy are weak and not reflected in partisan alignments (quadrant II), countries have been democratic for a long time (Costa Rica) or experienced milder forms of authoritarianism that left few organized residues once democracy was reinstated (Bolivia, Brazil, and the Dominican Republic after Balaguer). Few parties can look back favorably to a past authoritarian episode. Citizens and politicians see past dictatorial rule now as sufficiently benign, ineffective, and irrelevant for the present political debates to exclude mobilization of opinion or partisan divides around such historical episodes. It is not by accident that at least two of the three countries with an authoritarian episode in this quadrant have

[13] We cannot enter here into debates about whether the "prospective" regime divide in these countries reflects an emerging "post-liberal" approach to democracy, evident today in the rhetoric and reform efforts of left-populist movements that attempt to broaden or even challenge the institutions of representative democracy (Arditi 2008). The survey questions that we draw from here are more basic questions about support for democracy-in-general, parties, and elections, and they tap into what scholars from both sides of this debate would presumably regard as authoritarian dispositions.

elected former authoritarian rulers to be heads of state under by and large democratic circumstances (Balaguer in the Dominican Republic, Banzer in Bolivia).[14] And in Brazil, politicians associated with the military regimes of the 1970s and 1980s, José Sarney and Itamar Franco, could serve out the presidential terms of democratically elected politicians who died in office or were impeached on corruption charges.

The most difficult case in quadrant II is Bolivia. Since the mid-1990s, its democracy has been marked by intensifying doubts about the viability of democracy under the impression of what Gamarra (1996: 87) has called an "explosion of corruption," coming on the heels of more than a decade of democratic governance involving all three of the traditional major parties in various coalitional arrangements. At the time of our survey in 1998, Bolivia was exhibiting growing restlessness among political elites and new challenges by parties outside the circle of established contenders, particularly the leaders of the economically and culturally marginalized Indian highland population. The emerging conflicts intensified in the ensuing years up to this writing (cf. Domingo 2005; Mayorga 2005). If our survey had been taken in 2000 or after, Bolivia would probably have transferred into quadrants III or more likely IV in Figure 8.2 for reasons we probe into later.

Quadrant III covers countries where a subset of politicians still has doubts about democracy, but no party alignments organize these doubts around specific partisan alternatives. During the decades leading up to the 1997–98 legislators' survey, the two countries in this quadrant – Colombia and Mexico – evolved toward more competitive democracy from a restrained oligarchical compact between two parties and limited effective suffrage (Colombia, until 1974) or a thinly veiled single-party "electoralist" dictatorship (Mexico, at least until 1988). The old dominant cartel-party has stuck around, although many politicians in the former ruling parties now claim to have fully embraced democracy. At the same time, new challenges have appeared inside the party system and outside organized politics in social movements, armed insurrections, and terrorist attacks against the democratizing regimes. In Colombia, a de facto exclusion of many residents from political citizenship, the presence of clientelistic machines configured around pyramidal patron-broker-client relations tied to the Conservative and Liberal Parties, and the blatant murder of many oppositional politicians running for office outside the two major parties in the 1990s (cf. Kline 1996: 25; Archer 1995) certainly contributed to the long-festering armed conflict with guerrillas in

---

[14] Balaguer's last administration, which includes the time the survey was administered, clearly straddles the line between democratic and authoritarian. His reelection in 1994 was tarnished by fraud and a highly negative campaign; however, two years later he agreed to step down and allow new elections after an official investigation revealed the scope of the irregularities (Hartlyn 1998). During these last years, the Dominican Republic is rated by Freedom House as "partly free."

the countryside. The reach of state sovereignty and policy-making capacity remained limited, so that democratic institutions had control over few pressing issues on the political agenda (cf. Bejarano and Pizarro 2005). This may place in context the ambivalence of survey respondents in both major Colombian parties to questions about democracy.

In Mexico, only the 1994 presidential election of Ernesto Zedillo can be considered the first fully free and democratic election (cf. Domínguez and McCann 1996). While none of the major parties has challenged democracy since then, both PRI stalwarts and some former PRI politicians who moved on to other parties, particularly the PRD, may express their individual reservations about democracy in our 1998 legislators' survey. Furthermore, as previous chapters demonstrated, the old ruling parties and their new competitors have differed on issues of more lasting prospective salience than assessment of the past regime. Maybe for this reason, population surveys revealed already in 1994 that economic distribution had more salience for the actual crystallization of partisan constituencies than the regime divide (Domínguez and McCann 1996).

Explaining (Retrospective and Prospective) Political Regime Divides

The descriptive-interpretive distinction of four groups of Latin American countries points toward a short-term explanation of regime PPS. Countries in quadrants I and IV have the strongest regime divides, but they have experienced contrasting economic fortunes and reform trajectories. Table 8.9 reveals these patterns. We have placed groups of countries exhibiting strong regime divides with different levels of internal disagreement about democracy in the left two columns (groups I and IV from Figure 8.2), and countries with generally weak regime divides and varying levels of disagreement about democracy on the right (groups II and III). As a rule, in groups with strong regime divides (I and IV), short-term capacities and stakes for political mobilization of political conflict take on extreme values (high or low), whereas in the groups with weak regime partisan divides (II and III) values for these variables tend to be intermediate. We now have to work out the underlying logic of the intergroup differences.

Before moving to this explanation, we need to say a brief word about Bolivia, the interesting outlier in group II. On all the independent variables that we examine, Bolivia exhibits characteristics that would make it fall into group IV, with the expectation of both high partisan regime divides and strong controversy about the current merits of democracy, something we could not find in our 1997–98 dataset. In fact, the explanation we offer for the general pattern in the next paragraphs would lead us to predict that Bolivia would end up in group IV (strong regime PPS and intense dissent about democracy), and the subsequent events within the Bolivian polity

TABLE 8.9. *Regime Conflict and Short-Term Economic Performance*

	Group I: Argentina, Chile, Uruguay	Group IV: Ecuador, Peru, Venezuela [plus Bolivia]	Group III: Colombia, Mexico	Group II: (Bolivia), Brazil, Costa Rica, Dominican Republic [minus Bolivia]
Regime PPS	Strong	Strong	Weak	Weak
Disagreement about democracy	Weak	Strong	Strong	Weak
Capacity				
1998 per capita GDP ($1,000 at PPP)	9.8 (sd 1.9)	4.4 (sd 1.4) [3.9/sd 1.5]	6.9 (sd 1.2)	4.9 (sd 1.9) [5.7/sd 1.0]
Stakes				
Economic market liberalization 1985	0.70 (sd 0.10)	0.47 (sd 0.09) [0.47/sd 0.07]	0.58 (sd 0.00)	0.47 (sd 0.2) [0.48/sd 0.02]
Change in economic market liberalization 1985–95	+0.17 (sd 0.10)	+0.30 (sd 0.13) [+0.32/sd 0.11]	+0.22 (sd 0.01)	+0.36 (sd 0.05) [0.36/sd 0.06]
1997 GDP per capita, if 1980 = 100	138 (sd 0.32)	87 (sd 6.1) [88/sd 5.6]	116 (sd 12.7)	119 (sd 30.2) [127/sd 30.0]
Policy betrayal (Table 7.8)	0.88 (sd 0.96)	2.15 (sd 1.64) [2.15/sd 1.34]	1.94 (sd 1.88)	1.40 (sd 0.84) [1.02/sd 0.75]

between 2000 and 2005 reveal the onset of a severe regime crisis.[15] As a hypothetical exercise, therefore, we offer additional mean values on proximate causes of the configurations of regime divide for each of our four groups, as if Bolivia had shifted from group II to group IV (in brackets, in columns 2 and 4 of Tables 8.9 and 8.10). In many instances, this makes the contrasting group patterns stand out more starkly. Given the small number of cases, we do not report statistical significance tests for the group comparisons, but we do provide standard deviations within the groups that allow us to assess the robustness of intergroup differences to a limited extent.

In 1998 the strongest partisan regime divides prevailed in the richest (group I) and the poorest (group IV) countries. Moreover, the countries in the richest group (group I) also had the highest level of market liberalization, as measured by the Inter-American Development Bank's summary index both in 1985 and again in 1995 after a bout of further reforms. By contrast, the countries in group IV started with a very low level of market liberalization in 1985, but then made a huge leap in the following decade to end up with a level of liberalization on average only slightly below that of the countries in the other groups. A similar pattern applies to the countries in group II, the intermediate group without regime controversy.

Further contrasts between groups I (rich with regime partisan divide) and IV (poor with regime partisan divide) concern economic performance in the twenty-year period before our legislators' survey was taken. Group I has the overall best growth, although with substantial variation in the group (given Chile's spectacular performance), whereas group IV uniformly performs miserably, with all countries having a lower per capita GDP than at the beginning of the 1980s. Groups II and III again constitute intermediate cases, with the average in group II dragged down a bit if Bolivia is still included.

How can we make sense of these patterns and relate them to configurations of regime partisan divides? Group I is obviously a set of countries where economic reforms, on balance, paid off in improved performance by the time of the survey. Good performance reconciled initial friends and foes of democracy with the new political realities of electoral competition. Hence, while any objections to democracy that still exist are sharply focused around partisan divides between former supporters and opponents of authoritarian regimes, they have lost significance now and cooled off by

---

[15] In Latinobarometer annual surveys, the difference between the percentage of respondents who endorsed the statement that "democracy is preferable to any other kind of government" and the statement that "in certain circumstances an authoritarian government can be preferable to a democratic one" fell from 47 in favor of democracy in 1996 to an average 28 in 2004 and 2005, one of the worst records in Latin America. See the *Economist*, October 29, 2005, p. 29.

TABLE 8.10. *Regime Conflict and Long-Term Political Regime Development*

	Group I: Argentina, Chile, Uruguay	Group IV: Ecuador, Peru, Venezuela [plus Bolivia]	Group III: Colombia, Mexico	Group II: (Bolivia), Brazil, Costa Rica, Dominican Republic [minus Bolivia]
Regime PPS	Strong	Strong	Weak	Weak
Disagreement about democracy	Weak	Strong	Strong	Weak
Capacity				
1928 per capita GDP (standardized)	1.3 (sd 0.3)	−0.78 (sd 0.1) [−0.95/sd 0.4]	−0.59 (sd 0.36)	−0.93 (sd 0.4) [−0.75/sd 0.2]
Opportunity				
Electoral contestation 1945–73	20.3 (sd 12.4)	13.7 (sd 4.0) [11.3/sd 5.8]	11.5 (sd 3.5)	12.5 (sd 10.7) [15.3/sd 11.1]
Stakes				
Social policy expenditure in 1973 as % of GDP	12.9 (sd 1.3)	5.5 (sd 1.6) [5.0/sd 1.7]	6.0 (sd 0.6)	6.8 (sd 3.2) [7.9/sd 2.7]
Economic market liberalization 1970–74	0.42 (sd 0.08)	0.46 (sd 0.04) [.047/sd 0.04]	0.49 (sd 0.08)	0.49 (sd 0.07) [0.48/sd 0.09]
Change in economic market liberalization 1970/74–85	+0.29 (sd 0.15)	+0.01 (sd 0.05) [+0.00/sd 0.05]	+0.10 (sd 0.08)	−.000 (sd 0.06) [+0.01/sd 0.07]
Economic PPS (Table II.1, column 5.2)	2.3 (sd 1.2)	−1.7 (sd 0.6) [−2.0/sd 0.8]	−0.5 (sd 2.1)	−1.5 (sd 1.7) [−1.0/sd 1.7]

the late 1990s.[16] By contrast, in group IV, economic market liberalization started late and manifestly did not pay off in the following period. Both the great poverty of the countries and the late start may have been inauspicious for them to garner the benefits of market liberalization quickly. Not surprisingly, economic decline and immiseration of most members of society – including, for example, the erstwhile Venezuelan middle class – and the associated distributive struggles have contributed to a partisan based conflict about the merits of democracy that is waged in a prospective disposition: would it pay off for economic performance to replace democracy with authoritarian governance? As Coppedge (2005: 309–14) forcefully argues, a sense of moral outrage in the population about economic decline and the failure of the political elites to reverse it amplified disaffection with democracy.

Countries in group IV started out in great poverty with highly vulnerable social groups protected by a state-regulated economy with little market competition. This made liberalizing reforms hard to administer in a mode of responsible partisan governance, where politicians announce their policy intentions before elections, are victorious on that platform, and then implement substantial elements of their programs. Instead, vote-seeking politicians tended to indulge in populist rhetoric and then sneak reforms in through the back door after electoral victory. By contrast, after the initial success of market liberalization in group I, politicians went into elections with some confidence, defended market liberalizing reforms, and then delivered responsible partisan governance in that spirit. It is therefore no wonder that groups I and IV are also extreme opposites in their capacity to engage in responsible partisan governance (last row, Table 8.9). In group IV, the strong tendency of politicians to deceive voters fuels regime controversy and contributes to the formation of clear regime partisan divides even in countries where the experience of harsh authoritarian repression is missing. In group I, however, the relevance of past authoritarianism for political competition subsides; citizens live under comparatively successful democratic governments that procedurally conduct themselves closer to the practice of responsible partisan governance than the average government elsewhere in Latin America, and especially in group IV countries (where Bolivia fits in perfectly).

---

[16] We are necessarily painting in very broad strokes here. In Argentina there is a rollback of market reforms under Alfonsín in the mid-1980s, and it is clearly Menem's newer wave of reforms that brings renewed growth by the early 1990s. Even in Chile the reforms are necessarily halted during the Debt Crisis as the government assumes control of banks and liquidates the assets of failed conglomerates (Edwards and Cox Edwards 1991; Edwards 1995). The situation in Peru actually parallels the cases in group I somewhat, in that market reforms already had some payoff by the time of the survey, but the survey of course reflects the previous government takeover by Fujimori.

Overall, short-term economic policy and performance, in interaction with the perceived conduct of incumbent governments, provide considerable insight into the profiles of regime partisan conflicts in group I and IV countries. Countries that emerge from restrained electoral competition (Colombia and Mexico in group III) or that lack highly repressive authoritarian episodes in the recent past tend to display weak partisan regime divides and mixed controversy about democracy against the backdrop of economic policy choices and economic performance in the last two decades of the twentieth century that is mediocre by global standards but certainly less calamitous than that of countries in group IV (Bolivia excepted, if we keep it in group II). Short-term economic performance and government economic policies are thus undoubtedly a key mechanism contributing to the articulation of regime divides.

The different incidence of weak economic performance in late twentieth-century Latin America, however, can itself be linked to a causally prior genealogy of developments that ties the current articulation of regime divides to the long-term origins of economic programmatic party system structuration in Latin America. Table 8.10 tracks this connection. Group I polities with primarily "retrospective" regime divides were the most affluent countries before the depression of the 1930s (and right after World War II), far ahead of countries in all other groups. Also in group I countries, citizens and politicians accumulated the most experience with electoral contestation both before World War II and in the postwar decades of reconstruction until the oil crisis of 1973. Against the backdrop of relative affluence, urbanization, and political mobilization of lower- and middle-class constituencies in contested elections, governments in group I most vigorously expanded social policy benefits in the postwar period and implemented ISI strategies already in the 1940s and 1950s, which resulted in marginally lower levels of economic market liberalization in 1970–74 than even the highly state-regulated economies of other Latin American polities.[17] The particular sensitivity of the comparatively sophisticated economies of group I to the economic inefficiencies of ISI interventionist governance – manifested

---

[17] In poorer countries, and countries with less electoral competition, such as Brazil or Mexico, the crest of ISI strategies of economic development was not reached until the 1960s and 1970s. Because these countries operated from a generally much lower level of economic sophistication, ISI strategies may have paid off in economic growth still at a much later date than in Argentina, Chile, or Uruguay. Given the relative emphasis on mobile industrial and service sector employment in these countries and competitive pressures to move into human and physical capital-intensive economic sectors, even the same levels of political regulation of market activities as in less advanced Latin American economies may have had even more stifling consequences for economic performance than elsewhere. Students of ISI therefore often distinguish an initial phase of light consumer goods import substitution and a later phase of capital goods and service substitution, where economic performance due to political administration of the economy suffers most.

in balance-of-payments crises, capital flight, and bursts of hyperinflation in an environment of economic stagnation and growing unemployment – finally contributed to the installation of highly repressive "bureaucratic-authoritarian" regimes. Either rulers governing such regimes themselves (in Chile, most obviously, but to some extent also in Argentina and Uruguay) or democratic politicians in the aftermath of such regimes realized that ISI strategies had counterproductive economic and political consequences. Such results reduced public support of government incumbents, whether they were authoritarian usurpers or democratically elected, and gave politicians an opportunity to embrace major market liberalizing reforms earlier and more comprehensively in these countries than in the other groups of Latin American countries.

The shift in the IBD's economic liberalization index from 1970–74 to 1985 in the twelve countries provides evidence for this claim (Table 8.10). Only rulers in group I engaged in vigorous liberalization reforms between the early 1970s and 1985. While these measures were economically and politically very painful, economic performance particularly in the second half of the 1980s and the 1990s suggests that they eventually paid off (see Table 8.9). By contrast, the absence of early reforms set other Latin American countries on a lower trajectory of economic performance. When combined with high levels of initial poverty and destitution, as in countries belonging to group IV (plus Bolivia), the delay of reforms with correspondingly weak payoffs in terms of growth and employment for agonizingly long periods of time created the conditions for intensifying political conflicts about the viability of democratic governance toward the end of the twentieth century when our Latin American legislators' survey was taken. When politicians opted for sudden leaps of reform late and under often desperate economic conditions (Weyland 2002), they commonly did so as "policy switchers" without the benefits of responsible partisan governance (cf. Chapter 7). In some instances such moves failed to result in reforms, or profound reforms were unable to produce short-term payoffs (Bolivia, Ecuador, and Venezuela). Here, renewed regime conflicts prompted attempted or successful coups (Ecuador and Venezuela) or irregular, accelerated presidential turnover (Bolivia, Ecuador, and Venezuela). In the case of Peru, far-reaching reforms could be implemented only by a self-coup (*autogolpe*) of the sitting president Alberto Fujimori after a policy-switching maneuver in his first electoral term. Whether Bolivia is included or not, countries in group IV have both the weakest dispositions toward programmatic party competition on economic-distributive issues (Table 8.10) and a comparatively high potential for crystallizing conflicts around questions of political regime.

How are countries in groups II (minus Bolivia) and III situated between the experiences of groups I and IV? They were generally less poor than countries in group IV but not as wealthy as group I. They had as little market liberalization as group IV by 1985, but they then accelerated the reforms even more than in group IV. They did show, however, substantially better economic growth in the 1980–97 period and more penchant to abide by standards of responsible partisan governance. This may have made the difference in preempting or diluting political regime divides that have become so prominent in group IV. In all these regards, Bolivia is, of course, more typical of group IV.

Interestingly, countries in groups IV and III had the weakest Freedom House civil and political liberties scores in 1997. Ecuador, Peru, and Venezuela achieved an average of 3.3 on a 7-point scale with a value of 1.0 indicating full civil and political rights. Group I countries, under harsh authoritarian rule in the 1970s and 1980s, scored a much better average of 2.0. Group II countries clocked in at 2.5. Only Colombia and Mexico in group III did worse than group IV countries (3.3). But by 2004–5, group IV countries had fallen behind the rest of Latin America, lingering at a Freedom House average of 3.2. Argentina, Chile, and Uruguay in group I had moved up to 1.3, and Colombia and Mexico in group III to 2.5, just a whisker behind group II at 2.3. The "prospective" regime partisan divide appears to play itself out in negative consequences for civil and political liberties, anticipated and maybe wished for by some political actors in these countries. We are now beginning to consider the consequences of different levels of programmatic structuration of party competition, a topic that preoccupies us in the next chapter.

CONCLUSION

This chapter offers qualified support for the long-term learning theory of programmatic structuration forwarded in this volume. In the case of religious issues, we find strong evidence for an explanation emphasizing the long-term determinants of programmatic structuration in terms of the capacity of the electorate, the opportunities provided by repeated rounds of democratic experience, and the stakes of political conflict around issues of church-state relations. Where church-state conflicts occurred later and were more intense, and where corresponding levels of economic development and democratic experience provided an environment conducive to programmatic partisan mobilization, partisan divides around religious issues remain significant to the present. These long-term factors do not explain the presence of electorally powerful Christian Democratic parties across the twelve Latin American countries. Christian Democratic party success is instead the result of other strategic and historical conditions that seem to have little relationship to the church-state conflict. In several Latin American polities, religious issues are represented just as effectively or more so by non–Christian Democratic parties. Finally, there is little evidence that short-term economic and cultural catalysts might have affected the strength of religious PPS. This suggests either that religious PPS is not very susceptible to short-term change or that levels of religious PPS are already so low in comparison with more salient issues that even momentous changes in the politics and economy of Latin American countries make little difference for them.

In the case of political divides over democratic regime issues, we find only a very indirect link to long-term developments in Latin American politics. Regime issues are fairly transitory. To distinguish underlying causal patterns more clearly, we need to bring in an additional indicator of the relative disagreement among all politicians over the merits of democracy. Some party systems have "retrospective" divides in which parties have consistent, marginally different evaluations of democracy, based on their assessment of a recent episode of authoritarian rule, but legislators in all parties essentially agree on the current desirability of democracy. These party systems had long trajectories of development, experience with electoral contestation, and extensive ISI economic development strategies. The crisis of ISI in these countries resulted in spells of repressive authoritarian rule in which the new rulers advanced an agenda of economic liberalization which, for the most part, paid off in terms of sustained economic growth once these authoritarian rulers had been displaced by new democracies. Hence, partisan regime divides in such countries are largely retrospective and do not reflect continuing conflict about the merits of democracy.

In contrast, there is a set of countries with fairly strong partisan alignments along regime issues but more profound disagreements about the current viability of democracy. These "prospective" regime divides occur in Latin American countries with weak (Ecuador and Peru) or intermediate (Venezuela) long-term conditions for programmatic party competition – that is, weak economic development (at least outside the oil-dependent economy), limited experience with democratic contestation, and comparatively modest ISI development schemes or social policy reforms in the 1950s through 1970s. These countries went through milder dictatorships or stayed democratic in the 1970s and 1980s, delayed basic market-liberalizing economic reform until after 1985 if they underwent it at all, and suffered a deep economic crisis in the "lost decade" from which even the economic recovery of the 1990s elsewhere in Latin America brought scant relief.

The remaining countries in between these two groups in our Latin American comparison tend to have weak regime partisan alignments, paired with greater or lesser opinion divides over the value of current democracy. They have highly varied long-term background conditions for programmatic party structuration but, with the exception of Bolivia, share the experience of intermediate levels of economic performance and economic reform effort in the 1980s and 1990s. Unlike economic and to some extent religious divides, we concede that short-term factors seem to play a much stronger role in shaping the articulation of regime divides than they do with religion or economic policy.

A final question worth reconsidering is the relationship between regime and religious PPS. Initially it came to us as a surprise that the articulation of religious PPS was strongly aligned with distributive-economic PPS but not with regime PPS. If anything, we would have expected a close relationship between religious and regime divides given the traditional ties between conservative groups and the church, but this may have been undercut by the increasing distance the Catholic Church hierarchy has tried to place between itself and old, conservative antidemocratic forces in many Latin American polities.[18] The result may be a church whose clergy and members are both divided on regime issues, and military governments that avoid basing their claims to legitimacy on religious grounds. Of course, this does not rule out that in specific episodes of democratic transition the presence of a crosscutting religious divide and of Christian Democratic parties with considerable capacities for mobilization can make a difference.[19] But for the most part, regime PPS constitutes a phenomenon pretty much independent of religious PPS. At the end of the twentieth century in Latin America, many politicians with authoritarian sympathies are not pro-Catholic or given to religious appeals, and many politicians with strong religious views are not authoritarian.

A related question is the surprising weakness of long-term factors at explaining the patterns in regime PPS that we find here. While regime PPS can be tied to longer patterns of economic policy and development, particularly the early implementation of ISI in our small set of relatively developed countries, the pattern of retrospective and prospective regime PPS we find here suggests that partisan divides over issues of regime are ephemeral. Even in countries with harsh authoritarian experience and a relatively high tendency toward programmatic structuration, regime divides are weak. While we can only speculate here about the answer to this question, we are more inclined to take a positive view of our finding, seeing it as evidence of a general trend in Latin America toward acceptance of liberal democratic values and institutions. Whereas Latin American polities of a century ago held large constituencies of poor citizens and, more importantly, elites who subscribed to conservative notions of elitist government, today liberal ideas about the essential legal equality of all adult citizens have largely taken hold. Pockets of old practices remain, particularly in the form of a weak rule of law present throughout much of the region (Méndez, O'Donnell,

---

[18] The exception, of course, is Chile, where our data reveal a strongly reinforcing system of divides that combines economic-distributive, religious, and political regime considerations.

[19] In this regard, consider Mainwaring's (2003: 10–12) discussion of the role of Christian Democracy in transition games, as a force between the polarized alternatives of the authoritarian regime incumbents and radical democracy advocates who also have far-reaching redistributive ambitions. Christian Democrats can smooth the transition to democracy by lowering the fear of incumbents to lose everything, including their economic assets, when giving in to democracy.

and Pinheiro 1999; O'Donnell 2001), and few countries meet the high levels of overall support for democracy that one finds in the advanced industrial democracies (P. Smith 2005: 292–93), but basic principles of representative government, popular election, and civil liberties are relatively robust. While such positive diagnoses about Latin America have often turned out to be premature, many scholars have recently documented the surprising resilience of basic democratic forms of government in the region despite disappointing policy performance (Hagopian and Mainwaring 2005; Pérez-Liñán 2007; Mainwaring and Scully 2008). Popular mobilizations and elite (especially military) conspiracies still unseat presidents, but there is a marked tendency to play by the basic rules of the democratic game. Even the current populist regimes in Venezuela, Bolivia, and Ecuador have shown a surprising tendency to respect democratic forms and practices, especially in comparison to their forebears from the early and mid-twentieth century. Hence, while economic crises may chisel away at support for democracy at the margins, the level of disagreement we find in our set of countries is still relatively mild in absolute terms. This suggests that future authoritarian regimes will have a much higher threshold of policy performance to surpass if they hope to retain legitimacy, and that the deck will generally be stacked against those who avoid taking the electoral path to power. Authoritarians will increasingly come in "competitive authoritarian" and other softened, hybrid guises that leave less of a legacy.

None of this explanation applies to the other issues we have considered thus far. Questions over the appropriate forms of economic policy and the place of traditional religious institutions and values in public policy remain valid questions that can all be addressed from within the confines of democracy – they do not immediately challenge the basis of the regime. Hence, the traces left by early struggles over these issues can still be seen in party systems today, and we expect to see (and are seeing) the resurgence of these issues in partisan politics throughout the region as democracy maintains its hold. This does not ensure that party systems in the region will suddenly become programmatic; as we discuss in the Conclusion, conditions for the emergence and strengthening of programmatic forms of politics are still tenuous in many countries. But the existing programmatic content of party competition in these countries is likely to center on issues that are similar to the distributive and ideological conflicts of the past century and a half, and old party labels and platforms may acquire new force.

9

Programmatic Structuration and Democratic Performance

Herbert Kitschelt, Juan Pablo Luna, and Elizabeth J. Zechmeister

After empirically documenting the varying degrees to which Latin American party systems were programmatically structured in the late 1990s, our study has explained the observed cross-national pattern with a theory of programmatic alignments that emphasizes long-term investments in the development of partisan competition. Beyond this contribution to the research field on parties and party systems, our results gain significance for the comparative study of political systems if they also speak to questions of democratic performance and political economy. Do patterns of programmatic party structuring leave imprints on the democratic process, on political performance, and on the evaluation of democracy? If so, this would provide persuasive evidence that PPS, and more specifically economic PPS, the issue dimension that has the strongest profile in the greatest number of Latin American countries, is a critical intermediary mechanism shaping the empirical quality and possibly the durability of democracy.

We thus focus on economic party system structuration as the most powerful dimension of PPS in Latin America that may affect the quality (actual and perceived) and durability of democracies in the region. We address four baskets of phenomena: intensity and modes of political participation; stability and predictability of democratic competition; the quality of policy making and governance; and support for the democratic polity.

Concerning the first basket, the presence of programmatic partisan alternatives in elections clarifies the stakes of democratic competition and may tell citizens that it is meaningful and relevant to participate in democratic politics, to exercise their voice, and to turn out to vote. At the same time, effective programmatic partisan competition may dissuade dissatisfied citizens from seeking the "outside option" and choosing violent means against democratic incumbents.

With regard to the second basket, programmatic party competition both presupposes and reinforces the stability of partisan alternatives and institutionalization of parties. After all, building up a party's programmatic reputation takes time, and changing it may be cumbersome and slow. New party entrants, lacking clear programmatic reputations and evidence establishing their credibility, may find it difficult to get off the ground. Programmatic party systems hence tend to be less fragmented and more institutionalized.

The third basket deals with the conduct and achievements of the elected policy makers themselves. By enhancing the transparency of the stakes in the interparty competition and reducing the costs of attracting voters, at least when compared to purely clientelistic systems relying primarily on targeted material inducements to individual voters, democratic polities with high PPS may discourage politicians from relying on corruption to raise funds and help them accept a professionalized civil service and the rule of law. Such practices in turn may be associated with greater capacity of legislators to develop policy proposals and greater executive effectiveness in designing and implementing public policies.

Finally, patterns of participation, attributes of the partisan process of interest aggregation, and the quality of political governance should all feed into summary evaluations of democracy and its alternatives. If high PPS stimulates participation through "conventional" political channels, durable programmatic partisan alternatives, and an uncorrupted process of effective policy making, then high PPS should also result in greater support for democracy in general and a greater awareness of the role of parties, as well as more confidence in them.

To what extent may PPS be considered a cause rather than a complementary correlate or even a consequence of these democratic process and output features? To consider PPS a cause, it must temporally precede the democratic system feature we try to explain; the relationship must be grounded in a plausible micrologic; and the correlation must prove robust, when pitted against rival explanations that are themselves clearly exogenous to our focal causal variable.[1] In Chapters 6 and 7 we argued that features of economic PPS did not emerge at the same time as the current spell of democracy in Latin America but originated much earlier during the push for import-substituting industrialization that took on definitive institutional shape between the 1950s and 1970s in our twelve countries. In order to strengthen claims that causality runs from economic PPS to current features of democracy and not the other way around, we postdate our dependent variables in this chapter such that they succeed our observations of PPS by several years. Given that our PPS measure is from around 1998, this can be achieved conveniently with data that capture attributes of the democratic process and its assessment from 2002 to 2006.

---

[1] See Collier, Seawright, and Munck (2004) for a discussion of strategies to minimize the risks of causal endogeneity.

Even if we establish an association between economic PPS and democratic process features and explore controls, as much as this is feasible with a small N of twelve cases, there is always the possibility of omitted variables. For example, some unknown factor might have caused import-substituting industrialization (ISI)–social policy regimes in the post–World War II period and may have directly affected late twentieth-century features of Latin American democracies without working through the causal pathway from ISI–social policy regime through economic PPS to the quality of democratic process features. We think, though, that the burden of proof is on those who wish to challenge our argument that the observed attributes of democracy are unrelated to programmatic party structuring.

Chapters 6 and 7, of course, generate the equivalent of a selection model identifying the countries where we would expect high or low economic PPS in the late 1990s. Given our small number of cases, however, we cannot estimate an explicit selection model to separate two parts of the expected association between economic PPS and democratic process features in Latin American polities. One part is due to the prior selection processes that bring about high economic PPS, such as the configuration of ISI strategies with more inclusive social policies in the 1960s and 1970s that initially contributed to an urban class compromise but later may have made polities more prone to authoritarian takeover (Chapter 6). These determinants of PPS may exert an independent causal effect on contemporary democratic process features. The other part of the association between PPS and attributes of democratic polities is the effect of high economic PPS on democratic process features, once we have controlled for factors involved in the generation of high economic PPS in the first place. This residual value of PPS identifies the genuinely independent causal contribution of economic PPS to democratic polity features and their popular assessment. Only a very large sample would enable researchers to make some headway in sorting out causal effects of PPS in democratic polities, although even here we would struggle with the inherent difficulties of substantiating claims of causality based on observational data.

Given the limits of causal inference in our analysis, throughout this chapter we characterize the relationship between PPS and democratic process features as "associations," "correlations," and "complementary" attributes. This recognizes the fact that the attributes of democracy we examine may be due to (1) programmatic party system structuration as the cause; (2) a causally interactive, reciprocal process in which such attributes of democracy stimulate actors to choose higher or lower PPS, which then shapes party competition in turn; (3) a causal process involving selection into different levels of PPS, where PPS is endogenous to prior conditions; or (4) entirely separate variables that cause both PPS and democratic process features.

In order to reduce the probability of scenario (4), we introduce theoretically plausible controls and test their impact on all of our focal variables.

We consider here two rival hypotheses that may account for democratic process features without drawing on economic PPS or the selection process that stands behind it. The first is that the *current economic performance* of a Latin American polity, as captured by post-1998 per capita growth rates, may shape the quality of and public support behind a democracy. In Chapter 7, we showed that dismal economic performance in the "lost decade" and after may have undermined economic PPS in countries where prior conditions would lead us to expect moderate to strong PPS. But we also showed that good economic performance in countries with weak prior conditions would not build stronger economic PPS, at least not in the short and medium run spanning the 1980–98 time frame.

Overall, the relationship between economic performance and economic PPS is weak in our sample of countries. Nevertheless, growth may independently affect the nature of political participation, the volatility and institutionalization of parties, the capacities of countries to produce sound policies, and the public evaluations of democracy and its alternatives across our set of Latin American countries. Where economic performance is particularly dreadful, as manifested by high inflation or unemployment, the resulting fiscal crisis of the public sector may translate into sharply declining civil service wages, an increased propensity of public officials to seek bribes, and influential firms and interests manipulating the political process in favor of narrow rent-seeking provisions. Cumulatively, such politics may wreck trust in political institutions and undercut democratic allegiances altogether.[2] Strong economic growth, in turn, may reverse such practices and improve evaluations of democracy. We are focusing here on medium-term economic growth over the period of the "lost decade" of the 1980s and the 1990s until 1998. We do not report results for short-term growth in the year immediately before measurement of the quality of democracy variables, unless such short-term performance reveals a potential causal mechanism separate from the cumulative consequences of medium-term economic growth (e.g., spontaneous popular mobilization in the face of a declining economy or violence in an economic crisis).

A second rival hypothesis is that *levels of affluence* in the 1990s, not economic change rates (growth or contraction of the economy) or economic PPS, explain cross-national differences in democratic practices and evaluations. Where affluence is greater, elites expect little payoff from choosing authoritarianism, because running a complex economy based on increasingly sophisticated human capital requires voluntary compliance rather than coercion. Particularly the Latin American experience of often disastrous economic policy under military dictatorships may discourage the pursuit of alternatives to democracy. In this chapter we measure economic affluence

---

[2] Relationships among economic performance, trust, and system support have received a significant amount of scholarly attention (see, e.g., Mishler and Rose 1997, 2001a, 2001b).

as per capita GDP in both 1980 and 1998. The latter is contemporaneous with our PPS measure. But if causal relations become efficacious over time, a lagged GDP measure may be more appropriate for two reasons. First, it explicitly captures the causal hypothesis of a cumulative effect of affluence on democratic practices. With regard to economic PPS, we can claim a causal lag structure only indirectly by highlighting the long-term causes of party system structuration elaborated in Chapter 6 that lead back to political economic reforms and social policies in the middle third of the twentieth century. Second, 1980 per capita GDP is much less collinear with our economic PPS measure than is 1998 per capita GDP ($r = .40$ for 1980; $r = .75$ for 1998). Empirically, however, it turns out that the high collinearity between economic PPS and 1998 GDP per capita is not a problem when it comes to uncovering patterns of correlation; per capita GDP is surprisingly unrelated to most democratic regime qualities. In contrast, recent economic performance leaves a much bigger imprint on democratic quality features and emerges as a much stronger explanatory rival to economic PPS, when both are pitted against each other.

Given the small number of Latin American cases in our sample, we cannot systematically test all imaginable and theoretically plausible explanations of democratic quality features. Several theoretically grounded arguments caught our attention, but we do not report our empirical findings here because they fail to generate evidence that challenges our main conclusions. Among the alternative scenarios we explored are institutionalist arguments about democratic process features (electoral systems, legislative powers of the presidency) as well as a variety of political-economic characteristics that may shape democratic process features (income inequality, dependence of public revenue on raw material rents /"resource curse").

POLITICAL PARTICIPATION AND DEMOCRATIC ORDER

Where programmatic competition is more pronounced, at least critical sophisticated minorities in the electorate see the different party alternatives more clearly and may be encouraged to opt for or mobilize through electoral participation, rather than through violent channels, to articulate their political demands. Relatedly, when voters are linked to parties through programmatic representation, the mass public may feel more efficacious and subsequently more inclined to participate in politics. To gauge how citizens choose different profiles of political involvement, we rely here on composite governance indicators constructed by Kaufmann, Kraay, and Mastruzzi (2005), based on multiple expert surveys and calculated for several time points since 1996. We focus here on observations in 2002, that is, four years after our measure of economic PPS was taken; these measures appear in Table 9.1. Unfortunately, closer inspection of the ingredients in each measure reveals that they are grab bags of somewhat related but analytically

TABLE 9.1. *Patterns of Democratic Participation and Accountability, 2002*

	Political Stability and Nonviolence, 2002[a]	Voice and Accountability, 2002[b]	Turnout in National Legislative Elections, 2002 or Immediately Preceding Election
Argentina	27	57.6	72.9
Bolivia	42.7	50.0	72.1
Brazil	47	59.1	82.3
Chile	83.2	81.8	87.1
Colombia	3.8	30.8	43.5
Costa Rica	87.6	84.8	68.8
Dominican Republic	51.4	55.6	51.1
Ecuador	24.9	48.0	65.0
Mexico	52.4	59.6	63.6
Peru	23.8	52.5	80.5
Uruguay	78.9	77.8	91.3
Venezuela	16.2	37.9	56.6
Mean	44.91	57.96	69.57
Standard deviation	27.36	16.58	14.54
Correlation with economic PPS	.66	.72	.43
Correlation with 1980/1998 GDP per capita	.16/.25	.24/.40	.28/.39
Correlation with economic growth 1980–98	.39	.42	.12

[a] High values = stability and low violence.
[b] High values = strong voice.

Source: Columns 1 and 2: Kaufmann et al. (2005), World Bank Governance Indicators. Column 3: UNDP (2004).

diverse aspects of politics. Results have to be interpreted with the greatest caution.

Countries with powerful extremist movements and intense political violence receive low scores in Table 9.1. Lack of party system structuration in 1998 does indeed correlate strongly with democratic stability and nonviolence. Where parties do not offer programmatic alternatives, citizens are more likely to resort to violence. Economic PPS shows a much more pronounced relationship with these features than economic affluence or economic growth. Even when we examine economic growth in the immediate year or two preceding our observation of economic PPS (not shown here), it does not account well for the cross-national distribution of violence and instability. Some countries with high economic PPS, such as Uruguay and Costa Rica, had poor economic performance in 1996–98, yet maintained political stability and nonviolence then and in subsequent years. Democracies show considerable resilience to short-term economic crises, as long as they have high PPS values.

The second expert measure of "voice and accountability" in political regimes conveys a similar message. Where economic PPS is high, polities display more political voice and accountability, while economic growth or affluence appear to have only minimal influence on political participation and accountability relations. We have some hesitation, however, in using this voice and accountability index, as it combines a potpourri of indicators that include opportunities for political participation made possible by civil and political rights and the rule of law, on the one hand, but also measures of politicians' and governments' responsiveness to public demands and openness to scrutiny, on the other.

The voice and accountability index includes the Freedom House civil liberties and political rights scores and is highly correlated with that measure ($r = -.81$). Political stability or nonviolence is even more strongly related to voice and accountability ($r = .95$) so that both measures pick up similar democratic quality features. Freedom House scores (not shown here) taken by themselves are only weakly related to measures of economic PPS, economic growth, and affluence. Given an international environment in the 1990s in which Western democracies and international organizations punished a polity's deviation from basic democratic norms, political elites may not abandon the trappings of democracy lightly, even though the quality of democracy may suffer somewhat.

Do the data entitle us to claim a causal relation going from economic PPS to nonviolence and more voice and accountability in democracy? Or is the causal relationship reversed, such that societal peace and stability affect economic PPS? Given the small number of cases, only historical tracking of causal mechanisms could provide an exhaustive answer. Most likely, however, the record would bear out that many polities encountered social instability and violence that was allayed by the emergence of economic PPS – for example, in Costa Rica after 1949–50, in Chile after the 1930s, in Mexico after the 1920s, in Uruguay after the 1910s, and in Venezuela after the 1950s. The outlier is Argentina with little stability before, during, and after episodes of programmatic party competition. It appears therefore quite plausible that under conditions of higher economic PPS, citizens and politicians voice political demands through formal channels of democratic interest aggregation – parties and elections – more frequently than they do in polities where economic PPS is weak. Here violent and disruptive politics plays a much more decisive role. Further research would probe into the extent to which this has to do with clientelistic patronage politics that promote favoritism to small well-placed constituencies and intense conflicts over privileged access to scarce resources.

As a final measure of democratic participation, we report voter turnout in national legislative elections around 2002, give or take one or two years (Table 9.1). Under programmatic competition, citizens might feel encouraged to vote because the stakes are clear. Unfortunately, there are too many competing explanations of voter turnout (e g , Powell 1986; Jackman 1987, Franklin 2004) for which we cannot control in order to draw any consequences even if there were a robust empirical correlation between turnout and PPS. The insignificant correlations reported for turnout in Table 9.1 are meaningless, albeit in the correct direction. It appears that economic PPS may affect citizens' and elite members' fundamental choices concerning compliance with and participation in the democratic order. But PPS may have much less effect on voter turnout than other factors such as the level of competitiveness, the diffuseness of government (coalition) alternatives, or provisions for mandatory voting.

THE PROCESS OF PARTY COMPETITION

How does a greater or lesser emphasis on programmatic appeals by parties interact with the dynamics of party competition? Does programmatic competition make it more likely that parties persist and institutionalize or does it create a fluid market of partisan alternatives invoking ever changing issues?

We hypothesize here that the stability of the competitive framework (the rules of the game, the identity and durability of the players) and the emphasis of the competitors on programmatic competition are intrinsically intertwined. It may take a party a long time to build a programmatic reputation. During that period, stability of the competitive framework enables parties to persevere in their "ideology work" to build lasting reputations recognized by electoral constituencies. In turn, once parties' programmatic reputations have been established and are consequential for electoral campaigns, it becomes difficult for new entrants to challenge the established players. High PPS reinforces democratic stability and institutionalization. Because of the interdependence between programmatic structuration and stability of the party system, we are hesitant to consider economic PPS as a "cause" of stable parameters of party competition. Causality in this case is likely to run in both directions. Moreover, economic PPS may be a sufficient, though not necessary, condition for institutionalization in that predominantly clientelistic parties can also be firmly institutionalized.

Where elites offer clearer and more distinct policy packages and critical minorities of voters associate with parties on those grounds, we expect to find *less volatility over time* in the partisan alternatives among which voters choose, as well as more stability of voters' affiliation with specific partisan labels.[3] We are measuring here *net volatility*, calculated as the sum of absolute gains and losses sustained by all parties from one election to the next, divided by two (cf. Pedersen 1983). The indicator of electoral volatility employed here is a country average based on the two elections before 2004 (see Jones 2005). The measure combines both vote and seat volatility, with higher levels indicating greater levels of volatility.

Table 9.2, indeed, shows a mildly negative correlation between electoral volatility and economic PPS across the twelve Latin American democracies ($r = -.50$). But weak economic performance in the decades of the 1980s and 1990s shows a stronger link to electoral volatility, such that countries that experienced worse performance end up with greater volatility of partisan support even after the turn of the millennium.[4] Voters defect from parties that preside over accelerating economic misery and move on to new alternatives, possibly with each election that follows economic disappointments. In order to illustrate how economic performance trumps economic PPS as a predictor of electoral volatility, Table 9.2 shows a multiple regression analysis using economic PPS and economic growth as covariates.[5] We realize that a regression with two independent variables and twelve cases has at best descriptive value.

The effect of bad economic performance on electoral volatility is known from an important study of Latin American electoral volatility with a larger number of observations that did not include economic PPS as a predictor variable (Roberts and Wibbels 1999). But a number of the other variables Roberts and Wibbels found to affect party system volatility – such as average party age, polarization among parties and, in some statistical estimations (for presidential elections), party system fragmentation (negative) – may be

---

[3] Roberts and Wibbels (1999) suggest that parties with an ideological profile and a distinct constituency "anchor" the electorate, create loyalty, and decrease electoral volatility. In a similar way, we hypothesize that in those cases where voters link to parties along programmatic lines, voters will be less willing to switch parties from one election to the other.

[4] Whereas the economic shocks of the 1980s did contribute to high electoral volatility across the board, relevant case-by-case variation (in terms of the scope and timing of partisan turmoil) exists. Taking the four cases that suffered the most severe economic crises in the 1980s (Argentina, Bolivia, Peru, and Brazil), one finds a mixed record. While traditional parties persisted in Argentina (at least until the emergence of the Frente Grande in the 1990s), Peruvian historical parties experienced radical declines in terms of their electoral support in the aftermath of the economic crisis. In Brazil significant electoral volatility occurred, but the major parties of the 1980s managed to survive the crisis. In Bolivia, in turn, after 1985 and until recently, the main traditional parties also managed to command a large electoral share. In short, our data suggest that economic crises cause disruptions in voting patterns but do not speak to the nature or duration of these disruptions, which appears to vary across cases.

[5] Economic volatility is also closely related to policy switching, as operationalized in Chapter 7 ($r = .78$). Once economic conditions are bad and incumbents have been, or are in the process of being, thrown out, parties often harvest a windfall of support with populist slogans, but then turn around and deliver harsh economic stabilization programs. Obvious examples are Argentina (1989), Ecuador (several), Peru (1990), and Venezuela (1992).

TABLE 9.2. *Attributes of Party Systems*

	Electoral Volatility (averages based on elections before 2004)	Party System Fragmentation (averages based on two elections before 2004)	Current Party System Institutionalization I: 1998	Current Party System Institutionalization II
Argentina	27	3.18	2.03	65
Bolivia	35	5.21	1.74	56
Brazil	21	7.81	1.50	59
Chile	6	2.02	2.38	65
Colombia	11	5	1.85	60
Costa Rica	24	3.12	2.46	61
Dominican Republic	25	2.52	No data	74
Ecuador	27	6.71	1.43	53
Mexico	13	2.79	2.29	67
Peru	50	4.24	1.19	53
Uruguay	16	2.73	2.87	76
Venezuela	41	4.74	1.58	55
Mean	24.67	4.17	1.94	62
Standard deviation	12.74	1.79	.52	7.65
Correlation with economic PPS	−.50	−.74	+.84	+.64
Correlation with 1980/1998 GDP per capita	−.04 / −.47	−.24 / −.40	.34/.57	.22/.52
Correlation with economic growth 1980–98	−.60	−.72	.64	.69
Multivariate regression results				
Intercept	57.523	6.088	1.582	47.896
PPS	−1.022 (1.598)	−0.515[†] (0.213)	0.175[†] (0.057)	1.464 (0.950)
Change in GDP 1980–98	−0.29[†] (0.114)	−0.018 (0.015)	0.004 (0.004)	0.127[†] (0.068)
Adjusted R^2	0.466	0.519	0.659	0.477

Sources: Columns 1, 2, and 4: Jones (2005); column 3: Payne et al. (2002), p. 143. Multivariate regression results are based on a regression of column variables on PPS and change in GDP 1980–89. Data reported include the constant (intercept) and coefficients for PPS and change in GDP with standard errors in parentheses. [†] identifies coefficients that are statistically significant at a 5 percent confidence level.

related to economic PPS. Let us examine the relationships among economic PPS and two of these other variables, party system fragmentation and institutionalization, as potential indirect pathways through which programmatic party competition may stabilize a framework of democratic competition.

Table 9.2 reports party system fragmentation in Latin America, measured as the effective number of legislative parties in the two elections before 2004 (Jones 2005). The data reveal a pronounced negative relationship between party system fragmentation and economic PPS that, in multivariate analysis, trumps the almost equally pronounced negative bivariate relationship between economic performance and party system fragmentation. Higher economic PPS prevails in less fragmented party systems. A small number of large parties may have an easier time establishing their programmatic reputations, differentiating their programmatic appeals from each other ("polarization"), and outcompeting new entrants that are struggling to acquire a programmatic reputation. Of course, once again, we cannot exclude reverse causality, but even a circuit of mutual causation between higher economic PPS and lower party system fragmentation supports the point we are making in this chapter, namely the functional importance of PPS for the performance of democratic governance.

Table 9.2 also examines the relationship between economic PPS and two measures of contemporary party system institutionalization in 1998. Column 3 reports values from Payne et al. (2002: 143) where scores for institutionalization result from summarizing indicators of volatility, party identification, and support for party democracy in a single index of current party system institutionalization in Latin America. The data in the fourth column are from Jones (2005) who has drawn on work on party system institutionalization by Mainwaring and Scully (1995) to calculate an updated measure of this phenomenon. Jones uses both electoral and survey data to gauge the stability of a party system. His measure taps the depth of party roots, the legitimacy accorded to parties and elections, and the extent to which parties operate as organizations with routinized operations that are relatively independent of individual politicians. In a way, Jones's index constitutes an "omnibus" measure that sums up a lot of facets of the democratic policy process that contribute to democratic stability and that we disaggregate in indicators discussed in this chapter.[6]

Both measures of party system institutionalization are almost identical in terms of the cross-national variance they capture (r = .90). They are both

---

[6] Both Payne et al.'s (2002) and Jones's (2005) measures of party system institutionalization are different from the "historical" measure of party system institutionalization employed in Chapter 6 and derived from Mainwaring and Scully's (1995) scoring of the age of parties and their legislative seat share of historical parties, supplemented by values for the Dominican Republic and revised values for Colombia as a polity with highly constrained enfranchisement and party competition.

negatively correlated with party system fragmentation (r = −.74 and −.67) and with electoral volatility (−.56 and −0.57). Both economic performance from 1980 to 1998 and economic PPS are robustly correlated with institutionalization. But depending on which measure of institutionalization one employs as dependent variable in the multivariate regression, either economic PPS or economic growth emerges as the statistically significant and substantively more powerful predictor or correlate.

To summarize the patterns of democratic process features revealed by Table 9.2, economic PPS is intricately associated with lower electoral volatility, lower party system fragmentation, and higher party system institutionalization. But the effect of short-term and medium-term economic performance is equally strong or stronger. Overall, this pattern of associations makes sense in the context of our analysis of contemporary economic conditions that affect programmatic economic PPS already discussed in Chapter 7. Strong economic dislocations send shock waves through party systems that generate high volatility and consequently low party system institutionalization (several years out, as measured by the recent party system institutionalization variable). In party systems with at least moderately high long-term PPS, bad economic performance leads to an erosion or repositioning of established parties together with a partial displacement by new parties, as is demonstrated by the trajectories of Argentina and Venezuela and, to a certain extent, Costa Rica and Mexico. As we speculate in the conclusion, however, the preexistence of higher PPS may nevertheless generate a resilience of patterns of programmatic party competition that facilitates the regeneration of programmatic parties in later rounds of competition.

In contrast, in countries with low economic PPS, the way economic shocks translate into high volatility is not so much through turnover of large partisan blocks (preserving low fragmentation), but through the proliferation of numerous short-lived parties, none of which have much staying power even if they win in a single election. Examples in the 1990s and early 2000s are Bolivia, Ecuador, and Peru and, to some extent, Colombia. Countries with higher programmatic party system structuration do see increased volatility when they are struck by economic duress but generate still limited party system fragmentation. Countries with low economic PPS combine high volatility and extreme party system fragmentation under conditions of economic crisis.

Let us conclude by noting one glaring absence. As opposed to change rates, levels of economic development, whether measured in 1980 or in 1998, cannot account for patterns of party competition and democratic regime stability. At least within the constrained set of Latin American countries that range from lower to higher middle-income polities (with few exceptions), wealth differentials do not account for differences in the political process.

PROCESSES OF POLICY MAKING AND GOVERNANCE

Our third basket relates economic PPS to political-administrative governance and policy-making performance in Latin America. By now there is a huge literature on the relationship between political institutions – conceived as formal or informal operational rules according to which binding, authoritative political decisions are discharged and implemented – and economic performance. Does "good governance" – conceived as the absence of corruption; the rule of law with universal, predictable rules followed by state administrators and enforceable in independent courts; and government effectiveness in organizing and implementing authoritative decisions – translate into better economic growth, or is it growth that generates better institutions? Even with large and sophisticated datasets, the empirical literature on this question is shot through with problems of selection bias, recursive causality, and endogeneity (for a critique, see Glaeser et al. 2004). It is fiendishly difficult to sort out cause and effect.

Now let us make things even more complicated and throw party system structuration into the fray: do certain kinds of party competition, and especially those based on programmatic competition, substantially affect institutional quality and ultimately economic growth and income distribution, when compared to competition on a nonprogrammatic base (clientelistic, charismatic, or identified with descriptive traits of the politician)? It is obvious that with our twelve observations bounded to a single time point and a limited slice of the world's governments, we cannot possibly make a contribution to the causal research program on growth and institutions. If we can demonstrate, however, that there is a high statistical association between features of party system competition, governance institutions, and economic performance, we may at least motivate further investigations that take parties and party systems seriously as possible causes and as essential ingredients of the process in which governance and economic performance are ultimate outcomes in some combination.

There is a very sizable political economy literature that relates political institutions in democracies – such as electoral laws, the strengths of the executive vis-à-vis legislatures, or decentralization of government jurisdictions to subnational governments – to political performance features such as aspects of fiscal policy (size of state budgets, allocation between general, universal benefits and targeted benefits to special interests), or to institutional attributes such as quality of governance (e.g., Persson and Tabellini 2000, 2003; Iversen and Soskice 2006). But this literature usually operates with very simple conceptualizations of political parties choosing between strategies and policies in direct correspondence to unambiguous institutional incentives.

We have already seen in Chapter 7 that formal institutional arrangements (electoral laws, executive-legislative power division, and power sharing) do not directly translate into programmatic party competition. Maybe programmatic party competition is a theoretical mechanism that has causal force in its own right. There is certainly theory available or within reach that can identify a causal mechanism between party competition, democratic institutions, and government performance.

For example, where parties run on policies to win elections, incumbents have an incentive to enhance the efficiency and predictability of the political apparatus and improve policy outputs that affect their reelection chances. Especially close competition between rival parties competing on programmatic grounds may provide incentives for politicians to cut down on corruption, enhance the rule of law, increase judicial independence, and improve administrative professionalism and, in that process, improve government effectiveness (Geddes 1991). In a similar vein, however, better economic performance may ease the demand for corruption, as more wealth can be accumulated without resorting to illegal means, or at least improve a polity's reputation for transparency, rule of law, and government effectiveness. Furthermore, there might be unidentified conditions that bring about both better economic performance and more programmatic party systems. Likewise, in a high PPS environment based on institutionalized parties, party leaders are less likely to regard office holding as a one-shot game and more likely to see it as an iterated game in which reputations have to be built and defended. The iterative game involves an electoral process that rewards parties more than the individual politicians. Politicians thus have fewer incentives to go it alone or to break with programmatic commitments by defecting from party discipline in order to cater to small but well-organized rent-seeking interests.[7]

Finally, in the context of programmatic competition, citizens assisted by the mass media have at least a modicum of opportunities to monitor the relationship between parties' preelection promises and their record in office, compared to polities where competition involves clientelistic linkages or personalistic-charismatic appeals. In the latter, citizens gauge parties' achievements of accountability on the basis of private knowledge about often clandestine flows of material rewards to politicians' supporters. Under such conditions, a proliferation of corruption, regulatory ineffectiveness, and patrimonial governance is likely to pervade the polity.[8]

---

[7] Parties, as teams, may still find it advantageous at times to break programmatic precommitments (policy switching).

[8] Of course, we recognize that institutional design and strength may independently affect these variables. For example, with respect to corruption, scholars have posited that the balance of power among the branches of government (affecting horizontal accountability generally speaking and oversight of the executive office more specifically) and the design of the electoral system affect the severity of political corruption (see, e.g., O'Donnell 1998; Morgenstern and Manzetti 2003; Kunicova and Rose-Ackerman 2005). Other work has posited a conditional relationship whereby the combination of weak institutions and market-oriented reforms facilitates corruption (Manzetti 2003). Our argument is simply that the greater the

Our first attempt to assess the plausibility of such expectations is with data concerning corruption and the rule of law. The data in column 1 in Table 9.3 are taken from the 1997–98 Latin American legislators' survey and report the percentage of legislators in each country who consider fighting corruption as a priority policy issue. One would presume that the more corruption is practiced in a country, the more legislators find it urgent to address this issue. Indeed, there is an almost perfect negative correlation between this measure of legislators' concern and policy expert assessment scores for control of corruption reported by the World Bank in its Governance Indicators for 2002 ($r = -.91$) in the second column. We further include in columns 3 and 4 the World Bank's indices of "rule of law" and "government effectiveness," essentially measuring the rule-based accountability and professionalism of public administration and policy making.

The legislators' survey asks if politicians have had direct experience with corruption in their country. The World Bank's measure is based on multiple expert surveys judging the situation in each country assembled in "indices of indices" measuring control of corruption, rule of law, and government effectiveness of policy making. The high correlation between the two measures of corruption inspires confidence in the expert judgments, albeit with a qualification. It may well be that experts score countries' institutional practices with the benefit of hindsight after knowing its economic and political performance. The same cannot be said for our indicators of programmatic party system structuration, particularly economic PPS. The indicator is constructed objectively such that polities are assigned particular PPS scores without the benefits of knowing their policy process and outputs.

Table 9.3 shows a strong and robust relationship between indicators of institutional quality, measured four years out compared to the measure of economic PPS and programmatic party competition (economic PPS-2). By contrast, economic development in 1980 or 1998, and growth experience from 1980 through 1997, fare the same or even worse, including when pitted against PPS in a multiple regression model. While these bare statistical associations do not entitle us to draw any causal inferences, particularly not in the absence of a battery of controls that is necessarily missing in a twelve-country single-shot comparison, our findings are suggestive. Programmatic party competition deserves more research as a candidate cause of good political governance.

strength of programmatic party competition, the less politicians will be tempted to resort to extralegal or, at the least, low-quality governance options (in particular perhaps when institutional arrangements might otherwise facilitate such behavior). Further, the argument can and has been made that programmatic connections between voters and politicians strengthen oversight institutions, and vice versa. According to Moreno, Crisp, and Shugart (2003), "If legislators are either uninterested in national policy (excessively weak parties) or unaccountable to voters (excessively strong parties) they have little interest in exercising oversight and 'political control' over the executive."

TABLE 9.3. *Political Governance, 2002*

	Corruption as Priority Policy Issue, 1998 (% of legislators responding affirmatively)	Control of Corruption, 2002	Rule of Law 2002	Government Effectiveness, 2002
Argentina	91	27	26.5	36.8
Bolivia	99	25	30.1	32.8
Brazil	64	55.6	45.9	53.7
Chile	50	90.8	85.2	87.1
Colombia	83	37.8	24	41.3
Costa Rica	60	80.6	72.4	69.2
Dominican Republic	84	40.8	42.3	39.8
Ecuador	92	14.3	30.1	13.4
Mexico	88	51	47.4	65.7
Peru	72	50.5	38.7	37.3
Uruguay	39	77.6	68.4	71.1
Venezuela	94	17.9	15.8	9.5
Mean	76.3	47.41	45.40	46.48
Standard deviation	19.2	25.24	26.64	23.53
Correlation with economic PPS	−0.62	.66	.67	.67
Correlation with 1980/1998 GDP per capita	−0.29/−0.36	.20/.25	.12/.29	.15/.48
Correlation with economic growth 1980–98	−0.51	.66	.68	.71
Multivariate regression results				
Intercept	97.557	4.199	2.367	−2.313
PPS	−4.385† (2.710)	5.27† (3.121)	4.89† (2.509)	4.547† (2.610)
Change in GDP 1980–98	−0.196 (0.194)	0.390† (0.223)	0.365 (0.180)	0.438† (0.187)
Adjusted R²	0.323	0.481	0.544	0.582

Sources: Column 1: Legislators' survey 1997–98; Columns 2–4: Kaufmann et al. (2005), World Bank Governance Indicators. Multivariate regression results are based on a regression of column variables on PPS and change in GDP 1980–89. Data reported include the constant (intercept) and coefficients for PPS and change in GDP, with standard errors in parentheses. † identifies coefficients that are statistically significant at a 5 percent confidence level.

Table 9.4 provides us with a different lens through which to evaluate the relationship between economic PPS and our rival variables, on the one hand, and political governance in our Latin American countries, on the other. At the request of the Inter-American Development Bank, in 2003 several panels of social scientists engaged in a detailed exercise to assess the capacity of state executives and democratic processes across Latin America with objective performance indicators, data about formal institutional rules, public opinion data, and expert judgments. The resulting host of analytical papers is summarized in a major Inter-American Development Bank publication (Stein et al. 2006). The researchers assessed the capacity of legislatures to attract talented, well-informed legislators with technical expertise on policies, to pass competent judgment on policy alternatives, and to have the resources to oversee agencies. They also assessed the de facto autonomy of the judiciary on the basis of objective data covering terms and tenure of judicial appointments, as well as budget and salary conditions within the judiciary. Other researchers for the IDB engaged in an innovative comparative analysis of types and capabilities of public administration (civil service) across Latin America (summarized in Stein et al. 2006: 65–73). Finally, the coordinators of this project tied together different measures of government effectiveness and developed a Public Policy Quality Index.

Is there any plausibility to the claim that economic PPS in the arena of party competition affects features of legislative capability, judicial independence, civil service development, and public policy quality? Table 9.4 reveals that when it comes to these capacities of policy making and implementation, economic PPS displays only a substantively small and statistically insignificant correlation with such features of democracy. But it is stronger than the correlation of economic development levels or economic performance measures with state capacities. Only with respect to the public policy quality index, economic growth performance clearly trumps economic PPS as a predictor variable. But in this instance we may be facing the same problem of circularity of subjective expert judgments we already encountered: expert judgments of policy quality may be affected by twenty-twenty hindsight vision of economic performance in a specific country over the preceding twenty years.

Overall, the statistical associations reported in Table 9.4 are not impressive, even without further controls and probing into endogeneity issues. Of course, the complicated assessment of institutional capacities in the IDB report may be fraught with measurement error. The weak correlations between political capacity and performance indicators and either economic PPS or measures of economic performance suggest that unobserved processes of political mobilization and bargaining may be decisive to explain policy outputs, not just information about such relatively distant and abstract conditions as economic growth and economic PPS.

TABLE 9.4. *Political Capabilities, 2003–2005*

	Congressional Capabilities Index	De Facto Judicial Independence	Development of the Civil Service	Public Policy Quality Index
Argentina	Low (0)	.33	.50	Low (0)
Bolivia	Medium (1)	.56	.24	Medium (1)
Brazil	High (2)	.49	.68	High (2)
Chile	High (2)	.58	.59	Very high (3)
Colombia	High (2)	.53	.47	High (2)
Costa Rica	Medium (1)	.92	.49	High (2)
Dominican Republic	Low (0)	No data	.28	Medium (1)
Ecuador	Medium (1)	.39	.18	Low (0)
Mexico	Medium (1)	.71	.40	High (2)
Peru	Low (0)	.16	.16	Medium (1)
Uruguay	High (2)	.45	.48	High (2)
Venezuela	Medium (1)	.40	.37	Low (0)
Mean	1.08	.50	0.40	2.33
Standard deviation	0.79	.20	0.16	0.98
Correlation with economic PPS	.40	.29	.50	.41
Correlation with 1980/1998 GDP per capita	.09/.12	−.05/.02	.47/.68	−.20/.21
Correlation with economic growth 1980–98	.27	.01	.41	.67

Sources: Stein et al. (2006), IDB Report. Congressional Capabilities Index: 55; De Facto Judicial Independence: 88; Development of the Civil Service: 152, based on 68–72; Public Policy Quality Index: 134.

PUBLIC EVALUATIONS OF DEMOCRATIC POLITICS
AND REGIME STABILITY

We conclude our tour of political system features that may be closely related correlates, or maybe even effects, of PPS with an examination of indicators of *specific support for political parties* as a key mechanism of democratic interest aggregation and, next, of *general support for competitive party democracy* when pitted against authoritarian alternatives. If programmatic politics builds circuits of accountability that deliver a modicum of transparency in the interaction between politicians and voters, as well as a less corrupt and arguably more effective policy process that involves less violence, greater protection of civil and political rights, and more stability in the party system, then it is fair to expect that citizens living in polities with comparatively stronger economic PPS will show greater support for parties and democracy.

Table 9.5 reports the percentage of mass publics in our twelve Latin American countries (minus the Dominican Republic in the first dataset) who voice confidence in political parties in their countries (Latinobarómetro 1998 and 2002). This measure is obviously affected by both short-term performance-related and long-term systemic considerations reflected in the respondents' judgments. Only a time-series analysis could separate these elements neatly. The 1998 survey follows a period of relatively robust growth, whereas the 2002 survey was taken in the immediate aftermath of the Argentinean economic meltdown of 2000–2 and its regional reverberations.

Inspecting the data in Table 9.5 reveals a very low confidence in political parties across Latin America. Even in countries with comparatively strong confidence in the mission of political parties in a democratic order, it is barely one-third (Mexico, Uruguay), or even less than one-fifth of respondents (Argentina) who voice such views. The vast majority of respondents has little confidence in parties. Nevertheless, a fairly strong sense that parties are needed for democracy is widely and fairly uniformly recognized, given the mean endorsement of 2.82 over all twelve countries on a scale ranging from 1 to 4 for this item. Ecuador and Colombia are the outliers on the low side, Costa Rica and Uruguay those on the high side.[9] In a similar vein, mass publics in Latin America fairly uniformly admit that elections permit a choice among alternatives, with the glaring outlier of Bolivia, where a "party cartel" was about to be shunned away in elections subsequent to this survey.[10] At the same time, however, outside of Chile, Costa Rica, and Uruguay there is little faith in the integrity of elections. It is thus not clear whether the response pattern revealed by the data confirms or disconfirms Schattschneider's (1942: 1) famous dictum that "modern democracy is unthinkable save in terms of

---

[9] Moreover, as the UNDP data analysis demonstrates, respondents who clearly support democracy accept the necessity of parties much more than skeptics of democracy.
[10] We return to the Bolivian case in the Conclusion.

TABLE 9.5. *Public Opinions about the Political Process in Democracy, 1998/2002*

	Confidence in Political Parties		Parties Needed for Democracy	Elections Permit Choice	Are Elections Rigged?
	Percent High, 1998	Average Score, 1–4 Scale, 2002	Average Score, 1–4 Scale, 2002	Percent (very much) in Agreement, 2000	Percent "Yes" or "Do not know"
Argentina	16.6	1.24	2.73	67.2	52
Bolivia	19.9	1.40	2.82	55.7	69
Brazil	19.7	1.57	2.76	81.0	69
Chile	24.3	1.53	2.90	74.9	32
Colombia	16.9	1.53	2.14	73.8	79
Costa Rica	28.9	1.89	3.37	88.2	30
Dominican Republic	No data	1.74	3.09	85.2	No data
Ecuador	14.4	1.45	1.97	76.4	76
Mexico	33.4	1.65	2.81	73.1	70
Peru	16.7	1.63	3.04	80.2	78
Uruguay	34.6	1.98	3.39	87.1	28
Venezuela	15.4	1.74	2.86	87.6	74
Mean	21.9	1.57	2.82	77.6	59.7
Standard deviation	7.3	0.25	0.42	9.7	20.4
Correlation with economic PPS	.67	.33	.51	–.05	–.85
Correlation with 1980/1998 GDP per capita	.29/.32	.28/–0.7	.36/.21	.41/.07	–.33/–.53
Correlation with economic growth 1980–98	.47	.17	.24	.07	–0.64

Sources: Column 1: Latinobarómetro 1998; columns 2–4: Latinobarómetro 2002, as reported in UNDP (2004), *Statistical Compendium* (DVD ROM), table 141 (column 7), table 127, (p40st) and 132 (columns 4+5).

political parties." Generally, Latin American countries display a begrudging acceptance of parties and recognition of democratic choice, paired with low confidence in them. But we must keep in mind that equivalent surveys in established postindustrial democracies do not reveal all that much confidence in political parties either.

Examining the cross-national variation in Table 9.5 is difficult, because cross-national standard deviations are small, relative to the metric of each scale, and the national means are clearly on one side of the scale. Across the board, voters signal little party confidence but tend to admit that parties are necessary and that elections permit choice. Relating these patterns to our independent variables thus yields a very mixed picture. Cross-national variation is clearly not driven by economic affluence or economic performance since the beginning of the "lost decade."[11] The impact of economic PPS on perceptions of the specific functioning of parties appears not much greater, save with regard to 1998 confidence in political parties and especially electoral fraud.

Why does high economic PPS not coincide with more acceptance of and confidence in party democracy? Five countries preclude a high level of association between the structuring of party competition and endorsement of partisan democracy, in particular Argentina and Chile, where economic PPS would predict higher than average confidence and acceptance; and Colombia, the Dominican Republic, and Peru, where it would predict lower scores on these variables. In the former set of countries, repressive military rule in the 1980s and divisive, polarized democratic politics in the 1970s left sizable camps of citizens who now accept democracy but in principle justify authoritarian alternatives because they had previously supported military rule (see Chapter 8). This appears to affect their evaluation of party democracy. Conversely, the three countries where endorsement of party democracy appears stronger than expected in 2002 all rid themselves of highly unpopular presidents in competitive elections not long before the surveys were taken. The new incumbents could still bask in the afterglow of their victories.[12] Long-term patterns of economic PPS thus appear to have little leverage to explain specific evaluations of partisan democracy, with the exception of perceptions of electoral fraud.

The picture changes dramatically when we examine the assessment of democracy in Latin American countries more generally and more fundamentally. Economic PPS very robustly associates with higher preferences for democracy compared to authoritarian regimes as well as greater satisfaction with democracy, as currently practiced in Latin America. Although

---

[11] This finding did not change when we included the countries' rates of economic growth in 1998 through 2001 as predictors of 2002 measures of public opinion.

[12] A similar argument may explain the relative enthusiasm of Venezuelans for party democracy in 2002.

evaluation of particular collective actors in democracy, such as parties, may make it difficult for respondents to separate their general judgment on the principle that parties are needed to aggregate interests in democracy from the empirical practice of the specific entities that occupy their political stage, questions about basic support for democracy may be less affected by everyday politics. In these fundamental regime evaluations, the impact of long-term high economic PPS comes to the fore most clearly (Table 9.6).

The first column of Table 9.6 shows the percent of respondents to the 2002 Latinobarometer survey who have a democratic orientation. This measure, calculated by the UNDP (2004), is based on cluster analysis of eleven questions related to attitudes toward democracy.[13] The values reflect the percent of respondents whom the UNDP classifies as "Democrats," as opposed to "Ambivalents" or "Non Democrats." This value is by far highest in Uruguay, where 71.3 percent of respondents fall into this category. Several countries are grouped at values just above 50 percent: Argentina, Costa Rica, Mexico, and Peru. In contrast, Colombia (16.9 percent) and Ecuador (21.1 percent) have the lowest percent of Democrats.

We also present in Table 9.6 two of the individual components of the Democratic Orientation index. Respectively, these two columns show the within-country average response, coded on a 1–4 scale, to questions about preferring democracy over authoritarianism and the acceptability of a nondemocratic regime in order to solve economic problems. Higher values indicate more democratic responses. We again see that Uruguay and Costa Rica take top places. In contrast to the evaluation of parties, Argentina, with moderately high economic PPS, is no longer at the bottom of the pile, where we encounter Brazil, Colombia, and Ecuador, all polities with historically weak economic PPS. As before, there are outliers. Chile scores much lower than would correspond to its score of economic PPS. There is a convenient ad hoc explanation for this observation. Chile is the only Latin American polity where dictatorship delivered economic reform and growth, creating a large following for nondemocratic solutions (see Chapter 8). Venezuela scores very strongly as a result of widespread hopes to move the country out of its chronic decline after the reelection of Chávez to the presidency under a new constitution.

The first three measures of Table 9.6 thus tap general support for democracy, compared to authoritarian rule. They evidence moderately strong relationships with economic PPS that are stronger than those with current

[13] These eleven questions ask about the following: Is democracy preferable to authoritarianism (p32st); is democracy or economic development more important (p35st); is democracy indispensable for development (p37no2); is nondemocracy okay if it solves economic problems (p38stb); is a National Congress essential for democracy (p39st); are political parties essential for democracy (p40st); does democracy help with solving problems (p41st); and if the country has serious problems, should the president "not be limited by what the laws say" (p28ua), "secure order by force" (p28ub), "control the media" (p28uc), and "bypass Congress and the parties" (p28ud)?

TABLE 9.6. *Public Opinion about Political Regime Alternatives, 2002*

	Democratic Orientation (% of respondents)	Democracy Preferable to Other Regimes (mean score on a 1–4 scale)	No Turn Away from Democracy to Solve Economic Problems (mean score on a 1–4 scale)	Satisfaction with Democracy Index
Argentina	51.1	3.25	2.66	59
Bolivia	34.9	3.15	2.51	40
Brazil	30.6	2.97	2.14	47
Chile	40.7	3.14	2.54	53
Colombia	16.9	3.08	2.23	41
Costa Rica	53.8	3.63	2.67	59
Dominican Republic	48.3	3.44	2.48	No data
Ecuador	23.1	2.98	2.43	38
Mexico	54.4	3.22	2.55	47
Peru	54.8	3.24	2.52	41
Uruguay	71.3	3.52	2.94	66
Venezuela	54.5	3.5	2.67	53
Mean	44.53	3.26	2.53	49.45
Standard deviation	15.63	0.22	0.21	9.26
Correlation with economic PPS	.64	.50	.69	.84
Correlation with 1980–98 GDP per capita	.62/.40	.43/.15	.51/.30	.72/.73
Correlation with economic growth 1980–98	.19	.04	−.02	−.32

Sources: Columns 1–3: Latinóbarometro 2002, as reported in UNDP (2004), *Statistical Compendium* (DVD ROM), tables 126 (column 1), 127, p32st (column 2) and 127, p38stb (column 3); column 4: Hagopian (2005).

affluence or economic growth since the beginning of the "lost decade." Once again, values are somewhat lower than expected in Argentina and Chile, two countries with high or moderately high economic PPS but also with a retrospective regime divide resulting in substantial proportions of citizens that still justify past dictatorships. In addition, in some countries with weak economic PPS, the recent removal of unpopular presidents mildly boosts support for democracy beyond what would have been expected on the basis of the nature of party competition (the Dominican Republic, Peru, and Venezuela).

The relationship between economic PPS and the assessment of current democracy appears to be even stronger when we focus on a general measure of citizens' satisfaction with democracy (Table 9.6). Again, while our analysis does not permit us to make strong causal claims, it is plausible that a programmatically structured democratic polity makes citizens more likely to believe that the system follows transparent and unbiased rules (elections not rigged, Table 9.5) and therefore deserves the citizens' support, as captured by Hagopian's (2005) aggregate index based on indicators that tap citizens' attitude toward democracy, their electoral conduct, and their trust in government generally. Countries with the highest economic PPS scores, such as Uruguay, Costa Rica, and Argentina and, to a lesser extent, Chile, also generate a robust relationship to people's satisfaction with democracy. Among medium-high PPS countries, the only moderate outlier is the recently democratized Mexican state, where mistrust in democracy and elections is still quite pronounced. Countries with weak economic PPS are assembled at the bottom (Bolivia, Colombia, Ecuador, and Peru). Once again, neither economic levels nor change rates offer a powerful rival cross-sectional explanation, although affluence displays a strong relationship to Hagopian's index of democratic satisfaction.

Of all our attributes characterizing democratic processes and assessments in Latin America, these results may be most directly relevant not just to issues of democratic quality but also to system durability. The shallower and more fluid the connections between elites and mass public, the less committed the mass public is to the democratic regime; at worst, this situation may result in a citizenry that is more open to reversal to a more authoritarian system (Diamond 1996).[14] Although economic performance and the elites' ability to deliver on material promises also plays a role in stabilizing or

---

[14] Of course, under conditions of high poverty and inequality in Latin America, political regime stability, whether under dictatorship or a formal democracy that is confined to intra-oligarchical competition, may be more stable if the poor masses whose claims inspire the emergence of economic PPS in the party system are entirely excluded from representation (cf. Huber and Stephens 1999). In this scenario, democracy is consolidated precisely as subordinated classes lack effective channels of political representation, thereby keeping elite interests secure and threat perception low. Democracies where exclusion of large constituencies is no longer possible are caught in a dilemma. While high levels of PSS could potentially threaten a fragile democracy with parties pushing redistributive demands, the

undermining democracy, the integrity of the political process and the ability of parties to engage in economic PPS appear to play an independent role. It is heartening to find evidence that political elites positively influence support for the democratic regime by the manner in which they compete for political office – via programmatic party competition or not – and not only by a proven track record of delivery of economic goods or credible promises of more goods. Given our finding that economic PPS originates at rare political-economic junctures and builds up and persists over long periods of time (Chapter 6), it is debatable, however, whether politicians have more control over economic PPS than economic output.

CONCLUSION

In this chapter we have attempted to provide suggestive evidence, though not decisive empirical support, for a two-pronged argument. First, programmatic structuration of a party system constitutes a central element of the democratic process that is strongly associated with, if not causally responsible for, a range of attributes of democracy, such as patterns of political participation and competition, the quality of governance, and specific and general democratic regime support. Second, even if (some of) these features have not been historically caused by economic PPS as a prior condition, the latter constitutes a complementary attribute that functionally reinforces other characteristics of the democratic process. Economic PPS is a crucial attribute of high-performance democracies that generates a broad base of popular support.

Because our study covers only a single time point and our observations are confined to twelve countries, we cannot bring sophisticated statistical technology to bear on our effort to draw causal inferences. Selection bias and endogeneity problems are related hazards that make causal claims risky (cf. Collier, Mahoney, and Seawright 2004). In spite of these caveats, on the basis of a close observation of the timeline along which causal mechanisms unfold and on the basis of a consideration of rival explanations, we are confident that a case can be made for the causal efficacy of political party system structuration with respect to some, albeit not all indicators assembled in this chapter. Moreover, economic PPS is more robustly associated with attributes of democratic quality than rival economic hypotheses. Levels of wealth and development rarely ever account for cross-national variation in democratic quality among the Latin American countries. But the cumulative economic performance of Latin American countries since the beginning of the "lost decade" sometimes accounts for democratic quality features, either in competition with or complementing economic PPS (Table 9.7 for a summary).

---

absence of representative parties may encourage disgruntled masses to choose disruptive forms of protest outside the institutional framework of democracy.

TABLE 9.7. *Economic PPS and Economic Growth as Explanations of Democratic Politic Features*

	Explanatory Power of Economic PPS (complementary or causal relationship)	Explanatory Power of Economic Growth (1980–98, change of GDP per capita)
Political participation (Table 9.1)	Limited explanatory power of civil and political rights as well as electoral turnout; strong explanatory power of accountability and political violence	No explanatory power
Party system: Process features (volatility, fragmentation, institutionalization) (Table 9.2)	Moderate explanatory power, strongest for party system fragmentation and institutionalization	Strong explanatory power of economic performance, affecting volatility and institutionalization
Quality of political governance 2002 (Table 9.3)	Strong explanatory power	Strong explanatory power
Governmental capabilities 2002–4 (Stein et al. 2006) (Table 9.4)	Moderately limited explanatory power	Weak limited explanatory power
Specific regime legitimacy: Evaluation of political parties (Table 9.5)	Weak to moderate explanatory power	Little to no explanatory power
General diffuse regime legitimacy: Democracy compared to regime alternatives (Table 9.6)	Strong explanatory power	No explanatory power

Political party structuration has more impact on the political process of interest aggregation and democratic party competition, including general democratic regime support, than on operational legislative and executive capabilities to develop policies in Latin America (Table 9.4). Moreover, economic PPS in 1998 is not a good predictor of later economic performance. Tracking per capita economic growth from 1998 to the latest figures recorded in the Penn World Tables for 2003 or 2004 fails to show a correlation with economic PPS in Latin America. Also, programmatic party competition and stronger democratic regime support appear not to translate into a more egalitarian income and wealth distribution, a line of reasoning not documented in this chapter. The general absence of a distinct impact of economic PPS on socioeconomic well-being may have major implications for the future decay or rejuvenation of economic PPS in the Latin American region, a topic we discuss in the conclusion to this book.

In research not reported in this chapter, we also looked into the capacity of programmatic structuration in the religious and regime dimensions analyzed in earlier chapters to account for democratic quality features. Although religious PPS is strongly related to economic PPS, it shows much weaker empirical associations with indicators of democratic process quality and party or regime assessment than the latter. Religious PPS is a less salient and less powerful partisan divide in the Latin American region than economic PPS. Our indicators of regime PPS show next to no association with any of the democratic quality features, not even with those that directly concern satisfaction with democracy. The failure of regime and religious divides to complement specific attributes of the democratic process suggests that economic-distributive divides are critical for the structuring of Latin American party systems, at least in the second half of the twentieth century and well into the new millennium.

This chapter is designed more to motivate future research than to report conclusive findings and test theories in light of these findings. Programmatic party competition may contribute something to the quality of the democratic process that is not furnished by other processes and endowments, such as economic development or economic growth. PPS also seems to predict – better than its economic rivals – patterns of democratic support and involvement. This claim, however, requires a great deal more theoretical elaboration and empirical testing than we could provide in this project.

Conclusion

Herbert Kitschelt, Kirk A. Hawkins, Juan Pablo Luna,
Guillermo Rosas, and Elizabeth J. Zechmeister

Our study has characterized and explained patterns of programmatic party system structuration in twelve Latin American countries in the late 1990s in some detail. With data from this region, our analysis develops and explores, but does not comprehensively test, a more general argument about the formation of party systems that foster programmatic competition. Politicians and citizens can build programmatic parties only with great effort. Such effort results in programmatic partisan alignments only where politicians can construct "stakes" around widely shared but contested political-economic strategies of development and distribution or around conflicts concerning sociocultural or political governance.

Creating "stakes" that structure programmatic competition, in turn, requires voters and political entrepreneurs to possess capabilities and to seize opportunities to engage in electoral competition. Programmatic conflicts do not appear spontaneously but require a great deal of work over long periods of time. Once political-economic or sociocultural alignments lock into party system alignments, however, they can weather even episodes of profound exogenous shock and dislocation, such as times of authoritarian rule or new political-economic challenges. Such shocks were in evidence in Latin America in the 1960s and 1970s, when many electoral democracies reverted to military rule, and in the "lost decade" of the 1980s that spelled the end of import-substituting industrialization strategies.

But patterns of programmatic party competition are not forever: they do not "freeze" permanently. Sustained, severe economic decline, such as that experienced by Venezuela since the early 1970s, or long-term irreversible structural change in the economy, in demographics, or cultural practices eventually precipitate an erosion of existing partisan alignments, as politicians can no longer rally electoral support around waning political divides. New politicians rise up and instead attempt to seize on new divides to disorganize the existing winning parties and establish new alignments. What may follow is a period of programmatically unstructured politics or efforts by politicians to rebuild programmatic partisan alignments around new principles, typically based on new political-economic or cultural institutions that may then stabilize political alternatives for an extended period of time.

In contrast to Riker's (1986) voluntarist conceptualization of realignment, however, it is not sufficient that office-seeking politicians wish to dislodge a hegemonic party or party system. They need resources, opportunities, and a societal endowment that allows them to craft "stakes" that resonate with broad audiences. Our theoretical framework and our analysis thus neither endorse a caricature of historical path dependence that denies innovation in party systems nor further an extreme version of rational adaptation where new shocks and alignments of interests quickly and smoothly generate a new equilibrium. Programmatic party system development and reequilibration is a protracted process that often enough is stuck in disequilibrium.

In Latin America, the emergence of programmatic alignments around conflictual stakes applies not only to economic distributive issues but also to sociocultural issues, such as religion. By contrast, conflicts over the acceptability and viability of democracy itself (regime divide) rarely produce long-term alignments. Either such divides occur in the aftermath of a repressive authoritarian spell and fade away within less than a generation or they flare up as manifest crises of democracy when elites and mass movements challenge democratic modes of decision making and anticipate their replacement by an authoritarian alternative.

To be sure, programmatic competition has certainly not furnished the only accountability mechanism linking citizens and politicians even in countries where we detect a fair measure of PPS in the late 1990s. Even in the comparatively more programmatic polities, such as Chile and Uruguay, clientelistic exchange between voters and politicians has always constituted a common and powerful way of conducting the political business of generating supporters and inducing turnout in elections. We also recognize the powerful role that charismatic personalities play in Latin American party competition.

For students of Latin American politics, our characterization of partisan alignments in the region is particularly relevant only if it constitutes more than an inconsequential snapshot taken at an arbitrary point in time (1997–98). For students of partisan politics more generally, the study is relevant insofar as it speaks to general issues of partisan divisions and their transformation over time both within and beyond the region. Our conclusion intends to convince the reader that this is the case. First of all, our study argues that Latin America developed partisan divides over a long period of time. What we observe in the late 1990s can be accounted for not in terms of recent conditions but rather in terms of a cumulative buildup of capacities, opportunities, and political stakes over a number of decades throughout the twentieth century. Second, we engage in a brief comparison with postcommunist democracies in Eastern Europe. This exercise suggests that, in new party systems elsewhere, programmatic competition also tended to emerge in a more sharply articulated fashion where politicians and citizens were able to make investments in the construction of partisan alignments in earlier episodes of electoral contestation, albeit not always under fully democratic conditions. These investments filter through what in broad historical comparison may be a rather brief communist interlude lasting forty years from about 1946–49 to 1989–91. Third, our analysis is powerful if it can predict developments that follow the point in time at which we observe and explain party system structuration in Latin America. We therefore examine evidence gathered about Latin American party systems since 1998 and explore how recent developments can be related to the historical record of party system structuration and its underlying causal dynamic. Our analyses are based on our own reading of recent scholarship on these countries and on media accounts of current politics in the region. Rather than existing as an authoritative and rigorous set of analyses, these final prognostic considerations have an obvious speculative element and are intended to provoke new comparative research more than to postulate firm theoretical and empirical conclusions.

LATIN AMERICAN PARTY SYSTEMS AT THE END OF THE TWENTIETH CENTURY: RELEVANCE OF A HISTORICAL SNAPSHOT

Our study has been preoccupied with mapping programmatic party competition in the late 1990s in Latin America with four empirical indicators. Three of these indicators rely exclusively on politicians' construction of programmatic party differences (programmatic partisan divides, programmatic content of left-right semantics, and ideological party cohesion). Substantively, we found that, in those countries where there is any indication of programmatic structuring of party competition, economic-distributive issues about the allocation of property rights or the (re)distribution of revenues through social policies are most likely to give rise to programmatic partisan divides. To a much lesser degree, and only in a smaller subset of countries, we can also identify a religious divide that largely overlaps with the economic divide. Finally, in a few countries, we encounter a political regime divide, albeit one that comes in two very different flavors. In some countries, this divide *retrospectively* refers to past episodes of authoritarianism, the resurgence of which hardly any politician would have welcomed by 1998; in other countries, this divide *prospectively* points forward to the dismissal of existing democracy to replace it with some other political regime.

The empirical focus of our study is on political elites and their production of public political appeals that may evidence more or less programmatic partisan structuration. We do not provide a complete, independent assessment of party structuration within the electorate. Our analysis nonetheless demonstrates that, in some countries on some issues (e.g., Chile and privatization), programmatic party structuration at the elite level is mirrored by a similar organization at the mass level; in other cases (e.g., Ecuador and spending on public security), a *lack* of structuration at the elite level is mirrored by a similar state of disorganization at the mass level (see Chapter 4). Even in polities with comparatively sharply contoured programmatic party competition, a closer analysis might reveal that such divides are somewhat less pronounced at the level of parties' mass constituencies. In some cases, limited *congruence* between politicians' issue positions and those of their electoral constituencies may suggest not necessarily a misrepresentation of voter preferences by party politicians but relatively amorphous electorates with a limited propensity to divide along partisan issue appeals.

Moreover, our measure of programmatic party system structuration is relative and does not rule out the presence of other linkage mechanisms even in countries that score comparatively high on programmatic competition. As we have already mentioned, Chile and Uruguay, the two countries with the relatively highest economic PPS scores in the late 1990s, have always had clientelistic exchange mechanisms in their party systems. These have been more articulated in certain time periods. For example, historical accounts suggest that partisan competition in the 1950s relied relatively more on clientelistic exchange against the backdrop of an earlier era of intense programmatic party competition. Conversely, some countries with low structuration might have seen a run-up to short bursts of intensely programmatic politics, such as Bolivia's political mobilization in the 1940s, climaxing in the 1952 revolution. Nevertheless, the relative rank order of economic and religious programmatic party system structuration captured by our data in the late 1990s reflects average cross-national differences over longer time periods in the second half of the twentieth century.

Our book explains and empirically documents the scores on each empirical indicator of programmatic structuration measured in 1997–98. It then probes into different explanations that draw on durable, long-term, or recent, short-term features of political economy, institutions, and interest alignments in Latin American polities to identify causal mechanisms that might have brought about weaker or stronger profiles of programmatic partisan structuration. As our dependent variables, in the explanatory chapters we primarily construct summary indices of economic, religious, or regime party system structuration. At least for economic-distributive issues, let us here briefly review each indicator and the structure of causation we found for it. We then turn in a more roundabout way to our findings on religious and regime divides. In this context, we can address whether our investigation captures a pattern of competition at a fairly arbitrary point in time or says more about the formation and maintenance of partisan alignments in Latin America and in democratic party systems more generally.

Our first indicator of PPS in the late 1990s is the strength of partisan divides, as derived from discriminant analyses of legislators' policy positions in each Latin American country (Chapter 2). In at least six polities, socio-economic issues have some capacity to discriminate among parties' positions that ranges from strong (Chile and Uruguay) to intermediate (Argentina, Costa Rica, Mexico, and Venezuela), when compared to six countries where it is pretty much nonexistent in 1998 (Bolivia, Brazil, Colombia, the Dominican Republic, Ecuador, and Peru). In some countries within this second set – such as Colombia, the Dominican Republic, or Peru – economic issue divisions are not mapped onto partisan alternatives in 1998 but appear only in ideological divisions among legislators, regardless of their party affiliation (Figure 2.1). It appears these party systems cannot map and bundle economic-distributive divisions onto the space of party competition. A similar mismatch between moderately strong ideological divisions on the level of policy preferences among legislators and the absence of such division on the level of interparty competition also applies to the religious ideological division in Argentina, Bolivia, Brazil, the Dominican Republic, Ecuador, Peru, and Venezuela. Only with regard to regime divides is there relatively little discrepancy between ideological dimensions and partisan divides.

Our second indicator is the extent to which the left-right self-placements of legislators can be explained in terms of respondents' economic policy issue positions, as summarized by respondents' scores on the partisan discriminant functions (Chapter 3). The larger the power of discriminant functions to predict legislators' left-right self-placement, the more such formal placements have a substantive policy content that enables legislators to signal their issue stances to mass electorates. In Chile, Uruguay, Mexico, and Costa Rica, predominantly economic-distributive discriminant functions predict legislators' left-right self-placements quite well. In Argentina, they do so weakly. In the Dominican Republic and Venezuela, we cannot identify strong economic-distributive partisan divides in the late 1990s, but here issue positions on law-and-order or regime divides have a modest impact on legislators' left-right self-placements. None of the other countries have issue-based discriminant functions or show an association between such functions and left-right self-placements. In countries without programmatic partisan divides, the legislators' personal issue preferences may still predict their left-right self-placements (Table 3.3), but these personal judgments do not configure around political parties. Thus, in Bolivia, Colombia, and Venezuela, legislators are sharply divided according to left and right over economic-distributive issues. To the extent that partisan labels do not structure economic left and right in the late 1990s, voters cannot identify economic partisan positions by knowing a legislator's personal issue stances and her party affiliation.

Our third indicator measures the extent to which programmatic divisions among parties on policy issues, and particularly those that load on the economic-distributive partisan divides, are congruent with corresponding divisions in the average issue positions of different parties' electorates (Chapter 4). Elite-voter congruence would satisfy a minimal criterion of political representation. Because of data limitations, we could perform this analysis only for nine of our twelve countries. Moreover, we had to make many measurement decisions to construct theoretically reasonable summary scores of representation, whether concerning individual issues or aggregate baskets of issues. For example, representation should be expected primarily on issues that constitute partisan divides in a polity. But mass-level data do not include the same basket of issues we had at our disposal in the elite survey. We thus had to select individual issues that correspond between mass- and elite-level survey, always hoping to identify the most salient issues and measure congruence on those. When doing so, we find that where parties are divided over economic-distributive issues at the elite level, also electoral constituencies tend to be divided along similar lines, although there are outliers. Most glaringly, in Mexico in the late 1990s political parties do not represent the central tendency of their electorates' economic policy preferences. And Brazilian parties have a greater capacity for economic issue representation than one might expect from our analysis of partisan divides and left-right semantics.

Our final and probably most demanding measure of programmatic party system structuration examines the intraparty diffuseness or cohesion of legislators over policy issues, net of the parties' mean issue positions (Chapter 5). In general, we find that parties in Latin America tend to be programmatically highly diffuse, considering the mathematical endpoints of the scale and what is known about parties in other new party systems around the world, such as in Eastern Europe. Moreover, there is considerable cross-party variation within the same polities. Nevertheless, when we construct the national averages of internal party diffuseness on individual issues or entire issue baskets, such as economic distribution, across all parties within each Latin American polity, the resulting cross-national profile of countries with high and low diffuseness shows some similarity, though not very pronounced, to the cross-national profiles of economic partisan alignments and issue content of left-right placements (Figures 5.1. and 5.2).

Are our measures of party cohesion and party system structuration along programmatic lines mere snapshots of particular political and economic conditions in 1998 or are they reflective of durable, long-term alignments that built up in Latin America over decades and that prove hard to displace, at least in a short time span of a few years? And do they have any prognostic value to account for changes in Latin American partisan competition that can be observed in the now almost ten years since our detailed measures were taken?

If the observed cross-national profile of programmatic party structuring were purely conjunctural, resulting from short-term conditions prevailing around 1998 or at least no earlier than the period of Latin American (re)democratization since the late 1970s, we would not have found a striking and strong relationship of economic PPS to preceding political-economic developments in the 1920s through 1950s. Moreover, historical continuities in party organization (institutionalization) and alignments of partisan alternatives vividly demonstrate at the level of political action how micrologics of collective partisan mobilization build and persist over extended periods of time. Conversely, if short-term conditions had triggered the observed cross-national pattern of partisan alignments in the late 1990s, we should have been able to identify a causal relationship to at least one of the many plausible economic, institutional, or political mechanisms we have closely scrutinized throughout our research. Chapter 7 documents a fair range of failures to establish an association between recent economic, political, and cultural developments in Latin America and economic PPS in 1998, net of preceding distant and durable conditions. Similar efforts to account for religious divides with proximate conditions turn out to be no more successful. Still, we have refrained from documenting all of our many failed efforts to substantiate empirically what theoretically might have appeared as plausible arguments to establish causal links between proximate conditions and patterns of party competition in Latin America.

If one can specify appropriate intermediating mechanisms, it is plausible to infer that historically more distant economic and political conditions and actions set in motion the formation of partisan alignments that proved fairly sticky in Latin America over the course of several decades. The supremacy of such historically prior conditions when compared to the causal efficacy of more recent developments surfaces when we analyze the temporally more distant emerging capacities of political actors, their opportunities to mobilize in competitive elections in critical decades of the twentieth century, and their definition of stakes of the conflicts in those decades, all of which feed into the constitution and reproduction of political alignments well into the late 1990s.

In terms of *socioeconomic capacities for political participation*, differential economic development in Latin America before 1930 is a better predictor of economic PPS in 1998 than economic affluence between 1960 and 1998, albeit early development lacks a causal mechanism that would link it to the observed outcome. In terms of *political opportunities*, a long run of democratic party competition from World War II to the mid-1970s is more tightly associated with cross-national variation in economic PPS in 1998 than the duration of democracy since the mid-1970s. At the level of individual actors and organizations, there is a clear mechanism that connects the cause before 1975 to the consequences in the late 1990s. This mechanism is the survival of individual leaders, activists, and the rudiments of party organization through an era of often harsh authoritarianism in the 1970s and 1980s. Finally, in terms of the *stakes of the economic-distributive struggle*, the cross-national variation in the generosity of social policy achieved by 1973 trumps later comparative social policy efforts as predictors of 1998 economic PPS. Also in this regard, the causality runs not only through the "stickiness" of social policy programs but primarily through the survival of political actors and organizational coordination that had inspired the struggle for social protection in the post–World War II era and was not easily forgotten by citizens and political activists.[1]

With regard to religious PPS, we made the observation that a similar logic, but with different stakes, explains the long-run institutionalization of religious programmatic divides. Early socioeconomic capacities and political democratic opportunities set the stage for political actors to coordinate around issues of religion and secular political governance. Although the *stakes* of such struggles often precede socioeconomic development, they certainly inspire political struggles, once general conditions for political mobilization improve with a rising socioeconomic capacity of citizens to participate in territorial politics beyond the municipality, and more opportunities for electoral contestation open up.

The only divide that appears relevant in a subset of Latin American countries but is hard to account for in terms of distant origins and chains of mobilizational investments is regime antagonism. But rather than the long-term buildup of authoritarian experiences, it is the record and achievements of nondemocratic and democratic rulers in the recent past and the present that trigger regime divides over the desirability of democracy or autocracy. Retrospective support for past episodes of harsh dictatorship in countries such as Argentina, Uruguay, and especially Chile is tenacious but does not spill over into a negative assessment of the current and future promise of democracy. The situation is different in countries with current crises of corruption and economic performance, where substantial portions of the electorate lose faith in democracy, at least as it is practiced in their countries, and begin to defend or advocate authoritarian alternatives as a way to preserve some societal integrity and order.

It goes without saying that political alignments, including durable, tenacious socioeconomic divides, are not forever. Unlike what some scholars have made of the Lipset-Rokkan thesis of cleavage stability, the main question is not whether partisan alignments change, but when, why, how, and with what content. Ultimately, the rise and decline of political divides may not be controlled by the deliberative action of citizens and politicians – for

---

[1] Our argument concerning the enduring influence of the nature of ISI is consistent with that made by Kurtz and Brooks (2008), who argue that extensive ISI programs created constituencies that in combination with political factors account for current configurations of state-market relations in Latin America. While their dependent variable is not programmatic party politics, it is nonetheless worth noting that their argument and evidence resonate with our own.

example, Rikerian entrepreneurs who activate dormant divisions to dismantle hegemonic parties – but derive from long-term socioeconomic and institutional developments, albeit mediated by the cumulative effects of political choices that affect socioeconomic developments and their institutional governance. The construction of welfare states, for example, has left an imprint on preference distributions in postindustrial democracies.

Cumulative, incremental, and often anonymous political and economic changes that cannot be attributed to the actions of an extraordinary politician or party tend to erode and ultimately eliminate the dead hand of the past that constrains the dynamic of party system reconfiguration. Put under a magnifying glass that highlights the bustle of competitive democratic partisan politics at any given moment, there is always a great deal of activity by citizens and politicians that remains inexplicable in terms of durable, long-run alignments anchored in robust socioeconomic and institutional conditions and cumulative social and political developments. Thus, the disintegration of ISI strategies of economic development in Latin America since the 1980s, particularly where it was associated with more comprehensive welfare states, may not yet have fully eroded long-standing partisan alignments. Ultimately, however, these profound changes are likely to reconfigure partisan alignments more fundamentally than we could observe hitherto. We conjecture about this reconfiguration at greater length in the final section of this chapter.

Before we expand our analysis geographically and temporally to speculate about implications of the past for the future of Latin American party systems, let us address one last explanatory task we have shunned so far – namely, the empirical limits of long-term explanations revealed by our own dataset. Neither the Mexican nor the Brazilian party systems are particularly well explained in terms of the parsimonious and temporally interconnected causal mechanisms (long-term capacity, opportunity, stakes) that appear to work just about everywhere else in our Latin American polities. In Mexico, weak economic development before World War II, the country's long-term experience with hegemonic party rule, and the virtual absence of meaningful social policy until recently would lead us to predict a less structured and more inchoate party system than we actually observe in 1997–98. Yet our data show that Mexico had a fairly clear differentiation of partisan economic-distributive and religious issue positions, as well as an intense regime divide.

The puzzle here lies not so much with our first two factors facilitating long-term learning. The country's economic development in the first half of the twentieth century is not that far off from levels congruent with the prediction of moderately strong economic PPS. And the PRI-dominated party system still offered opportunities for opposition politicians to learn to coordinate around alternative parties in many rounds of electoral quasicompetition. Indeed, when the hegemonic party system began to open up in

the 1980s, it was precisely politicians in parties that had existed for a number
of decades who began to take advantage of the new electoral opportunities
to win legislative office and to go beyond a niche existence as minorities in
national and regional legislatures or local councils by winning subnational
executive offices (governorships, mayoralties). The advantages of long-term
electoralism even benefited a new party, the leftist PRD, which emerged from
a field of at times long-standing small leftist opposition parties, enriched by
a dissenting faction that split from the ruling party in opposition to its
leadership's pursuit of economic liberalization.

The greatest explanatory problem with Mexico's PPS is the stunningly low
level of social policy exhibited by Mexico's budgets, that is, an extremely
low score on the variable that proxies for the "stakes" and thus the mechanism allowing politicians to coordinate around economic-distributive policy
alternatives (this variable is aggregate social policy expenditure, which is
based on data by Kaufman and Segura-Ubiergo 2001, and Evelyne Huber
and John Stephens – see Chapter 6, especially Table 6.6). But the social
policy measure may be somewhat misleading. The Mexican ruling party
promoted functional equivalents of risk-hedging social policy, that is, institutions that protected vulnerable social groups, particularly in the countryside, from loss of income and livelihood. This applies especially to the *ejido*
system of communal land tenure that was incorporated into land reform
policies since at least the era of President Cárdenas. The *ejido* offered a modicum of social protection from market forces to the vast mass of peasants
in the Mexican countryside. Laws allowing the privatization of communal land, together with the international opening of Mexico's agriculture
through the North American Free Trade Agreement (NAFTA), disman-
tled this protection and fueled a predictable political polarization around
"stakes" that manifested itself in the consolidation of the leftist PRD and
the emergence of ethnically based insurgency in poor agrarian provinces,
especially Chiapas. While proximate causes of open rebellion have to be
sought in facilitating processes that enabled aggrieved peasants to overcome
their collective action problems, the underlying structural triggers have to
do with the reversal of the distributive prospects faced by poor former constituencies of the PRI or disenfranchised ethnic minorities through market
liberalization.

For the urban population, substitute a bloated clientelistic state apparatus
and employment in the state-owned oil industry for the protective shield of
the rural *ejido* system, and the PRI did establish an ark of protective measures
that began to constitute the political-economic "stakes" of programmatic
partisan conflict, particularly under President de la Madrid in the 1980s,
when the PRI embarked upon an open course of market liberalization with
little initial effort to compensate the losers. The various targeted welfare
programs implemented by his successors, Salinas and Zedillo, all intended
to maintain PRI support among the poor, especially in competitive electoral

districts (cf. Magaloni et al. 2007), could not entirely compensate for the decline of social protection and the great potential for configuring political controversy around distributive economic issues seized upon by opposition parties of the right (PAN) and the left (PRD).

In contrast to the Mexican case, in the late 1990s Brazil exhibited a level of economic PPS that was substantially lower than one might have expected on the basis of our temporally interconnected causal variables. True, Brazil was a comparatively poor Latin American country until the 1960s (see Table 6.1), but it had a *long run of competitive party democracy* from 1946 to 1964. Moreover, repression in the subsequent two decades of rule by military junta (1964–85) was sufficiently mild most of the time to permit the continuation of some partisan politics and local or state-level competition, albeit under partisan labels licensed by the junta itself. Finally, in the early 1970s Brazil had an *expenditure level for social policies* that put it just under the average of the entire Latin American country cohort (Table 6.6) but certainly not in the lowest quarter, as would have to be the case for our causal variable to predict a programmatically inchoate party system. Brazilian social policy expenditure then grew dramatically over the subsequent twenty years. Hence, the "stakes" of a distributive conflict that could be mapped onto the party system were certainly there and had built up cumulatively over decades.

The conventional explanation for Brazil's low level of programmatic party competition has to do with electoral institutions that personalize the vote (e.g., Ames 2001; Mainwaring 1999). As we remarked in Chapter 7, even if this explanation works for Brazil, it cannot account for differentials of economic PPS across the cohort of Latin American countries that we have examined. Furthermore, it could not account for the increasing programmatic structure that more recent analyses find in Brazil in the absence of major institutional changes (cf. Hagopian, Moraes, and Gervasoni 2009; Lyne 2007). It is therefore appropriate to look for ways to tackle the conundrum of Brazil's reported lack of programmatic party competition. We propose three alternative explanations.

First, there may be a validity problem with the measure of welfare state expenditure in Brazil. In Brazil it was the expansion of the state apparatus under Getulio Vargas and beyond that drove social policy innovation, not the rise of labor and other "popular" movements, as in Argentina or Chile (Segura-Ubiergo 2007: 62–63). As a consequence, the Brazilian ruler concentrated a very high proportion of benefit entitlements on a small segment of the labor force, the civil service. With social policy "stakes" so highly concentrated on a small beneficiary group, politicians defending the interests of that group have almost certainly not relied on programmatic appeals in their efforts to attract votes beyond the privileged core constituency and instead turned to clientelistic politics to buy off the support of those disadvantaged by a particularistic welfare state. Economic development in the 1980s and

1990s, however, makes it more expensive for politicians to satisfy a growing number of increasingly demanding rent seekers so that nonclientelistic strategies to get the vote become relatively more attractive (cf. Lyne 2007; 2008).

Second, the Brazilian "anomaly" may as well derive from a measurement problem involving our dependent variable, economic PPS. There is consensus among Brazil observers that the party that lent a modicum of programmatic focus to the Brazilian party system since the early 1990s is the Workers' Party (PT) led by President Lula da Silva. But for most of its existence, the PT hovered in the vicinity of only 10 percent of national electoral support in legislative elections, leaving much of the rest of the electorate to be divided among programmatically "inchoate" parties. In the new millennium as well, the PT remained far from winning electoral pluralities, let alone majorities of legislative seats in national assembly elections. Global party system measures, such as the index of economic partisan divides (Chapter 2), tend to submerge this programmatic bit of Brazilian party competition and drown it in a sea of clientelistic and personalistic competitors. While our measure of low economic PPS is operationally correct, it ignores the disproportional substantive importance of that one party. De facto, the PT has lent substantial programmatic structure to the whole competitive system by generating a leftist pole against a field of clientelistic establishment parties.

Third, it may be that the gradual and partial transition from clientelistic to more programmatic politics in Brazil since the early to mid-1990s is not yet adequately captured in our survey data. Though they are not without critics, recent empirical studies of legislative roll-call voting claim to find increasing discipline of caucus loyalty among members of Parliament and a decline of partisan turnover that at least indirectly suggests rising programmatic structuration in Brazilian party competition (Figueiredo and Limongi 2000; Morgenstern 2004; Lyne 2005, 2008; Hagopian et al. 2009; Desposato 2006). Advocates of a change thesis tend to account for these dynamics of greater economic-distributive programmatic partisan competition over time by highlighting the reduction in government patronage resources that accompanied economic liberalization and the development of an urban middle class; over time, and perhaps jointly, these policies negatively affected the supply and demand for nonprogrammatic politics (cf. Lyne 2008). The remaining roadblock to higher PPS is the particularistic nature of the Brazilian welfare state, but even here reforms under Cardoso and Lula have begun to undermine the prevalence of civil service and rent-seeking occupational group preferences in order to place social policy on a more universalistic track. This momentum has produced a substantial increase in social policy expenditure as well from 1973 to the late 1990s, one that exceeds growth of social policy expenditure in all other Latin American countries in relative terms (see Table 6.6) and even in absolute terms (aside from Uruguay), although it began from a low base value.

Viewed in this light, neither the Brazilian nor the Mexican cases falsify the theoretical framework we have found useful to account for differential patterns of programmatic party competition across Latin America. Instead, these cases offer rich texture to flesh out the conditions and details that spell out how long-term buildup of economic capacities, political opportunities, and political-economic stakes interact in the construction of programmatic politics.

GENERALIZING THE MODEL BEYOND LATIN AMERICA: THE POSTCOMMUNIST EXPERIENCE

Generalizing the theoretical framework applied to Latin America requires finding adequate empirical referents for the key concepts employed in the Latin American study. Ideally, they would be exactly the same operational variables as those employed for the Latin American region. But there may be reasons why contextual conditions in countries or entire regions call for a different and more appropriate operationalization of variables to provide a fair test of the theoretical propositions.

Let us turn to postcommunist Eastern and Central Europe for this purpose, the only region for which we have empirical data on a few countries' PPS scores measured in ways that are at least approximately similar to those created for our twelve Latin American countries. For these additional countries we have politicians' detailed scores of party positions on a wide variety of issues. We can then develop roughly equivalent indicators of PPS, such as the strength of discriminant functions that employ parties' policy positions to differentiate among party labels, the extent to which policy-based discriminant functions also predict respondents' left-right positions, and the average standard deviations of the policy positions supported by members of the same party across the spectrum of parties on salient issues. A detailed comparison of the indicators can be based on Kitschelt et al. (1999) and Kitschelt and Smyth (2002).

Survey results from the mid-1990s indicate that, in five postcommunist countries for which such data exist, PPS is at least as high as or higher than in the most structured Latin American polities (Chile and Uruguay), but that there is nevertheless pronounced cross-national diversity within the region. The Czech Republic has the highest programmatic structuration (focused on economic-distributive issues), followed by medium-high levels in Hungary and Poland (more configured around sociocultural issues and national identity, in addition to economics) and by comparatively lower PPS (intermingling economic-distributive, sociocultural, and national identity issues) in Bulgaria and Russia (see Kitschelt et al. 1999 and Kitschelt and Smyth 2002). Now let us consider how each of our long-term causal factors squares with these results, beginning with the opportunities for democratic competition.

To operationalize opportunities for and experience with multiparty electoral competition in Eastern Europe, it obviously makes little sense to select the post–World War II period of 1945 to 1973, a time when Latin America witnessed its first burst of democratization, to identify intraregional variation. Following extremely brief episodes of post–World War II electoralism in only a handful of countries (Czechoslovakia and Hungary and, to an even lesser extent, Poland), Stalinism snuffed out any semblance of political competition. Moreover, if our theoretical argument is correct, the single rounds of open or semiopen competition in these three countries should by themselves make little difference for the performance of politicians and voters in coordinating parties around programmatic claims after the collapse of communism and of the Soviet Union in 1989–91.

To give the opportunity thesis a valid chance in the postcommunist region, one needs to draw on the interwar period (1919–39) and establish the extent to which political regimes across the region permitted longer stretches of full democracy (Baltics, 1919–late 1920s; Bulgaria, 1919–23; Czechoslovakia, 1919–38; Germany, 1919–33; Poland, 1919–26) or at least partially free electoral competition for legislative seats in semi-authoritarian tutelary regimes, such as in the Baltic countries in the 1930s, Poland after 1926, Hungary during the entire postwar era, and, more arguably, some regions of newly created Yugoslavia for at least some of that time. This contrasts with the experience of much of Southeastern Europe where, starting in 1919 or the early 1920s, opportunities for party formation under conditions of competitive elections virtually vanished (Albania, Bulgaria, Romania/Moldova, and arguably parts or all of Yugoslavia, as well as the pre–World War II constituent elements of the Soviet Union, that is, Belarus, Russia, Ukraine, Armenia, Georgia, and all of the Central Asian Republics). For the five postcommunist countries with data on PPS, opportunities for electoral party competition in the interwar period are in fact closely aligned with the articulation of programmatic party competition in the 1990s. Given the temporal distance, this correlation, of course, does not prove causality without further probing into intermediating mechanisms.

While opportunities offer considerable leverage in accounting for within-region variation in two different regions, we certainly cannot maintain that the extensiveness of electoral experience accounts for cross-regional variation in economic PPS in the 1990s. Latin American countries accumulated as much or more experience with electoral party competition after World War II than their East European counterparts did during the interwar period, yet even the most persistently democratic Latin American countries achieve no more programmatic structuration than the lowest East European countries in our admittedly small comparison sample. What, if not opportunities for democratic competition, could account for such cross-regional differences? These come into sharper relief when we turn to the other distant explanatory variable we have employed in our analysis of Latin

TABLE 10.1. *Early Twentieth-Century Literacy and Late Twentieth-Century Programmatic Party Structuration (literacy rates in parentheses)*

	Latin America	Eastern Europe
High PPS		Czech Republic (88)
Moderately high PPS		Hungary (69)
		Poland (68)
Intermediate PPS	Uruguay (51)	Bulgaria (30)
	Chile (44)	Russia (29)
Intermediate-low PPS	Argentina (51)	
	Costa Rica (36)	
	Mexico (24)	
	Venezuela (28)	
Low or absent PPS	Brazil (35)	
	Colombia (34)	
	Dominican Republic (23)[a]	
	Ecuador (33)	
	Peru (24)	
	Bolivia (19)	
Correlation of literacy with PPS measure	.73 (economic PPS-2) (N = 12)	.99 (ordinal ranking, 3/2/1 of the three tiers of PPS; N = 5)
	.83 (N = 17)	

[a] Extrapolated backward from 1930 figures, based on the average increase of literacy in the remaining Latin American countries. The literacy rate is defined as the percentage of individuals fifteen and older that can read and write at least simple statements about everyday life.

Source: Janos (2000: 140, 167); Kappeler (1992: 337); Astorga, Bergés, and FitzGerald (2004: 32).

America – early economic development ("capacity" for PPS) – as well as when we examine the more proximate political-economic sources of high partisan conflict around economic-distributive issues, namely, the comprehensiveness of social policies to protect citizens from the vagaries of uncertain market incomes and to offer a minimum standard of living for the worst-off ("the stakes").

We do not have comparable per capita GDP data in the 1920s for both Latin America and Eastern Europe, but there are fairly reliable figures on literacy rates starting around 1900. Literacy is closely related to income at any given moment in time, but not perfectly. Literacy may also pick up an important element of "bureaucratic state capacity," as successful literacy achievements manifest the ability of governments to institute extensive, complex, and costly systems of basic education that rely on a substantial deployment of sophisticated civil servants and a tax-extractive bureaucracy. Table 10.1 arranges countries in both regions by rough levels of PPS in the 1990s and literacy rates around 1900 (in parentheses). We see that in

East (Central Europe), both literacy rates then and PPS rates nearly 100 years later are higher than in Latin America. A strong correlation prevails within each region and across regions. It is, of course, too historically distant to suggest a causal mechanism that accounts for observed cross-regional differences.

Let us then search for a more proximate explanation that builds on this foundation. Higher levels of development, which meant the beginnings of substantial industrialization, and more opportunities for electoral contestation in the interwar period (Eastern Europe) or the post–World War II period (Latin America) promoted the development of stronger labor movements, net of ethnocultural and religious divides – both of which remained subordinate in the two regions. These forces, in turn, had a greater tendency to press for comprehensive, inclusive social policy reforms, but in Eastern Europe the intraregional diversity was transformed, and temporarily even suppressed, by the advent of communism and the imposition of Stalinism between 1946 and 1953. Stalinism did create ultracomprehensive welfare states in the entire region that protected people from capitalist labor markets once and for all.

Moreover, building on the communist status quo of hermetically controlled welfare societies, the introduction of liberal-capitalist elements of competition required a much sharper break with the political-economic status quo in Eastern Europe than in Latin America to achieve a system of economic regulation in which market contracting would be the dominant mechanism of allocating scarce resources. It is therefore not surprising that the general level of programmatic stakes concerning economic-distributive policies in democratic party competition in the 1990s tends to be higher in postcommunist Eastern Europe compared to always basically capitalist Latin America.[2] This explanation is crude but elegant in its simplicity. Accounts of postcommunist variation within Eastern Europe, however, do require finer analytical arguments that build on precommunist legacies (economic development, precommunist political regime opportunities for collective action, state formation) and examine how they were refracted by the communist regimes themselves. The literature on "varieties of communism," of course, cannot be reviewed in this conclusion to show these effects on postcommunist regimes.[3] Critical for our interregional comparison of PPS levels in

---

[2] More specifically, if ownership constitutes a bundle of rights beyond formal title to an asset, in Latin America private juridical personalities tended to have a much larger share of the rights to deploy, alienate, and collect residual income (profit) from a formally owned asset than under communism.

[3] See comprehensively for this literature Møller (2007). This literature also suggests that we consider the prospect of EU membership as a potential cause of greater programmatic structuration in postcommunist polities, so to speak as an anticipatory adaptation of patterns of political competition prevailing within the EU. Let it be said here only briefly why this

electoral contestation is the relevance of political-economic stakes, as shaped by post–World War II regime trajectories.

Add on as one final consideration the *repressiveness of nondemocratic regimes* that undercuts opportunities for electoral contestation. In Latin America, we found no relationship, or a slightly *positive* one between the repressiveness of nondemocratic regimes and subsequent economic PPS in democratic polities during the 1990s. As a creative adaptation of the bureaucratic authoritarianism thesis, we explained this relationship as mostly endogenous to prior conditions of stronger labor movements, more extensive welfare states, more intense distributive struggles, and ultimately a vigorous military backlash against socialist challenges that, in muted shape, reasserted themselves in programmatic partisan alternatives after redemocratization in the 1980s. This reassertion was possible only because, on a global scale, even the horrid crimes of the Chilean and Argentinean juntas qualify them at most as "intermediate" and intermittently repressive dictatorships, when compared to Stalinist purges and Cultural Revolutions that physically liquidated essentially all internal forces of opposition in an entire polity over a period of time that often lasted for a generation or more, such as in most republics of the former Soviet Union and in some of its Southeast European satellites.

If it could be quantified, during communism repression ranged from an "intermediate" level that marked the upper bounds of regime violence within Latin America all the way to extremes of state-instigated political violence and terror unparalleled anywhere in Latin America. Whereas in Latin America the opposition to authoritarian regimes was mostly displaced and muted, under communism it was physically liquidated or prevented from ever organizing even in the smallest cultural clubs. And in Latin American countries where the opposition was only temporarily silenced, but tolerated at a low level or displaced through emigration, it bounced back all the more vigorously in the process of reinstating democracy. By contrast, after extremely repressive communist regimes, there was no displaced opposition, no offspring of that opposition, and nothing for a newly emerging opposition to build upon. It is not surprising, therefore, that among formerly communist states, variation in levels of communist regime repressiveness, ranging from intermediate to very high, display a stark *negative* relationship with programmatic party competition after 1989–91: the more repressive,

argument is unlikely to matter for our cross-regional comparison. Russia, with the least structured competition in the within-region comparison of postcommunist Europe, certainly had no prospects of joining the EU, yet its structuration is still greater than that of just about any Latin American democracy and almost the same as that of the postcommunist country with the least promising conditions for high PPS from a perspective of domestic conditions, yet an EU joiner (Bulgaria). More generally, patterns of party system structuration vary across all postcommunist countries with reasonable prospects of joining the EU, looked at from the vantage point of the mid-1990s before formal entry negotiations began.

the less programmatic party competition. Viewed over the whole spectrum ranging from nonrepressive democracies via intermediately repressive dictatorships to extremely repressive despotisms, the functional form of the relationship of regime to programmatic competition is likely to be curvilinear. If we examine Latin America and the communist region separately, this functional form is obscured by the limited range that the independent variable (repressiveness) covers within each region.[4]

On the basis of the cursory comparison between Latin America and Eastern Europe, we suggest that our theoretical framework for analyzing the formation of programmatic partisan divisions in democratic party systems has substantial promise to explain *variation within regions* elsewhere than in Latin America and *variation between regions* in global comparison across space, and perhaps also over time. Of course, many, but not all countries within the postcommunist and Latin American regions share characteristics that make it likely to observe at least a modicum of programmatic competition in some of them – namely, the presence of relative "middle income" affluence, often achieved and indicated by high literacy levels in the first half of the twentieth century; a substantial record of electoral contestation in some earlier period of the twentieth century; and more or less comprehensive social policies to counteract market risks to wage labor. As we explore regions of the world with hitherto low income, no democratic experience, and very little social policy, however, chances to encounter programmatic party competition may be minimal. Instead of sharply contoured programmatic parties, mechanisms of democratic accountability are more likely to rely on clientelistic practices of direct exchange. In fact, given these endowments and trajectories, intensifying democratic contestation and the growing capacity of political entrepreneurs to invest in partisan organizational infrastructure may initially entrench clientelistic competition (cf. Kitschelt and Wilkinson 2007).

THE FUTURE OF LATIN AMERICAN PARTY SYSTEM STRUCTURATION

A theoretical argument is attractive when it allows generalization not only in space but especially in time. After all, nothing is more interesting (and difficult) to predict than the future. Let us therefore turn to this ultimate frontier and speculate about the fruitfulness of arguments developed in this study in order to account for big shifts in party competition that are in the process of taking place in Latin America since our main empirical data were recorded in 1997–98. Most studies advertise as part of their attractiveness that they work with the "latest" data on a research object. We, however, treat it as an advantage that a data record can be assembled that lies after

---

[4] Of course, questions of collinearity and endogeneity still make it doubtful whether intensity of repression has exerted an independent effect on democratic party competition.

our main point of analysis. This will permit in the not-too-distant future a serious "out of sample" test of the theoretical argument offered in this study. For now, in this conclusion, we offer only a preview of what the terms of such an evaluation of our theory might entail. Examining Latin America from the vantage point of 2008, what changes have taken place with regard to the independent variables that are key for the prediction of programmatic party competition? And what would we need to find in order to confirm or disconfirm the theoretical framework exemplified by a "historical" study of programmatic party competition in late twentieth-century Latin America?

The argument we propose here comes in several parts. First, the buildup of capacity (income, education) and opportunity (repeated, uninterrupted rounds of democratic party competition) does continue to matter for the future of programmatic party system structuration. More affluent countries and democracies without constitutional crises and breakdowns of the competitive process are more likely to acquire higher levels of PPS. The critical difference for future prospects of programmatic party system competition, however, turns on the ability of politicians to recast the *strategic stakes of politics* that constitute divisions among competing forces. The old political-economic agenda relating to social policy and ISI and the corresponding partisan divides have become obsolete, or at least in need of major recasting, in the aftermath of the "lost decade" of development and the collapse of domestically centered development strategies with high state interventionism in the marketplace. But what issues and development strategies can be seized upon by politicians as more timely alternatives for constituting partisan issue agendas and organizing political competition around conflict generating programmatic "stakes"?

As we argued for the emergence of the social policy–ISI divide, the definition of stakes of political conflict is in part endogenous to preceding levels of development and political opportunity. But the link between them and the articulation of stakes needs to be spelled out. In Latin America, the critical tie for programmatic party system structuration in the twentieth century was the political mobilization of urban wage labor forces around social protection within the broader setting of import-substituting industrialization strategies. This happened primarily in the more urban and affluent countries with some experience of electoral competition. Parties were able to lock in programmatic competitive alignments only where politicians that organized a modicum of social protection on the basis of formal social policies prevailed. Once such policies were in place, they were much more closely related to the maintenance of programmatic party competition than the subsequent economic growth or democratic regime durability in Latin American polities.

With the crisis of ISI since the "lost decade" of development in the 1980s, a new framing of programmatic alternatives is on the agenda. What may be the content of such alternatives, and what are the conditions that enable parties to develop new political alignments around them? The crisis of ISI was initially answered by the rallying cry of the "Washington consensus" strategy proposed by the international financial institutions – the World Bank and the International Monetary Fund – to bring about macroeconomic fiscal and monetary stabilization (balanced budgets, positive real interest rates), regulatory liberalization of economic transactions (domestic and international trade), and asset privatization in Latin American economies (Williamson 1990). The extent to which Latin American countries implemented this Washington agenda is empirically captured by the Inter-American Development Bank liberalization indices of Latin American economies we have repeatedly employed in preceding chapters (Morley et al. 1999). Stabilization and liberalization progressed sooner or later in most of our countries and eventually arrived at a fairly high plateau by 1995. The exception to this rule is Venezuela, where liberalization was arrested substantially below the level reached everywhere else in the comparison cohort.

While the broad array of liberalization measures removed inefficiencies generated by rent-seeking special interests in many Latin American countries, it is fair to say that the (partial) implementation of liberalization alone has not consistently restored Latin American economies to a new growth trajectory. Several criticisms of this strategy have come to the fore, and their consideration yields a spectrum of new policy alternatives that may more fully and more permanently shape political stakes in Latin American party competition. Critics have argued that in most Latin American countries economic liberalization has remained incomplete and has not been associated with a first "Washington plus" component of requisite structural economic reform – namely the construction of regulatory institutions of "good governance," ensuring the rule of law through predictable, professional bureaucracies and courts that enforce property rights efficiently and counteract corruption. Only in an environment of well-defined and enforceable property rights will market transactions thrive and businesses invest confidently (World Bank 1997). Other critics have argued that the removal of impediments to market exchange, by itself, does not help Latin American economies to build up comparative advantages that would enable them to compete internationally and create sustained growth. The construction of comparative advantage requires greater policy efforts to promote human capital formation (education and training at all levels, health care) and to build physical infrastructure, with all those measures together improving total factor productivity, but also to address the stark inequalities and high levels of poverty common in many Latin American countries (Kuczynski and Williamson 2003). Such public investment strategies in human capital de facto involve a substantial income redistribution toward the poor by taxing the affluent in order to build the capacities of the needy to become productive participants in dynamic, competitive market economies.

TABLE 10.2. *Policy Alternatives in Twenty-first-Century Latin American Party Competition*

| | Investments into Institutions of "Good Governance"[a] | |
	Rather Little	A Great Deal
Investments into policies of social capital formation[b]		
Rather little	Status quo politics "Politics of drift"	Washington Consensus Mark I+. "Institutional liberalism"
A great deal	"Neosocialism"	Washington Consensus Mark II: "Social liberalism"

[a] Professional administration, courts, regulatory agencies, police.
[b] Education, health care, physical infrastructure.

Taken together, the need for market-complementary institutions and human capital development opens up a new policy space that includes four ideal-typical options (Table 10.2). Politicians need to decide whether to invest in mechanisms of good governance. Such policies would benefit private business in a competitive marketplace but hurt the often-bloated sectors of civil service employment in Latin America. The promotion of good governance may have an ambiguous impact on the informal sector of such economies in which many poor and unskilled people operate. It would subject them to tax and regulatory authorities but also grant them protections and formal property rights that might enhance investment opportunities. Politicians also need to decide how much and in what way to invest in human capital and physical infrastructure. A broad-based strategy of social investment would make lower-income formal- and informal-sector employees the main beneficiaries. Potential losers, at least in the short run, are more affluent social strata and private businesses that would have to supply the (tax) funds to finance these investments.

Political partisan alignments may now open up between advocates of each of the four strategies inscribed in Table 10.2, depending on whether politicians embrace the priority of institutional governance reform and social investment. The starkest contrasts are along the diagonals of the table. One diagonal pits a politics of the status quo that does nothing to invest in good governance or social infrastructure and may be wedded to traditional strategies of clientelistic exchange, against a reformist "social liberalism" that benefits business in the market by building regulatory institutions of governance but also invests in social infrastructure to empower the poor in the market economy. The other diagonal contrasts a pure politics of economic liberalism, supplemented by investments into institutions of good governance, but absent empowerment strategies for the less well-off ("institutional liberalism"), against a "neosocialist" politics of public social investment with little

TABLE 10.3. *Affluence, Economic Performance, and Economic PPS*

	Economic Growth, 1980–2004: Per Capita GDP (1980 = 100)		
	<100	100–145	>145
Economic affluence, 2005: PPP per capita GNI ($US)			
<6,500	Bolivia[a] Ecuador Peru[a] Venezuela		
<9,700		Colombia Brazil	Dominican Republic[a]
≥ 9,700	Argentina	Costa Rica Uruguay Mexico	Chile

[a] Time series for growth covers only six years (1998–2003), not seven years (1998–2004), as in the other countries.

Sources: Per capita growth: Heston, Summers, and Aten 2006; PPP per capita GNI: World Development Indicators 2006.

emphasis on constructing market institutions. Of course, one might also conceive of competitive divides that pit status quo politics against neosocialism or pure institutional liberalism against social liberalism.

Can we specify conditions under which some of these options appear more likely and politicians identify stakes that crystallize into programmatic partisan divides? Let us begin with a simple economic argument that yields a striking fit of patterns in our twelve-country set. Politics does not come into play here yet. If we reflect on the mechanisms, however, that translate economic conditions into new political alignments, we inevitably need to refer to political partisan processes of constructing programmatic appeals. In that regard, we argue that preexisting levels of programmatic party system structuration in the twentieth century in Latin America influence the pathways by which politicians construct their new programmatic appeals in the first decade of the twenty-first century.

Table 10.3 juxtaposes the per capita economic growth of our Latin American cohort between 1980 and 2004 (or 2003 in several instances) with current (2005) per capita gross national income at purchasing power parity, taking as our cutpoints 0.5 standard deviations below or above the cohort mean on both variables. We can discern distinct clusters of countries that give us a lead to flesh out a political story about the interrelation between economics and partisan competition in Latin America. In the northwest corner of the table are four poorer countries with very weak economic performance in the last quarter century. They also have historically weak economic PPS in their party systems. In the southeastern corner are four countries (Chile, Costa Rica, Mexico, and Uruguay) with less bad or even exceptionally good economic performance in the last quarter century, above-average levels of affluence, and comparatively strong economic PPS in the late twentieth century. In between we find the remaining three to four countries (depending on where we might situate Argentina) with trade-offs between greater affluence and better economic performance in the quarter century under examination. They displayed low levels of economic PPS (Colombia and the Dominican Republic, and arguably Brazil) to intermediate levels (Argentina and arguably Brazil). Do these patterns coincide with strategies of political competition in the twenty-first century and differential levels of programmatic party competition?

Each of the two clusters and the residual grouping appear to gravitate empirically toward different sets of policy strategies and alternatives. Whereas the affluent, above-average economic performers tend to articulate programmatic competition that pits institutional liberalism against social liberalism, in the poor below-average performers, politicians come to the fore in the early twenty-first century who assert neosocialist politics against a politics of nonprogrammatic drift. In the remaining intermediate countries, we tend to see politics devoid of programmatic competition (Colombia and the Dominican Republic), or a politics that contrasts a potpourri of social liberalism, with elements of neosocialism, against that of institutional liberalism or politics of drift (Argentina and Brazil).

Now let us bring politics back into this picture by considering the effects of existing party systems on these trajectories. Preexisting levels of economic PPS in the late twentieth century may influence the strategic appeals of politicians confronted with different economic conditions through at least three causal mechanisms. First, where institutionalized parties with programmatic commitments vested into the social policy conflict exist, politicians have at their disposal partisan vehicles and organizational resources to advertise their message. Rather than writing these off, politicians may try to modify such parties' appeals to make them suitable to an era with new political-economic challenges. Starting from a welfarist-populist or socialist-redistributive platform, it should be easier to move to social liberalism than any other option in the possibility space. Conversely, partisan politicians having advocated a politics of drift or of pure market liberalism are arguably more likely to embrace an institutional liberalism than any of the other options.

Second, as we examined in Chapters 6 and 7, in countries with greater economic-distributive PPS originating in the era of ISI development strategies in the 1950s and 1960s, market-liberalizing economic reforms began earlier in the late 1970s and were far more advanced by 1985 than in countries with little programmatic structuring (cf. Tables 6.4 and 6.6). Where liberal reforms happened earlier, by the 1990s they were not only institutionally locked in more securely than elsewhere, but they were also more likely to have produced economic efficiency gains by the late 1990s that translated into a modicum of broad-based popular acceptance of reforms. Thus, in countries with early market liberalization even politicians aiming to attract the losers of market liberalization were careful not to promise a return to populist policies of the past, but to build and improve on market liberalism via social liberalism rather than a blanket rejection of market-based reforms à la "neosocialism."

By contrast, countries without much programmatic party system structuration tended to be late adopters of liberalization. Other than eliminating hyperinflation, these reforms came too late to produce tangible material payoffs in terms of growth and employment for much of a country's population even by the late 1990s. Hence, where economic liberalism tended to provide more pain than gain and only feeble economic recoveries in the 1990s, democratic partisan competition generated a more unrestrained neosocialist backlash. This was all the easier in low economic PPS party systems, as economic reforms were identified more with the individual incumbent of the presidency deploying his or her party as a personal campaign tool rather than with parties as institutionalized forces of collective action with credible political appeals independent of leader personalities of the day.

Third, where politicians have promoted a neosocialist backlash against market liberalism, it may look like a powerful programmatic partisan mobilization only superficially. Upon closer inspection, the implementation of neosocialist reforms is destined to erode programmatic partisan competition and reconstitute powerful clientelistic linkages between citizens and politicians. Much of neosocialist spending is discretionary, targeted spending on neighborhood projects and services (Hawkins, Rosas, and Johnson 2009; Penfold-Becerra 2007). There is nothing that is more conducive to clientelistic webs of particularistic exchanges than the promotion of nonroutine, targeted projects. Whatever semblance of a professional-bureaucratic operating procedure according to universalistic norms may have existed before, it most likely started to decay under the weight of neosocialist targeted spending programs. In addition, most leaders currently taking neosocialist stances have entered office through the vehicle of populist movements, adopting a rhetoric that pits the putative "will of the people" against a "diabolical," antidemocratic elite. This populist discourse, together with the exigencies of charismatic leadership, creates inevitable tensions within the movement that make it difficult to institutionalize. The folk wisdom that guides the movement (not to mention the leader who embodies it) coexists uneasily with the sophisticated ideologies of leftist intellectuals, and enthusiastic followers and their leader may reject a party apparatus staffed by professional politicians (Hawkins forthcoming).

In other words, while the "stakes" for programmatic competition in an age disillusioned by the apparent failure of both ISI strategies and purely neoliberal policies clearly appear to grow on the horizon where the neosocialist discourse wins followers and government office, these countries also have extremely poor capabilities (income, education, occupational skills) and only recent experience with the practicalities of political mobilization and (programmatic) party building. As a consequence of raising the stakes of neosocialism, it even appears that socioeconomic capabilities stagnate and decline, in an environment of inflation and unemployment, and that opportunities for democratic competition are stifled, as the incumbent neosocialist rulers tilt the playing field in their favor. Stakes of interparty conflict are not entirely endogenous to the development of capacities and opportunities. There appears to be a complicated causal interplay among opportunities, stakes, and capabilities.

By undermining professional bureaucratic governance in favor of partisan patronage, by dismantling political rules of checks and balances that lend some transparency and accountability to executive action, and by building a regulatory economic apparatus that displaces competitive market contracting by discretionary political allocation of scarce economic resources, neosocialism reasserts the power of clientelistic ties, whether within a framework of democratic politics or after engineering a regime shift to semi-authoritarianism with power centralization around a plebiscitarian presidency. In the rest of this section we explore how these general expectations fit the recent trajectory of the cases we have analyzed in this volume. Readers have to keep in mind, of course, that our argument is at best probabilistic and ignores the inevitable element of creative leadership and the unique constellation of actors, all of which cannot be reduced to our capabilities-opportunities-stakes framework.

Strong Preexisting Programmatic Partisan Structuration: Institutional versus Social Liberalism

Countries with strong and medium-strong preexisting economic PPS include above all Chile and Uruguay, and to a lesser extent Argentina, Costa Rica, and Mexico. Within this group of countries it is possible to distinguish two subsets of cases. Let us first analyze the countries of the Southern Cone where we found, on average, greater levels of PPS (in particular in Chile and Uruguay).

These are countries that went through bureaucratic authoritarian regimes in the 1970s, after having experienced increasing levels of political polarization in the 1960s and 1970s. Indeed, in Argentina and Chile populist or even socialist governments were in power in the early 1970s (Perón in Argentina and Allende in Chile); in Uruguay the leftist Frente Amplio (FA) started challenging the traditional party system after obtaining close to 20 percent of the vote in its first election in 1971. These three countries also witnessed the emergence of guerrilla movements in the late 1960s. In the context of the Cold War, these increasing levels of leftist mobilization and political polarization prompted an authoritarian backlash that crystallized around repressive military juntas bent upon uprooting the leftist challenge through political repression and (with differences across cases) promoting the implementation of market-liberal reforms.

Particularly in Chile, the military implemented a full-fledged program of market liberalization, radically dismantling ISI. These reforms eventually brought about widely felt economic improvements by the late 1980s and early 1990s. Factors including the self-critique that several leftist organizations launched following the defeat of Allende's government and leftist leaders' experiences living in political exile in social-democratic Europe compelled much of the political left in Chile to moderate its view regarding economic policy appeals. A move away from wholesale rejection of the market-liberalizing economic policies engineered by the military junta (which were also protected through "authoritarian enclaves" written into the 1980 constitution) facilitated the transition to democracy, as authoritarian incumbents no longer had to fear total expropriation of their societal constituencies under a new political regime. The act of moderating platforms so as to appeal to centrist voters also improved the left's chances of winning elections. The left thus underwent a dramatic transformation toward social liberalism that accepted basic parameters of market capitalism, provided the latter were restrained by policies of social protection and human capital investment. Although the regime divide (between supporters of the Pinochet regime and those of pro-democratic forces that coalesced around the center-left Concertación) continues to split both mainstream partisan pacts more forcefully, the rightist Alianza por Chile could be seen as representing an institutional-liberal policy stance that opposes the current center-left government's social-institutional program.

In Uruguay, where we also found relatively high levels of PPS, the military junta did pursue trade and capital liberalization. However, it did not engage in significant privatization, state, or social policy reform attempts. As a result, much of the ISI complex was still in place after re-democratization. With a relatively weak private industrial sector even when sheltered under ISI, public employment, a relatively generous welfare state, and an ever expanding pension system constituted the key pillars of the Uruguayan model. Those three pillars were primarily financed through raw material exports, especially cattle. Politically, public employment and pensions were the primary clientelistic handouts that traditional parties historically provided to their followers. After the return to democracy a significant proportion of the population was still entitled to ISI benefits. In a representative democracy that escaped the patterns of hyperpresidentialism and delegation that prevailed in the region in the 1990s, the organizations of ISI beneficiaries allied with FA to oppose (successfully in many instances) the liberalizing attempts that both traditional parties engaged in when confronting increasing budget deficits, inflation, and economic stagnation. Therefore, the emergence of a veto coalition identified with FA and opposed to reformist attempts provided greater levels of PPS to a system historically character-ized as composed of two catchall and clientelistic parties. As a result of this process of programmatic strengthening, two party families consoli-dated in the system and started competing to capture the median voter. The first was represented by the mainstream factions of the Blanco and Col-orado parties and endorsed a reformist stance that partially resembles our institutional-liberal ideal type. The second, represented by the left, began to crystallize in a social-institutional stance that is currently advanced by the FA government headed by Tabaré Vázquez. This social-institutional stance emerged from a complex process of programmatic moderation that occurred when the party was in the opposition during the 1990s and which resulted, primordially, from the electoral strengthening of moderate factions within the FA.

Because of its comparatively weaker party system institutionalization combined with widespread clientelistic practices in national and subnational politics (Levitsky 2003; Wibbels 2005), as well as the ineffectiveness of the military government in pushing market liberal reforms in the early 1980s, Argentina does not quite fit the simplified template that broadly applies to Chile and Uruguay. Argentina can be included in the cohort of countries with an expected transition of competition to social liberalism versus insti-tutional liberalism only with qualifications. Argentina's overall economic record in the quarter century until 2005 has been much worse than that of the other four countries with medium to high economic PPS in Latin Amer-ica (see Table 10.3). The big push to market liberalization did not come under military rule in the early 1980s as in Chile, but during the presidential incumbency of the formerly populist Justicialists under Menem, starting in 1989. The reforms resulted in some immediate economic gains, but were marred by corruption and a lack of liberal institution building. They were also sufficiently inconsistent and incomplete enough to precipitate a deep financial crisis by the turn of the millennium.

Meanwhile, though the Alianza between the UCR and the FREPASO defeated the Justicialists in 1999 on the basis of a social-institutional pro-grammatic stance, this effort was quickly delegitimized in government as a result of the economic collapse of 2002. This failure has granted the Justicial-ists a hegemonic position in national politics, with a jockeying of different factions to capture the flags of institutional or social liberalism. Social liberal factions would reclaim the Justicialists with Kirchner as president. Given the circumstances of economic crisis and high growth of poverty in the after-math of the financial crisis, however, the Kirchner wing's interpretation of Peronism embraces more populist and redistributive policy elements than appears to be common for social liberal partisan alternatives in the other Latin American countries with historically higher economic-distributive PPS, and it has made much less investment (perhaps even a de-investment) in institutions that foster the rule of law. At the same time, the dominant current in the Argentinean Peronist party does not appear ready to embrace the entire neosocialist agenda. In turn, the opposition has remained weak and divided, between institutional-liberal (e.g., López-Murphy, Macri) and social-institutional alternatives (e.g., the ARI). The hegemony and programmatic heterogeneity of the PJ and the programmatic inconsistency of a weak opposition have further contributed to diminish programmatic distinctions between governing and opposing forces. To sum up, in Argentina as in the other cases of medium to high preexisting economic PPS, the breakdown of old alignments did not give way to a direct neosocialist challenge. However, differing from cases with relatively higher PPS (Chile and Uruguay), both the patterns of party competition and the overall quality of democratic governance seem somewhat less promising in this case.

The two remaining cases in this group did not go through bureaucratic regimes in the 1970s and early 1980s and show only intermediate levels of preexisting PPS. Beyond this commonality, significant divergences also exist among them.

In Mexico, within a hegemonic party regime with some programmatic structuration, the backlash against economic populism and redistribution took place during the de la Madrid and Salinas presidencies, beginning in the 1980s. As in Argentina, the same party that was responsible for implementing ISI (the PRI) was the one that embarked on market reforms. Both the moderate economic improvements that followed these reforms in the early 1990s and the moderating effects that Mexico's protracted transition to democracy have exerted on the opposition to the PRI helped configure a centripetal competitive dynamic between the governing party and its electoral rivals.[5] In this case, however, the opposition to the reformist PRI split between two currents, one more clearly concerned with the social dimension (the PRD, which recently has, under the leadership of López-Obrador, moved from a social-institutional stance to one that more closely resembles a neosocialist platform) and the other, electorally successful in 2000 and 2006, more concerned with the institutional dimension and the completion of transition to electoral democracy (the PAN, which can be portrayed in terms of its economic platform as a liberal institutional party). In Mexico, as in the case of Argentina, the internal heterogeneity of the PRI and the split of the opposition might have jointly contributed to lessen programmatic distinctions in the party system.

---

[5] For an empirical analysis of this process in Mexico, see Greene (2007) who shows that improving democratic prospects, in turn, attracts more centrist partisan activists into the opposition parties in regimes transitioning from authoritarianism. This, in turn, makes it more likely for the opposition to win elections, albeit with restraints on their programs of economic and political change.

Costa Rica is the one country in this group of intermediate to high economic PPS polities that witnessed uninterrupted free and fair elections since the late 1950s. Here party competition was structured around two essentially catchall parties (the PLN and the PUSC), which gravitated toward a narrow band of center-left and center-right policy alternatives by the 1980s, but configured around a status quo of low market liberalization of the economy. Since the mid-1990s, citizen's support for these political parties has begun to erode, during a period when economic performance problems also emerged. Both phenomena have compelled politicians to abandon the status quo and embrace unpopular market reforms. From 1990 to 2002, the PUSC (Christian Democrats) pushed relatively hard for reforms, with the PLN generally opposing them, in spite of losing three out of four elections in that period. In the most recent election the traditional bipartisan system disappeared with the collapse of the PUSC, precipitated in part by a series of corruption scandals involving government officials. By a very close margin, former president and PLN leader Oscar Arias was again elected to the presidency, this time after running a campaign centered on institutional liberalism. Under the current presidency of Oscar Arias, the formerly social reformist PLN has thus emerged as the new party of institutional liberalism, whereas PLN dissidents who objected to the party leadership's willingness to embrace market liberalization began to construct a new social liberal alternative. As these recent events illustrate, the Costa Rican party system has gone through considerable turmoil since the mid-1990s. It still remains to be seen if a programmatic restructuring of the party system is on its way in the country. However, it is clear that party system turmoil did not end up breeding the type of polarization between a neosocialist force and advocates of the status quo that is currently seen in the countries that had weak preexisting economic PPS.

Overall, the extent of preexisting economic PPS weighs in on the realignment of democratic partisan politics in these Latin American countries through different channels and mechanisms. It favors a reconfiguration of politics around the alternatives of institutional versus social liberalism. Organizational inertia, persistence, and relative depersonalization of partisan politics are as important here as the timing of economic liberalization in higher PPS countries and the economic performance of these countries since the 1980s. The conflict between social liberalism and institutional liberalism is the configuration most likely to deliver the stakes that will underlie PPS into, at least, the near future.

Weak Preexisting Programmatic Structuration: From Neosocialism to a Clientelistic Politics of Drift

Poorer countries with unambiguously feeble economic partisan structuration in the late 1990s include the four Andean states of Bolivia, Ecuador, Peru, and Venezuela. All four exhibit weak to extremely weak economic performance in the past quarter century. Three of these four had military dictatorships in the 1970s, yet none with as repressive or as decidedly market-liberalizing approaches to economic policy as can be found in countries with greater economic PPS. Post-ISI economic reforms came here either late and suddenly (particularly in Ecuador and Peru) or only in a hesitant fashion, starting relatively early but breaking off at a much lower level than in other countries (Venezuela and Bolivia).[6] They were almost invariably identified with individual presidential personalities rather than with institutionalized parties. In contrast to polities with more programmatic parties, among which only Argentina experienced an episode of irregular presidential transitions in 2001, all four countries with weak or absent economic-distributive PPS went through a variety of "irregular" presidential replacements or attempted military coups or "self-coups" of sitting presidents, disrupting the constitutionally specified provisions of electoral politics and representation. Before the advent of neosocialism, the leading political parties in all four polities fit the template of status-quo-oriented clientelistic parties with little capacity or ambition to invest in good governance or human capital formation.

Given the accelerated tempo, comparatively late timing, and personalization of leadership in market-liberal reforms advanced by clientelistic parties in this group of countries, it is no accident that corruption and other legal violations characterized the process of market liberalization, further discrediting the policies in the eyes of many citizens. World Bank Governance Indicators for the 1996 to 2006 period (Kaufmann et al. 2007) invariably identified Bolivia, Ecuador, and Venezuela as the most corrupt countries in our Latin American comparison set. Peru is ranked within the next tier of countries with only slightly less bad governance, together with Argentina, Brazil, Colombia, the Dominican Republic, and Mexico. Only intermediate or high economic PPS countries Costa Rica, Chile, and Uruguay receive comparatively favorable governance marks.

The confluence of corruption, weak economic performance (measured by hyperinflation or lack of growth and employment creation), and weak preexisting PPS generated the explosive mix in which Latin American neosocialism and its populist vehicles have thrived (Hawkins forthcoming).[7] The

---

[6] In Bolivia, market reforms were implemented relatively early, since 1985.

[7] As Hawkins (forthcoming) emphasizes, populist discourse and the neosocialism position are not equivalent, and populist movements can come in leftist and rightist varieties. The causes of populist movements generally and the recent neosocialist "wave" are very similar, however. Populist movements require a context featuring widespread violation of the rule of law, and policy failures such as catastrophic economic performance provide important catalysts. Insofar as the rule of law also aids in the process of economic development and the consolidation of democracy, it serves as a causal antecedent for PPS. Thus, we can expect (low) PPS and recurrent populism to be intertwined phenomena in Latin America. The direct relationship between populism and programmatic structuration is less clear, though. Low PPS may be a *consequence* of populism, in that populist leaders and their followers tend to

failure to successfully reinforce the rule of law provided a backdrop of injustice against which the populist appeal resonated with unusual force, and it further undermined the minimal structural conditions required for market-based growth. Notoriously weak economic performance in Bolivia, Ecuador, Peru, and Venezuela therefore helped to further the popular sense of political malaise. Economic crisis and perceived bad governance fueled backlashes against incumbent politicians; citizens quickly came to perceive market liberalization as policy failure. Hence incumbent politicians were sooner or later confronted with a new breed of neosocialist political entrepreneurs who created their own electoral vehicles from scratch, but whose message of cosmic struggle against conspiring enemies almost instantly resonated with large audiences. Neosocialist challengers have won power in three of these four countries now, and in the remaining one (Peru) the challenger remains a formidable foe of the incumbent, traditional party. In at least two of the four countries (Ecuador and Bolivia), political liberalization granting increased freedom and opportunity to the large indigenous populations and their gradual political mobilization around independent movement organizations and proto-parties throughout the 1980s and 1990s, most clearly exemplified by Pachakutik in Ecuador, may have provided another stimulus for neosocialist politics (Yashar 1998). The mobilization of indigenous people antedates neosocialism but nonetheless had a redistributive economic policy bent early on and, in some instances, groomed future neosocialist electoral leaders (cf. Van Cott 2005, 2008; Yashar 2005).

Note that our explanation for the initial rise of neosocialism rules out several alternatives. Neosocialism is certainly not a reaction to vigorous market liberalization per se. Only two of the four countries had vigorous market liberalization to begin with, and that came belatedly on the heels of long crises (Bolivia and Peru). In both Ecuador and especially Venezuela, conventional politicians embraced anemic economic liberalization programs that ran into a great deal of opposition. Especially Venezuela fell far behind most other Latin American countries in the process of market liberalization by 1995 before neosocialism began to organize in the electoral space. It was a case of nonreform, or only very partial reform, coupled with economic failure. Neosocialist rhetoric blaming economic liberalization for Venezuela's massive economic decline in the 1980s and 1990s is truly a case of "perverse learning."

Neosocialism is also not a response to the presence of substantial oil and gas resources that would make neosocialism a plausible appeal by eliminating the need for redistribution through taxation (cf. Weyland 2007). In Venezuela, the biggest Latin American oil exporter, neosocialism began to

---

reject institutionalized forms of political organization. Yet low PPS may also be an additional *cause* of populism, in that it reduces the barriers to entry for third-party outsiders with diffuse platforms.

emerge more in response to depressed oil prices and intensifying resource scarcity in the 1990s. Ecuador is only a minor world market supplier (0.4 million barrels a day) and not likely to finance extravagant social programs even with sustained high oil prices, given the size of Ecuador's population and increasing domestic oil consumption. In Bolivia, the rise of ethnically based neosocialist movements antedates the prospects of a natural-gas-driven revenue bounty. Peru, finally, where the left economic nationalist Ollanta Humala almost won the presidency in 2006, has always been an energy importer with little prospect of reversing that situation.

While hydrocarbon rents may not explain the origins of the rise of neosocialism, Weyland's (2007) argument may be significant to account for the prospective persistence of neosocialism in the twenty-first century. Once the appeal of neosocialism resonates with the mass of poor voters, the presence of escalating nontax revenues makes plausible some of the more outrageous neosocialist promises and helps these governments conceal the economic inefficiencies of administered resource allocation. However, nontax revenues become an impediment to, rather than a catalyst for, sustaining neosocialism as a programmatic partisan appeal, because they allow the new movement to rely on clientelistic exchange mechanisms to stay in power. This concerns our last point, the long-term consequences of neosocialism for programmatic party competition.

Neosocialism has a tendency to undermine programmatic party competition because the implementation of its program may inevitably bring about its replacement by clientelistic political practices. This applies to both neosocialist demands for constitutional reform and neosocialist plans for political-economic reform. The neosocialist constitutional effort to dismantle all checks and balances – such as legislatures with meaningful capacities to exercise oversight and control the executive, independent constitutional courts, elected subnational governments, and autonomous central banks – and make presidents the sole fountain of political authority, vested with an unencumbered capacity to make rules and allocate resources, undercuts the transparency and thus the accountability of democratic rule. It encourages patronage politics and government through informal networks configured around the office of the presidency. Extreme political centralization makes it impossible for organized opposition forces to win subnational government offices as a check on the federal government or use a minority role in the legislature to control the executive. Neosocialist constitutional reform thus removes the level playing field of interparty competition.

Additionally, the political-economic reforms of neosocialism – such as nationalization of strategic economic sectors, including natural resource producers; control of the financial sector; regulation of prices for basic food stuffs and fuels; and state management of external trade and capital flows – create many points of discretionary power to be placed in the hands of public officials who may either be elected partisans or be supervised and appointed by partisans. This opens the door to clientelistic politics serving rent-seeking constituencies through the channels of partisan patronage.

Control of natural resource rents may give neosocialist governments an additional lease on life, even if their constitutional objectives generate a political backlash and their economic governance structures produce inefficiencies that ultimately result in weak economic performance (high inflation, unemployment, decline of export-oriented industries). Neosocialists heed the "Washington plus" strategic advice to invest in human capital but do so within a framework of governance that undercuts democratic civil and political liberties as well as economic efficiency. Ultimately, this does not seem to be a path for either stable economic development or the creation of PPS.

The Residual Group: Weak Programmatic Structuration, but No Neosocialism

This leaves us with a residual group of arguably three or four of our twelve Latin American countries that unambiguously fit neither the neosocialist camp – with high poverty, weak economic performance, and little preexisting programmatic party system structuration – nor the camp of more affluent countries with better economic performance and a minimum of preexisting programmatic partisan articulation that permits political parties to articulate a novel divide between institutional and social liberalism.

We already discussed Argentina as a borderline case to the group of countries with institutionalized parties adapting programmatic party competition to new conditions. If we follow assessments of Brazilian politics that attribute more programmatic structuration to its party competition than our measures detect, Brazil, like Argentina, may actually be a marginal case gravitating to the group of countries in which partisan divides are crystallizing around the alternatives of institutional and social liberalism. Not only do general levels of economic development and the persistence of uninterrupted democratic competition in Brazil now favor programmatic politics, but also political-economic reform of the welfare state, particularly the civil service pension funds, may begin to pull Brazil out of the realm of heavily clientelistic politics. The deradicalization of the Workers' Party after its capture of the office of the presidency in 2002 may promote a divide between institutional and social liberalism, provided that internal organizational mechanisms within the party continue to prevent it from irreversibly compromising its programmatic appeal and adopting clientelistic patronage politics (on the PT, see Hunter 2007; Samuels 2004).

The remaining two countries, the Dominican Republic and Colombia, both historically lack firm alignments of programmatic partisan competition and instead practice predominantly clientelistic politics of partisan accountability. Nevertheless, both countries have accumulated an outstanding record of economic performance within the region over the past generation – through 2009 (cf. Table 7.6) – that improved their citizens' "capabilities." Economic improvements certainly also contributed to preempt the rise of strong neosocialist movements in the two countries. Moreover, an expanding period of continuous electoral party contests under democratic conditions since the 1980s has offered "opportunities" for the construction of parties with programmatic appeals. At the same time, however, it is challenging for political parties to elaborate the stakes and build programmatic parties where none existed before. Whether "stakes" lead to high PPS is not deterministically set, nor is the causality that links capabilities and opportunities to stakes unilinear, making stakes the endogenous result of capabilities and stakes.

Colombia, arguably, is the hardest case to gauge. Never a political economy fully beholden to ISI strategies, its governments embarked on market liberalization early and gradually. They delivered some economic improvement in the 1980s, but further benefits were sapped by the government's low-level civil warfare against opposition forces tied to the radical left and/or the drug trade. Insofar as these guerrilla armies embrace leftist programmatic appeals, they externalize what might emerge in other polities as a neosocialist challenge to the incumbent parties within the sphere of electoral competition. Indeed, since the 1970s, armed opposition groups from time to time ventured into electoral politics and out again, sometimes after paramilitary forces on the side of the government killed their candidates. Most recently, the Revolutionary Armed Forces of Colombia (FARC) inaugurated an electoral wing in 2000, with the explicit aim to appeal to poor Colombians by demands for economic redistribution. Although since the 1990s Colombia's party system went through the disintegration of its historical duopoly of liberal and conservative parties in favor of a highly volatile, fragmented landscape of parties by the time of the legislative and presidential elections of 2006, no major neosocialist contender appeared. It remains to be seen if the center-left Polo Democrático (with a social institutional agenda) will succeed in becoming a viable opposition force to the strong leadership of President Álvaro Uribe and if, in doing so, it will further stick to its moderate center-left agenda. As long as the low-level civil war persists in Colombia, these special circumstances impede the emergence of a strong neosocialist challenger in the electoral arena, although economic and political conditions appear otherwise ripe for the successful entry of such an alternative.[8] On the other hand, should the conflict be brought to a successful conclusion, conditions for PPS seem uncertain.

---

[8] Since the 1980s, leftist political forces have oscillated between participation in the electoral arena and an armed struggle against the government.

LATIN AMERICAN PARTY POLITICS IN PERSPECTIVE

Where parties installed comparatively comprehensive social policy programs for wage earners in the formal sector of the economy during the heyday of import-substituting industrialization, they helped to sustain at least a modicum of programmatic party competition all the way into democratic party politics of the 1990s. By then, however, political-economic challenges had changed and made ISI strategies obsolete. It appears possible that politicians in established parties under favorable conditions can modify their political appeals and reconfigure the programmatic alignment of party systems. They may supplant the old polarities with new competition between institutional and social liberalism. Not only moderate economic affluence and an undisturbed process of electoral competition for office but also a legacy of programmatic party structuration and party institutionalization facilitate this reorientation toward a new political alignment.

By contrast, in polities where the ISI era left little legacy of programmatic party structuration, neosocialist challenges pitted against a clientelistic politics of drift have reigned supreme. This occurs only where a range of empirically interconnected facilitating conditions appeared as well: economies performing badly throughout much of the quarter century after 1980 and belatedly, followed by hurried policies of market liberalization that are advanced by highly personalistic presidential governments and often shrouded in a cloud of corruption scandals. But the opportunities for turning such developments into sustained programmatic party competition look less than auspicious. The ideological momentum of neosocialism itself promotes constitutional, institutional, and political-economic reforms that subvert programmatic party competition. And even if the neosocialist bid to recast Latin American polities ultimately collapses, it is unclear whether its heirs will be able to construct programmatic alternatives, given the strategic circumstances under which they may have to wrest power from neosocialist incumbents.

A serious analysis of the partisan alignments that might succeed the prevailing patterns of party competition in Latin America in the late twentieth century has to await another study. All we can do is advance hypotheses that suggest how partisan alignments in an earlier era might help shape subsequent transformations of political divides when new political-economic challenges emerge.

Appendix A

Description of Variables, Data Issues, and Research Design

The objective of this book is to uncover the degree of programmatic structure in Latin American legislative party systems. To this purpose, we primarily analyze data from the 1997 Parliamentary Elites of Latin America (PELA) project (see Chapter 4 for discussion and use of a second data source, the 1998 Latinobarometer survey). The 1997 PELA survey was directed by Manuel Alcántara (Universidad de Salamanca) and financed by Spain's Comisión Interministerial de Ciencia y Tecnología. The Salamanca questionnaire was administered in eighteen countries, including almost all of continental Latin America, and codes responses to 104 questions in 257 variables. A total of 1,197 Latin American legislators participated in the surveys, all of them national representatives to their country's lower chamber at the time of the interview (or to the unicameral legislature in the case of Costa Rica, Ecuador, El Salvador, Guatemala, Honduras, Nicaragua, Panama, and Peru).

Because of their coverage and substantive contents, the Salamanca surveys represent a quantum leap in our knowledge of Latin American legislatures. Not only do they allow the chance to explore the idiosyncrasies of legislators in different countries, but their common design permits systematic, cross-national comparisons among legislative bodies. In exploring the programmatic structure of party systems in the region, we thoroughly exploit the wealth of information contained in the Salamanca surveys regarding attitudes, opinions, beliefs, values, party membership, policy preferences, and left-right placement of Latin American legislators. In accordance with the explanatory purpose of this book, we also develop summary measures of different traits of programmatic structure and carry out simple statistical analyses of these indicators.

Yet, despite their originality and importance, the Salamanca surveys are still limited instruments in a few important respects, such that a naive use of information therein might lead to mistaken conclusions about Latin American party systems. Because we purport to infer the extent and causes of programmatic structure in Latin America from analyses of these data, it is essential that we specify the shortcomings of these surveys and clearly convey the solutions that we have adopted. Moreover, we have purposefully disregarded some of the information contained in the Salamanca surveys, particularly that pertaining to five Central American legislatures and Paraguay. A few words regarding the reasons behind our selection of cases and variables are therefore in order. In particular, in the first section of this appendix we present a discussion of selection issues with respect to national cases, substantive topics for cross-national exploration, and political parties. In the second section of this appendix, we discuss two additional challenges presented by the data: sampling defects and missing values. For further reference, Appendixes B and C contain variable descriptions and the English translation of the relevant portions of the Salamanca questionnaire, whereas Web Appendixes D and E (at www.cambridge.org/9780521114950) provide a breakdown of all variables by political party and further information about the political party weights used in some of our analyses.

SELECTION ISSUES

National Cases

For the purpose of cross-national comparison, we kept twelve of the eighteen countries covered by the Salamanca surveys: Argentina (with 68 respondents), Bolivia (74), Brazil (69), Chile (94), Colombia (63), Costa Rica (52), Dominican Republic (62), Ecuador (71), Mexico (123), Peru (87), Uruguay (73), and Venezuela (69). We excluded five Central American countries and Paraguay because of one or more of the following reasons. First, two countries had samples too small to be amenable to the quantitative techniques of analysis we apply to the cases we have included in our sample. In Guatemala, the survey reports only 11 cases. In Panama, there are 53 respondents, but they are distributed over more than seven parties such that no analysis is possible for all but the largest two parties. Second, we ran into the problem of lack of variation on key indicators. This applies to El Salvador, which we had originally planned to include despite its small number of respondents (46). A further problem in the Salvadoran survey is that legislator samples are absolutely out of line with actual party shares in the national legislatures (see our subsequent discussion of sampling problems). Thus, the Salvadoran sample extremely overrepresents the Christian Democrats to the detriment of ARENA, the FMLN, and smaller parties in the national legislature.

Third, among the six deleted cases, there are several polities with little or no exposure to any sort of moderately open electoral contestation over the course of their twentieth-century history until the mid-1990s. These countries had never experienced a period of open democratic competition for any time in the twentieth century. Furthermore, their levels of contestability of political rule in the decades preceding the 1990s, as measured by political rights and civil liberties to organize challenges to the government, was very low. Thus, throughout these decades Paraguay and Nicaragua earned substantially lower Freedom House scores of political and civil rights than even Mexico, the long-term least democratic country in the sample of cases included in our comparison.

Finally, for Central American countries a number of the explanatory indicators we employ in later chapters are missing that are readily available for the polities we are covering in our study. This applies especially to political-economic measures of import-substituting industrialization, social policy, and economic liberalization. Thus, lack of key indicators eliminated Honduras (67 respondents), Nicaragua (56), and Panama (55) from our analysis. Our deletion of these cases reflects, among other things, the relatively sparse attention research on Latin American politics has given to the Central American polities.

Nevertheless, our sample includes more than 90 percent of the Latin American population. Despite the exclusion of Paraguay and much of Central America, our twelve-country sample is fairly representative, as it includes countries with large and small indigenous minorities, low- and middle-income economies, and long-standing democracies or societies with lengthy histories of party competition alongside countries that have transited to democracy more recently and some others with dubious democratic credentials at least for some time period.

Substantive Topics (Issue Bundles)

The Salamanca databases include ample information on a wide range of substantive policy issues that potentially are of paramount importance in contemporary Latin American politics. Of all the available data, we eliminated some variables when confronted with too many missing values or too little variation, dropping them from all twelve country datasets in order to maintain cross-national comparability. This left us in possession of a long list of indicators, which cover a sufficiently wide field of subjects that we could not conceive of any subject of policy debate left entirely ignored by the array of issue questions included in the questionnaire.

Let us briefly introduce the twenty-seven indicators we settled on to convey the potential menu of political, economic, and cultural concerns that legislators in the region might entertain (Appendix B identifies each of our variables according to its Salamanca label and a brief mnemonic; Appendix C displays an English translation of the relevant portions of the questionnaire).

In the beginning stages of our research we were largely agnostic about the relative political importance of different issues in different countries and the ways different issues relate to each other in the policy preference schedules of individual respondents and political parties. As a matter of convenience and conceptual parsimony, we grouped them in three bundles – economic, social, and cultural – with further distinctions among several issue subcategories. As it turned out – and is discussed in detail in Chapter 2 – a number of these "baskets" of issues indeed are approximately coherent in a number of our Latin American countries, in the sense that respondents' policy positions are coherent on items that belong to the same basket. Whether clusters of economic, political, and cultural issues translate into partisan divides, however, turns out to be quite a different matter.

Economics

1. *Economic governance* (indicators v49, v50):[1] This bundle contains two questions about preferred ownership patterns in industry and provision of services. We consider that this bundle evokes opinions on the optimal locus of economic activity. In other words, rather than signaling legislators' opinions regarding public versus private ownership of means of production, this dimension conveys the faith that a legislator places on the self-regulating market either as a means to achieve economic growth or as a desirable outcome that requires no further justification.

2. *Social protection* (indicators v64, v65, v69, v70, v71, v72, v150): A related aspect of government intervention in economic activity is the provision of social safety nets, state-sponsored mechanisms aimed at alleviating the risk that market participants bear in case of an adverse economic outcome. These six variables elicit legislators' opinions on the appropriateness of government action to subsidize basic foodstuffs and control prices, foster job creation, provide unemployment insurance and basic social security, supply cheap housing, and prioritize welfare over security.

3. *Economic nationalism* (indicators v54, v57, v59, v61): Indicators v57 (*US investment best*), v59 (*EU investment best*), and v61 (*LA investment best*) ask legislators about their tolerance to foreign ownership of strategic privatized firms. Thus, these variables conflate two issues: the desirability of foreign direct investment, on the one hand, and the possibility of *foreign* control of *strategic* industries, on the other. Thus, when legislators report negative answers to these questions, we cannot know if they are against all foreign direct investment (i.e., whether they are financial isolationists) or whether they would avoid it only in strategic industries (i.e., whether they are economic nationalists). Some interpretive context can be added by considering v54 (*let IMF in*), which elicits opinions on whether national governments should

---

[1] In the interest of easier replication of our findings, we keep the original indicator labels in the Salamanca surveys, which are all prefixed by "v."

accept conditions imposed by international financial institutions in order to secure access to financial support. For example, individuals who dislike foreign direct investment but are not ideologically opposed to IMF conditionality clauses should probably be considered economic nationalists, rather than financial isolationists. Because of our results in later chapters, we keep the "economic nationalism" label to refer to these four issues.

Political Regime

1. *Authoritarianism* (indicators v11, v15, v26, v32): This dimension captures legislators' commitment to democracy as the proper way to solve political disputes and thus taps into preferences about regime form and about the subjective limits to political dissent. Note however that v26 (*parties not superfluous*) might be interpreted not as tapping into authoritarian propensities at all but into preferences for a system where the relationship between citizens and governments is not mediated by parties. In this interpretation, legislators with high scores on indicator v26 might not be opposed to democracy, whatever they mean by it, but to parties as the main vehicles of political representation. Notice as well that v32 (*justice doesn't work*) could in principle be related to the indicators that make up our law-and-order issue bundle, rather than to authoritarian propensities.

2. *Law and order* (indicators v34, v35, v87, v168): We include in this dimension four variables that prima facie tap into legislators' views on threats to the state or to society. Yet we have only diffuse expectations about how these variables should relate to one another. For one, two of these variables are feeling thermometers (v34 and v35), and two are "salience" measures (v87 and v168). Moreover, though we can conceive of a legislator preferring to endow the state with absolute authority to combat delinquency (v34), labor unrest (v35), violence (v87), and corruption (v168), we think it is more likely that legislators will look at these sources of threat differentially – and would therefore, for example, favor strong state responses to delinquency but not to corruption. In any case, this dimension comprises indicators that reflect "loose" ideological tolerance for threats to the status quo.

Culture

1. *Religious/secular* (indicators v210, v235, v236, v240): This dimension reflects differences of opinion on the importance of upholding traditional values versus adopting more secular or socially progressive views on morality. A more daring interpretation would see this factor as a reflection of nineteenth-century struggles on the proper

place of the Catholic Church in the body politic, perhaps even as the ideological remnant of a structural church-state cleavage (Lipset and Rokkan 1967; Dix 1989).

2. *Postmodernism* (indicators v90, v92): Because these issues elicit responses about the environment and human rights, we name this dimension after Inglehart (1997), though we hasten to add that its contents might be only loosely related to his original meaning. Notice, first, that the previous religious-secular dimension might already capture some of the traits that belong in this "value-based cleavage" (Knutsen 1989). In addition, these two indicators do not code legislators' stances on human rights or environmental issues; rather, they ask legislators how salient these issues are. By including indicators v90 and v92 in the original design matrix, we implicitly assume that legislators who consider these issues as salient tend to have similar views on them. This is, admittedly, a heroic assumption, and we are willing to make it only in a first approximation to the study of legislative ideologies. Moreover, wording on indicator v90 confounds two separate issues, namely, human rights and minority rights.

Throughout the book, we examine the importance of economic-distributive concerns, preferences regarding political regime, and cultural dispositions in shaping the programmatic structure of Latin American political party systems. Where appropriate, we disaggregate this abstract categorization to single out some of the most conspicuous twenty-seven issues, that is, those over which legislators in different countries most disagree. In general, however, we consider this very inclusive collection of issues as comprising the "meat and bones" of everyday politics in Latin America at the end of the twentieth century. Finally, we also analyze information on party membership (v132b) and left-right self-placement of legislators (v234).[2]

Political Parties

In most sections of the book, we have disregarded information about small parties in national legislatures. Where appropriate, we explain how this decision changes our inferences about the programmatic structure of party systems. This decision was ultimately driven by the theoretical desire to study the traits of "historical" parties and of newer but electorally relevant parties in each legislature, even at the peril of ignoring parties that seem marginal today but might swell to paramount importance in the future. Aside from this theoretical rationale, however, defects of design in the Salamanca surveys mean that smaller parties (i.e., those with marginal seat shares in national

---

[2] Web Appendix D (at cambridge.org/9780521114950) also contains summary statistics of left-right self-placement broken down by party.

congresses) are at times overrepresented in the samples, whereas larger parties are underrepresented (see the subsequent entry on sampling problems). Small sample sizes per party are not problematic when the purpose is to infer characteristics of the legislature as a whole (provided, of course, that one adopts some solution to the sampling problem). At times, however, the samples for small parties include such a low number of observations that any effort to infer individual party characteristics from them, such as a party's location in a policy issue space relative to other parties, is meaningless. Thus, the statistical imperatives of gathering relatively informative samples also motivated our decision to banish smaller parties.

In consequence, we adopted a simple rule of thumb to determine which parties to include in our study: those with six respondents or less were dropped from our investigation.[3] As simple rules of thumb go, this one has desirable characteristics. First, as we already mentioned, it drops parties about which we cannot say anything meaningful because of small sample size. Second, it eliminates most parties with marginal representations in national legislatures, which are usually those with regional ties or single-issue advocacy positions, important in voicing political preferences of electoral minorities, but seldom prevalent in the national scene (e.g., the Mexican Partido de los Trabajadores). The potential drawbacks of such a rule are less troublesome than we had anticipated. First, although we feared that too many (overrepresented) small parties would be retained in our study (i.e., parties with seven or more respondents but only minor representation in legislatures), a glance at the parties that made the cut shows that this is not the case (see Web Appendix E at www.cambridge.org/9780521114950). The opposite situation of dropping "historically important" parties underrepresented in the sample occurs in only a limited number of cases.[4] Second, small parties accurately represented in the samples, and for which we have at least seven observations, are kept in our study. Here, the most conspicuous instance is the Pachakutik, a relatively new but influential party in Ecuador which held less than 10 percent of seats in the 1997 legislature but which contributed eight observations to the sample and was therefore kept in our study. Of the forty-one parties that met the requirement of having at least seven respondents, only ten have less than ten observations.[5]

Be this as it may, we recognize that our selection rule may introduce some bias in our measures of programmatic structuration. If we assume that very small parties cater to special interests and single-issue concerns, they would

[3] These parties are: UCD (Argentina); MBL, Conciencia de Patria, and SyD (Bolivia); PSB, PCdoB, PTB, and PPB (Brazil); ID, FRA (Ecuador); PT (Mexico); AP, Renovación (Peru); and Nuevo Espacio (Uruguay).

[4] In our view, the only conspicuous omission is Peru's Acción Popular, whose star had waned by the late 1990s.

[5] Web Appendix E also contains information on sample size for all parties included in our analysis.

contribute little to the programmatic structuring of the party system in a polity. Hence, in those countries where a larger proportion of legislators belongs to small parties, and were consequently dropped from our analysis, our measures of party system programmatic structuration might actually overstate the true level a bit more than in polities where the proportion of small parties eliminated from our analysis is less substantial.

DATA ISSUES

Our theoretical desire to include all relevant information was at times trumped by defects in the Salamanca surveys. These defects could have irrevocably damaged our inferences about programmatic structure in Latin America had we simply dropped all troublesome indicators. We found, however, that most of these defects could be lessened, if not totally eliminated, through common methodological fixes. We discuss two issues related to measurement error in the introduction to Part I of the text. In the following section, we discuss our solutions to two additional problems: sampling issues and missing values.

Sampling Problems

One of our central concerns is that the sampling procedure used to gather the Salamanca surveys might potentially lead to biased inferences regarding the degree of programmatic structure in Latin American legislative party systems. We have thus taken special care to detect and correct one damaging source of sample bias, namely, the over- or undersampling of some parties in the different country samples. As can be gleaned from Web Appendix E (at www.cambridge.org/9780521114950), sample sizes vary cross-nationally in both absolute and relative terms, from a low of 52 observations in Costa Rica (ca. 90 percent of the legislature) to 123 in Mexico (ca. 25 percent). Though the survey targeted politicians from all political parties represented in a country's national assembly, the sampling procedure did not yield samples that mirror the relative importance of political parties in the various legislatures. Needless to say, sampling error would naturally produce differences in the seat and sample proportions of different parties. However, a look at Web Appendix E suggests that actual *legislative party shares* and *sample party shares* sometimes differ by large margins. Three notable exceptions are Costa Rica, Uruguay, and Venezuela, where the sample proportion of legislators from each party closely mirrors each party's seat share in congress. In the other nine legislatures, however, the mismatch between a party's legislative and sample shares can be relatively high.

We do not endeavor to correct the problem of over- or undersampling when our purpose is to infer characteristics of individual parties. However, over- or undersampling of parties might introduce bias in our inferences regarding characteristics of legislative party systems as a whole. For example, one could falsely conclude that economic-distributive concerns are paramount in a legislature if extreme left-leaning and extreme right-leaning legislators are overrepresented in the sample (and, of course, if these extremists do stress heavily the importance of economic-distributive concerns). Fortunately, there seems to be no consistent bias across countries in the representation of small over large parties or leftist over rightist parties. To strengthen this argument, we regressed the difference between sample and actual party shares on indicators of *left-right party placement, secular-religious orientation,* and the *legislative seat share* of all parties with seven or more respondents in the Salamanca surveys.[6] When all parties are pooled together in a single dataset, none of these indicators is a statistically significant predictor of the amount of over- or undersampling.

However, erroneous sampling might still lead to biased inferences within countries. Dropping overrepresented respondents at random within each country would solve this problem, but would also lead to a high rate of attrition in the database and consequent efficiency losses in our estimators. In order to avoid loss of information, we prefer to weight each observation by the party share of seats in a legislature. Thus, if p_i is party i's share of seats in a legislature and s_i its sample proportion, then $w_{ji} = p_i/s_i$ is the weight attributed to each legislator j in party i. If w is close to 1, then information provided by the weighted observation is similar to that provided by the original, unweighted observation, which we do not consider problematic. This is true for most parties in most countries, and particularly in the twelve legislatures that we analyze.

Web Appendix E displays the weights that we employ in our analyses. Weights are about normally distributed, with mean 1 and standard deviation 0.28 (within-country weights are not independent but constrained to add up to unity, hence explaining why the mean weight is precisely "1"). The

---

[6] We use the *left-right party placement* indicator in the Salamanca survey ($v132$). This question asks respondents to place their own party along a 10-point left-right continuum (we average a party's score over all respondents). *Secular-religious orientation* is Coppedge's dichotomous coding of parties as "secular" or "religious" (Coppedge 1998b). *Seat share* is the actual share of legislative seats that a party held at the time of the survey. The regression pools together thirty-eight parties (three parties in the Dominican Republic, included in the rest of our analysis, are herein excluded because we lack *secular-religious orientation* scores for them). Regression results follow ($N = 38$, $F(3, 34) = 1.52(0.23)$, root MSE = 0.08).

	Coefficient	Standard Error	t	P > |t|	[95% Conf. Interval]	
Left-right	.0218	.0168	1.30	0.203	−.01231	.0559
Secular	−.0031	.0087	−0.35	0.727	−.0208	.0146
Seat share	−.0015	.0010	−1.46	0.154	−.0036	.0006
Constant	−.0651	.0595	−1.09	0.281	−.1859	.0557

only conspicuous cases of misrepresentation among the forty-one parties in our twelve national samples occur in Bolivia, where the MNR, ADN, and MIR have weights of 0.363, 1.639, and 2.021, respectively, all of which are at least two standard deviations away from the mean.[7] Whenever we use these weights in our analyses, we are in fact downplaying the significant oversampling of MNR legislators by discounting each observation by two-thirds, and we are concurrently treating MIR respondents as if they each yielded two observations in order to balance their relative paucity in the Bolivian sample. Throughout the text, we explicitly acknowledge the use of these weights whenever they are included in our empirical analyses.

Aside from the lack of correspondence between seat and sample shares, we have reason to believe that the sampling procedure employed by data collectors might have been partially affected by networks among legislators. It is conceivable that after completing a survey the interviewer might have followed the interviewee's lead to contact similarly minded colleagues. This kind of "snowball" data-collection could result in a sample that does not fully reflect the diversity of legislators' positions within a party. If this is indeed the case, we should tend to find greater within-party cohesion than actually exists on issues and on left-right party and self-placements. However, we are not overly concerned about the effects of this kind of sampling insofar as we are dealing with small universes (in general, no more than 200 legislators, except in Argentina, Brazil, and Mexico) and in most countries the survey involves from 13.5 percent (Brazil) to 91.2 percent (Costa Rica) of the legislature.[8]

Missing Values

A few indicators in our twelve samples included relatively high numbers of nonresponses, sometimes as many as 20 percent of the observations.[9] For example, sixteen out of sixty-eight legislators in Argentina did not provide a response on v50 (*privatize services*). As can be seen in Web Appendix D (at www.cambridge.org/9780521114950), nonrespondents include five

---

[7] Again, because weights are not independent within a country, overrepresentation of one party includes underrepresentation of other parties, and vice versa. If we exclude Bolivian parties from the estimation of the distribution of weights, w is then normally distributed with mean of 0.97 and standard deviation of 0.19.

[8] Moreover, nonrandom samples from small universes are much less problematic than non-random samples from large universes simply on account of the fact that they cover a larger segment of the population (Kalton 1983). Furthermore, we have no reason to believe that interviewers in the Salamanca project would have anticipated the theoretical questions we are asking in our analysis of the dataset and, with this knowledge, could have biased their choice of interviewees toward specific parties or specific individuals inside political parties. The Salamanca survey was originally designed to study political careers of Latin American legislators, not the programmatic structure of party competition.

[9] This is the case in eight of the 324 variables in our full 27 × 12 database: v50 in Argentina; v57 in Brazil; v57, v59, and v61 in Chile; v49 and v240 in Ecuador; and v50 in Uruguay.

Justicialistas (out of twenty-four), three UCR legislators (out of nineteen), four *Frepasistas* (out of eleven), and four respondents from excluded "minor" parties. In most cases, there is no relevant difference in cross-party rates of nonresponse. In other words, a legislator's propensity to abstain from responding to a particular question does not seem to be determined by his party membership. (The exceptional cases are v49 [*privatize industry*] and v240 [*I'm very religious*] in Ecuador, where nonrespondent rates are moderate across parties, but extremely high among Pachakutik legislators. Less drastically, many Frente Amplio legislators in Uruguay also abstained from responding to v50.)

Ideally, we would have carried out sophisticated imputation procedures in each of the twelve national samples to substitute for missing values. We were unable to do so because of the relatively low variables-to-observations ratio in each national sample. As a more viable alternative, we substituted missing values with the mean of the within-country distribution of each variable. Thus, if indicator x in country j includes a subset of k missing values, each of these missing elements is substituted with the mean of x_j estimated from observed values. This procedure will produce unbiased inferences if missing values are missing completely at random, which seems to be an accurate description of the pattern of missing values in most countries and therefore an assumption we make. Only in the exceptional cases mentioned previously (v49 and v240 in Ecuador) can we not say that missing values are random. In these circumstances, inferences from a sample with mean-substituted missing values will be biased. By increasing the number of observations with mean values, we narrow the distribution of within-country responses for each variable. Indeed, party average positions within a country will be closer together after substituting mean for missing values.

With regard to the postimputation within-party distribution of variables, parties that are on average closer to the grand average of the full legislature will appear to be more coherent (i.e., their distribution will be narrower) than before substituting missing with mean values. However, this same correction will increase within-party distributions for "extreme" parties, those whose legislators are on average farther away from the grand mean. In general, our measures of within-party coherence will reflect this bias, with extreme parties appearing less coherent, and centrist parties more coherent, than they really are (Chapter 5 deals with this issue in more detail). Because of the reasons already stated, we base our analysis on mean-value imputed datasets, but we certainly acknowledge the limitations imposed by this decision as a caveat to our research.

CONCLUSION

The Universidad de Salamanca's Parliamentary Elites survey represents an extraordinary opportunity to analyze and compare political parties and party systems across Latin America. In this volume, we explore a wide range of questions on current issues and political discourse that allow us to assess the programmatic structure of parties and party systems. However, the data on which we base our analysis are not perfect. In a few countries, key political parties are undersampled; the samples within parties might not be random, but rather the result of "snowballing"; and on a few variables we find usual problems (aggravated by our small sample sizes) of missing observations.

We have described here a variety of corrections that increase the accuracy of the inferences we draw. Individual responses are weighted to reflect actual seat shares, and we have chosen to exclude parties with extremely small representation in the various national samples from our analysis. The empirical chapters in Part I each use a variety of techniques to determine the political relevance of particular issues within each country. In a few chapters, some of these general corrections are eschewed in favor of more relevant techniques. We are however keenly aware that imperfect observational data cannot be entirely corrected, and that descriptive inferences based on faulty data may be biased. Where possible, we have made an effort to determine the direction of these biases. Ultimately, the best proof of the pertinence of using the Salamanca databases is our ability to generate theoretical insights into the programmatic character of party competition in the region.

Appendix B

List of Variables

Economic governance/privatization
    v49   Privatize industry
    v50   Privatize services

Social protection/social policy
    v64   Price controls bad
    v65   Do not sponsor job creation
    v69   Do not provide housing
    v70   Do not provide social security
    v71   Do not provide unemployment insurance
    v72   Basic subsidies bad
    v150 More guns, less butter

Financial openness/closure
    v54   Let IMF in
    v57   US investment good
    v59   European investment good
    v61   Latin American investment good

Law and order
    v34   Delinquency/robbery are threats
    v35   Labor unrest threatens democracy
    v87   Violence an important problem
    v168 Corruption always existed

Traditional values/cultural libertarianism
    v210 I go to church
    v235 No abortion
    v236 No divorce
    v240 I'm very religious

Postmodern sensibilities

    v90   Human/minority rights are important

    v92   Environmental issues are important

Authoritarian propensities

    v11   Democracy is never the best system

    v15   Elections are never the best way

    v26   Parties not needed for democracy

    v32   Justice doesn't work

Other variables

    v234   *Left-right self-placement* is a continuous variable in the range 1 (left) to 10 (right).

    v132b *Parties* are a series of dummy variables specific to each country.

Appendix C

English Translation of Relevant Portions of the Salamanca Survey

Variable 049–
"In this actual economic moment, which of the following criteria best summates your personal attitude toward the issue of privatization of state industry? Choose only one criterion."

- Privatize all state industries.
- Privatize only those industries that produce scarce profits.
- Privatize all the industries that are not strategically relevant to the development of the nation.
- Leave things in their current state.
- Other [specify]
- Does not know [cannot read]
- No response

Variable 050–
"Also, along the same line, which of the following criteria best approximates your personal attitude toward the theme of privatization of public services? Choose only one criterion."

- Privatize all public services.
- Privatize only those services of scarce profits.
- Privatize all public services except services that are highly necessary to the majority of the populace.
- Leave things in their current state.
- Other [specify]
- Does not know [cannot read]
- No response

Variable 054–
"In the processes of economic reorganization, the actions of diverse international organizations have been debated. In principle, what is the level of intervention in the national economy that you consider appropriate for

supranational institutions like the World Bank or International Monetary Fund? [Await response]. And what about the Inter-American Development Bank?"

- Complete/total
- Very strong
- Moderate
- Low
- None
- Does not know
- No response

Variable 057, 059, and 061–
"In the privatization process that your national economy is currently undergoing, where do you prefer capital investment to come from?"

Variable 057–From the United States

Variable 059–From countries in the European Union, excluding Spain

Variable 061–From Latin American countries in your immediate geographic region

Variable 064, 065, 069, 070, 071, and 072–
"Of the following functions that I will read to you, at which level do you believe the state should intervene? Signal 1 for the minimum level of intervention and 5 for the maximum."

Variable 064–Price controls

Variable 065–Giving jobs to those who want to work

Variable 069–Providing housing for citizens

Variable 070–Giving general social security coverage

Variable 071–Providing security in the form of unemployment coverage

Variable 072–Subsidizing products and services that are considered basic needs

Variables 087, 090, and 092–
"I will now name a series of problems that are common to many Latin American countries. Please indicate the importance that you give to each of the following issues in the case of your country. Situate each on a scale of 1 to 5, with 1 indicating little importance and 5 indicating maximum importance."

Variable 087–Citizen violence and insecurity

Variable 090–Human rights or the rights of ethnic or cultural minorities

Variable 092–The environment

Variable 132–
"Let us return to utilizing the column scale that goes from 'left' to 'right.'
How would you place your personal political party on this scale?"

(Scale of 1 to 7).

Variable 150–
"Please indicate your level of conformity, according to the subsequent scale,
with the following affirmations."

[1] Strongly disagree

[2] Somewhat disagree

[3] Somewhat agree

[4] Strongly agree

[99] Does not know

[88] No response

Variable 150–The budget dedicated to the armed forces should be reduced
gradually to dedicate that spending to other societal costs.

Variable 168–
"In recent times, corruption has acquired a very strong presence in the
public life of a number of countries. Please indicate your level of conformity
or agreement with the following affirmations on a scale from 1 to 5, with 1
indicating that you completely disagree and 5 that you strongly agree."

Variable 168–Corruption has always existed and will continue to exist.

Variable 210–
"Approximately how frequently do you attend religious services?"

- At least once a week
- Various times throughout the month
- Irregularly, but various times a year
- Very rarely or almost never
- Never
- Does not know
- No response

Variable 234–
"Let us once again return to utilizing the column scale that goes from 'left'
to 'right.' In which column would you locate yourself?"

Variable 235–
"What is your personal opinion about abortion? Choose only one response."

- In favor of complete liberalization
- Should be permitted only for some specified cases under the law
- Should never be permitted
- Does not know
- No response

Variable 236–
"What is your personal opinion related to divorce? Choose only one response."

- In favor of complete liberalization
- Should be permitted only in some specified cases under the law
- Should not be permitted under any circumstances
- Does not know
- No response

Variable 240–
"In accordance with your religious sentiment and beliefs, in which column would you locate yourself with 1 being indifferent in respect to which religion and 10 being a strong, practicing religious person?"

Bibliography

Abel, Christopher. 1987. *Política, Iglesia y Partidos en Colombia: 1886–1953.* Bogotá: Universidad Nacional de Colombia.

Acemoglu, Daron, Simon Johnson, and James A. Robinson. 2001. "The Colonial Origins of Comparative Development. An Empirical Investigation." *American Economic Review* 91: 1369–1401.

Acemoglu, Daron, and James Robinson. 2006. *Economic Origins of Dictatorship and Democracy.* Cambridge: Cambridge University Press.

Achen, Chris. 1977. "Measuring Representation: Perils of the Correlation Coefficient." *American Journal of Political Science* 21: 805–15.

1978. "Measuring Representation." *American Journal of Political Science* 22: 477–510.

Adams, James. 2001. *Party Competition and Responsible Party Government.* Ann Arbor: University of Michigan Press.

Adams, James, Samuel Merrill III, and Bernard Grofman. 2005. *A Unified Theory of Party Competition.* Cambridge: Cambridge University Press.

Adsera, Alicia, and Carles Boix. 2001. "Trade, Democracy, and the Size of the Public Sector: The Political Underpinnings of Openness." *International Organization* 56: 229–62.

Alcántara Sáez, Manuel, ed. 2008. *Politicians and Politics in Latin America.* Boulder, CO: Lynne Rienner.

Alchian, Armen. 1950. "Uncertainty, Evolution, and Economic Theory." *Journal of Political Economy* 58(3): 211–21.

Aldrich, John. 1983. "A Downsian Spatial Model with Party Activism." *American Political Science Review* 77: 974–90.

1995. *Why Parties? The Origin and Transformation of Party Politics in America.* Chicago: University of Chicago Press.

Aldrich, John, and Keith Rohde. 2001. "The Logic of Conditional Party Government." In Lawrence C. Dodd and Bruce I. Oppenheimer, eds., *Congress Reconsidered*, pp. 269–92. Washington, DC: CQ Press.

Alesina, Alberto. 1988. "Credibility and Convergence in a Two-Party System with Rational Voters." *American Economic Review* 78: 796–805.

Alesina, Alberto, Reza Baqir, and William Easterly. 1999. "Public Goods and Ethnic Divisions." *Quarterly Journal of Economics* 114: 1243–84.

Alesina, Alberto, Arnaud Devleeschauwer, William Easterly, Sergio Kurlat, and Romain Wacziarg. 2003. "Fractionalization." *Journal of Economic Growth* 8(2): 155–94.

Alonso, Paula. 2000. *Between Revolution and the Ballot Box: The Origins of the Argentine Radical Party in the 1890s.* Cambridge: Cambridge University Press.

Alvarez, R. Michael, and Charles H. Franklin. 1994. "Uncertainty and Political Perceptions." *Journal of Politics* 56: 671–88.

American Political Science Association (APSA). 1950. "Toward a More Responsible Two-Party System: A Report of the Committee on Political Parties." *American Political Science Review* 44(3), part 2, suppl.: 1–97.

Ames, Barry. 1995. "Electoral Strategy under Open-List Proportional Representation." *American Journal of Political Science* 39: 406–33.

2001. *The Deadlock of Democracy in Brazil.* Ann Arbor: University of Michigan Press.

Annett, Anthony. 2001. "Social Fractionalization, Political Instability, and the Size of Government." *IMF Staff Paper* 48(3).

Archer, Ronald. 1995. "Party Strength and Weakness in Colombia's Besieged Democracy." In Scott Mainwaring and Timothy Scully, eds., *Building Democratic Institutions: Party Systems in Latin America*, pp. 164–99. Stanford, CA: Stanford University Press.

Arditi, Benjamin. 2008. "Arguments about the Left Turns in Latin America: A Post-Liberal Politics?" *Latin American Research Review* 43: 59–81.

Arrow, Kenneth. 1963 [1951]. *Social Choice and Individual Values.* 2nd ed. New York: John Wiley & Sons.

Astorga, Pablo, Ame R. Bergés, and Valpy FitzGerald. 2004. "The Standard of Living in Latin America during the Twentieth Century." *University of Oxford Discussion Papers in Economic and Social History* 54.

Auza, Nestor Tomás. 1966. *Católicos y Liberales en la Generación del Ochenta.* Cuernavaca: Centro Intercultural de Documentación.

Barnadas, Joseph M. 1987. "La Reorganización de la Iglesia ante el Estado Liberal en Bolivia." In E. Dussel, J. Klaiber, F. A. Rojas, J. M. Barnadas, J. M. Vargas, M. M. Marzal, C. Romero, C. Tovar, J. M. Alvarez, and M. Arias, eds., *Historia General de la Iglesia en América Latina*, vol. 8: *Perú, Bolivia y Ecuador*, pp. 308–24. Salamanca: CEHILE/Ediciones Sígueme.

Bartolini, Stefano, and Peter Mair. 1990. *Identity, Competition and Electoral Availability: The Stabilisation of European Electorates, 1885–1985.* Cambridge: Cambridge University Press.

Bejarano, Ana María, and Eduardo Pizarro. 2005. "From 'Restricted' to 'Besieged': The Changing Nature of the Limits to Democracy in Colombia." In Frances Hagopian and Scott Mainwaring, eds., *The Third Wave of Democratization in Latin America: Advances and Setbacks*, pp. 235–60. Cambridge: Cambridge University Press.

Biles, Robert E. 1975. *Patronage Politics: Electoral Behavior in Uruguay.* Baltimore: Johns Hopkins University Press.

Birnir, Johanna Kristin, and Donna Lee Van Cott. 2007. "Disunity in Diversity. Party System Fragmentation and the Dynamic Effect of Ethnic Heterogeneity in Latin American Legislatures." *Latin American Research Review* 42: 99–125.

Bobbio, Norberto. 1996. *Left and Right: The Significance of a Political Distinction.* Trans. Allan Cameron. Chicago: University of Chicago Press.

Boix, Carles. 2003. *Democracy and Redistribution.* Cambridge: Cambridge University Press.

Boix, Carles, and Susan Stokes. 2003. "Endogenous Democratization." *World Politics* 55: 517–49.

Brooks, Sarah. 2009. *Social Protection and the Market in Latin America: The Transformation of Social Security Institutions.* Cambridge: Cambridge University Press.

Brown, David S., and Wendy Hunter. 1999. "Democracy and Social Spending in Latin America, 1980–92." *American Political Science Review* 93: 779–90.

Bruhn, Kathleen. 1997. *Taking on Goliath: The Emergence of a New Left Party and the Struggle for Democracy in Mexico.* University Park: Pennsylvania State University Press.

Bulmer-Thomas, Victor. 1994. *The Economic History of Latin America since Independence.* Cambridge: Cambridge University Press.

Butler, David, and Donald Stokes. 1969. *Political Change in Britain.* New York: St. Martin's Press.

Buxton, Julia. 2001. *The Failure of Political Reform in Venezuela.* Burlington, VT: Ashgate Publishing.

Cai, H., and Daniel Treisman. 2001. "State Corroding Federalism: Interjurisdictional Competition and the Weakening of Central Authority." Unpublished manuscript, University of California, Los Angeles.

Caillaud, Dominique, and Jean Tirole. 2002. "Parties as Political Intermediaries." *Quarterly Journal of Economics* 117: 1453–89.

Cain, Bruce E., John A. Ferejohn, and Morris P. Fiorina. 1987. *The Personal Vote: Constituency Service and Electoral Independence.* Cambridge, MA: Harvard University Press.

Camp, Roderic Ai, ed. 2001. *Citizen Views of Democracy in Latin America.* Pittsburgh: University of Pittsburgh Press.

Campos Salas, Dagoberto. 2000. *Relaciones Iglesia-Estado en Costa Rica: Estudio Histórico Jurídico.* San José, Costa Rica: Editorial Guayacán Centroamericana, S.A.

Carey, John M. 1996. *Term Limits and Legislative Representation.* Cambridge: Cambridge University Press.

Carey, John M., and Mathew Soberg Shugart. 1995. "Incentives to Cultivate a Personal Vote: A Rank Ordering of Electoral Formulas." *Electoral Studies* 14(4): 417–39.

eds. 1998. *Executive Decree Authority.* Cambridge: Cambridge University Press.

Chandra, Kanchan. 2004. *Why Ethnic Parties Succeed: Patronage and Ethnic Headcounts in India.* Cambridge: Cambridge University Press.

2007. "Counting Heads." In Herbert Kitschelt and Steven Wilkinson, eds., *Patrons, Clients, and Policies,* pp. 84–109. Cambridge: Cambridge University Press.

Cobb, Roger W., and Charles D. Elder. 1973. "The Political Uses of Symbolism." *American Politics Research* 1: 305–38.

Collier, David, ed. 1979. *The New Authoritarianism in Latin America*. Princeton, NJ: Princeton University Press.

Collier, David, and Ruth Berins Collier. 1991. *Shaping the Political Arena*. Princeton, NJ: Princeton University Press.

Collier, David, and Steven Levitsky. 1997. "Democracy with Adjectives: Conceptual Innovation in Comparative Research." *World Politics* 49(3): 430–51.

Collier, David, James Mahoney, and Jason Seawright. 2004. "Claiming Too Much: Warnings about Selection Bias." In Henry E. Brady and David Collier, eds., *Rethinking Social Theory: Diverse Tools, Shared Standards*, pp. 85–102. Lanham: Rowman and Littlefield.

Collier, David, Jason Seawright, and Gerardo L. Munck. 2004. "The Quest for Standards: King, Keohane, and Verba's *Designing Social Inquiry*." In Henry E. Brady and David Collier, eds., *Rethinking Social Theory: Diverse Tools, Shared Standards*, pp. 21–50. Lanham: Rowman and Littlefield.

Collier, Ruth Berins. 1999. *Paths toward Democracy: The Working Class and Elites in Western Europe and South America*. Cambridge: Cambridge University Press.

Colomer, Josep, and Luis E. Escatel. 2005. "La Dimensión Izquierda-Derecha en América Latina." *Desarrollo Económico* 45(177): 123–36.

Conover, Pamela J., and Stanley Feldman. 1981. "The Origins and Meaning of Liberal/Conservative Self-Identifications." *American Journal of Political Science* 25(4): 617–45.

Converse, Philip E. 1964. "The Nature of Belief Systems in Mass Publics." In David Apter, ed., *Ideology and Discontent*, pp. 206–61. London: Free Press of Glencoe.

1969. "Of Time and Partisan Stability." *Comparative Political Studies* 2: 139–61.

Converse, Philip, and Roy Pierce. 1986. *Political Representation in France*. Cambridge, MA: Belknap Press at Harvard University Press.

Coppedge, Michael. 1994. *Strong Parties and Lame Ducks: Presidential Partyarchy and Factionalism in Venezuela*. Stanford, CA: Stanford University Press.

1996. "The Rise and Fall of Partyarchy in Venezuela." In J. Domínguez and A. F. Lowenthal, eds., *Constructing Democratic Governance in Latin America and the Caribbean in the 1990s, Part III*, pp. 3–19. Baltimore: Johns Hopkins University Press.

1998a. "The Evolution of Latin American Party Systems." In Scott Mainwaring and Arturo Valenzuela, eds., *Politics, Society, and Democracy*, pp. 171–96. Boulder, CO: Westview.

1998b. "The Dynamic Diversity of Latin American Party Systems." *Party Politics* 4: 547–68.

2003. "Venezuela: Popular Sovereignty versus Liberal Democracy." In Jorge I. Domínguez and Michael Shifter, eds., *Constructing Democratic Governance in Latin America*, 2nd ed., pp. 165–92. Baltimore: Johns Hopkins University Press.

2005. "Explaining Democratic Deterioration in Venezuela through Nested Inference." In Frances Hagopian and Scott Morgenstern, eds., *The Third Wave of Democratization in Latin America: Advances and Setbacks*, pp. 289–316. Cambridge: Cambridge University Press.

Costner, Herbert L. 1965. "Criteria for Measures of Association." *American Sociological Review* 30(3): 341–53.

Cotler, Julio. 1986. "Military Interventions and 'Transfer of Powers to Civilians' in Peru." In Guillermo O'Donnell, Philippe C. Schmitter, and Laurence Whitehead, eds., *Transitions from Authoritarian Rule: Latin America*, pp. 148–72. Baltimore: Johns Hopkins University Press.

1995. "Political Parties and the Problems of Democratic Consolidation in Peru." In Scott Mainwaring and Timothy Scully, eds., *Building Democratic Institutions: Party Systems in Latin America*, pp. 323–53. Stanford, CA: Stanford University Press.

Cox, Gary W. 1997. *Making Votes Count*. Cambridge: Cambridge University Press.

Cox, Gary W., and Scott Morgenstern. 2002. "Epilogue: Latin America's Reactive Assemblies and Proactive Presidents." In Scott Morgenstern and Benito Nacif, eds., *Legislative Politics in Latin America*, pp. 446–68. Cambridge: Cambridge University Press.

Craig, Ann L., and Wayne A. Cornelius. 1995. "Houses Divided: Parties and Political Reform in Mexico." In Scott Mainwaring and Timothy Scully, eds., *Building Democratic Institutions: Party Systems in Latin America*, pp. 249–97. Stanford, CA: Stanford University Press.

Cusak, Thomas, and Torben Iversen. 2000. "The Causes of Welfare State Expansion: Deindustrialization or Globalization." *World Politics* 52: 313–49.

Dahl, Robert. 1989. *Democracy and Its Critics*. New Haven: Yale University Press.

Dalton, R. 1985. "Political Parties and Political Representation: Party Supporters and Party Elites in Nine Nations." *Comparative Political Studies* 18: 267–99.

Degregori, Carlos Iván. 2003. "Peru: The Vanishing of a Regime and Challenge of Democratic Rebuilding." In Jorge I. Domínguez and Michael Shifter, eds., *Constructing Democratic Governance in Latin America*, 2nd ed., pp. 220–43. Baltimore: Johns Hopkins University Press.

Desposato, Scott W. 2006. "Parties for Rent? Ambition, Ideology, and Party Switching in Brazil's Chamber of Deputies." *American Journal of Political Science* 50(1): 62–80.

Diamint, Rut. 2003. "The Military." In Jorge Domínguez and Michael Shifter, eds., *Constructing Democratic Governance in Latin America*, 2nd ed., pp. 43–73. Baltimore: Johns Hopkins University Press.

Diamond, Larry. 1996. "Is the Third Wave Over?" *Journal of Democracy* 7: 20–37.

2002. "Thinking about Hybrid Regimes." *Journal of Democracy* 13: 21–35.

Diamond, Larry, Juan J. Linz, and Seymour Martin Lipset, eds. 1989. *Democracy in Developing Countries*. Vol. 4: *Latin America*. Boulder, CO: Lynne Rienner.

Dix, Robert. 1989. "Cleavage Structures and Party Systems in Latin America." *Comparative Politics* 22: 23–37.

1992. "Democratization and the Institutionalization of Latin American Political Parties." *Comparative Political Studies* 24: 488–511.

Domingo, Pilar. 2005. "Democracy and New Social Forces in Bolivia." *Social Forces* 83: 1727–43.

Domínguez, Jorge, and James McCann. 1996. *Democratizing Mexico: Public Opinion and Electoral Choices*. Baltimore: John Hopkins University Press.

Downs, Anthony. 1957. *An Economic Theory of Democracy*. New York: Harper and Row.

Dresser, Denise. 1996. "Mexico: The Decline of Dominant-Party Rule." In Jorge I. Domínguez and Abraham F. Lowenthal, eds., *Constructing Democratic Governance: Mexico, Central America, and the Caribbean in the 1990s*, pp. 159–84. Baltimore: Johns Hopkins University Press.

Duverger, Maurice. 1954. *Political Parties*. London: Methuen.

Edwards, Sebastian. 1995. *Crisis and Reform in Latin America: From Despair to Hope*. New York: Oxford University Press.

Edwards, Sebastian, and Alejandra Cox Edwards. 1991. *Monetarism and Liberalism: The Chilean Experiment*. Chicago: University of Chicago Press.

Elster, Jon. 1979. *Sour Grapes*. Cambridge: Cambridge University Press.

Esaiasson, P., and K. Heidar. 2000. *Beyond Westminster and Congress: The Nordic Experience*. Columbus: Ohio State University Press.

Esping-Anderson, Gøsta. 1990. *The Three Worlds of Welfare Capitalism*. Princeton, NJ: Princeton University Press.

Estévez, Federico, and Beatriz Magaloni. 2000. "Legislative Parties and Their Constituencies in the Budget Battle of 1997." *Working Paper in Political Science* 2000–01, ITAM, D.F.

Evans, Geoffrey, Anthony Heath, and Mansur Lalljee. 1996. "Measuring Left-Right and Libertarian-Authoritarian Values in the British Electorate." *British Journal of Sociology* 47: 93–112.

Evans, Geoffrey, and Stephen Whitefield. 1998. "The Evolution of Left and Right in Post-Soviet Russia." *Europe-Asia Studies* 50: 1023–42.

Fearon, James D. 1999. "Electoral Accountability and the Control of Politicians. Selecting Good Types versus Sanctioning Poor Performance?" In Bernard Manin, Adam Przeworski, and Susan C. Stokes, eds., *Democracy, Accountability, and Representation*, pp. 55–97. Cambridge: Cambridge University Press.

Figueiredo, Angelina Cheibub, and Fernando Limongi. 2000. "Presidential Power, Legislative Organization, and Party Behavior in Brazil." *Comparative Politics* 32: 151–70.

Fiorina, Morris P. 1997. "Voting Behavior." In Dennis C. Mueller, ed., *Perspectives on Public Choice: A Handbook*, pp. 391–414. Cambridge: Cambridge University Press.

Fitch, J. Samuel. 1998. *The Armed Forces and Democracy in Latin America*. Baltimore: Johns Hopkins University Press.

Fleury, Christopher J., and Michael S. Lewis-Beck. 1993. "Anchoring the French Voter: Ideology Versus Party." *Journal of Politics* 55: 1100–9.

Fox, Jonathan. 1994. "The Difficult Transition from Clientelism to Citizenship." *World Politics* 46: 151–84.

Franklin, Mark. 2004. *Voter Turnout and the Dynamics of Electoral Competition in Established Democracies since 1945*. Cambridge: Cambridge University Press.

Freidenberg, Flavia, Fátima García Díez, and Iván Llamazares Valduvieco. 2008. "The Determinants of Intraparty Ideological Differences." In Manuel Alcántara Sáez, ed., *Politicians and Politics in Latin America*, pp. 161–71. Boulder, CO: Lynne Rienner.

Gamarra, Eduardo A. 1996. "Bolivia. Managing Democracy in the 1990s." In Jorge I. Domínguez and Abraham F. Lowenthal, eds., *Constructing Democratic Governance*, pp. 72–98. Baltimore: Johns Hopkins University Press.

Gamarra, Eduardo A., and James M. Malloy. 1995. "The Patrimonial Dynamics of Party Politics in Bolivia." In Scott Mainwaring and Timothy Scully, eds., *Building Democratic Institutions: Party Systems in Latin America*, pp. 399–433. Stanford, CA: Stanford University Press.

Geddes, Barbara. 1991. "A Game Theoretic Model of Reform in Latin American Democracies." *American Political Science Review* 85(2): 371–92.

2003. *Paradigms and Sand Castles: Theory Building and Research Design in Comparative Politics*. Ann Arbor: University of Michigan Press.

Gerring, John, Philip Bond, William T. Barndt, and Carola Moreno. 2005. "Democracy and Economic Growth. A Historical Perspective." *World Politics* 57(3): 323–59.

Gibson, Edward L. 1996. *Class and Conservative Parties: Argentina in Comparative Perspective*. Baltimore: Johns Hopkins University Press.

1997. "The Populist Road to Market Reform: Policy and Electoral Coalitions in Mexico and Argentina." *World Politics* 49(3): 339–70.

Gillespie, Charles G. 1986. "Uruguay's Transition from Collegial Military-Technocratic Rule." In Guillermo O'Donnell, Philippe C. Schmitter, and Laurence Whitehead, eds., *Transitions from Authoritarian Rule: Latin America*, pp. 49–71. Baltimore: Johns Hopkins University Press.

Gillespie, Charles G., and Luis Eduardo González. 1989. "Uruguay: The Survival of Old and Autonomous Institutions." In Larry Diamond, Juan Linz, and Seymour Martin Lipset, eds., *Democracy in Developing Countries*, vol. 4: *Latin America*, pp. 207 46. Boulder, CO: Lynne Rienner.

Glaeser, Edward L., Rafael La Porta, Florencio López-de-Silanes, and Andrei Shleifer. 2004. "Do Institutions Cause Growth?" *Journal of Economic Growth* 9(3): 271–303.

González G., Fernán E. 1977. *Partidos Politicos y Poder Eclesiástico: Reseña Histórica 1810–1930*. Bogota: Editorial CINEP.

González, Luis E. 1991. *Political Structures and Democracy in Uruguay*. South Bend, IN: University of Notre Dame Press.

1995. "Continuity and Change in the Uruguayan Party System." In Scott Mainwaring and Timothy Scully, eds., *Building Democratic Institutions: Party Systems in Latin America*, pp. 138–63. Stanford, CA: Stanford University Press.

Gordon, Stacey B., and Gary M. Segura. 1997. "Cross-National Variation in the Political Sophistication of Individuals: Capability or Choice?" *Journal of Politics* 59: 126–47.

Greene, Kenneth F. 2007. *Why Dominant Parties Lose: Mexico's Democratization in Comparative Perspective*. Cambridge: Cambridge University Press.

Greif, Avner. 2006. *Institutions and the Path to the Modern Economy: Lessons from Medieval Trade*. Cambridge: Cambridge University Press.

Grofman, Bernard. 2004. "Downs and Two-Party Convergence." *Annual Review of Politics* 7: 25–46.

Gudmundson, Lowell. 1996. "Costa Rica: New Issues and Alignments." In Jorge I. Domínguez and Abraham F. Lowenthal, eds., *Constructing Democratic Governance: Mexico, Central America, and the Caribbean in the 1990s*, pp. 78–91. Baltimore: Johns Hopkins University Press.

Gwynne, Robert N. 1985. *Industrialization and Urbanization in Latin America*. London: Routledge.

Haggard, Stephan. 1990. *Pathways from the Periphery*. Ithaca, NY: Cornell University Press.

Haggard, Stephan, and Robert Kaufman. 1992. *The Politics of Economic Adjustment: International Constraints, Distributive Conflicts, and the State*. Princeton, NJ: Princeton University Press.

1995. *Political Economy of Democratic Transitions*. Princeton, NJ: Princeton University Press.

2008. *Development, Democracy, and Welfare States: Latin America, East Asia, and Eastern Europe*. Princeton, NJ: Princeton University Press.

Haggard, Stephan, and Mathew D. McCubbin, eds. 2001. *Presidents, Parliaments, and Policy*. Cambridge: Cambridge University Press.

Hagopian, Frances. 1996. "Traditional Power Structures and Democratic Governance in Latin America." In Jorge I. Domínguez and Abraham F. Lowenthal, eds., *Constructing Democratic Governance: Latin America and the Caribbean in the 1990s*, pp. 64–86. Baltimore: Johns Hopkins University Press.

1998. "Democracy and Political Representation in Latin America in the 1990s: Pause, Reorganization, or Decline?" In F. Agüero and J. Stark, eds., *Fault Lines of Democracy in Post-Transitional Latin America*, pp. 85–120. Miami, FL: North-South Center Press.

2004. "Economic Liberalization, Party Competition and Elite Partisan Cleavages: Brazil in Comparative (Latin American) Perspective. 2004." Paper prepared for the Workshop on the Analysis of Cleavages and Party Competition, Duke University, April.

2005. "Conclusions. Government Performance, Political Representation, and Public Perceptions of Contemporary Democracy in Latin America." In Frances Hagopian and Scott P. Mainwaring, eds., *The Third Wave of Democratization in Latin America: Advances and Setbacks*, pp. 319–62. Cambridge: Cambridge University Press.

Hagopian, Frances, Carlos Gervasoni, and Juan Andrés Moraes. 2007. "From Patronage to Program: The Emergence of Party-Oriented Legislators in Brazil." Working Paper No. 344. Kellogg Institute, University of Notre Dame.

2009. "From Patronage to Program: The Emergence of Party-Oriented Legislators in Brazil." *Comparative Political Studies* 42(3): 360–91.

Hagopian, Frances, and Scott P. Mainwaring, eds. 2005. *The Third Wave of Democratization in Latin America: Advances and Setbacks*. Cambridge: Cambridge University Press.

Hall, Peter, and David Soskice, eds. 2001. *Varieties of Capitalism: The Institutional Origins of Comparative Advantage*. New York: Oxford University Press.

Harmel, Robert, and Kenneth Janda. 1982. *Parties and Their Environments*. New York: Longman.

Hartlyn, Jonathan. 1988. *The Politics of Coalition Rule in Colombia*. New York: Cambridge University Press.

1998. *The Struggle for Democratic Politics in the Dominican Republic*. Chapel Hill: University of North Carolina Press.

Hawkins, Kirk A. 2003. "Sowing Ideas: Explaining the Origins of Christian Democratic Parties in Latin America." In Scott Mainwaring and Timothy Scully, eds., *Christian Democracy in Latin America: Electoral Competition and Regime Conflicts*, pp. 78–120. Stanford, CA: Stanford University Press.

Forthcoming. *The Discourse of Populism: Venezuela's Chavismo in Comparative Perspective*. Cambridge: Cambridge University Press.

Hawkins, Kirk A., Guillermo Rosas, and Michael E. Johnson. 2009. "The *Misiones* of the Chávez Government in Venezuela." In Daniel Hellinger and David Smilde, eds., *Bottom Up or Top Down? Participation and Clientelism in Venezuela's Bolivarian Democracy*. Durham, NC: Duke University Press.

Held, David. 1987. *Models of Democracy*. Cambridge: Polity Press.

Heston, Alan, Robert Summers, and Bettina Aten. 2006. Penn World Table Version 6.2, Center for International Comparisons of Production, Income and Prices at the University of Pennsylvania, September.

Hinich, Melvin J., and Michael C. Munger. 1994. *Ideology and the Theory of Political Choice*. Ann Arbor: University of Michigan Press.

Horowitz, Donald. 1985. *Ethnic Groups in Conflict*. Berkeley and Los Angeles: University of California Press.

Huber, Evelyne, and Fred Solt. 2004. "Success and Failures of Neoliberalism." *Latin American Research Review* 39: 150–64.

Huber, Evelyne, and John Stephens. 1999. "The Bourgeoisie and Democracy: Historical and Comparative Perspectives." *Social Research* 66: 759–88.

2001. *Development and Crisis of the Welfare State*. Chicago: University of Chicago Press.

Huber, John. 1989. "Values and Partisanship in Left-Right Orientations: Measuring Ideology." *European Journal of Political Research* 17: 599–621.

Huber, John, and Ronald Inglehart. 1995. "Expert Interpretations of Party Space and Party Location in 42 Societies." *Party Politics* 1: 73–111.

Hunter, Wendy. 2007. "The Normalization of an Anomaly. The Workers' Party in Brazil," *World Politics* 59: 440–75.

Huntington, Samuel P. 1968. *Political Order in Changing Societies*. New Haven: Yale University Press.

Hurley, P. A., and K. Q. Hill. 2001. "Beyond the Demand-Input Model: A Theory of Representational Linkages." Paper presented at the annual meeting of the Midwest Political Science Association, San Francisco, August 30–September 2.

Inglehart, Ronald. 1997. *Modernization and Postmodernization: Cultural, Economic, and Political Change in 43 Societies*. Princeton, NJ: Princeton University Press.

Inglehart, Ronald, and Hans D. Klingemann. 1976. "Party Identification, Ideological Preference and the Left-Right Dimension among Western Mass Publics." In Ian Budge, Ivor Crewe, and Dennis Farlie, eds., *Party Identification and Beyond: Representations of Voting and Party Competition*, pp. 243–73. Chichester: Wiley Press.

Inglehart, Ronald, and Dusan Sidjanski. 1976. "The Left, the Right, the Establishment and the Swiss Electorate." In Ian Budge, Ivor Crewe, and Dennis Fairlie, eds., *Party Identification and Beyond*, pp. 215–42. London: Wiley Press.

Inglehart, Ronald, and Christian Welzel. 2005. *Modernization, Cultural Change, and Democracy: The Human Development Sequence*. Cambridge: Cambridge University Press.

Inter-American Development Bank. 1981. *Economic and Social Progress in Latin America: 1980–81 Report*. Washington, DC: Inter-American Development Bank.

Isaacs, Anita. 1996. "Ecuador. Democracy Standing the Test of Time?" In Jorge I. Domínguez and Abraham F. Lowenthal, eds., *Constructing Democratic Governance: South America in the 1990s*, pp. 42–57. Baltimore: Johns Hopkins University Press.

Iversen, Torben. 1994a. "The Logics of Electoral Politics: Spatial, Directional and Mobilizational Effects." *Comparative Political Studies* 27: 155–89.

1994b. "Political Leadership and Representation in West European Democracies: A Test of Three Models of Voting." *American Journal of Political Science* 38: 45–74.

Iversen, Torben, and David Soskice. 2006. "Electoral Institutions and the Politics of Coalitions: Why Some Democracies Redistribute More Than Others." *American Political Science Review* 100 (2): 165–82.

Jackman, Robert. 1987. "Political Institutions and Voter Turnout in the Industrial Democracies." *American Political Science Review* 81(2): 405–23.

Jacoby, W. G. 2002. "Liberal–Conservative Thinking in the American Electorate." In M. X. Delli Carpini, L. Huddy, and R. Y. Shapiro, eds., *Political Decision-Making, Deliberation and Participation*, Research in Micropolitics, vol. 6. Oxford: Elsevier.

Janda, Kenneth, and Desmond King. 1985. "Formalizing and Testing Duverger's Theories on Political Parties." *Comparative Political Studies* 18: 139–69.

Janos, Andrew. 2000. *East Central Europe in the Modern World: The Politics of the Borderlands from Pre- to Post-Communism*. Stanford, CA: Stanford University Press.

Johnson, Gregg B., and Brian F. Crisp. 2003. "Mandates, Powers and Policies." *American Journal of Political Science* 47: 128–42.

Jolliffe, Ian T. 1986. *Principal Component Analysis*. New York: Springer-Verlag.

Jones, Mark. 1995. *Electoral Laws and the Survival of Presidential Democracies*. Notre Dame, IN: University of Notre Dame Press.

1997. "Evaluating Argentina's Presidential Democracy: 1983–1995." In Scott Mainwaring and Matthew Soberg Shugart, eds., *Presidentialism and Democracy in Latin America*, pp. 259–99. Cambridge: Cambridge University Press.

2002. "Explaining the High Level of Party Discipline in the Argentine Congress." In Scott Morgenstern and Benito Nacif, eds., *Legislative Politics in Latin America*, pp. 147–84. Cambridge: Cambridge University Press.

2005. "Political Party and Party System Institutionalization and Salient Partisan Cleavages in Latin America." Paper presented at the annual conference of the Midwest Political Science Association, April 7–10.

Kalton, Graham. 1983. "Models in the Practice of Survey Sampling." *International Statistical Review* 51: 175–88.

Kappeler, Andreas. 1992. *Russland als Vielvölkerreich. Entstehung, Aufstieg, Zerfall*. Munich: C. H. Beck.

Kaufman, Robert, and Alex Segura-Ubiergo. 2001. "Globalization, Domestic Politics, and Social Spending in Latin America. A Time-Series Cross-Section Analysis." *World Bank* 53(4): 553–87.

Kaufmann, Daniel, Aart Kraay, and Massimo Mastruzzi. 2005. "Governance Matters IV: Governance Indicators for 1996–2004." The World Bank Institute, World Bank Policy Research Working Paper No. 3630.

2007. "Governance Matters VI: Governance Indicators for 1996–2006." The World Bank Institute, World Bank Policy Research Working Paper No. 4280.

Kiewiet, Roderick, and Matthew McCubbins. 1991. *The Logic of Delegation: Congressional Parties and the Appropriations Process.* Chicago: University of Chicago Press.

King, Gary, Robert O. Keohane, and Sidney Verba. 1994. *Designing Social Inquiry: Scientific Inference in Qualitative Research.* Princeton, NJ: Princeton University Press.

Kirchheimer, Otto. 1966. "The Transformation of the Western European Party Systems." In Joseph LaPalombara and Myron Weiner, eds., *Political Parties and Political Development*, pp. 177–200. Princeton, NJ: Princeton University Press.

Kitschelt, Herbert. 1989a. *The Logics of Party Formation.* Ithaca, NY: Cornell University Press.

1989b. "The Internal Politics of Parties. The Law of Curvilinear Disparity Revisited." *Political Studies* 37: 400–21.

1992. "The Formation of Party Systems in East Central Europe." *Politics and Society* 20: 7–50.

1994. *The Transformation of European Social Democracy.* Cambridge: Cambridge University Press.

1995a. (in collaboration with Anthony J. McGann). *The Radical Right in Western Europe.* Ann Arbor: University of Michigan Press.

1995b. "The Formation of Party Cleavages in Post-Communist Democracies. Theoretical Propositions." *Party Politics* 1: 447–72.

2000a. "Citizens, Politicians, and Party Cartellization. Political Representation and State Failure in Post-Industrial Democracies." *European Journal of Political Research* 37: 149–79.

2000b. "Linkages between Citizens and Politicians in Democratic Polities." *Comparative Political Studies* 33: 845–79.

2002. "New Challenges in the Study of Political Representation: Comment on G. Bingham Powell, Jr., 'Citizens, Elected Policymakers and Democratic Representation: Two Contributions from Comparative Politics.'" Working Paper. Duke University, Durham, NC.

2003. "Accounting for Postcommunist Regime Diversity. What Counts as a Good Cause?" In Grzegorsz Ekiert and Stephen Hanson, eds., *Legacies of Communism*, pp. 49–86. Cambridge: Cambridge University Press.

2007. "The Demise of Clientelism in Affluent Capitalist Democracies." In Herbert Kitschelt and Steven Wilkinson, eds., *Patrons, Clients, and Policies*, pp. 298–321. Cambridge: Cambridge University Press.

Kitschelt, Herbert, and Staf Hellemans. 1990. "The Left-Right Semantics and the New Politics Cleavage." *Comparative Political Studies* 23: 210–238.

Kitschelt, Herbert, Zdenka Mansfeldova, Radoslaw Markowski, and Gábor Tóka. 1999. *Post-Communist Party Systems: Competition, Representation, and Inter-Party Cooperation.* Cambridge: Cambridge University Press.

Kitschelt, Herbert, and Regina Smyth. 2002. "Programmatic Party Cohesion in Emerging Postcommunist Democracies: Russia in Comparative Context." *Comparative Political Studies* 35(10): 1228–56.

Kitschelt, Herbert, and Steven Wilkinson, eds. 2007. "Citizen-Politician Linkages: An Introduction." In Kitschelt and Wilkinson, eds., *Patrons, Clients and Policies: Patterns of Democratic Accountability and Political Competition*, pp. 1–49. Cambridge: Cambridge University Press.

Klecka, William R. 1980. *Discriminant Analysis*. Beverly Hills, CA: Sage.

Klein, Herbert S. 1969. *Parties and Political Change in Bolivia*. Cambridge: Cambridge University Press.

Kline, Harvey F. 1996. "Colombia: Building Democracy in the Midst of Violence and Drugs." In Jorge I. Domínguez and Abraham F. Lowenthal, eds., *Constructing Democratic Governance: South America in the 1990s*, pp. 20–41. Baltimore: Johns Hopkins University Press.

Klingemann, Hans D. 1979. "The Background of Ideological Conceptualization." In Samuel H. Barnes, Max Kaase, et al., eds., *Political Action: Mass Participation in Five Western Democracies*, pp. 255–77. Beverly Hills, CA: Sage.

Knutsen, Oddbjørn. 1989. "Cleavage Dimensions in Ten West European Countries. A Comparative Empirical Analysis." *Comparative Political Studies* 21: 495–534.

  1997. "The Partisan and the Value-Based Components of Left-Right Self-Placement: A Comparative Study." *International Political Science Review* 18: 191–225.

Kornblith, Miriam, and Daniel H. Levine. 1995. "Venezuela: The Life and Times of the Party System." In Scott Mainwaring and Timothy Scully, eds., *Building Democratic Institutions: Party Systems in Latin America*, pp. 37–71. Stanford CA: Stanford University Press.

Korzeniewicz, Roberto Patricio. 2000. "Democracy and Dictatorship in Continental Latin America during the Interwar Period." *Studies in Comparative International Development* 35: 41–72.

Kriesi, Hanspeter. 2004. "Political Context and Opportunity." In David A. Snow, Sarah A. Soule, and Hanspeter Kriesi, eds., *The Blackwell Companion to Social Movements*, pp. 67–90. Oxford: Blackwell.

Krishna, Anirudh. 2007. "Politics in the Middle: Mediating Relationships between the Citizens and the State in Rural North India." In Herbert Kitschelt and Steven Wilkinson, eds., *Patrons, Clients, and Policies*, pp. 141–58. Cambridge: Cambridge University Press.

Kuczynski, Pedro-Pablo, and John Williamson, eds. 2003. *After the Washington Consensus: Restarting Growth and Reform in Latin America*. Washington, DC: Institute for International Economics.

Kunicova, Jana, and Susan Rose-Ackerman. 2005. "Electoral Rules and Constitutional Structures as Constraints on Corruption." *British Journal of Political Science* 35(4): 573–606.

Kurtz, Marcus J., and Sarah M. Brooks. 2008. "Embedding Neoliberal Reform in Latin America." *World Politics* 60(2): 231–80.

Larrea, Juan Ignacio. 1954. *La Iglesia y el Estado en el Ecuador (La personalidad de la Iglesia en el Modus Vivendi celebrado entre la Santa Sede y el Ecuador)*. Seville: Escuela de Estudios Hispano-Americanos.

Latinobarómetro. 1998. Latinobarómetro 1998. Unpublished raw data. Santiago, Chile: Corporación Latinobarómetro.

2002. Latinobarómetro 2002. Unpublished raw data. Santiago, Chile: Corporación Latinobarómetro.

Laver, Michael. 2005. "Policy and the Dynamics of Party Competition." *American Political Science Review* 99: 263–82.

Lehoucq, Fabrice. 2005. "Costa Rica: Paradise in Doubt." *Journal of Democracy* 16(3): 140–54.

Levitsky, Steven. 2001. "Inside the Black Box. Recent Studies of Latin American Party Organization." *Studies in Comparative International Development* 36: 92–110.

2003. *Transforming Labor-Based Parties in Latin America: Argentine Peronism in Comparative Politics.* Cambridge: Cambridge University Press.

Levitsky, Steven, and Maria Victoria Murillo. 2003. "Argentina Weathers the Storm." *Journal of Democracy* 14: 152–66.

Levitsky, Steven, and Lucan Way. 2002. "The Rise of Competitive Authoritarianism." *Journal of Democracy* 13: 51–65.

Lieberson, Stanley. 1985. *Making It Count: The Improvement of Social Research and Theory.* Berkeley: University of California Press.

Lijphart, Arend. 1995. *Electoral Systems and Party Systems: A Study of Twenty-seven Democracies, 1945–1990.* Oxford: Oxford University Press.

1999. *Patterns of Democracy.* New Haven: Yale University Press.

Lindert, Peter. 2004. *Growing Public: Social Spending and Economic Growth since the Eighteenth Century.* Cambridge: Cambridge University Press.

Linz, Juan, and Alfred Stepan. 1996. *Problems of Democratic Transition and Consolidation: Southern Europe, South America and Post-Communist Europe.* Baltimore: Johns Hopkins University Press.

Lipset, Seymour Martin, and Stein Rokkan. 1967. "Cleavages Structures, Party Systems, and Voter Alignments. An Introduction." In Lipset and Rokkan, eds., *Party Systems and Voter Alignments: Cross-National Perspectives,* pp. 1–64. New York: Free Press.

Lluberes, Antonio, S.J. 1998. *Breve Historia de la Iglesia Dominicana: 1493–1997.* Santo Domingo: Editora Amigo del Hogar.

Loaeza, Soledad. 2003. "The National Action Party (PAN): From the Fringes of the Political System to the Heart of Change." In Scott Mainwaring and Timothy R. Scully, eds., *Christian Democracy in Latin America: Electoral Competition and Regime Conflicts,* pp. 196–246. Stanford, CA: Stanford University Press.

Londregan, John. 2000. *Legislative Institutions and Ideology in Chile's Democratic Transition.* Cambridge: Cambridge University Press.

López-Maya, Margarita. 1997. "The Rise of *Causa R* in Venezuela." In Douglas A. Chalmers, ed., *The New Politics of Inequality in Latin America: Rethinking Participation and Representation,* pp. 117–43. New York: Oxford University Press.

Lora, Eduardo. 2001. "Structural Reforms in Latin America. What Has Been Reformed and How to Measure It." Inter-American Development Bank. Update of Working Paper 348.

Luna, Juan Pablo. 2007. "Frente Amplio and the Crafting of a Social Democratic Alternative in Uruguay." *Latin American Politics & Society* 49(4, Winter): 1–30.

Lupia, Arthur, and Mathew D. McCubbins. 1998. *The Democratic Dilemma*. Cambridge: Cambridge University Press.

Luskin, Robert C. 1990. "Explaining Political Sophistication." *Political Behavior* 12(4): 331–61.

Lynch, John. 1986. "The Catholic Church in Latin America, 1830–1930." In Leslie Bethell, ed., *The Cambridge History of Latin America*, vol. 4: *c. 1870 to 1930*, pp. 527–96. Cambridge: Cambridge University Press.

Lyne, Mona M. 2005. "Parties as Programmatic Agents. A Test of Institutional Theory in Brazil." *Party Politics* 11: 193–216.

2007. "Rethinking Economics and Institutions: The Voter's Dilemma and Democratic Accountability." In Herbert Kitschelt and Steven Wilkinson, eds., *Patrons, Clients and Policies: Patterns of Democratic Accountability and Political Competition*, pp. 159–81. Cambridge: Cambridge University Press.

2008. *The Voter's Dilemma and Democratic Accountability: Explaining the Democracy-Development Paradox*. University Park: Pennsylvania State University Press.

Madrid, Raúl L. 2008. "The Rise of Ethnopopulism in Latin America." *World Politics* 60(3): 475–508.

Magaloni, Beatriz. 1997. "The Dynamics of Dominant Party Decline: The Mexican Transition to Multipartyism." Ph.D. dissertation, Department of Political Science, Duke University.

Magaloni, Beatriz, Alberto Díaz-Cayeros, and Federico Estévez. 2007. "Clientelism and Portfolio Diversification: A Model of Electoral Investment with Applications to Mexico." In Herbert Kitschelt and Steven Wilkinson, eds., *Patrons, Clients and Policies: Patterns of Democratic Accountability and Political Competition*, pp. 182–205. Cambridge: Cambridge University Press.

Magaloni, Beatriz, and Alejandro Moreno. 2003. "Catching All Souls: The Partido Acción Nacional and the Politics of Religion in Mexico." In Scott Mainwaring and Timothy Scully, eds., *Christian Democracy in Latin America: Electoral Competition and Regime Conflicts*, pp. 247–74. Stanford, CA: Stanford University Press.

Mainwaring, Scott. 1999. *Rethinking Party Systems in the Third Wave of Democratization: The Case of Brazil*. Stanford, CA: Stanford University Press.

2003. "Party Objectives in Authoritarian Regimes with Elections or Fragile Democracies: A Dual Game." In Scott Mainwaring and Timothy R. Scully, eds., *Christian Democracy in Latin America. Electoral Competition and Regime Conflicts*. pp. 3–29. Stanford, CA: Stanford University Press.

2006. "The Crisis of Representation in the Andes." *Journal of Democracy* 17: 13–27.

Mainwaring, Scott, Ana María Bejarano, and Eduardo Pizarro Leongómez. 2006. *The Crisis of Democratic Representation in the Andes*. Stanford, CA: Stanford University Press.

Mainwaring, Scott, Daniel Brinks, and Aníbal Pérez-Liñán. 2001. "Clarifying Political Regimes in Latin America, 1985–1999." *Studies in Comparative International Development* 36: 37–65.

Mainwaring, Scott, G. O'Donnell, and J. S. Valenzuela, eds. 1992. *Issues in Democratic Consolidation: The New South American Democracies in Comparative Perspective*. Notre Dame, IN: University of Notre Dame Press.

Mainwaring, Scott, and Aníbal Pérez-Liñán. 1997. "Party Discipline in the Brazilian Constitutional Congress." *Legislative Studies Quarterly* 22(4): 453–83.

2003. "Level of Development and Democracy: Latin American Exceptionalism, 1945–1996." *Comparative Political Studies* 36(9): 1031–67.

2005. "Latin American Democratization since 1978." In Frances Hagopian and Scott P. Mainwaring, eds., *The Third Wave of Democratization in Latin America: Advances and Setbacks*, pp. 14–61. Cambridge: Cambridge University Press.

Mainwaring, Scott, and Timothy Scully. 1995. "Introduction: Party Systems in Latin America." In Scott Mainwaring and Timothy Scully, eds., *Building Democratic Institutions: Party Systems in Latin America*, pp. 1–35. Stanford, CA: Stanford University Press, 1995.

eds. 2003. *Christian Democracy in Latin America: Electoral Competition and Regime Conflicts*. Stanford, CA: Stanford University Press.

2008. "Latin America: Eight Lessons for Governance." *Journal of Democracy* 19(3): 113–27.

Mainwaring, Scott, and Mathew S. Shugart. 1997. *Presidentialism and Democracy in Latin America*. Cambridge: Cambridge University Press.

Mainwaring, Scott, and Edurne Zoco. 2007. "Political Sequences and the Stabilization of Interparty Competition. Electoral Volatility in Old and New Democracies." *Party Politics* 13(2): 155–78.

Mahoney, James. 2001. *The Legacies of Liberalism: Path Dependence and Political Regimes in Central America*. Baltimore: Johns Hopkins University Press.

Mansbridge, Jane. 2003. "Rethinking Representation." *American Political Science Review* 97(4): 515–28.

Manzetti, Luigi. 2003. "Political Manipulations and Market Reforms Failures." *World Politics* 55(3): 315–60.

Marx, Anthony. 1997. *Making Race and Nation: A Comparison of the United States, South Africa, and Brazil*. Cambridge: Cambridge University Press.

May, John D. 1973. "Opinion Structure of Political Parties: The Special Law of Curvilinear Disparity." *Political Studies* 21: 135–51.

Mayhew, David R. 2000. "Electoral Realignments." *Annual Review of Political Science* 3: 449–74.

Mayorga, René Antonio. 2005. "Bolivia's Democracy at the Crossroads." In Frances Hagopian and Scott Mainwaring, eds., *The Third Wave of Democratization in Latin America: Advances and Setbacks*, pp. 149–78. Cambridge: Cambridge University Press.

McClintock, Cynthia. 1989. "Peru: Precarious Regimes, Authoritarian and Democratic." In Larry Diamond, Juan J. Linz, and Seymour Martin Lipset, eds., *Democracy in Developing Countries*, vol. 4: *Latin America*, pp. 335–86. Boulder, CO: Lynne Rienner.

McGuire, James W. 1997. *Peronism without Perón: Unions, Parties, and Democracy in Argentina*. Stanford, CA: Stanford University Press.

Mecham, J. Lloyd. 1966. *Church and State in Latin America: A History of Politico-Ecclesiastical Relations*. Rev. ed. Chapel Hill: University of North Carolina Press.

Méndez, Juan E., Guillermo O'Donnell, and Paulo Sérgio Pinheiro. 1999. *The (Un)Rule of Law and the Underprivileged in Latin America*. Notre Dame, IN: University of Notre Dame Press.

Merrill, Samuel, III, and Bernard Grofman. 1999. *A Unified Theory of Voting: Directional and Proximity Spatial Models.* Cambridge: Cambridge University Press.

Middlebrook, Kevin J., ed. 2000. *Conservative Parties, the Right, and Democracy in Latin America.* Baltimore: Johns Hopkins University Press.

Miller, Gary, and Norman Schofield. 2003. "Activists and Partisan Realignment in the United States." *American Political Science Review* 97(2): 245–60.

Miller, W. E., R. Pierce, J. Thomassen, R. Herrera, S. Holmberg, P. Esaiasson, and B. Wessels. 1999. *Policy Representation in Western Democracies.* Oxford: Oxford University Press.

Miller, W. E., and D. Stokes. 1963. "Constituency Influence in Congress." *American Political Science Review* 57: 165–77.

Mishler, William, and Richard Rose. 1997. "Trust, Distrust and Skepticism: Popular Evaluations of Civil and Political Institutions in Post-Communist Societies." *Journal of Politics* 59(2): 418–51.

2001a. "Political Support for Incomplete Democracies: Realist and Idealist Theories and Measures." *International Political Science Review* 22(4): 303–20.

2001b. "What Are the Origins of Political Trust? Testing Institutional and Cultural Theories of Post-Communist Societies." *Comparative Political Studies* 34(1): 30–62.

Moe, Terry. 1984. "The New Economics of Organization." *American Journal of Political Science* 23(4): 739–77.

Møller, Jørgen. 2007. "The Post-Communist Tri-Partition, 1990–2005: Contrasting Actor-Centered and Structural Explanations." Ph.D. dissertation, Department of Political Science, European University Institute.

2009. *Post-Communist Regime Change: A Comparative Study.* London: Routledge.

Moreno, Alejandro. 1998. "Party Competition and the Issue of Democracy: Ideological Space in Mexican Elections." In Mónica Serrano, ed., *Governing Mexico: Political Parties and Elections*, pp. 38–57. Oxford: Institute of Latin American Studies.

1999. *Political Cleavage: Issues, Parties, and the Consolidation of Democracy.* Boulder, CO: Westview Press.

2003. *El Votante Mexicano: Democracia, Actitudes Políticas y Conducta Electoral.* Mexico, D.F.: Fondo de Cultura Económica.

Moreno, Ericka, Brian F. Crisp, and Matthew Soberg Shugart. 2003. "The Accountability Deficit in Latin America." In Scott Mainwaring and Christopher Welna, eds., *Democratic Accountability in Latin America*, pp. 79–131. Oxford: Oxford University Press.

Morgenstern, Scott. 2004. *Patterns of Legislative Politics: Roll-Call Voting in Latin America and the United States.* Cambridge: Cambridge University Press.

Morgenstern, Scott, and Luigi Manzetti. 2003. "Legislative Oversight: Interests and Institutions in the United States and Argentina." In Scott Mainwaring and Christopher Welna, eds., *Democratic Accountability in Latin America*, pp. 132–70. Oxford: Oxford University Press.

Morgenstern, Scott, and Benito Nacif, eds. 2002. *Legislative Politics in Latin America.* Cambridge: Cambridge University Press.

Morgenstern, Scott, and Stephen Swindle. 2005. "Are Politics Local? An Analysis of Voting Patterns in 23 Democracies."*Comparative Political Studies* 38(2): 143–70.

Morley, Samuel, Roberto Machado, and Stefano Pettinato. 1999. "Indexes of Structural Reform in Latin America." *ECLAC Economic Development Division.* LC/L.1166, January.

Munck, Gerardo L., and Jay Verkuilen. 2002. "Conceptualizing and Measuring Democracy." *Comparative Political Studies* 35: 5–34.

Nacif, Benito. 2002. "Understanding Party Discipline in the Mexican Chamber of Deputies: The Decentralized Party Model." In Scott Morgenstern and Benito Nacif, eds., *Legislative Politics in Latin America*, pp. 254–84. Cambridge: Cambridge University Press.

Nathan, Andrew J., and Tianjian Shi. 1996. "Left and Right with Chinese Characteristics: Issues and Alignments in Deng Xiaoping's China." *World Politics* 48: 522–50.

Nichter, Simeon. 2008. "Vote Buying or Turnout Buying? Machine Politics and the Secret Ballot." *American Political Science Review* 102(1): 19–32.

Norris, Pippa. 2004. *Electoral Engineering: Voting Rules and Political Behavior.* Cambridge: Cambridge University Press.

North, D. 1990. *Institutions, Institutional Change, and Economic Performance.* Cambridge: Cambridge University Press.

O'Donnell, Guillermo. 1973. *Modernization and Bureaucratic Authoritarianism: Studies in South American Politics.* Berkeley: Institute of International Studies, University of California.

1994. "Delegative Democracy." *Journal of Democracy* 5: 55–69.

1998. "Horizontal Accountability in New Democracies." *Journal of Democracy* 9(3): 112–26.

2001. "Democracy, Law and Comparative Politics." *Studies in Comparative International Development* 36(1): 7–36.

O'Donnell, Guillermo, Philippe C. Schmitter, and Laurence Whitehead, eds. 1986. *Transitions from Authoritarian Rule: Comparatie Perspectives.* Baltimore: Johns Hopkins University Press.

Ozbudun, Ergun. 1970. *Party Cohesion in Western Democracies: A Causal Analysis.* Beverly Hills, CA: Sage.

Page, B. I., and R. Y. Shapiro. 1983. "Effects of Public Opinion on Policy." *American Political Science Review* 77: 175–90.

Payne, J. Mark, Daniel Zovatto G., Fernando Barrillo Flórez, and Andrés Allamand Zavala. 2002. *Democracies in Development: Politics and Reform in Latin America.* Washington, DC: Inter-American Development Bank and International Institute for Democracy and Electoral Assistance.

Pedersen, Mogens. 1983. "Changing Patterns of Electoral Volatility in European Party Systems, 1948–1977: Explorations in Explanation." In Hans Daalder and Peter Mair, eds., *Western European Party Systems: Continuity and Change,* pp. 29–66. Beverly Hills, CA: Sage.

Penfold-Becerra, Michael. 2007. "Clientelism and Social Funds: Evidence from Chávez's Misiones." *Latin American Politics and Society* 49(4): 63–84.

Pérez-Liñán, Aníbal. 2007. *Presidential Impeachment and the New Political Instability in Latin America.* Cambridge: Cambridge University Press.

Persson, Torsten, and Guido Tabellini. 2000. *Political Economics: Explaining Economic Policy*. Cambridge, MA: MIT Press.

2003. *The Economic Effects of Constitutions*. Cambridge, MA: MIT Press.

Piattoni, Simona, ed. 2001. *Clientelism, Interests, and Democratic Representation*. Cambridge: Cambridge University Press.

Pierson, Paul. 2000. "Increasing Returns, Path Dependence, and the Study of Politics." *American Political Science Review* 94: 251–68.

2003. "Big, Slow-Moving, and Invisible, Macrosocial Processes in the Study of Comparative Politics." In James Mahoney and Dietrich Rueschemeyer, eds., *Comparative Historical Analysis in the Social Sciences*, pp. 177–207. Cambridge: Cambridge University Press.

2004. *Politics in Time: History, Institutions, and Social Analysis*. Princeton, NJ: Princeton University Press.

Pike, Frederick. 1967. "Church and State in Peru and Chile since 1840: A Study in Contrasts." *American Historical Review* 73(1): 30–50.

Polity IV Project. 2007. *Political Regime Characteristics and Transitions, 1800–2007*. [computer file; version p4v2007] Severn, MD: Center for Systemic Peace.

Pollack, Marcelo. 1997. "Jaime Guzmán and the Gremialistas: From Catholic Corporatist Movement to Free Market Party." In Will Fowler, ed., *Ideologues and Ideologies in Latin America*, pp. 151–70. Westport, CT: Greenwood Press.

Poole, Keith T., and Howard Rosenthal. 1997. *Congress: A Political-Economic History of Roll-Call Voting*. Oxford: Oxford University Press.

2001. "D-Nominate after 10 Years: A Comparative Update to Congress: A Political-Economic History of Roll-Call Voting." *Legislative Studies Quarterly* 26(1): 5–29.

Popkin, Samuel L. 1994. *The Reasoning Voter: Communication and Persuasion in Presidential Campaigns*. Chicago: University of Chicago Press.

Powell, G. Bingham, Jr. 1982. *Contemporary Democracies: Participation, Stability, and Violence*. Cambridge, MA: Harvard University Press.

1986. "American Voter Turnout in Comparative Perspective." *American Political Science Review* 80(1): 17–43.

1989. "Constitutional Design and Citizen Electoral Control." *Journal of Theoretical Politics* 1: 107–30.

2000. *Elections as Instruments of Democracy: Majoritarian and Proportional Visions*. New Haven: Yale University Press.

2001. "Democratic Representation: Two Contributions from Comparative Politics." Paper presented at the annual meeting of the American Political Science Association, San Francisco.

2004a. "The Chain of Responsiveness." *Journal of Democracy* 14(4): 91–105.

2004b. "Political Representation in Comparative Politics." *Annual Review of Political Science* 7: 273–96.

Power, Timothy J. 2000. *The Political Right in Postauthoritarian Brazil: Elites, Institutions, and Democratization*. University Park: Pennsylvania State University Press.

Przeworski, Adam. 1991. *Democracy and the Market: Political and Economic Reforms in Eastern Europe and Latin America*. Cambridge: Cambridge University Press.

Przeworski, Adam, Michael E. Alvarez, Jose Antonio Cheibub, and Fernando Limongi. 2000. *Democracy and Development*. Cambridge: Cambridge University Press.

Przeworski, Adam, and Fernando Limongi. 1997. "Modernization: Theory and Facts." *World Politics* 49: 155–83.

Przeworski, Adam, S. Stokes, and B. Manin, eds. 1999. *Democracy, Accountability, and Representation*. Cambridge: Cambridge University Press.

Ranney, Austin. 1962. *The Doctrine of Responsible Party Government*. Urbana: University of Illinois Press.

Remmer, Karen L. 1989. *Military Rule in Latin America*. Boston: Unwin, Hyman.

2002. "The Politics of Economic Policy and Performance in Latin America." *Journal of Public Policy* 22: 29–59.

Rial, Juan. 1996. "Uruguay: From Restoration to the Crisis of Governability." In Jorge I. Domínguez and Abraham F. Lowenthal, eds., *Constructing Democratic Governance: South America in the 1990s*, pp. 133–46. Baltimore: Johns Hopkins University Press.

Rice, Roerta, and Donna Lee Van Cott. 2006. "The Emergence and Performance of Indigenous Peoples' Parties in South America. A Subnational Statistical Analysis." *Comparative Political Studies* 39: 709–32.

Riker, William. 1982. *Liberalism versus Populism*. San Francisco: Freeman.

1986. *The Art of Political Manipulation*. New Haven: Yale University Press.

Roberts, Kenneth M. 1998. *Deepening Democracy? The Modern Left and Social Movements in Chile and Peru*. Stanford, CA: Stanford University Press.

2000. "Party-Society Linkages and Democratic Representation in Latin America." Paper presented at the conference on Threats to Democracy in Latin America, University of British Columbia, Vancouver.

2002. "Social Inequalities without Class Cleavages: Party Systems and Labor Movements in Latin America's Neoliberal Age." *Studies in Comparative International Development* 36(4): 3–33.

Roberts, Kenneth, and Erik Wibbels. 1999. "Party Systems and Electoral Volatility in Latin America. A Test of Economic, Institutional, and Structural Explanations." *American Political Science Review* 93: 575–90.

Robertson, David. 1976. *A Theory of Party Competition*. New York: Wiley.

Rock, David. 1975. *Politics in Argentina, 1890–1930: The Rise and Fall of Radicalism*. Cambridge: Cambridge University Press.

Rodden, Jonathan. 2004. "Comparative Federalism and Decentralization: On Meaning and Measurement." *Comparative Politics* 36: 481–500.

Rodden, Jonathan, and Erik Wibbels. 2002. "Beyond the Fiction of Federalism: Macroeconomic Management in Multi-tiered Systems." *World Politics* 54(4): 494–531.

Rodríguez Iturbe, José. 1968. *Iglesia y Estado en Venezuela (1824–1964)*. Caracas: Instituto de Derecho Publico, Universidad Central de Venezuela.

Roland, Gérard. 2004. "Understanding Institutional Change: Fast-Moving and Slow-Moving Institutions." *Studies in Comparative International Development* 38: 109–31.

Roquié, Alain. 1987. *The Military and the State in Latin America*. Berkeley: University of California Press.

Rosas, Guillermo. 2005. "The Ideological Organization of Latin American Legislative Parties: An Empirical Analysis of Elite Preferences" *Comparative Political Studies* 38: 824–49.

Ross, Michael. 2001. "Does Oil Hinder Democracy?" *World Politics* 53: 325–61.

Rudra, Nitra. 2008. *Globalization and the Race to the Bottom in Developing Countries: Who Really Gets Hurt?* Cambridge: Cambridge University Press.

Rueschemeyer, D., E. Huber, and J. Stephens. 1992. *Capitalist Development and Democracy.* Chicago: University of Chicago Press.

Safford, Frank. 1985. "Politics, Ideology, and Society in Post-Independence Spanish America." In Leslie Bethell, ed., *The Cambridge History of Latin America,* vol. 3: *From Independence to c. 1870,* pp. 347–422. Cambridge: Cambridge University Press.

Salazar Mora, Orlando, and Jorge Mario Salazar Mora. 1991. *Los Partidos Políticos en Costa Rica.* San José, Costa Rica: Editorial Universidad Estatal a Distancia.

Samuels, David. 2003. *Ambition, Federalism, and Legislative Politics in Brazil.* Cambridge: Cambridge University Press.

2004. "From Socialism to Social Democracy. Party Organization and the Transformation of the Workers' Party in Brazil." *Comparative Political Studies* 37: 999–1024.

Sani, Giacomo, and Giovanni Sartori. 1983. "Polarization, Fragmentation, and Competition in Western Democracies." In Hans Dalder and Peter Mair, eds., *Western European Party Systems: Continuity and Change,* pp. 307–40. Beverly Hills, CA: Sage.

Schattschneider, E. E. 1942. *Party Government.* New York: Farrar and Rinehart.

Schmitt, H., and J. Thomassen. 1999. *Political Representation and Legitimacy in the European Union.* Oxford: Oxford University Press.

Schofield, Norman. 2003. "Valence Competition in the Spatial Stochastic Model." *Journal of Theoretical Politics* 15: 371–83.

2004. "Equilibrium in the Spatial 'Valence' Model of Politics." *Journal of Theoretical Politics* 16: 447–81.

Schofield, Norman, and Itai Sened. 2006. *Multiparty Democracy: Elections and Legislative Politics.* Cambridge: Cambridge University Press.

Scully, Timothy J. 1992. *Rethinking the Center: Party Politics in Nineteenth- and Twentieth-Century Chile.* Stanford, CA: Stanford University Press.

Segura-Ubiergo, Alex. 2007. *The Political Economy of the Welfare State in Latin America: Globalization, Democracy, and Development.* Cambridge: Cambridge University Press.

Seligson, Mitchell. 2002. "Trouble in Paradise: The Impact of the Erosion of System Support in Costa Rica, 1978–1999." *Latin American Research Review* 37(1): 160–85.

Shapiro, Ian. 2003. *The State of Democratic Theory.* Princeton, NJ: Princeton University Press.

Shefter, Martin. 1994. *Politics Parties and the State: The American Historical Experience.* Princeton, NJ: Princeton University Press.

Short, R. P. 1984. "The Role of Public Enterprises: An International Statistical Comparison." In R. Floyd, C. Gray, and R. P. Short, eds., *Public Enterprise in Mixed Economies. Some Macroeconomic Aspects,* pp. 110–99. Washington, DC: International Monetary Fund.

Shugart, Matthew Soberg. 1998. "The Inverse Relationship between Party Strength and Executive Strength: A Theory of Politicians' Constitutional Choices." *British Journal of Political Science* 28: 1–29.

Shugart, Matthew Soberg, and John Carey. 1992. *Presidents and Assemblies*. Cambridge: Cambridge University Press.

Shugart, Matthew Soberg, and Martin P. Wattenberg, eds. 2001. *Mixed-Member Electoral Systems: The Best of Both Worlds?* Oxford: Oxford University Press.

Smith, Brian H. 1982. *The Church and Politics in Chile: Challenges to Modern Catholicism*. Princeton, NJ: Princeton University Press.

Smith, Peter. 2005. *Democracy in Latin America: Political Change in Comparative Perspective*. New York: Oxford University Press.

Sniderman, Paul M., Richard A. Brody, and Philip Tetlock. 1991. *Reasoning and Choice: Explorations in Political Psychology*. Cambridge: Cambridge University Press.

Snyder, James M., Jr., and Michael M. Ting. 2002. "An Informational Rationale for Political Parties." *American Journal of Political Science* 46: 90–110.

Stein, Ernesto, and Mariano Tommasi. 2005. "Democratic Institutions, Policymaking Processes, and the Quality of Policies in Latin America. Inter-American Development Bank." Unpublished manuscript, Washington, DC.

Stein, Ernesto, Mariano Tommasi, Koldo Echebarría, Eduardo Lora, and Mark Payne, coordinators. 2006. *The Politics of Policies: Economic and Social Progress in Latin America; 2006 Report*. New York: Inter-American Development Bank.

Stimson, James. 2005. *Tides of Consent: How Public Opinion Shapes American Politics*. Cambridge: Cambridge University Press.

Stokes, Susan. 1995. *Cultures in Conflict: Social Movements and the State in Peru*. Berkeley: University of California Press.

1996. "Peru: The Rupture of Democratic Rule." In Jorge I. Domínguez and Abraham F. Lowenthal, eds., *Constructing Democratic Governance: South America in the 1990s*, pp. 58–71. Baltimore: Johns Hopkins University Press.

1999. "What Do Policy Switches Tell Us about Democracy?" In A. Przeworski, S. Stokes, and B. Manin, eds., *Democracy, Accountability, and Representation*, pp. 98–130. Cambridge: Cambridge University Press.

2001. *Mandates and Democracy: Neoliberalism by Surprise in Latin America*. Cambridge: Cambridge University Press.

2005. "Perverse Accountability. A Formal Model of Machine Politics with Evidence from Argentina." *American Political Science Review* 99(3): 315–25.

2007. "Political Clientelism." In Carles Boix and Susan Stokes, eds., *Oxford Handbook of Comparative Politics*, pp. 604–25. Oxford: Oxford University Press.

Swift, Jeannine. 1978. *Economic Development in Latin America*. New York: St. Martin's Press.

Taagepera, Rein, and Matthew Shugart. 1989. *Seats and Votes*. Cambridge: Cambridge University Press.

Tarrow, Sidney. 1996. "States and Opportunities: The Political Structuring of Social Movements." In Doug McAdam, John D. McCarthy, and Mayer N. Zald, *Comparative Perspectives on Social Movements: Political Opportunities, Mobilizing*

Structures, and Cultural Framings, pp. 41–61. Cambridge: Cambridge University Press.

Teichman, Judith A. 2001. *The Politics of Freeing Markets in Latin America*. Chapel Hill: University of North Carolina Press.

Thelen, Kathleen. 1999. "Historical Institutionalism and Comparative Politics." *Annual Review of Political Science* 2: 369–404.

2003. "How Institutions Evolve: Insights from Comparative Historical Analysis." In James Mahoney and Dietrich Rueschemeyer, eds., *Comparative Historical Analysis in the Social Sciences*, pp. 208–40. Cambridge: Cambridge University Press, 2003.

Thomassen, Jacques. 1994. "Empirical Research into Political Representation." In Kent Jennings and Thomas Mann, eds., *Elections at Home and Abroad*, pp. 237–64. Ann Arbor: University of Michigan Press.

Thornton, Mary Crescentia. 1973. *The Church and Freemasonry in Brazil, 1872–1875: A Study in Regalism*. Westport, CT: Greenwood Press.

Treisman, Daniel. 2002. "Defining and Measuring Decentralization: A Global Perspective." Department of Political Science, University of California, Los Angeles.

United Nations Development Programme (UNDP). 2004. *Democracy in Latin America: Towards a Citizens' Democracy*. New York: UNDP.

Van Cott, Donna. 2005. *From Movements to Parties in Latin America: The Evolution of Ethnic Politics*. Cambridge: Cambridge University Press.

2008. *Radical Democracy in the Andes*. Cambridge: Cambridge University Press.

Weissberg, Robert. 1978. "Collective versus Dyadic Representation in Congress." *American Political Science Review* 72: 535–47.

Weyland, Kurt. 2002. *Politics of Market Reform in Fragile Democracies*. Princeton, NJ: Princeton University Press.

2007. "Politics and Policies of Latin America's Two Lefts. The Role of Party Systems versus the Resource Bonanza." Paper prepared for the annual meeting of the American Political Science Association, Chicago, August 30–September 2.

Whitehead, Laurence. 1986. "Bolivia's Failed Democratizstion, 1977–1980." In Guillermo O'Donnell and Philippe Schmitter, eds., *Transitions from Authoritarian Rule: Latin America*, pp. 49–71. Baltimore: Johns Hopkins University Press.

Wibbels, Erik. 2001. "Federal Politics and Market Reform in the Developing World." *Studies in Comparative International Development* 36: 27–53.

2005. *Intergovernmental Conflict and the Economic Reform in the Developing World*. Cambridge: Cambridge University Press.

Wilkinson, Steven. 2007. "Explaining Changing Patterns of Party-Voter Linkages in India." In Herbert Kitschelt and Steven Wilkinson, eds., *Patrons, Clients, and Policies*, pp. 110–40. Cambridge: Cambridge University Press.

Williams, Edward J. 1967. *Latin American Christian Democratic Parties*. Knoxville: University of Tennessee Press.

Williamson, John. 1990. "What Washington Means by Policy Reform." In John Williamson, ed., *Latin American Adjustment: How Much Has Happened?*, pp. 5–20. Washington, DC: Institute for International Economics.

Wipfler, William. 2001. "The Catholic Church and the State in the Dominican Republic." In Armando Lampe, ed., *Christianity in the Caribbean: Essays on Church History*, pp. 191–228. Kingston: University of the West Indies Press.

Wong, Joseph. 2004. "Democratization and the Left. Comparing East Asia and Latin America." *Comparative Political Studies* 37: 1213–37.

World Bank. 1997. *World Development Report 1997: The State in a Changing World*. Oxford: Oxford University Press.

2003. *Inequality in Latin America and the Caribbean: Breaking with History?* Washington, DC: World Bank.

2006. "World Development Indicators 2006." Washington, DC: World Bank.

Yashar, Deborah. 1995. "Civil War and Social Welfare: The Origins of Costa Rica's Competitive Party System." In Scott Mainwaring and Timothy Scully, eds., *Building Democratic Institutions: Party Systems in Latin America*, pp. 72–99. Stanford, CA: Stanford University Press.

1998. "Contesting Citizenship: Indigenous Movements and Democracy in Latin America." *Comparative Politics* 31(1): 23–42.

2005. *Contesting Citizenship in Latin America: The Rise of Indigenous Movements and the Postliberal Challenge*. Cambridge: Cambridge University Press.

Zaller, John. 1992. *The Nature and Origins of Mass Opinion*. Cambridge: Cambridge University Press.

Zechmeister, Elizabeth. 2003. "Sheep or Shepherds? Voter Behavior in New Democratic Contexts." Ph.D. dissertation, Duke University.

2004. "'Left' and 'Right' in Latin America: A Cross-National Q-Method Study." Paper prepared for the annual meeting of the Latin American Studies Association, Las Vegas, October 7–9.

2006. "What's Left and Who's Right? A Q-Method Study of Individual and Contextual Influences on the Meaning of Ideological Labels." *Political Behavior* 28(2): 151–73.

Index

Achen, Chris, 121
AD (Acción Democrática/Democratic
    Action) (Venezuela), 66, 93, 103,
    163, 199, 255, 266
administrative professionalism. *See*
    democracy, effects of PPS, on
    good governance
ADN (Acción Democrática
    Nacionalista/ National
    Democratic Action) (Bolivia),
    156, 163, 166, 350
Albania, 319
Alcántara, Manuel, 341
Aldrich, John, 22
Alianza (Alianza Trabajo, Justicia y
    Educación/Alliance Labor,
    Justice and Education)
    (Argentina), 139, 332
Alianza por Chile (Alliance for Chile)
    (Chile), 140, 331
Allende, Salvador, 217, 330, 331
Ames, Barry, 217
APRA (Alianza Popular Revolucionaria
    Americana/American Popular
    Revolutionary Alliance) (Peru),
    92, 166, 175, 176, 193
Argentina
    authoritarian regime, 217
    church-state conflict, 246
    clientelism, 205–6
    cohesion, 156, 157, 159

democracy, attitudes toward, 300,
    302
democracy, quality of, 29
economic development, 181, 192–93,
    225
economic partisan divide, 77, 80–81,
    92–93
labor movement, 193–94
landed oligarchies, 54
law and order, attitudes toward, 79
left-right labels, 100, 105, 107, 110,
    151, 158
party discipline, 65
political representation, 135, 136,
    137, 139
programmatic party structuration,
    173
regime divide, attitudes toward, 83
religiosity, 87, 94
social policy, 189, 198
Arias, Oscar, 334
Armenia, 319
Austria, 29
authoritarian regimes
    consequences for regime divide, 265,
    266, 313
    long-term consequences for PPS,
    37–38, 184, 322–23
    short-term consequences for PPS, 44,
    216–17
autogolpe, 266